Fools' Crusade

'Diana Johnstone has written a "must" book for progressives, and for anybody who wants to cut through the remarkable structure of disinformation regarding the Kosovo war and its background that has been institutionalized in the West. With a willingness to confront and weigh evidence on topics usually treated with great superficiality, and with a breadth of knowledge matched by few writers in the field, Johnstone's study will be an eye-opener for many. She works with a critical framework that does not take NATO-friendly assumptions, pre-fabricated history, and filtered and decontextualized evidence as premises and truth (or the whole truth). The result is an excitingly original and powerful book and an essential corrective to a remarkable body of propaganda that dominates thought in the Free World.' —*Edward S. Herman*

Fools' Crusade

Yugoslavia, NATO and Western Delusions

Diana Johnstone

Monthly Review Press
New York

Library of Congress Cataloging-in-Publication Data
is available from the publisher

Monthly Review Press
146 West 29th Street, Suite 6W
New York, NY 10001
www.montlyreview.org

This book was simultaneously published in the
United Kingdom by Pluto Press, London

ISBN 1-58367-084-X

Contents

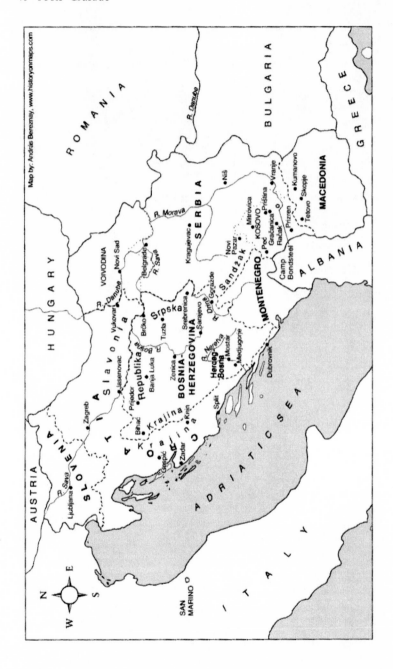

Introduction

TURNING POINTS

At the end of November 1999, an important new movement against "globalization" emerged in massive protests against the World Trade Organization meeting in Seattle. Strangely enough, only months earlier, when NATO launched its first aggressive war by bombing Yugoslavia, there had been remarkably little protest. Yet NATO's violent advance into southeast Europe was precisely related to the globalization process opposed in Seattle. Few seemed to grasp the connection. Was it really plausible that overwhelming military power was being wielded more benevolently than overwhelming economic power? Or that the two were not in some way promoting the same interests and the same "world order"?

Apparently, many people on the left, who would normally defend peace and justice, were fooled or confused by the claim that the "Kosovo war" was waged for purely humanitarian reasons. The altruistic pretensions of NATO's Kosovo war served to gain public acceptance of war as the appropriate instrument of policy. This opened the way for the United States, in the wake of 11 September 2001, to attack Afghanistan as the opening phase of a new, long-term "war against terrorism".

The bombing of Yugoslavia marked a turning point in the expansion of U.S. military hegemony. For the first time, a European country was subjected to the type of U.S. intervention usually reserved for Central America. It also marked the end of Germany's postwar inhibition about foreign military intervention, and saw Germans returning to the scene of Nazi crimes with a clear conscience. For the first time, NATO abandoned its defensive posture and attacked a country that posed no threat to its member states, outside the NATO treaty area, and without seeking UN Security Council authorization. International law was circumvented in the name of an alleged higher moral imperative. A precedent was set. When the United States subsequently arrogated the right to bomb and invade Afghanistan on moral grounds, its NATO allies could only meekly offer to tag along. In a world with no more legal barriers

1

to might proclaiming itself right, there was nothing to stop a U.S. president from using military force to crush every conceivable adversary.

For all its dubious origins, the 1991 Gulf war against Iraq was waged against a militarized single-party dictatorship, condemned by the United Nations for invading another country. And yet, remarkably, the war against Yugoslavia aroused less public protest than the war against Iraq.[1] A significant difference was that the war against Yugoslavia was waged by the political center-left. The NATO governments were mostly led by liberals and "Third Way" social democrats. The attack on Serbia was endorsed by politicians and intellectuals identified with the left, who exhorted the public to believe that the United States and its allies no longer made war to advance selfish interests, but might be coaxed into using their overwhelming military might to protect innocent victims from evil dictators. This caused considerable confusion in the very segments of public opinion that would normally be expected to oppose war. In most Western countries, only a few drastically weakened fragments of left-wing movements and isolated individuals still remembered that humanitarian intervention, far from being the harbinger of a brave new century, was the standard pretext for all the Western imperialist conquests of the past. The left was too confused, feeble, or isolated to provide a vigorous challenge to the official claim that the NATO war against Yugoslavia marked a new era in global morality. On the contrary, much of the most pertinent challenge came from right-wing analysts, whose minds were kept relatively clear, either by awareness of traditional *realpolitik* or by libertarian suspicion of official propaganda. Not since the Socialist Parties of Europe rallied to their governments' war programs in 1914 has the left opposition to war collapsed so ignominiously and with such good conscience.

WAR REHABILITATED

The message that war was once again an acceptable instrument of politics was all the more resounding in that it was delivered by center-left governments composed of those very political parties – Social Democrats and Greens – which in the 1980s had attained a large measure of ideological hegemony within their generation in both Eastern and Western Europe by holding out the promise of a peaceful world. On the eve of the Soviet implosion, there was talk of a "peace dividend" in the form of resources that could henceforth be diverted from military production to meeting social needs. With the fall of the Berlin Wall in 1989, the big Western peace movements of the 1980s seemed to consider that their job was done. Because the period of superpower stand-off had been called the Cold *War*, the expectation was widespread that ending it would bring a new era of peace and disarmament.

This turned out to be a brief mirage. A decade after the fall of the Berlin Wall, U.S. military spending again resumed its upward spiral, "Star Wars" was back on the agenda, Washington was pressuring its allies to spend more on armaments, NATO was expanding eastwards, and the United States was using military diplomacy to gain influence across the southernmost tier of the former Soviet Union.

Recently rewarded with a peerage and the post of NATO Secretary General for his incomparable performance as British defense secretary during the Kosovo conflict, former Labour Party disarmament advocate George Robertson declared on 2 December 1999: "The time for a peace dividend is over because there is no permanent peace in Europe or elsewhere." This acceptance of war was couched in moral terms: war was not only inevitable, it was good. NATO had taken it upon itself to overrule the postwar international legal order set up around the United Nations and decree unilaterally that war was no longer the scourge of mankind, the worst of all "humanitarian catastrophes", but rather, when employed by enlightened Western powers, the proper means to protect "human rights" and punish the wicked. The last war of the twentieth century was a promise of more war in the century to come. That promise was fulfilled with a vengeance with the attack on Afghanistan and President Bush's vow to pursue war against "evil", with no end in sight.

"During the Cold War, we would not have gotten ourselves involved in a dispute like the one in Kosovo", one commentator observed.[2] "In the days when the Soviet Union contained us, power realities would have kept the U.S. from interfering. It is because we are now free to indulge in backing up our ideals and sympathies with cruise missiles that we are there." In choosing to get involved, without any obligation to do so, and in disregard of the UN Charter and international law, "the United States is not serving any particular interest of its own. It is acting out of altruism. This is a new kind of approach to the use of power in world politics.

It was called for by a line of U.S. presidents, from Wilson to Bush to Clinton, who consider this to be a new era in world politics, in which the rules have changed."

In Kosovo, wrote a mainstream American columnist, the United States and its allies "intervened without UN authorization, in violation of Serbian sovereignty and probably of international law". But this was nothing to be "hung up" about, since "Sometimes the only way to stop bad men from doing bad things is with force. Lawyers won't get the job done."[3] The scenario is straight out of a classic Western movie: "bad men" must be stopped from doing "bad things", presumably by "good men" – and women, of course. A "new era in world politics"? Or the same old story?

THE HUMANITARIAN ILLUSION

For years, a chorus of non-governmental organizations and commentators reproached the United Nations, Europe, and the U.S. government for failing to take action, which came to be understood as *military* action. As a result, NATO intervention appeared to be a response to public demand. NATO's 1999 war was presented to the public as a happy ending to the serial drama of Yugoslavia as recounted by the media throughout the previous decade. Many significant factors were systematically ignored. Other elements, sometimes distorted and sometimes simply untrue, were constantly repeated. The result was a collective fiction told and retold, written and rewritten, by very many people, including reporters under pressure to meet deadlines, editors further simplifying the story for readers assumed to be both ignorant and impatient, paid propagandists and public relations officers, pontificating commentators, prejudiced editorialists, ambitious politicians, outright liars – as well as by talented opportunists and conformists sensitive to the direction the wind was blowing and the buttered side of the bread. Endlessly repeated, this collective fiction has become a formidable myth perpetuated by the powerful institutions and individuals whose own credibility is at stake in its maintenance. The fictional saga of Yugoslavia in the 1990s goes something like this:

Yugoslavia was a "prison of peoples" where the Serbs oppressed all the others. It was destroyed by the rise of an evil leader, Slobodan Milošević, who set out to create a "Greater Serbia" by eliminating other peoples in a process called "ethnic cleansing". Those other peoples sought to escape, by creating their own independent states. The Yugoslav army, actually Serbian, invaded them. In Bosnia, the invading Serbs tried to drive out the Muslims, who wanted to perpetuate an exemplary multi-ethnic society. The Serb ethnic cleansing killed 200,000 unarmed Muslims while the international community looked on and even prevented the Muslims from arming in self-defense. At Srebrenica, the United Nations allowed the Serbs to commit genocide. Only U.S. bombing forced Milošević to come to the negotiating table at Dayton. The resulting agreement brought peace and democracy to multi-ethnic Bosnia. However, the international community had failed to save the Albanian majority in Kosovo from apartheid. In 1998 Madeleine Albright warned that NATO must intervene to keep Milošević from "doing in Kosovo what he could no longer get away with in Bosnia".[4] In January 1999, Serbian security forces massacred defenseless civilians in the Kosovo village of Račak, awakening the NATO governments to the need to act to stop genocide. After the turning point of Račak, the Serbs were summoned to peace negotiations in Rambouillet, in France. Milošević stubbornly refused to negotiate. NATO had no choice but to start bombing Yugoslavia. Masses of Albanians were deliberately driven out according to a preconceived plan called "Operation Horseshoe". Finally, Milošević gave in, and NATO liberated the Kosovars from their oppressors. Conclusion: from now on, humanitarian intervention constitutes a principal mission for NATO, as the military arm of an international community henceforth committed to protection of human rights.

Almost everything about this tale is false. Unfortunately, disproving falsehoods, especially established falsehoods, is a hard task. What has been repeated over and over becomes "obviously true". Very many facts challenging the dominant myth have been reported by news agencies. But such reports are not the ones that major mainstream media highlight. They mostly end up in the wastebaskets of editorial rooms or deleted from computer screens. Those who have believed and helped spread such belief by public advocacy cannot easily reverse themselves. The collective fiction creates its own collective defense. Once the Yugoslav imbroglio was dramatized as a new version of the Nazi Holocaust, any effort to return to reality was stigmatized as the equivalent of "Holocaust denial", and critics were dismissed as "revisionists" and "negationists", comparable to apologists for Nazi crimes.

GLOBALIZATION AS U.S. HEGEMONY

The economic and institutional factors that animated the Cold War in the United States remained as vigorous as ever after the collapse of the Soviet Union. More so, in fact. The military-industrial complex was intact and triumphant. It no longer had to counter domestic fears that an arms race could lead to war with the other nuclear superpower. While one superpower, exhausted, dropped out of the arms race, the other looked ahead to unlimited opportunities. In the words of Madeleine Albright, "What's the point of having this superb military ... if we can't use it?"[5] The use of military power had to be justified, however. There was to be no "conversion" of military industry to production of civilian goods. The only conversion was ideological: the identification of new enemies and threats.

With the Soviet communist challenge to the capitalist system lying in ruins, U.S. leaders had no reason to accept the sort of "historic compromise" with socialism apparently imagined by the discarded transition leader Mikhail Gorbachev and various European social democrats. Soviet-style political command of the economy had been discredited by incompetence, corruption, and the absence of democratic control or even availability of accurate information. The former Soviet Bloc countries became "transition" countries, as they scrambled to learn how to play the liberal capitalist game. A minority of well-placed individuals made fortunes. Millions of people in the former Soviet Bloc lost their jobs as well as security as basic social services disintegrated.[6]

The elimination of the Soviet system was seen as the triumph of a single dominant model of social, political, and economic organization, imposed by the United States. The uncontested hegemony of the U.S. model is the meaning of "globalization" as it is being carried out by Western transnational corporations, supported by "this superb military".

Globalization has meant worldwide empowerment of the transnational private sphere, dominated by ever more powerful corporations, financial institutions, and wealthy individuals.[7] The function of government is reduced to creating conditions favorable to private investment. This is accomplished by deregulation, privatization of public service, and cutbacks in public spending for social welfare. Every activity must offer prospects for competitive return on investment capital or be abandoned. Throughout the world, government policies are judged, approved, or condemned decisively not by their populations but by "the markets", meaning the financial markets, movements of investment capital outside all political control. Foreign investors rather than domestic voters decide policy.

As the ability of nation-states to protect the interests of their citizens declines, the importance of citizenship diminishes in turn. The democratic process is unable to provide citizens with the protection they need to earn a decent living, stay healthy, and educate their children. In compensation, group identities of all kinds offer the prospect of mutual assistance, protection, or at least solace to populations struggling to cope with changes beyond their control. People turn to identity groups – national, religious, "ethnic", etc. – for protection. It is surely not by chance that in the post-communist era one of the most successful forms of socio-economic organization has been the cross-border Mafia, based on national or ethnic loyalty.

Meanwhile, regulatory functions are transferred to a new international bureaucracy, totally outside any democratic process. Globalization is advanced institutionally by such bodies as the International Monetary Fund and the World Trade Organization, which set the rules and arbitrate between the dominant economic powers. These institutions severely limit the power of governments to protect public interests, whether citizens' welfare or the environment, from the demands of private business. The stalled "Multilateral Agreement on Investment" (MAI) would go even further in shifting vital political decision-making power to the private sector, acting in obscure, non-elected bureaucratic tribunals.

CONVERSION OF THE THREAT

In a mono-polar world, a "threat" is anything that might weaken the hegemony of the single superpower. Under President George W. Bush, this has been made explicit. However, the main thrust of U.S. foreign policy has been essentially the same for over half a century. The gist is that the liberal capitalist model favored by the United States is the only permissible model for future development. Large parts of the world may lag far behind, but there must be no viable attractive alternative. Chaos is preferable to the wrong kind of order. Elimination of any viable alternative model of economic development is the essence of "globalization", just as it was the prime motive for the protracted war against communism. Communism was only one form of the basic, intolerable alternative: a government of a sovereign state determined to control its own resources and markets. The existence of the communist "threat" was an ideological asset to the United States, which could use certain aspects of the Soviet system, notably its harsh repression of political dissent, as the justification for its own intervention, even in places such as Central America where U.S. intervention was already the rule before communism existed. Control of oil resources, not "communism", was the reason why the CIA engineered the military overthrow of the bourgeois reformist government of Mohammed Mossadegh in Iran in 1953. Control of the fruit plantations was the reason why the CIA engineered the overthrow of the reformist government of Guatemala in 1954. The communist threat was an all-purpose ideological excuse.

In Vietnam, the United States failed in its most ambitious project: to impose a Western-style, Catholic-led satellite regime on the territory of an Asian nation whose population was already fully mobilized to liberate itself from a century of colonial oppression. The project failed ignominiously. Nevertheless, the destruction wrought by bombs, napalm, and chemical defoliants, followed by economic sanctions and a cynical alliance with China, prevented Vietnam from emerging as an attractive alternative model of development. After the semi-failure in Vietnam, a shift took place, toward a mixture of edifying rhetoric and destructive action. The great lesson of Vietnam drawn by American strategists was that it was easier to arm a guerrilla movement than to combat one, and easier to destroy an unfriendly state than to build a friendly one. Nation-building was abandoned in favor of destruction pure and simple. The following period was marked by the use of every possible means to sabotage undesirable regimes: criminal mercenaries, drug traffickers, obscurantist religious fanatics. Jonas Savimbi in Angola, the Contras in Nicaragua, death squads throughout Latin America, even Pol Pot after his defeat by the Vietnamese benefited from more or less covert aid from the CIA, while American diplomats preached the gospel of human rights to the world. The *chef d'œuvre* of that policy of destruction was undoubtedly the use of Islamic mujahidins in Afghanistan to entrap the Soviet Union – the declared goal of Jimmy Carter's openly cynical advisor, Zbigniew Brzezinski.[8]

Gorbachev was already in power and seeking an historic compromise with the West and a way out of Afghanistan when the United States dramatically reinforced the mujahidin in 1986 by supplying them with Stinger missiles able to shoot down Soviet planes. The only U.S. aim was to humiliate the Soviets as much as possible, afterwards abandoning Afghanistan to chaos and misery, and at the mercy of obscurantist tribal warlords.

Between Democratic and Republican administrations there is no fundamental difference, even though the Democrats often prefer to stress positive and ambitious goals such as "nation-building" and "human rights". Republicans tend to stress national interests and threats from enemies: communists, the Evil Empire and, starting with Reagan, the "war against terrorism". Presidents come and go but the continuity of U.S. policy is ensured by a small elite of policy-makers who remain outside party politics – and often outside public view. An influential member of this foreign policy establishment is Morton Abramowitz, whose career has involved him with both the Afghan mujahidin and Kosovo Albanian rebels. In 1986, as assistant secretary of state for intelligence and research in the Reagan administration, Abramowitz helped arrange delivery of the Stinger missiles. The collapse of the Soviet Union obliged U.S. policy-makers to redefine the "threat" justifying foreign intervention. The "war on terrorism", launched by President Reagan in the early 1980s, was suffering by the end of the decade from a dearth of active terrorists. As president of the Carnegie Endowment for International Peace in the early 1990s, Abramowitz headed a project to develop a new U.S. foreign policy for the post-Cold War era.[9] Rather than simply identifying "threats", especially at a time when few threats could be seen, a successful new policy needed to combine promotion of U.S. interests with proclamation of American "ideals".

"American ideals and self-interest merge when the United States supports the spread of democracy around the globe – or what we prefer to call 'limited' constitutional democracy, meaning rule by a government that has been legitimized by free elections", was the conclusion of the Carnegie experts, summed up in the Endowment's 1992 publication *Self-Determination in the New World Order*. "The vision of a 'new world order' since 1990 has been a world with one superpower – the United States – in which the rule of law supplants the rule of the jungle, disputes are settled peacefully, aggression is firmly met by collective resistance, and all people are justly treated." This future "rule of law" is not to be confused with existing international law. Rather, it will be developed under U.S. influence. "International law – as it always has done – will respond and adjust to the behavior of nations and the actions of multilateral institutions."[10] A major feature of this "new world order" will be the weakening, even the destruction, of national sovereignty, the basis of existing international law. The sovereignty of the single superpower cannot be seriously challenged, but for other nations, the concept may be outdated.

The sovereign nation is being broken down subtly by the pressures of economic globalization. It may also be undermined from within, by domestic insurgencies. In the post-Cold War world, the Carnegie Endowment study noted, "groups within states are staking claims to independence, greater autonomy, or the overthrow of an existing government, all in the name of self-determination". In regard to these conflicts, "American interests and ideals compel a more active role." This may go so far as military intervention when self-determination claims or internal repression of such claims lead to "humanitarian calamities".[11] In the future, the authors announced in 1992, "humanitarian interventions will become increasingly unavoidable". The United States will have the final word as to when and how to intervene. "The United States should seek to build a consensus within regional and international organizations for its position, but should not sacrifice its own judgment and principles if such a consensus fails to materialize."

This text is significant because it expressed the vision of precisely the people who later led the United States and NATO into the Kosovo war. The selected experts included Richard Holbrooke and Madeleine Albright, among others, who were to become senior officials in the Clinton administration. One of the two co-authors of *Self-Determination in the New World Order*, David Scheffer, became Albright's special ambassador for war crimes issues. The other, Morton Halperin, served as the State Department policy planning director, offering advice on war with Serbia. Another participant in the Carnegie project, Leon Fuerth, former Vice President Al Gore's foreign policy expert, was put in charge of administering sanctions against Serbia.

Abramowitz continued to act from behind the scenes as an *eminence grise* for Albright. He helped found the high-level

International Crisis Group, a chief policy designer for Bosnia and Kosovo. He was omnipresent behind the scenes of the Kosovo drama, both in making policy and in shaping elite business, government, and media opinion. He acted as an advisor to the Kosovo Albanian delegation at the Rambouillet talks, whose programmed breakdown provided the pretext for NATO bombing.

The same group of advisors that theorized military intervention for "humanitarian" reasons went on to make it happen. Events in Kosovo were influenced and interpreted to fit the pattern of a "humanitarian calamity" requiring U.S. military intervention. Perhaps this was sincere, in line with the psychological tendency to see, in an obscure field of vision, whatever one expects to see. One way or another, the prophets fulfilled their own prophecy.

The relationship between Afghanistan in 1979 and Kosovo in 1999 is uncanny. In both cases, out in front there was the discourse on human rights, and in the background, drug traffickers, retrograde clan warlords, and even Osama bin Laden. It is noteworthy that until the 11 September attacks, the United States had consistently chosen to ally with the most obscurantist fundamentalist Islamic fanatics, whose center is Saudi Arabia, against nationalist secular governments. Islamic fundamentalism is compatible with U.S. globalization in that it cares nothing for national boundaries and does not threaten to establish national governments that can serve as a progressive model of alternative development. The plight of Afghan women was of no concern to the Western champions of "human rights" so long as the enemy was the Soviet Union, whose support of the education of girls and women incurred the murderous wrath of the U.S.-backed "freedom fighters".

Osama bin Laden belongs to the same category of enemies as the former Panama strongman Manuel Noriega: discarded assets. After being used to serve U.S. aims, they turned out to have aims of their own. But a superpower can use almost everything. The war against discarded assets provides an opportunity to strike moral poses against the crimes formerly tolerated or encouraged by the United States in its fight against the other category of enemies: potential alternatives.

In a way, Yugoslavia became an enemy *both* as a discarded asset *and* as a potential alternative. When the Soviet Bloc collapsed, non-aligned Yugoslavia lost its value to the West as a strategic asset. As a nominally socialist country with considerable Third World relationships thanks to its leading role in the Non-Aligned

Movement, Yugoslavia could be seen as a potential alternative model. If the country held together, it might stand in the way of Western plans for the region. Perhaps the potential Yugoslav "threat" was an illusion. But its disintegration settled the matter, and destroying the country provided a useful exercise for future operations.

HUMANITARIAN MISSIONARIES

The United States had intervened aggressively abroad before there was a "communist threat" and would continue to do so afterwards. Both imperialism and anti-imperialism existed over a century ago, before there were any communist parties. But in the 1990s, much of what remained of the left had forgotten the critique of imperialism, abandoned all critical scrutiny of geostrategic *realpolitik*, and focused on moral and ideological issues related to "identity politics".[12] With no clear economic policy of their own, left-wing parties were reduced to providing the "human face" for neoliberalism. This took the form of receptiveness to cultural diversity and opposition to racism. In Western Europe, a Eurocentric campaign celebrating "human rights" was used to discredit "Third Worldism". The adversary was no longer social injustice caused by unchecked economic power, but evil caused by bad people who adopted wrong ideas. The catch was that this approach, applied to foreign countries, can all too easily be used to justify intervention, leading back to imperialism at its most aggressive.

The exclusive focus on moral and humanitarian issues, with an emphasis on victims, was fostered by a certain privatization of progressive activism during the last quarter of the twentieth century. As political parties and mass movements declined, single-issue movements grew. These in turn engendered non-governmental organizations (NGOs) taking the form of small (or in some cases large) businesses using advertising to "sell" their good works to donors, whether private or public. The requirements of fund-raising favor consensual causes with immediate emotional appeal. Moreover, while NGOs may benefit from the aura of relative innocence related to being "non-governmental", all of them are by no means strictly "non-governmental". Many depend on contracts from governments. Some ostensible "NGOs" are set up by governments to intervene in the political affairs of other countries.

An important example is the National Endowment for Democracy. Created in 1983 by the Reagan administration, the NED receives an annual tax-exempt appropriation from the Congress, and funds citizens of foreign nations working to make their countries more "democratic" according to American "free market" standards. In Yugoslavia, the NED generously funded Albanian separatists in Kosovo and the anti-Milošević opposition in Serbia. Human Rights Watch, closely linked to U.S. policy-making, repeatedly launched inflammatory and unsubstantiated accusations against the Yugoslav government. Internationally active humanitarian NGOs were in the forefront of the demand for "humanitarian intervention". The fact that the calls for military intervention seem to come initially not from any government but from private voices of conscience in the media, in humanitarian NGOs, and in policy advisory groups helps preserve the illusion that eventual military action must be a disinterested response to moral imperatives. Suspicion of governments contributes to the credibility of these private entities, which, however, may be less open than government agencies to public scrutiny or democratic decision-making. Operating across borders, some charitable groups tend to perceive national sovereignty as little more than an obstacle to their own operations. Based in the rich NATO countries, operating in poorer countries, the direction of their intervention is the same as that of NATO, acting as policeman of the new world order. Such NGOs risk playing a role similar to that played in the past by Christian missionaries, as both a pretext and justification for military expeditions and imperialist conquests.[13] When, as in Bosnia-Herzegovina or Kosovo, military intervention leads to an international protectorate, Western NGOs are granted a prominent role in local administration and receive a large share of public and private donations.

Such are some of the factors that contributed to a readiness on the part of the public in general and the left in particular to accept, even to demand, NATO military intervention in Yugoslavia. The notion that the end of the Cold War had saved the world from the danger of war, that democracy was victorious, and that only a little more effort was needed to rid the world of "evil", distorted the ability to understand what was really happening in Yugoslavia and what was really at stake.

ABOUT THIS BOOK

The purpose of this book is to provide information and analysis to dispute the belief that NATO intervention in Yugoslavia was beneficial. This requires calling attention to aspects of the Yugoslav crisis and conflicts that are either distorted or neglected in mainstream commentary. The objective is not to recount the whole story (impossible in a book of this length), but to put the story in perspective. The inevitable selectivity may be reproached as evidence of a "pro-Serb" bias. Inasmuch as the dominant mainstream bias has been blatantly anti-Serb, this is unavoidable in an effort to recover a fair balance. However, for what it is worth, I can state at the outset that I am not "for" or "against" any people as such. All peoples have their own variants, their own ways of expressing human qualities and weaknesses. I am "pro-Serb" only if that means that I consider the Serbs to be human beings like everybody else, neither better nor worse. I have no personal connection with any party to the Yugoslav conflicts. The only thing that may have inspired a special sympathy for Serbs is the fact that they have been subjected in recent years to an altogether extraordinary campaign of racist calumny by commentators and politicians in NATO countries. The slander of an entire people is an injustice for which there is no court of appeal other than public opinion.

My main thesis is that the intervention of the NATO powers in Yugoslavia, far from being a last-minute rescue, was from the start a major driving factor in the tragic course of events. At best, the Great Powers intruded with all the helpfulness of bulls in a china shop. At worst, they deliberately stirred up fear and hatred in order to serve their own interests. Because of the constant interplay of past and present events in the Balkans, I have chosen an order that is not strictly chronological. Thus in the first two chapters, I plunge into the most burning issues: first, the responsibility for the wars of disintegration, and second, the question of criminal justice. In the third chapter, I describe the differences between various forms of nationalism within Yugoslavia. The fourth chapter is devoted primarily to the role of Germany. The fifth chapter analyzes the interplay between the Albanian nationalist movement in Kosovo and the Western powers, leading to NATO military intervention. In the final chapter, I draw attention to factors putting the Yugoslav events into the context of ongoing world conflicts.

1 The Yugoslav Guinea Pig

Why Yugoslavia? How did the Serbs go from being the heroic little people who stood up to empires and Nazis in defense of freedom, to being the "new Nazis", pariahs of the Western world? What were the faults and weaknesses inside Yugoslavia that account for the conflicts of the 1990s? What did the Europeans and Americans do to contribute to the mess? A complex interplay of internal and external errors and ambitions contributed to the Yugoslav disaster.

Despite concentrated media attention and the publication of book after book, the West managed for a decade *not to see* many of the most significant factors in Yugoslavia.

1. INVISIBLE SERBIA

Bill Clinton, 1999 Memorial Day speech:

> In Kosovo we see some parallels to World War II, for the government of Serbia, like that of Nazi Germany, rose to power in part by getting people to look down on people of a given race and ethnicity, and to believe they had no place in their country, and even no right to live.

Slobodan Milošević, 28 June 1989, at the commemoration of the 600th anniversary of the battle of Kosovo Polje:

> Never in history did Serbs alone live in Serbia. Today more than ever before, citizens of other nationalities and ethnic groups

are living here. That is not a handicap for Serbia. I am sincerely convinced it is an advantage. National structure is changing in this direction in all countries in the contemporary world, especially in developed countries. More and more, and more and more successfully, citizens of different nationalities, different faiths and races are living together. Socialism in particular, being a progressive and just democratic society, should not allow people to be divided by national or religious identity ... Yugoslavia is a multinational community, and it can survive only on condition of full equality of all nations that live in it ... Equal and harmonious relations among Yugoslav peoples are a necessary condition for the existence of Yugoslavia and for it to find its way out of the crisis and, in particular, they are a necessary condition for its economic and social prosperity.

Here we have the contrasting words of two successful politicians, who each in his own country rose to be president with the reputation of being more clever than scrupulously truthful. Which one, in this particular case, is the bigger liar?

In all simplicity, the answer has to be Clinton, because whether or not what Clinton says in this speech is true depends on what Milošević said in order to rise to power. And this speech of Milošević is the prime example, referred to in countless books, editorials, and articles, of the Serbian nationalist rhetoric by which Milošević supposedly rose to power. But what he actually said does not fit the description given by Clinton.[1]

Milošević: a fictional character

Throughout the 1990s, Western political leaders and media collaborated in the creation of a fictional character bearing the name "Slobodan Milošević".

"He is the man who started the war" and won elections "with promises of a Greater Serbia and with lurid propaganda about international conspiracies against Serbia ...".[2] For Daniel Jonah Goldhagen, Milošević was an "extreme nationalist" and a "genocidal killer" who spread "dehumanizing beliefs" in pursuit of "an eliminationist project". On 26 March 1999, Vice President Al Gore described Milošević as "one of these junior-league Hitler types who tries to hold on to power by stirring up hatred among his own people". Former British prime minister Margaret Thatcher went further: "We are not dealing with some minor thug", she insisted.

"Milošević's regime and the genocidal ideology that sustains it represents ... a truly monstrous evil ... which must be totally defeated ..."[3]

Media critic Philip Hammond observed that within 24 hours of the start of NATO bombing, "the Yugoslav president had been described by the UK press as a 'Warlord', a 'Serb butcher', the 'Butcher of Belgrade', the 'Butcher of the Balkans', 'the most evil dictator to emerge in Europe since Adolf Hitler', a 'psychopath', a 'Serb tyrant', a 'psychopathic tyrant', 'evil', 'a man of no mercy', and a 'former communist hardliner'. Casting around for insults, the *Star* added that he was 'dumpy'."[4]

On 13 October 1998, Bill Press, representing 'the left' versus Pat Buchanan on CNN's "Crossfire", said NATO had to intervene militarily against the "evil" Milošević because "He only understands the use of force like Saddam Hussein." General Wesley Clark, not surprisingly, also drew the conclusion from "dealing with Milošević over a long period of time" that "he only listens to one thing; that's the use of force".

The French were not lagging behind. French media during the days of bombing informed the public that Milošević was "a serial ethnic cleanser", "a butcher dictator", "an international terrorist", "a disciple of Stalin and Hitler", "a dictator of the most horrible sort", "a cold-blooded animal" and other descriptions more difficult to translate.[5] The rather ordinary physical appearance of this contemporary Caligula was cited as evidence of his evil character: "Everything in his physical appearance indicates that the man has no feelings. His heavy build speaks of the brutality of the warlord."[6]

This torrent of abuse tells us very little about Milošević, but a great deal about the political culture of the West, which allows its opinion-makers to resort to the most primitive level of insult.

Still, since nobody is perfect, and certainly not the leader of a "transition" country, the question arises: What was really wrong with Milošević?

What was really wrong with Milošević

What was *really* wrong with Milošević is indeed closely related to what was wrong with the Serbian people as Yugoslavia began to come apart at the seams in the 1980s: they were extremely divided. Serbs were geographically divided between the various Republics of the Yugoslav Federation: Serbia and Bosnia and Croatia, not to mention Macedonia (where lines of ethnic identity between Slavs were sometimes nearly impossible to draw) and Montenegro, whose principal inhabitants, the Montenegrins, are basically Serbs. They were subjectively divided between two identities, Yugoslav and Serb. Historically, they were divided in several ways, and most bitterly between World War II partisans and Chetniks (respectively, the communist and royalist guerrilla movements opposing Nazi occupation ... and each other). They were divided in outlook and interests between rural and urban inhabitants. And finally, in the wake of Titoism, they were politically divided between left projects to reform socialism and "centrist" projects to revive the parties and political traditions of the pre-communist past.

When a nation is deeply divided, the leader who can succeed is the one whose ambiguity can create a semblance of unity. The ability to be "all things to all men" is often the key to political success. What was *really* wrong with Milošević was also his biggest political asset: his ambiguity. When he rose to prominence in 1987 and emerged victorious in the struggle for leadership of the Serbian League of Communists, transformed it into the Serbian Socialist Party and then won Serbia's first postwar multiparty elections in 1990, he seemed to be able to square all the circles. He was the political magician who could get rid of communist "bureaucracy" but maintain a reassuring continuity, defend both Serbian interests and Yugoslavism, combine reformed socialism with economic privatization.

Multiparty elections were also held for the first time in 1990 in Croatia and Bosnia-Herzegovina. Genuine nationalist parties won those elections. Franjo Tudjman's party was clearly the party of Croatian nationalism. Muslim, Serb and Croat nationalist parties dominated the parliament of Bosnia-Herzegovina. In contrast, the genuine Serbian nationalist party, Vojislav Šešelj's Serbian Radical Party, came in far behind Milošević's Socialist Party. The voters of Serbia rejected nationalism. This fact was pushed out of sight by repeated description of Milošević as an "extreme nationalist". In the single-minded search for confirmation of this pre-judgment, there has been little effort to make a balanced assessment of Milošević's intentions and those of his adversaries.

Nationalism was the principal taboo in the Serbian League of Communists. Any mention of the interests of Serbs as such was considered unacceptable. The Kosovo problem broke this taboo because, following the death of Tito, a resurgence of militant Albanian nationalism in the early 1980s had made national identity a tangible issue in the autonomous province. Serbs living in Kosovo felt discriminated against, intimidated by the Albanian majority, and under pressure to sell their homes and farms to Albanians and move away. The economic downturn aggravated the problem, as the richer republics (Slovenia, Croatia) balked at continuing to contribute to development funds for the province, where unemployment and population growth were far greater than in the rest of Yugoslavia. Kosovo was a burden for the republic of Serbia, which the others did not want to share. But merely to acknowledge that Kosovo was a problem for Serbs was to break the taboo and entail the accusation of "Serbian nationalism", an accusation which could then be used to justify other nationalisms. Indeed, the very reason why the Serbian communists were so strenuously opposed to any mention of Serb national interest was awareness that accusations of Serbian "nationalism" could be exploited by secessionists in other national groups, endangering the whole Yugoslav Federal State.

Milošević's sin was that he used the Kosovo question to wrest leadership of the Serbian League of Communists away from the man in line for the job, Belgrade party leader Dragiša Pavlović. Denying accusations of nationalism, Milošević said it was wrong to "label us Serbian nationalists because we want to, and really will, resolve the problem of Kosovo in the interests of all the people who live there" and condemned Serbian nationalism as "a serpent deep in the bosom of the Serbian people" that would harm the Serbian people by isolating them.[7]

Supporters of Pavlović bitterly resented Milošević's rise to prominence and played a key role in characterizing him as an "extreme nationalist".[8] This accusation was eagerly welcomed and passed on to the West by supporters of Slovenian, Croatian, and Albanian leaders who had their own reasons for wanting to secede, but who used the "Serb threat" as the acceptable public excuse. However, outside the particular context of the Serbian League of Communists, the concept of "extreme nationalism" conveys positions and attitudes quite remote from those of Milošević. At the very least it suggests hostile chauvinism such as that of the French nationalist Jean-Marie Le Pen, at the most the murderous racism of Adolf Hitler. By such association of ideas, the legend grew of the rise of an aggressive racist dictator in Serbia.

What was really wrong with Milošević was a mixture of optimism and ambiguity not uncommon among ambitious politicians. He was often described as better at tactics than at strategy. His claim to be able to resolve the problem of Kosovo was based on illusion. He continued to preach unity, but offered no program for achieving it. He was never able to resolve the Kosovo problem as he promised, in the interests of all the people who live there. The problem was no doubt much more difficult than he realized. Whether he or anyone else could have solved it is a matter of speculation. In his ten years in office, first as president of Serbia and then as president of Yugoslavia, Milošević also failed to solve the grave economic problems he set out to solve in the first place. As a former banker, Milošević persistently gave priority to the economy. Far from being a useful distraction, the wars of Yugoslav disintegration and the international sanctions that followed were insurmountable obstacles to any coherent economic policy. Economic troubles were a prime cause of the clash of nationalisms, which in turn made problems even more intractable.

2. INVISIBLE ECONOMIC CAUSES

During the 1990s, Yugoslavia was disparaged as a sort of mini-USSR which was taking too long to abandon communism. This was ironic since Yugoslavia had been the first to leave the Soviet Bloc and go its own way. While autocratic in its political system, Tito's Yugoslavia had been able to take advantage of its unique intermediate position between East and West, North and South, to experiment at home and to profit internationally as the only European member of the Non-Aligned Movement. The communists counted on economic development to overcome past national antagonisms. This was not without success, until sharp economic decline was precipitated by failed efforts to adapt to the world capitalist system.

Outside the Soviet Bloc since shortly after it was formed, Yugoslavia had developed its own style of liberal socialism, characterized by "workers' self-management", a "social property" sector in between the state and private sectors, market mechanisms, and much greater personal freedom for citizens, notably the freedom to travel abroad and work in Western countries. Living standards were higher than in most other Eastern European countries and compared favorably with Portugal.[9] Yugoslavia was not a demoralized satellite of Moscow, but a proud leader of the Non-Aligned Movement. Its citizens were welcomed everywhere in the world, East and West. Its engineers worked on development projects in Third World countries, its academics taught in German and American universities, its "guest workers" blended readily into Western society wherever they went. Yugoslavs were not eager to become "Western" because they thought they already were. This was not a prodigal son to be welcomed back into the fold with celebrations; it was not repentant enough for that.

Precisely because Yugoslavia was not part of the Soviet Bloc, it had easily received substantial credits from the West to finance industrial modernization in order to export to Western markets. However, Western markets remained largely inaccessible. After 1979, interest rates skyrocketed on the massive dollar lending of the previous decade. Yugoslavia fell into the same "debt trap" that had strangled Latin American countries. Because the country was dependent on imports even for its own domestic industry, the need to keep up payments on foreign debt took priority among policy-makers. Belgrade was obliged to accept the dictates of the International Monetary Fund. Therefore, during the 1980s, the relatively high living standards of the Yugoslav people underwent the shocks of IMF austerity policies. The cost of basic necessities rose while social services were cut back and jobs eliminated. Strikes and work stoppages increased sharply. But protests were not directed against the growing Western influence. Instead, economic hardship tended to be blamed on domestic politicians – either on the ruling communists or, increasingly, on the "other" nationalities. Susan Woodward has provided a masterly description of this process, which by the end of the 1980s had resulted in "a breakdown in all elements of the domestic order, political disintegration and rising nationalism".[10]

Scapegoating economic reforms

Rather than fostering democratic free enterprise, the IMF reforms encouraged clannishness, nepotism and unfair mutual recriminations between social groups – which in multinational Yugoslavia meant *national* groups. As Woodward observed, the liberal economic reforms

> increased the use of personalistic criteria in access to jobs and goods, as well as the barriers to collective political action for change. Pressures to employ relatives, finding scapegoats on the basis of social prejudice, antifeminist backlash, and rightwing

nationalist incidents became more common. Resentment against those with political sinecures – or what were assumed to be party-based privileges – was informed by old stereotypes (for example, the belief that Serbs dominated political offices).[11]

One of the reactions of Yugoslavs to the economic stress of the 1980s was to blame other national groups – and in particular, to blame the Serbs, by reviving the old belief that Serbs ran the government. This stereotype, left over from the "first Yugoslavia" (1919–41), had not been true for well over a generation. Tito's Yugoslavia was built on a policy of deliberately reducing Serbian influence. The "key" system of national quotas ensured even distribution of public office between the various nationalities. Serbian dominance of Yugoslavia after World War II was a myth.

In the 1990s, this myth took on an added dimension in the version of Yugoslavia's troubles spread abroad by secessionist Slovenians, Croats, and Albanians in order to win Western sympathy. Serbs were equated with communists, to create the impression that the desire to escape from Yugoslavia was identical with the desire to escape from communism. This wildly misleading equation was well designed to appeal to the anti-communist prejudice of ignorant Western media and politicians.

The claim that Serbia under Milošević was the last bastion of communist dictatorship in Europe was particularly ironic inasmuch as Milošević had come to power with the support of Western banks and the U.S. government precisely because he was an economic liberal and political conservative who might have the authority to implement the reforms they wanted.[12] However, to do so, certain basic political changes had to be made, notably revision of the 1974 version of the Yugoslav Constitution which paralysed the Federal Government and made reform impossible. By granting effective veto power to Serbia's autonomous provinces of Voivodina and Kosovo, the 1974 Constitution made it impossible for Serbia to carry out serious reform. Kosovo's local leaders, predominantly Albanian, were most reluctant to accept reforms. Therefore, whether they realized it or not, the Western bankers and diplomats demanding that Belgrade enact major liberal reforms were also calling for the very measure – revocation of Kosovo's autonomy as defined in the 1974 Constitution – which the West would subsequently denounce as an unacceptable Serbian aggression against the "Kosovars".

A chain of causality led from the "debt trap" to the IMF reforms to the economic crisis of the 1980s to the nationalist explosion of the 1990s. But it remained invisible. All the troubles could be blamed on "nationalism", or an evil demon named "Milošević". This is characteristic of the "globalization" process. Outside powers dictate policies, and local authorities take the blame for the consequences. Worse still, the troubles caused are transformed into further arguments for "globalization". National governments are discredited. Only the "International Community" knows what is best for everyone.

3. INVISIBLE CROATIA

In 1990, Franjo Tudjman was elected president of Croatia. His new party, the Croatian Democratic Union (HDZ), was pledged to break away from Yugoslavia and form an independent Croatian state. Tudjman had the strong political and financial support of the Croatian émigré community, including direct descendants of the fascist Ustashe movement which ran the "Croatian Independent State" set up in 1941 following the Nazi invasion of the Kingdom of Yugoslavia. He also enjoyed very effective diplomatic support from Germany and the Vatican. Croatia had a large Serbian population (over 12 per cent of the total). Serbs had been targeted for liquidation by the Ustashe; men, women, and children had been slaughtered. The Serbs of Croatia were bound to be alarmed at the sight of Ustashe exiles returning triumphantly to a Croatia which rapidly restored the symbols of the dread 1941 state – notably the red and white checkerboard flag, which to Serbs was the equivalent of the Nazi swastika. Such symbolic gestures were followed by more concrete measures, notably the dismissal of Serb employees from civil service positions, and outright attacks on persons and property by uncontrolled gangs of provocateurs deliberately reviving the 1941 campaign to rid Croatia of its Serb population.

Throughout the autumn of 1990, Tudjman's government was secretly pursuing a huge illegal arms smuggling operation to transform the new police force, called the Croatian National Guard, into the army of the future independent Croatian state. The operation was run by a former senior officer of the Yugoslav People's Army (JNA), Martin Špegelj, who wanted to use the Croatian armed force to lay siege to JNA barracks and force the officers and men to transfer their loyalty to Croatia.

On 9 January 1991, full taped proofs of Špegelj's operations were set before a meeting of the Yugoslav presidency. It was clear that "by now the Croatian countryside was bristling with weapons that had been secreted or stolen from JNA warehouses or smuggled across the Croatian-Hungarian border".[13] It could not be denied that creating a separate army was an act of high treason and a step toward civil war. The government of any country would be expected to combat such moves. But Yugoslavia under the 1974 Constitution had a joint presidency, a ruling body composed of representatives from each of the Federation's six republics and the two autonomous regions, with its own rotating president – a formula for inaction. The current president of the rotating presidency, Borisav Jović of Serbia, proposed instructing the JNA to disarm the paramilitaries. At this point, the Croatian member of the Yugoslav presidency, Stipe Mesić (who succeeded Tudjman as president of Croatia in 2000), made a proposal illustrating the skill at legalistic subtlety perfected by Croatian political culture during centuries of obstructionism under Hungarian rule. To the order to disarm paramilitaries, Mesić succeeded in adding the word "illegal". This enabled the Croatian government not to carry out the order, arguing that its paramilitaries were not "illegal".

On 17 January 1991, the United States made a decisive intervention on behalf of Croatian secession. The U.S. ambassador to Belgrade, Warren Zimmermann, informed Jović that the United States would not accept any use of force to disarm the paramilitaries. Only "peaceful" means were acceptable to Washington. The Yugoslav army was prohibited by the United States from using force to preserve the Federation, which meant that it could not prevent the Federation from being dismembered by force.

This extraordinary intervention was contrary to all customary diplomatic usage. The United States had never presumed to prohibit Spain from using force against Basque separatists, the United Kingdom from using force against the IRA, Sri Lanka from using force against the Tamil Tigers, Turkey from using force against Kurdish separatists ... And of course, the United States considers Abraham Lincoln its greatest president for using force against the secessionists of the southern Confederacy. Zimmermann's ban was presented as proof of U.S. devotion to "peace" and "peaceful means". However, peace was not the result. Deprived of its sworn mission to preserve Yugoslav unity, the Yugoslav People's Army was doomed to disintegrate into fragments fighting each other on behalf of Yugoslavia's various constituent peoples.

The decisive fact was that Yugoslavia had lost its strategic importance as a potential thorn in the side of the Soviet bloc. Up until then, this strategic importance had ensured Tito's Yugoslavia of generous financial credits (the source of the debt crisis) and indulgence in regard to whatever human rights abuses might be deemed necessary to hold the country together. This was because intelligence specialists predicted that Yugoslav disintegration would enable Moscow to gain controlling influence over the southern Republics.[14] Once there was no more Soviet bloc, Yugoslavia lost its special status in the State Department and was being dumped back into the heap of "southeastern Europe". In April 1989, the new U.S. ambassador, Warren Zimmermann, arrived in Belgrade with instructions to deliver "a new message: Yugoslavia no longer enjoyed the geopolitical importance that the United States had given it during the Cold War".[15] Zimmermann had worked at the CSCE (Conference on Security and Cooperation in Europe, later the OSCE) where he had specialized in the human rights aspect of the Helsinki agreement.[16] From now on, Yugoslavia would be confronted with the same strict scrutiny of alleged human rights abuses that had helped the United States and its allies select the future leadership of other Eastern European countries from among friendly "victims" such as Vaclav Havel and the Polish Solidarnosc leaders. Instead of standing in the forefront of liberalization of state socialism, Yugoslavia was suddenly seen as the laggard in the rapid plunge of ex-Soviet bloc countries into "shock treatment" capitalism.

Throughout the 1980s, Slovenian leaders had been working to detach their republic from Yugoslavia for purely economic reasons. Croatian nationalists in exile, with Tudjman as their champion back home, had been plotting for decades to revive the "independent State of Croatia". Faced with such well-organized, well-financed and internationally supported secession projects, Milošević wavered. There was no comparable Serbian national project. Most Serbs would surely have preferred to preserve the Yugoslav Federation intact. But was this possible, when the United States was banning the use of force? Moreover, far from enthusiastically volunteering to fight for a mythical "Greater Serbia", Serbian students were massively rejecting military service. Rather than be drafted into a civil war, educated youth fled the country in droves – 200,000 is the accepted estimate. Still, Serbs in Serbia could not simply turn their backs on their cousins in Croatia who felt threatened by a renewal of "ethnic cleansing". Obliged to improvise a policy in reaction to Slovenian and Croatian secessionism, Milošević chose what seemed to be a middle course, a compromise. He would accept the secession of Slovenia as a *fait accompli*, go along with the secession of the Croats as unstoppable, but then offer to extend Yugoslav military protection to Serbs in the Serb-inhabited border lands of Croatia, which were already in open armed revolt against Tudjman's new Croatia.

"It is not our intention to prevent the Croats or any other nation from leaving Yugoslavia," Milošević told Belgrade University professors on 21 March 1991, "but we are not going to allow anybody to drag the Serbs out with them against their will". The Serbian government was "clearly for respect of the right to self-determination including secession", but "applied equally to all Yugoslav nations". This was a reference to the Yugoslav Constitution, which explicitly stated that Yugoslavia was constituted by its *narodi*, a word meaning "nations" or "peoples".

The term *narod* as understood in the Balkans is extremely hard to grasp elsewhere and is a source of endless confusion and misunderstanding. *Narod* means a people with the cultural attributes of a nation – notably a common language. In Yugoslavia, the *narodi* were the peoples whose principal political home was in Yugoslavia: Serbs, Croats, Slovenians, Montenegrins, Macedonians, and, after 1970, a new "nationality" called "Muslims". In addition, a second term, *narodnost* (plural *narodnosti*) designated nationalities whose main political home was in another state: Albanians, Hungarians, Bulgarians, Turks, Slovaks, and so on. All enjoyed cultural rights, centering on use of their mother tongue in schools, lawcourts, cultural establishments, and so on. Yugoslavia defined itself as a "multinational" country, not as "multi-ethnic", or "multicultural".

The Serbian argument was that only the peoples who joined together to form Yugoslavia could decide to take it apart. Self-determination was the right of the peoples, not of the republics, regarded as arbitrary administrative units, drawn by the communists without popular consultation. This was a hard argument for people outside Yugoslavia to grasp, although it was a reasonable interpretation of the country's complex laws and traditions. Thus, Milošević argued, "the Serbs should also decide in a referendum whether they do or do not want Yugoslavia. If the Serbs in Croatia decide in a referendum that they wish to live in a Croatia outside Yugoslavia we are not going to oppose that. We are resolved to respect all the human and civil rights of all Yugoslav citizens."

For this position of compromise, neither insisting on preserving Yugoslavia intact nor accepting Croatian independence without satisfying the Serb minority, Milošević has been widely blamed for the break-up of Yugoslavia and all the conflicts that followed. March 1991 has been described as "the decisive month", when "Milošević set the country on the course to war".[17]

Rejection of the Ustashe symbols revived by Tudjman was sharpest in the Serb-inhabited rural regions along the old "military frontier", the *Vojna Krajina*, a rugged, mountainous area which for centuries separated two, often warring, empires: the Ottoman Turkish empire to the southeast and the Habsburg Empire to the northwest. Serb peasant-soldiers had been granted homesteads there centuries ago by the Habsburgs to defend the frontier. Memories of Ustashe massacres of Serbs were vivid. Tudjman rebuffed attempts to obtain guarantees of rights for the Serb population.[18] They held their referendum and demanded autonomy. While the majority of Serbs living in the capital, Zagreb, preferred to pursue negotiations to protect their rights, Krajina Serb leaders impatiently reverted to their centuries-old tradition of armed self-defense. However mistaken, this was not a Serbian invasion of Croatia. The Serb rebellion, as it gained support from Belgrade, was masterfully exploited by Tudjman to portray the long-planned Croatian secession as a defensive resistance to "Greater Serbia".

The evidence is overwhelming that Tudjman set out quite deliberately to create "Greater Croatia", including parts of Bosnia-Herzegovina and perhaps parts of Serbia as well.[19] Tudjman's ambitions were seconded by an apparently united Croatian nationalist movement, millions of dollars of support from the Croatian diaspora, as well as by Germany and the Vatican. Milošević had no such outside support. Despite a confident façade, Milošević was improvising, while Tudjman knew exactly what he wanted.

THE GHOSTS OF GOSPIĆ

When fighting broke out in Croatia in 1991, the situation was confused. Western media coverage was selective. Foreign reporters needed an interpretive framework. This could be obtained in Zagreb, where Tudjman's information agency staffed by helpful English-speaking Croats from Canada and the United States offered a clear interpretation and reports on events to back it up. Thanks to such selective guidance, certain significant events were neglected by international media.

Gospić is the main crossroads town in the Lika river valley, a farming area surrounded by mountains in southwestern Croatia on the western fringe of the *Krajina*. With its mixed population of Croats and Serbs, Gospić has a special place in the collective memory of Croatian Serbs. It was at an Ustashe party meeting in Gospić on 22 July 1941, only three months after Hitler's *blitzkrieg* invasion put an end to the first Yugoslavia, that the minister for education and culture of the newly created "Independent State of Croatia", Mile Budak, described how Croatia was to be purified of non-Croatians within ten years.[20] For non-Croats, he said, "we have three million bullets. We shall kill one part of the Serbian population, expel another, and the rest we shall convert to the Roman Catholic religion. Thus the new Croatia will get rid of all the Serbs in its midst, and all that will be left will be an evil memory ..." This was no idle threat. The Ustashe had already begun to carry it out. Hundreds of thousands of Serbs were murdered or transported to death camps.

Half a century later, Gospić again became a scene of terror. Serbs made up over half the town's population of some 15,000 people. Croatian separatists staged violent demonstrations and besieged the barracks of the Yugoslav People's Army. Two Albanian officers, Ahmet Krasniqi and Agim Çeku, reportedly played a leading role in betraying the JNA garrison to the Croatian separatists, thus depriving local Serbs of protection. This was an early manifestation of an operational alliance between Croatian and Albanian nationalists.

Several years later, Krasniqi was named by Kosovo Albanian secessionist leader Ibrahim Rugova's prime minister-in-exile, Bujar Bukoshi, to head the Armed Forces of the Republic of Kosova, a rival to the "Kosovo Liberation Army" (UÇK). Krasniqi was assassinated in the Albanian capital of Tirana in September 1998, apparently by agents of the UÇK.[21]

Çeku joined the new Croatian army and rose to high rank. In 1995, after undergoing training by "retired" U.S. military officers on contract to the Zagreb Defense Ministry, Çeku helped command "Operation Storm" which emptied the Krajina of its Serb population.[22] Çeku gained a fearful reputation by leading particularly brutal massacres of Serbs in the Lika region. This same Çeku was named commander of the UÇK during the 1999 NATO war against

Yugoslavia and on 21 January 2000 was sworn in as chief of the "Kosovo Protection Corps", the theoretically tamed UÇK.

After the fall of the JNA garrison in 1991, a number of Serb citizens, fearing for their safety, left the town, but were persuaded to return by Croatian authorities, who guaranteed their security. Shortly thereafter, in late September 1991, over 120 Gospić Serbs, including prominent professors and judges, were abducted and murdered, their bodies destroyed or hidden. "It was a warning to Serbs – they were no longer safe in Croatia."[23] According to Croatian human rights activists, this was the first major massacre of civilians in the Yugoslav civil wars.[24] Earlier in 1991, there had been armed clashes, casualties, and attacks on villages in order to secure defense lines. But this was the first massacre carried out as a deliberate act of "ethnic cleansing", designed to frighten the Serb population of Croatia into fleeing. Yet, it was ignored by the world's media. The name of Gospić never became part of the litany of atrocities repeated by news media covering Yugoslav wars. The expression "ethnic cleansing" was taken up by the Western media months later, solely in reference to Serb treatment of Muslims in Bosnia.

Western media ignored the 1991 Gospić massacre until the late summer of 1997 when a disgruntled former policeman, Miro Bajramović, decided to reveal all.[25] Bajramović said his paramilitary unit was sent to Gospić in September 1991 with orders from the Croatian Interior Ministry to spread terror among the region's 9,000 Serbs. The paramilitaries were commanded by Tomislav Merčep, a notorious member of Tudjman's nationalist party who openly revived the slogans and gestures of the fascist Ustashe. "The order for Gospić was to perform ethnic cleansing, so we killed directors of post offices and hospitals, restaurant owners and many other Serbs", Bajramović told the Split-based opposition weekly *Feral Tribune*. "Executions were performed by shooting at point-blank range. We did not have much time. The orders from our headquarters were to reduce the percentage of Serbs in Gospić." Bajramović estimated his unit had liquidated some 90–100 people in less than a month, mostly Serb civilians but also a few anti-nationalist Croats. "I am responsible for the death of 86 people", Bajramović said. "I killed 72 people with my own hands. Among them were nine women."

Bajramović told his story to protest against the failure of the Croatian state to reward him for his services. Other paramilitary leaders got rich, he complained; Merčep had started out with nothing, but now possessed two houses in Zagreb, two apartments and a house on Brač island. But Bajramović had nothing, no job, "but my children eat just like Merčep's do".

Merčep was famous in Croatia. His gang of killers were called the "Croatian knights" by an admiring public. Gospić and Lika was not his only theater of operations. "In early October 1991 Tomislav Merčep's death squad descended on the Pakrac Valley ... entrusted with the task of exterminating the Serbs in the Pakrac region", the Association of Independent Media (AIM) reported nine years later.[26] Serbs were taken from their homes, tortured in the dressing room of the football club "Jedinstvo", and then killed. Members of "Merčep's gang" seemed to be untouchable so long as Tudjman remained in power, and the *Feral Tribune* was even ordered by a court to pay Merčep a large sum (130,000 kuna, about $26,000) for "anguish sustained" by a detailed report of Pakrac crimes published in mid-1995. Only after Tudjman's death was an inquiry opened, setting off furious demonstrations by Croatian nationalists protesting "defamation of the Patriotic War". The Croatian public was "like an ostrich" about the crimes of "our boys", AIM noted.

Six months after his revelations, Bajramović was still in prison, where he was reportedly being subjected to frequent beatings and intense psychological torture by his Croatian jailers. But no moves were being taken to prosecute the crimes he had disclosed. This information came from three former Croatian soldiers, all from Gospić, who risked their lives to take evidence of Croatian massacres of Serbs to the International Criminal Tribunal in The Hague. Their evidence included videotapes showing Croatian forces killing civilians and documents that "implicate senior Croatian officials, including Defense Minister Gojko Šušak, in the killings".[27]

The three – Milan Levar, the former commander of a reconnaissance intelligence unit, Zdenko Bando, a former military police commander, and Zdenko Ropac, a former secret intelligence police officer – told *New York Times* correspondent Chris Hedges that they had witnessed "scores of abductions and killings in and around the town of Gospić during Croatia's 1991 war of independence from Yugoslavia. They say that hundreds of ethnic Serbs, as well as Croats who opposed the nationalist movement, were executed and buried in mass graves around Gospić by the Croatian army, paramilitary groups and the police."

Bando told Hedges that he was "in a position to see everything that was happening" and that "the orders to carry out these killings came to us from the Ministry of Defense". The three men found it "inexcusable" that "those who committed these crimes were never punished, in fact they were promoted within the military, the police and the political structure. They remain in power." The abductions and murders were carried out by "the scum of the town", who were primarily interested in looting the homes and property of the Serbs and Croats they killed. Levar deplored the fact that in order to get rich, those people had "killed my town – the town of my father and grandfather". He feared it would never revive.

These very precise accusations by credible, identified witnesses in a position to know the facts and testifying against crimes committed by *their own* nation, not by the "other side", were treated by the International Criminal Tribunal in a lackadaisical fashion. In cases involving Muslim accusations against Serbs, the Tribunal gave priority to protection of witnesses for the prosecution, even allowing them to remain anonymous. No such interest was shown in protecting these Croats who put themselves at risk to produce solid evidence of crimes against Serb civilians.

Since approaching the Tribunal in August 1997, the three said that they received almost daily death threats, they had been repeatedly beaten by unidentified assailants, their vehicles had been firebombed. Yet the Tribunal had failed to provide them and their families with protection. Two of them had fled their native town of Gospić because of attacks, while the Tribunal was taking so long to investigate that local authorities had time to destroy evidence.

"We do not understand what is going on", Levar told the *New York Times* in early 1998. "We have been branded traitors. We live under constant pressure. The police chief in Gospić and the local army commander are war criminals. What kind of protection can we expect from these men?"

Eighteen months later, on 28 August 2000, Milan Levar was murdered by an explosion in the front yard of his Gospić home. In a short dispatch, Reuters noted that "Levar was the only Croat so far to testify to the International Criminal Tribunal for the Former Yugoslavia about mass executions of Serbs at his hometown of Gospić during Croatia's independence war."

The Hague Tribunal remained indifferent to publicizing or prosecuting the well-documented Croatian ethnic cleansing of Serbs at the very start of the Yugoslav conflicts. Whereas in January 2001,

Tribunal prosecutor Carla Del Ponte insisted relentlessly that The Hague must have priority over Serbian courts in trying Serbs (notably Milošević), the same Tribunal waived any priority over trying Croats. Carla Del Ponte decided that Croatian tribunals could be trusted to do justice. This disinterest on the part of the Tribunal prevented people in the West from understanding the way the war began in Croatia, when massacres of Serbs inevitably revived memories of Ustashe genocide and provoked reactions of self-defense. These reactions in Serb-inhabited areas of Croatia (Krajina, Slavonia) were stigmatized as "Serbian aggression", and used by Croatian propaganda to win international support.

4. GREATER SERBIA OR SMALLER YUGOSLAVIA?

For a short time, in 1991 and 1992, when events moved too fast for people to follow, it was unclear where defending Yugoslavia left off and creating a hypothetical Greater Serbia began. The official policy of Belgrade was to preserve the Yugoslav Federation. But the Federation was shrinking. Slovenia's secession, essentially unopposed (see Chapter 4), caused deep confusion in the Yugoslav People's Army, whose mission was to preserve the Federation as a whole. What was left, and where was the line to be drawn? Croatia's secession raised the problem of the large swathes of Serb-inhabited territory whose people preferred to remain part of Yugoslavia. Preserving Yugoslavia, or most of it, was the first meaning of the slogan "All Serbs in one state". But the slogan might also be realized in a smaller Yugoslavia, without Slovenia and even without Croatia – except for the mainly Serb areas.

The situation itself was ambiguous. Croatia's "Patriotic War" was a war of secession, transformed by the Serb revolts into a war to preserve the integrity of the republic's territory. From the Serb standpoint, it was a war to preserve, if not all of Yugoslavia, then as much of it as possible, including in particular those parts of Croatian territory inhabited mainly by Serbs, or (as in the case of southern Dalmatia, including Dubrovnik) considered by Serbs and Montenegrins to be part of *their* historic lands, not part of Croatia.

In the crucial years 1990–92, the majority of people in Yugoslavia were profoundly confused as to what was happening. Since the Yugoslav People's Army was increasingly uncertain as to what it should defend, the Serb front lines in Croatia were joined by a rag-tag lot of paramilitaries, made up of football fan clubs, thugs, and eccentric nationalists who emerged as if from a folklore museum complete with World War II Chetnik regalia and fueled by large quantities of *šlivovica*. These picturesque ruffians made a profound impression on foreign reporters, who took them as proof of the "extreme nationalism" of Serbs as a whole. The Croatian nationalist militia were more neatly dressed. Both the Serbian and Croatian paramilitaries, plausibly blamed for the worst atrocities committed during the civil war, were joined by "soldiers of fortune" from other countries attracted by some interpretation of the "cause" at stake and by the prospect of making war.

A look at the map shows that the failed attempt to detach the "Serbian Republic of Krajina" from Croatia was less an attempt to create "Greater Serbia" than an effort to solidify a "Smaller Yugoslavia". The Serb-inhabited Croatian Krajina bordered, not Serbia, but the Bosnian Krajina, even more solidly Serb. The two Krajinas were politically linked by the same political party, more conservative and nationalist than Milošević's Serbian Social Party. Their maximum political aim was to stay in Yugoslavia.

In mid-1992, following international recognition of an independent Bosnia-Herzegovina, the Yugoslav People's Army formally pulled out of Bosnia. Thereupon, Serbia and Montenegro alone proclaimed a new Federal Republic of Yugoslavia. The two "Serb Republics" in the Croatian Krajina and in Bosnia-Herzegovina were left out. The West failed to acknowledge that this amounted to a formal renunciation of "Greater Serbia", or even of medium-sized Yugoslavia.

During the period of the Yugoslav break-up, Milošević managed to co-opt Serbian nationalism, while keeping his distance from nationalist ideology. It may be suggested that he thereby prevented the rise of such a truly nationalist leader as Vojislav Šešelj. Surely one thing that made Milošević's "Serbian nationalism" so unbearable to so many critics (foreign and domestic) was that he played the nationalist card, not to get rid of the socialist system, but to hang on to it, or more precisely to hang on to scraps of it – both positive scraps such as remnants of social protection and negative scraps such as the patronage system and control of key institutions including the police and state media. Meanwhile, the negative scraps were also retained by Presidents Kučan of Slovenia, Tudjman of Croatia and Gligorov of Macedonia who had all, like Milošević, been prominent communists in Tito's Yugoslavia. Like the others, Milošević abandoned the collapsing League of Communists to form a new party and win election in multiparty elections. The significant difference was that Milošević's Serbian Socialist Party actually retained some interest in socialism and never had any powerful Western sponsors.

Throughout his period in office, Milošević continued to preach a mixture of Yugoslav multinationalism and reformist economic optimism.[28] After the more truly nationalist Bosnian Serb leadership, defying Belgrade's advice, stubbornly rejected the Vance–Owen peace plan in May 1993, an exasperated Milošević dropped the nationalist component of his political support in search of accommodation with the West (the search that led to the Dayton peace settlement in 1995).[29] From then on, the political tone of the ruling coalition was increasingly influenced by the avant-garde "Yugoslav United Left (JUL)" party set up by his wife, Mirjana Marković. The JUL was a "yuppie" party, some of whose elite members were involved in the more or less illegal trading ventures necessitated by the need to get round international sanctions, but whose doctrine was a perfect compendium of modern leftist "politically correct" ideas and multicultural togetherness, resolutely anti-nationalist.

Milošević's ambiguity enabled him to win elections, but not to unite the Serbs, who throughout remained so divided that for a long time, a strong and not implausible argument for retaining the existing government was simply that the alternative might be civil war. Much more could no doubt be said about what was wrong with Milošević. If using criminals for dirty tasks makes him a criminal, then he may be considered a criminal – but surely no more (or rather, less) than the late President Tudjman of Croatia or President Alija Izetbegović of Bosnia, widely regarded as a saint. All of them used, or at least allowed, paramilitary groups and gangsters to do their dirty work, but only the Serb known as "Arkan" enjoyed the spotlight of Western media. Unlike others, Milošević was virtually forced to resort to extra-legal means to enable his country to survive despite severe economic sanctions. But there is no trace in his words or deeds of the "dehumanizing beliefs" and the "eliminationist project" attributed to him by crusaders against a fictional "Serbian nationalism".[30]

5. INTEGRATING EUROPE, DISINTEGRATING YUGOSLAVIA

From 1989 to 1991, as the Yugoslav crisis was coming to a head, the European Community was absorbed in taking its economic and political integration a step further to become the European

Union. The terms of this Union were spelled out in a clumsily elaborate treaty finally signed in Maastricht (Netherlands) on 7 February 1992. The main significance of the Maastricht Treaty was to lock the EU member states into a monetarist economic policy from which there was no way out, but it was presented to the public as a brave step toward a peaceful democratic new Europe that would emerge as the wonder, even the salvation, of the world. Most of the European politicians involved in the Maastricht process and specialized journalists reporting on it seemed to subscribe wholeheartedly to this vision.

Belief in the European Eldorado was perhaps even more fervent in those East-Central European countries which, from being satellites of the Soviet Union, yearned to attach their orbits to Brussels. It was a moment when "Europe" – short for European Union – exercised an overwhelming attraction on the political classes from Estonia to Bulgaria. Yugoslavia had not been a Soviet satellite, but there too "Europe" was the center of political attraction – with unexpectedly catastrophic results.

First, while political leaders in all of Yugoslavia saw membership of the European Union as their medium-term goal, this did not have the unifying effects that might have been expected. The country's relatively prosperous and market-oriented economic development, as well as its geographic position between Italy and Greece, would have seemed to make Yugoslavia the most eligible of Eastern European countries to join the European Union. There was, however, no clear program for integrating Yugoslavia. The only practical course available leading toward EU membership was the economic austerity program of Yugoslav prime minister Ante Marković, recommended by the IMF and Harvard economist Jeffrey Sachs, which, by cutting the federal budget and public expenditures, was drastically undermining the influence of the federal government and precipitating a takeover of political leadership by the governments of the various republics.[31] At this point, the richest of the republics – especially Slovenia, but also Croatia – saw their chance to "jump the queue" and get into the European Union ahead of the others by cutting themselves off from the rest of Yugoslavia.

Second, and simultaneously, the European Union appeared to Western-oriented Yugoslavs as the *deus ex machina* that would somehow produce solutions to their economic problems and national antagonisms. Yugoslav intellectuals who wanted to preserve and democratize the federation often seemed to count on "Europe" to come to their rescue. In reality, the "Europeans" were totally absorbed in their own affairs. To foreigners who approached the European oracle for answers to their problems, the answer was always the same: "respect human rights". This was all very worthy, but usually beside the point.

What could "Europe" have done? The answer in principle is simple, although the application would have been complex. It could have offered Yugoslavia's people and politicians a prospect of an overall solution to their supposed problems of coexistence by offering a clear, feasible program for integration of *all* of Yugoslavia – all the republics, simultaneously – into the European Union. Such a program would have had enormous political impact, by giving arguments to non-nationalist, non-separatist leaders ready to foster cooperation rather than rivalry between the various segments of the country. This could have prevented the civil wars and justified the European Union's claim to be the core of a new era of peace and democracy for the continent.

In reality, as conflict mounted in Yugoslavia at the turn of the decade, European Community leaders seemed to have no idea what was going on. Just as it was pursuing European integration as the greatest of all historic advances, the European Community contributed decisively to the disintegration of the Yugoslav federation.

The Badinter Commission

The desultory approach of the European Community (soon to be the European Union) was to set up troubleshooting bodies supposed to go off and solve the problem without bothering anybody too much. In Brussels on 27 August 1991 the EC set up an "International Conference for Peace In Yugoslavia", whose first chairman was former UK Conservative foreign secretary Lord Carrington, and an "Arbitration Commission". Within the framework of the Conference, responsible authorities were supposed to submit their differences to this Commission. It was composed of five members chosen among the presidents of the Constitutional Courts of EC member states. At the time, Germany was calling the shots in the Balkans, insisting on rapid diplomatic recognition of independent Slovenia and Croatia. The Arbitration Commission was a French idea, which President François Mitterrand privately described to the Serbs as a way to enable their strong legal case to prevail over their public relations weakness. The presidency of the Arbitration

Commission was entrusted to Robert Badinter, a friend of Mitterrand and president of the French Constitutional Court, who personified a radical idealistic current of jurists. For Badinter, the opportunity to advance international jurisprudence seems to have been more interesting than mediating Balkan conflicts in the light of the ambiguous Yugoslav Constitution. Whatever his intentions, Badinter's function came down to providing a pseudo-legal gloss to the European Union's opportunistic consent to the destruction of Yugoslavia demanded by Germany.[32]

Despite its name, the Commission never engaged in genuine "arbitration" between the disputing parties in Yugoslavia, as some had hoped. Instead, without any legal base other than an executive mandate from EC foreign ministers (at a time when the EC did not yet have any common foreign policy), the Commission issued "opinions" which, although not legally binding on anybody, in fact ended up providing the legalistic arguments used by the International Community in its treatment of the Yugoslav problem. No doubt unwittingly, the five distinguished jurists of the Badinter Commission, in their ten opinions issued between December 1991 and July 1992, contributed to a vague new jurisprudence in which subjective moralistic criteria may be invoked to justify the destruction of old countries and the recognition of new ones.[33]

As if to relieve the EC member states of their grave responsibility, the Badinter Commission declared that: "the effects of recognition by other States are purely declaratory". In reality, recognition was a major issue precisely because it was clear that it would have a major impact on events. Advocates of hasty recognition of the secessionist republics claimed that this would prevent civil war in Yugoslavia by settling the matter once and for all. But the real impact of hasty diplomatic recognition was not to stop the fighting, but rather to formally transform a *civil war* into an *international conflict*, thus allowing international intervention. The impact was to destroy the prospect of neutral mediation and further polarize the conflict.

The Badinter Commission failed to confront the central legal question of the Yugoslav crisis, explicitly raised by Belgrade. In the summer of 1991, while Slovenian and Croatian independence were in suspension at Europe's request, the Serbian government submitted three questions to the Commission for its opinion:

1. Who can be the subject of the right to self-determination from

the standpoint of international public law, a nation or a federal unit? Is the right of self-determination a subjective collective right or the right of a territory?

2. Can secession be a legal act from the standpoint of the United Nations and other relevant legal rules?

3. Are the demarcation lines between constituent parts of a federal state (provinces, cantons, states, *Länder*, republics and the like) borders in the sense of international public law?

The Serbian government raised these questions to call attention to the fact that international law does not, in fact, recognize the right of self-determination in the form of *secession* of an administrative unit within a federal state (such as California within the United States or North-Rhine Westphalia within the Federal republic of Germany). According to the Serbian interpretation of the Constitution, the Federation having been formed by constituent peoples (*narodi*), reversal of this process, in the form of secession, was the privilege of those peoples, and not of the administrative units, the republics. This was the point of contention. The Croatian government argued that secession was the right of the republics. Croatian leaders naturally were bent on retaining the whole of the territory included within the administrative boundaries of the Republic of Croatia as drawn by Tito's partisans during World War II. The constitutional ambiguities were such that a legal argument could be made on both sides. A balanced mediation would at least have recognized the problem and perhaps called for patient negotiation.

However, these official questions from the Serbian government were never answered. Instead, on 29 November 1991, the Badinter Commission issued its First Opinion, which sounded the death knell of Federal Yugoslavia by announcing that "the Federative Socialist Republic of Yugoslavia is engaged in a process of dissolution".[34] This step was unprecedented in international law. By declaring Yugoslavia to be "in a process of dissolution" (the terms "disintegration" and "dismemberment" were also used), the legal status of Yugoslavia was simply dismissed, giving the signal for rival claimants to the remains to seize as much territory of the "disintegrating" country as they could.[35] It then went on to advise everybody to settle things peacefully with respect for human rights and the rights of minorities.

In regard to the question of what new states should be recognized in place of the "disintegrating" Yugoslavia, it abandoned the traditional realistic criteria for diplomatic recognition (control of territory) and substituted a politically correct wish list: commitment to the rule of law, democracy, human rights, disarmament, nuclear non-proliferation, the rights of ethnic minorities, and so on. Of course, anybody claiming to set up a new state can readily pledge commitment to such values, but this is no proof of aptness to organize and govern a state within defined territorial borders. In any case, these criteria were ignored by the very European democracies which had mandated the Badinter Commission to define them. Croatia, which the Badinter Commission found wanting, was recognized anyway, and Macedonia, which was found to meet the standards, was not (because of Greek objections to the name "Macedonia", which could imply claims to Greek territory). These criteria served above all to ease the conscience of the European countries. Whatever the disastrous results of the dissolution, they could rest assured that they had meant it to be for the best.

The purpose of law is not to create Utopia, but to set out reasonably fair rules which, by their regularity, let people know what to expect in particular situations, and so avoid perils. As the American Civil War illustrated, unnegotiated secession can lead to terrible conflict. For this reason, it has long been part of the tradition of states not to recognize such secessions, in order not to encourage either separatist movements by minorities or repression by central governments of minorities which might seek secession. By their treatment of Yugoslavia, the EU member states' governments deviated drastically from the procedures they could be expected to adopt in regard to themselves in such places as the Basque Country or Corsica, or in regard to Flemish separatists in Belgium or the Northern Italian League which would like to separate what it calls rich "Padania" from the rest of Italy. The Badinter Commission avoided questions of legal principle by resorting to an interpretation of fact: Yugoslavia was "in a process of dissolution". This in effect deprived the Serbs of recourse to legal norms. Only facts could count – facts obtained by force.

After recognizing independent Slovenia and Croatia, the Western powers proceeded, in early April 1992, to recognize Bosnia-Herzegovina as an independent state, even though it was very far from meeting the main traditional criterion for such recognition: a central government in control of its territory and accepted by its population. Indeed, from the very start, Bosnia-Herzegovina could be seen to be in "a state of dissolution" itself. This did not seem to matter. On the other hand, the central part of Yugoslavia which clearly was a state, the part which had *not wanted* to disintegrate and still called itself Yugoslavia – was not recognized.

Accepting the *fait accompli* of the secession of the other republics, the governments of Serbia and Montenegro drafted a new Constitution for the Federal Republic of Yugoslavia (FRY) which was promulgated in the Federal Assembly on 27 April 1992. The new Constitution emphasized the equality of all its citizens, regardless of religion or national origin, and at the same time provided extensive cultural rights for a number of national minorities. The human rights criteria of the EU and the Badinter Commission were fully met – but to no avail.

Whereas in other cases (notably Russia with the dismantling of the Soviet Union), the center of a diminished federal or unified state was recognized as its successor, the West denied this status to the third Yugoslavia. Apparently, it inherited only the "disintegration" declared by the Badinter Commission. The effects of the Badinter Commission on Serbia and truncated Yugoslavia were considerable. A British legal scholar has observed: "The view that the SFRY underwent a process of dismemberment was also undoubtedly influential as regards the United Nations' determination that the FRY should not continue automatically the membership of the former SFRY in the UN."[36]

The Badinter Commission was the first instance of the tendency, prolonged in exacerbated form by the "International Criminal Tribunal for former Yugoslavia", to forgo diplomacy in favor of proscriptive legal measures applied from above in the name of the "International Community". In practice, this Community, while claiming to represent impartial justice, listened to the arguments of its favorites and ignored others, without any fair hearing and without the unbiased arbitration that might have contributed to a reasonable settlement. In those years in EU circles, Yugoslavia could only be "the former Yugoslavia", and to use the term "Yugoslavia" without the obligatory "former" was taboo in polite company.

6. MULTICULTURAL BOSNIA VERSUS MULTICULTURAL YUGOSLAVIA

Having decisively contributed to the violent disintegration of multicultural Yugoslavia, the West proceeded to idolize one of the fragments as a multicultural Eden: the central Yugoslav republic of Bosnia-Herzegovina. As Misha Glenny observed, "The decision by the European Community to recognize Slovenia and Croatia pushed Bosnia into the abyss."[37] For complex historic reasons, deeply rooted in the consciousness of the people, the balance in Bosnia depended on its insertion in a balanced Yugoslavia. It was openly and widely predicted that the violent break-up of Yugoslavia was certain to be most violent and bloody in what Glenny called "the paradise of the damned": Bosnia-Herzegovina. Whereas to Western outsiders the Serb–Croat conflict might look like a feud between two retrograde nationalisms, Bosnia introduced the pathos of innocent victims caught between two fires. The Bosnians were indeed victims, but the question of who was responsible was complex. The Europeans who had unwittingly contributed to the disaster were certainly not eager to take the blame, and the easiest place to shift it all was to the Serbs.

The secession of Slovenia and Croatia unbalanced the Yugoslav Federation, increasing the relative weight of Serbia. This was not to the liking of Muslim or Croat leaders in Bosnia-Herzegovina, nor to the government of Macedonia. Muslim and Macedonian leaders were nevertheless reluctant to risk plunging into a bloody and uncertain civil war by declaring independence. At this point, cautious and constructive outside mediation might have avoided war through negotiations to preserve the federation, while avoiding excessive domination by Serbia. However, instead of pursuing "arbitration", as it had supposedly been set up to do, the European Union's Badinter Commission pushed Bosnia-Herzegovina toward the exit – and war – by calling for a referendum on independence. It did not matter to the IC that such a referendum violated the constitution of Bosnia-Herzegovina itself, which stipulated that such a decision could be taken only by agreement between the republic's three "constituent peoples": the Muslims, the Croats and the Serbs. The Westerners simply never grasped the significance of "constituent peoples" in Yugoslavia. The Bosnian Serbs were vehemently opposed to secession from Yugoslavia. They considered that without their consent as a "constituent people", secession and the referendum were illegal. Rather than pay attention to the arguments on both sides, Western media and government egged on the Muslim secessionists, who thereafter considered the West morally bound to get them out of the mess it had plunged them into.

In March 1991, a full year before Bosnia-Herzegovina was precipitated into independence, Tudjman and Milošević held a meeting in the Voivodina town of Karadjordjevo where they are accused of having privately agreed to divide Bosnia-Herzegovina between Serbia and Croatia. Tudjman made no secret of this intention. Integrating southwestern Herzegovina, with its overwhelming Croatian Catholic population, was an essential part of the long-range project for Greater Croatia. Tudjman owed it to the Herzegovina lobby, nationalist émigrés from southwestern Herzegovina who had made a crucial contribution to his rise to power and held top positions in his regime. As for Milošević, at this point he seems to have been navigating without a compass and was above all trying to maintain the impression at home that he was defending Serbia's interests by working things out with leaders of the other republics. Ironically, however, as part of the limitless demonization of Milošević, Tudjman was subsequently criticized not so much for having proposed the division (which he admittedly did), but for having made a deal with Milošević. The Serbian leader, as the source of all evil, was assumed to have been the source of such a diabolical scheme.

But if Yugoslavia was indeed "in a state of disintegration", what would have been so terrible about a negotiated territorial division between Croatia and Serbia to spare the people of Bosnia-Herzegovina the horrors of civil war? There had never in history been an independent Muslim Bosnia-Herzegovina. The designation of "Muslims" as an official "nationality" was a recent innovation. The Muslims were Serbs or Croats who had converted to another religion. Until the 1971 census, Orthodox Serbs made up the relative majority in Bosnia-Herzegovina, and Serb peasants still owned most of the land.[38] Tudjman's initial claims had the merit of being limited to areas inhabited mostly by Croats, in contrast to the "Greater Croatia" of the Nazi years, which had incorporated *all* of Bosnia-Herzegovina. As part of the 1941–44 "Independent State of Croatia", Bosnia-Herzegovina had been the scene of the most horrendous massacres and bitterest fighting between Chetniks, partisans, and various fascist armies and militias. Only the heavy hand of Titoist "brotherhood and unity" had dulled the bitter memories, now ready to emerge. The additional fact that Bosnia was the center of the Yugoslav arms industry ensured that civil war there would be fearful.

To avoid such a war, dividing the territory between Serbia and

Croatia was not necessarily a scandalous idea. It would have required guaranteeing that the full religious freedom already enjoyed by Bosnian Muslims would be safeguarded – by no means a difficult matter. Serbs and Croats had no objection to living with Muslims as neighbors; their objections were to living as potentially second-class citizens of a Muslim *state* – another matter altogether. However, dividing Bosnia could never be seriously discussed, because the Great Powers had arbitrarily decreed that Yugoslavia had to be torn apart along the lines of its existing internal borders, and the U.S. government weighed in on the side of Muslim dominance of that unified state.

The referendum called for by the Badinter Commission created a deep misunderstanding of the situation in world public opinion. Superficially, it seemed that the people of Bosnia-Herzegovina had decided "democratically" for independence, by referendum. By boycotting the referendum, the Serbs appeared to the outside world to be at best bad sports who refused to play the democratic game, and at worst racists who rejected "multicultural Bosnia". However, the Serbs were protesting against a procedure that was unconstitutional, although this made no impression on the West, despite its devotion to "the rule of law". Just as profoundly deceptive was the fact that the Croatian vote was interpreted by the West as a vote in favor of an independent multicultural Bosnia, when in reality it was a vote to detach Bosnia-Herzegovina from Yugoslavia with a view to attaching Croatian portions to Croatia – which is what was actually done.

In March 1992, as Bosnia-Herzegovina was about to explode, thanks to the EU-sponsored referendum, EC leaders made a last-minute attempt to patch things up. Portuguese diplomat José Cutilheiro proposed a compromise to the Muslims, Serbs, and Croats to accept Bosnia-Herzegovina as an independent state while organizing it into "cantons", on the Swiss model. The "Lisbon Accord" was far from perfect. It was not clear how to draw lines in a way that would make sense in terms of both ethnic composition and administrative viability. In any case, the Lisbon compromise would have created a *more* unitary republic of Bosnia-Herzegovina than the one that emerged from the Dayton Accords after four and a half years of war.

The cantonization proposal was signed on 18 March 1992, by Izetbegović, Karadžić, and Boban on behalf of the Muslim, Serb, and Croat communities respectively. It was accepted by all three parties as a compromise to avoid civil war. The Serbs and Croats accepted recognition of independent Bosnia-Herzegovina within existing boundaries, which they did not want, in exchange for "cantonization", which the Muslim party did not want. The compromise did not satisfy Mr. Izetbegović because (in the words of U.S. ambassador to Yugoslavia, Warren Zimmermann) it would have "denied him and his Muslim party a dominant role in the republic". Ambassador Zimmermann hastened to call on Izetbegović in Sarajevo to discuss the Lisbon Accord. "He said he didn't like it, I told him, if he didn't like it, why sign it?" Zimmermann recalled later.[39] Apparently only too glad to be encouraged to hold out for more, Izetbegović reversed his position and withdrew his support for the Lisbon Accord.

What was the full intent or effect of the U.S. ambassador's remark? Opinions differ. The fact remains that the same U.S. ambassador who first prohibited the Yugoslav People's Army from maintaining the unity of Yugoslavia, then went on to encourage Izetbegović's party to fight to maintain the unity of Bosnia-Herzegovina. Morally and practically, this was contradictory. Practically, it made no sense at all: the Yugoslav People's Army, if not opposed by NATO powers, would have been able to hold Yugoslavia together, obliging the parties thereafter to reach peaceful accommodation. Izetbegović's Muslim forces, in contrast, while stronger than admitted, were clearly *not* able to hold Bosnia-Herzegovina together without considerable outside military assistance.

The European Union itself never gave full support to the cantonization plan scuttled by Izetbegović with U.S. encouragement. In the West, Bosnia-Herzegovina was not so much a difficult problem needing careful solution as a subject for moral indignation. In the European Parliament, cantonization was denounced as a betrayal of the supposed European ideal of multiculturalism, which could allegedly be served only by maintaining Bosnia-Herzegovina as a unified, centralized state. This demand merged with the interests of the Muslim party in wielding its influence over a large, united territory. Muslims were against partition, for the simple and obvious reason that it would reduce the size of a predominantly Muslim state. Cannily, however, their American-educated representatives couched this aim in the language of "multi-" this and "multi-" that. Nevertheless, it was always clear, throughout the subsequent negotiations led mainly by Cyrus Vance and David

Owen, that some sort of territorial division was inevitable. Without an agreement to work this division out peacefully, the prospect served only to encourage "ethnic cleansing", in view of an eventual division of territory along ethnic lines.

With Alija Izetbegović and his Muslim party, the Party of Democratic Action (SDA), the U.S. government had found its own client (or pawn) to back in the silent rivalry between Western powers over the remains of "disintegrating" Yugoslavia. If Germany had its own client, Croatia, the United States now had one of its own.

Without the promise of superpower backing, Izetbegović might have felt obliged to work out a compromise with other parties in Bosnia-Herzegovina. The United States never delivered on Zimmermann's implicit promise to ensure Izetbegović a dominant role in a unified Bosnia-Herzegovina. However, behind the scenes it helped him arm his military forces, with considerable input from Islamic states and mujahidin fighters, while portraying his cause to the world as one of pure martyrdom. This double role was greatly facilitated by the U.S. branch of Izetbegović's party, represented by Bosnia-Herzegovina's first ambassador to the United Nations, Mohammed Sacirbey, who was in fact an American. The Sacirbegović (Sacirbey) family were politically active anti-communist Muslims who emigrated to the United States when Mohammed was seven years old. His father ran the U.S. branch of Izetbegović's SDA. The young Sacirbey was living in New York when he was given the high-profile UN post in the spring of 1992. The Izetbegović and Sacirbegović families belonged to the Muslim upper class (the "beg" in Bosnian names comes from the Turkish title "bey") who had enjoyed elite privileges during the centuries of Ottoman Turkish rule and were considered more safely anti-communist than the Bosnian Serb descendants of downtrodden peasants.

Being allied with the Bosnian Muslims had obvious political and geostrategic advantages for the United States. It helped cement Washington's crucial strategic alliance with Turkey, as well as with other Muslim countries in the arc reaching across Central Asia and including the petroleum reserves of the Caspian region. "The central focus of U.S. policy is Turkey, which Washington recognizes as the major regional power with considerable potential for expansion", the BBC's correspondent in the region Misha Glenny wrote at the time.[40] "America's policy is explained by its strategic and economic interests in the Mediterranean and the Middle East

– from now on, the Turks are the key nation in the region. This is bad news for the Greeks and bad news for the Serbs." Bosnia provided a miniature "Slav versus Muslim" conflict, which could be appreciated by analogy to eventual rivalries with Russia in Turkey's expanding sphere of influence among the Turkish-speaking peoples of the former Soviet Union, and all the way into China. It was also a useful demonstration that, despite unshakable support for Israel and the ongoing destruction of Iraq, the United States was not anti-Muslim. The pro-Muslim Bosnia policy actually facilitated practical cooperation between the Clinton administration and the Muslim countries which financed the Muslim cause and furnished both arms and fighters – some of the same mujahidin that the United States had supported in Afghanistan in pursuit of Brzezinski's strategy to weaken the Soviet Union by its "soft underbelly", that is, the predominantly Muslim southern tier. Since many Muslim states from Saudi Arabia to Brunei are important sources of oil and petrodollars, cooperation with them in a holy cause could only be good for business.

The Bosnian Muslim connection received strong political support from segments of the Israeli lobby because it promised to strengthen the crucial strategic US–Israeli–Turkish alliance in the Middle East. This attitude was expressed very frankly in a January 1996 column by *New Republic* editors Jacob Heilbrunn and Michael Lind, who wrote:[41]

> ... instead of seeing Bosnia as the eastern frontier of NATO, we should view the Balkans as the western frontier of America's rapidly expanding sphere of influence in the Middle East. ... The fact that the United States is more enthusiastic than its European allies about a Bosnian Muslim state reflects, among other things, the new American role as the leader of an informal collection of Muslim nations from the Gulf to the Balkans. The regions once ruled by the Ottoman Turks show signs of becoming the heart of a third American empire.

Heilbrunn and Lind predicted with remarkable foresight: "The main purpose of NATO countries, for the foreseeable future, will be to serve as staging areas for American wars in the Balkans, the Mediterranean and the Gulf."

The U.S. patronage to the Muslims of Bosnia was a subtle thorn in the side of the European Union. Indirectly bringing Turkey back into its former Balkan colonies was consistent with strong U.S. support for Turkish membership of the European Union. This support is embarrassing to the EU members states, who for the most part do not dare openly admit that they don't want Turkey to join, for various reasons, not least because of the impact on wages, demographics, and employment in the Western countries of unlimited entry of Turkish workers. More immediately, by standing on the sidelines and criticizing every proposal tabled as unfair to the Muslim side, the United States helped scuttle European efforts to end the conflict.[42]

On the rhetorical level – which was dominant in the early Clinton years – verbal support for the Muslims was an indispensable gauge of liberal sensibility, anti-racism, and concern for human rights. A number of politicians, intellectuals, and cultural figures throughout the West elevated support to "the paradise of the damned" to the touchstone of modern humanitarianism.

The Bosnia cult

The reality was complex, and steeped in lies, myth, and history. The reporters sent to report on the "siege of Sarajevo" were mostly too new to the region to be able to distinguish truth from lies. The mass media wanted a simple story. This meant something with "human interest", a pathetic story of innocent victims on one side and an evil villain on the other. Soon all photos of bereaved civilians were identified as Muslim, even if they were Serb. The story was easier to sell if it was clear who the "good guys" were and who the "bad guys".

However, the Bosnia cult that developed between 1992 and 1995 went far beyond the reporting, biased or otherwise, of the mass media. Sarajevo became the last stand of the intellectuals aspiring to continue the tradition of the *intellectuels engagés* of the twentieth century. The term echoed Jean-Paul Sartre, but the precise models were those who had defended the Republican side in the Spanish Civil War: André Malraux, Ernest Hemingway, George Orwell ... Like the tradition, the Bosnia movement was strongest in France and in circles in the United States that take the French *intellectuel engagé* as model. On one level, Bosnia aroused such passion because in Sarajevo, visiting Westerners found people just like themselves, in dramatically perilous circumstances. These were *Europeans*, suddenly elevated from their contemporary function as prosperous consumers to tragic victims of war. For all the protests that war was not supposed to happen to Europeans any more, the excitement generated cannot have been entirely unwelcome to a generation with no cause more inspiring than the common currency. A real aversion to war might have led journalists and writers to find in Bosnia merely the destructive chaos that can result when human beings fail to manage their collective affairs in a sensible way. Instead, they flocked to embrace "Bosnia" as a cause of great significance: indeed *the* cause of their generation. A cause worthy of yet more war.

"Bosnia was and always will be a just cause", wrote David Rieff, who has expressed as well as anyone the ideology of the Bosnia cult.[43] By "Bosnia", Rieff meant above all the *value of multiculturalism*, which, in his mind, was exemplified in Bosnia-Herzegovina where it was the object of "genocide". Armed with this conviction, he did what he could to fit reality into it, lopping off pieces, discounting unwelcome contradictions, padding an inadequate factual basis with passionate writing.

Rieff's conviction was all the more rapid in that it pre-dated his discovery of its apparent embodiment in Bosnia. He had left the United States in order to write about the effect of non-European refugees and immigrants on Europe, firmly persuaded in advance of the imperative need to transform old Europe into a new Europe that was "genuinely multicultural and multiracial". Rieff was openly and fervently convinced that Europe must become another United States, a melting pot. He had gone to Europe "in search of this 'Americanization' of the European future" with the "didactic conviction that in the twenty-first century we would all be polyglot or we would kill one another off".[44]

This is a rather extraordinary conviction, and comes down to saying, "within a century, everybody must be like me, or else we will all kill each other". However, it converged with that of a number of European intellectuals who viewed Bosnia through the distorting lens of Europe's immigrant problem. The sudden idealization of Bosnia-Herzegovina was closely related to a preoccupation with a current problem of vital importance in countries such as France: assimilation of Muslim immigrant populations. Television viewers suddenly discovered a romantic Sarajevo, populated by gentle, blue-eyed Muslims, practicing musical instruments in comfortable apartments – people "just like us". These people would be perfect neighbors, and their lukewarm European Islam seemed to offer the ideal model for successful assimilation.

The notion that "Bosnia" represented the model for Western Europe's integration of its Muslim immigrants helps explain the vehement hostility that arose against the Bosnian Serbs, accused of destroying this model society out of sheer racist nationalism. It accounts for the extreme passion expressed in the 1994 slogan adopted by Bosnia's European champions, "Europe lives or dies in Sarajevo". Multicultural Sarajevo was represented as a test case for the survival of European integration in the broadest sense. Through this lens, many Europeans almost automatically and without reflection identified Muslims with the underdogs: with the exploited immigrant workers in contemporary Western Europe, or with the victims of Europe's colonial wars (notably Algeria) in the past. Looking further back, the Serbs were subliminally equated with the Crusaders who had carried war against Islam to the Holy Land. These identifications were false and even ironic. The Crusades were a strictly Roman Catholic undertaking, which had culminated in the ruin of the capital of Eastern Orthodox Christianity, Constantinople. And there was nothing in common between poor Muslim immigrants in Western Europe and the leaders of Izetbegović's party, representatives of the old ruling families who made up the elite of the province under the Ottoman Empire.

Rieff was thus by no means alone in his passion, as he rightly recalls, explaining why he and "many other foreign writers, photographers and television journalists" kept choosing "to spend time on the Bosnian side":[45]

> We did not just think that what was going on was a tragedy – all wars are tragic – but that the values that the Republic of Bosnia-Herzegovina exemplified were worth preserving. Those ideals, of a society committed to multiculturalism (in the real and earned rather than the American and prescriptive sense of that much overused term), and tolerance, and of an understanding of national identity as deriving from shared citizenship rather than ethnic identity, were precisely the ones which we in the West so assiduously proclaim.

If these ideals were so worth preserving, why had there been no such ardent crusade for preserving *Yugoslavia*? Timing must have something to do with it. The idealists who discovered Bosnia after the proclamation of Yugoslavia's dissolution never quite realized that their multicultural ideals had been the mainstay of Titoist Yugoslavia, and that Bosnia-Herzegovina was the most "Titoist" part of the country. If "brotherhood and unity" was a forced slogan, it was most forced of all in Bosnia-Herzegovina, where memories of the killings of World War II were sharpest.

Recognition of the fears and antagonisms that made the three communities wary of each other could have been a step toward security guarantees to reassure them all. Instead, all had to try to deal with the West's illusion of Bosnia-Herzegovina as a paradise lost. Some tried to expose the illusions, others to exploit them. Certain realities were taboo. The Serbs, with memories of Muslims being recruited to the Nazi SS "Handžar" division to slaughter Serbs during the war, did not want to be a minority in a Muslim state. Nor did the Croats, although they were more discreet about it.

Muslim leaders, in contrast, were in favor of a unitary state for Bosnia-Herzegovina. This was natural. Since Muslims were the relative majority, they could hope to dominate a unitary state, and the more territory it covered, the better. This meant willingness to include Serb-inhabited and Croat-inhabited areas in a single political unit. (Thus the oft-repeated quip, "Why should I be a minority in *your* state, when *you* can be a minority in *mine*?") With the help of US-based public relations experts, this perfectly reasonable (in terms of self-interest of a Muslim state) attitude was presented as proof of devotion to multicultural tolerance in contrast to the "racism" of the Serbs.

Ideals versus facts

The idealization of Bosnia rested on the impression that Sarajevo had been an ideal "multicultural" society before being attacked by bigoted Serbs, and that Izetbegović and his Muslim party were the true defenders of that multiculturalism. None of these assumptions could withstand confrontation with basic facts available to all observers but resolutely ignored by the devotees of the Bosnia cult.

First of all, if the people of Sarajevo were indeed the embodiment of modern multiculturalism, why had 90 per cent of its citizens voted, the first chance they got (in December 1990), for one of the three nationalist parties, Muslim, Serb, or Croat? This does not prove that they were all "nationalists" by any means, much less that they favored the civil war that ensued. Rather, it indicates a measure of mutual distrust, and fear, that is not wholly compatible with a "multicultural paradise". In reality, only the truly mixed residents of Tuzla had shunned the nationalist parties and elected a non-nationalist, social democratic mayor, Selim Beslagić. But Tuzla was a dingy industrial town, without the romance of Sarajevo. Politically, Sarajevo was divided along cultural lines, far more than Belgrade, for instance, also a "multicultural" capital. Moreover, the cultural divide in Sarajevo was geographical; throughout the "siege", the city was divided between Muslim-held and Serb-held areas, each shelled and sniped at by the other, with the civilians in both sides suffering the same hardships. But the media were lodged in the Muslim-held center (which included Croatian and Serb minorities who were not allowed to leave, as well as the city's more attractive monuments) and ignored the Serb-populated sections in the more modern suburbs.

In May 1992, Muslim soldiers and snipers won a decisive early skirmish in their victorious battle for media support by frightening foreign journalists out of the Serb-controlled suburb of Ilidža, location of the Bosna hotel, first choice of foreign visitors to Sarajevo. In face of this danger, international correspondents were pulled out, and when they came back, they settled into the Holiday Inn in Muslim-held central Sarajevo. In that setting, they naturally identified with the cause of the local defenders, the Muslims. The "Sarajevo" on the world's television screens was the Muslim center of the city. The Serbian suburbs, whose inhabitants were undergoing the same fears and deprivations, became invisible.

To Westerners who had identified Bosnia-Herzegovina as the shrine of multiculturalism, any division was outrageous and unacceptable, since it implied the triumph of nationalism over multiculturalism. But not every division attracted the indignation of the humanitarians. In the opening stages of the civil war in Bosnia-Herzegovina, Tudjman sent the Croatian army to occupy southwestern Herzegovina. Extreme right-wing Croatian nationalist militia drove the Serb population out of Mostar. The ethnically cleansed Croat territory was declared "Herceg-Bosna" on 3 July 1992, and *de facto* annexed to Croatia, with Croatian police, flag, currency, and postage stamps. While this went on, the Western powers politely looked the other way. Having determined that only the Serbs stood in the way of an ideal unified Bosnia-Herzegovina, the "International Community" steadfastly ignored the existence of Herceg-Bosna and its ethnically purified Croatian Catholic population – even though all through the civil war, busloads of international pilgrims continued to converge on the Herceg-Bosna village of Medjugorje, to visit the scene of contemporary "visions of the Virgin Mary". There a flourishing tourist economy lived off scenes of mystical "ecstasy" skillfully stage-managed by the local Franciscans. Millions of pilgrims to Medjugorje bought "Herceg-Bosna" stamps (no "Bosnia-Herzegovina" stamps were available in Herceg-Bosna post offices, where only the Croatian flag flew) with Croatian currency for Catholic postcards to mail back home, without ever encountering a trace of the "multicultural" Bosnia-Herzegovina they were theoretically visiting. This total removal of a large piece of Herzegovina from the authority of Sarajevo was artistically cloaked under the "Federation" which the United States forced the Croat and the Bosnian Muslim leaders to sign. The "Federation" was a means for both to isolate the Serbs, the better to continue to fight each other unobserved.

As to the devotion to multicultural society of Izetbegović's followers, Rieff himself admitted that their "commitment ... to the values of multiculturalism and their belief in civil society had been far less firm" before Bosnia's recognition by the West in April 1992, and "began to wane in late 1994". He explained this short-lived commitment by the fact that "the Izetbegović government's strategy was to try to get the West to intervene militarily". Particularly in Central Bosnia, he acknowledged, "the Islamic fundamentalists became more and more important as the conflict dragged on ..."[46] But neither Rieff nor the other Bosnia enthusiasts stopped to consider that the extreme fragility of the Islamic party's devotion to multicultural values might explain why Serbs (and Croats) did not want to remain under a government headed by Izetbegović.

The Bosnian capital was a mirage for visiting dignitaries, "Potemkin Sarajevo" in the words of a president of the journalists' association of Bosnia-Herzegovina, who fled for his life to Norway in 1992.[47] The media reproduced photographs of the grandfatherly Izetbegović, but not his words, such as in this March 1994 speech:[48]

> In one of our respectable newspapers I read that our soldiers are dying for a multicultural coexistence, that they are sacrificing their lives so we can live together. Multicultural togetherness is all very well, but – may I say this openly – it is a lie! We cannot lie to our people or deceive the public. The soldier in combat is not dying for a multinational coexistence ...

Some 5,000 Muslim volunteers who came via Vienna to fight for Izetbegović, many of them veterans of Afghanistan, were certainly not interested in defending "multiculturalism".[49] Nor were the thousands of recent immigrants to Sarajevo from the Sandžak region of Serbia itself, more or less fanatic Muslims who adhered to Izetbegović's Islamic party and provided much of its most militant leadership. The fact that Izetbegović enjoyed the active support of these Muslims from outside Bosnia, *against* a large part of the indigenous Bosnian Muslim population, was also of little interest to Western enthusiasts.

David Rieff's mother, Susan Sontag, actually attempted to turn Sarajevo into the Bosnia cult's vision of it by going there and staging Samuel Beckett's "Waiting for Godot", in an apparent snipe at the "International Community" which was slow to rush to the awaited rescue. Meanwhile her son seemed little concerned to separate fact from fiction in his zeal to prove his tragic thesis that Bosnia was the best of all multicultural societies, being subjected to "genocide", and that "the Serbs were the villains of the war".[50] The press corps in the Holiday Inn knew that "to be fair and to be impartial are not the same thing",[51] what mattered was to work up enough public indignation to force the West to intervene militarily on behalf of the Muslims. After his first trip to Bosnia in September 1992, to write for an American magazine on "ethnic cleansing", Rieff returned repeatedly, "resolved to write as frankly incendiary a narrative as I could", with the idea that what he wrote could end the slaughter. Rieff had no doubt: "ethnic cleansing was not just a war crime, it was genocide, pure and simple".[52] But two pages later: "Ethnic cleansing was in part about making these routes secure from guerrilla attack." That sounds more like war than genocide.

"Genocide" was a leitmotif of this "frankly incendiary" narrative, which did not fail to compare "the Serbs" to the Nazis and the Khmer Rouge.[53] Such rhetoric inflated into the Cause of the century what was perhaps only a brutal little civil war for control of contiguous territory in a mountainous province chock full of arms factories and men trained in guerrilla war, occasionally aided by outside mercenaries: thousands of Muslim mujahidin fighting for Allah, a smattering of Russian Slavophiles rushing to the aid of the Serbs, and various European neo-Nazis inspired by Tudjman. They were inevitably joined by local criminals and psychopaths taking advantage of the chaos to rape and pillage under cover of one "cause" or the other. All this made Bosnia-Herzegovina a dangerous place, so dangerous that a large part of the population, Muslim, Serb, or Croat, wished or managed to escape from it. This was a disaster, but not exactly "genocide".

Rieff evidently considered the genocide charge so self-evident that he made no effort to prove it. He simply repeated the figure that everyone else repeats: 200,000 dead. "Two hundred thousand Bosnian Muslims die, in full view of the world's television cameras", according to Rieff.[54] This is obvious hyperbole, inasmuch as however many Bosnian Muslims died, this did not happen "in full view of the world's television cameras". As to the oft-repeated and never verified statistic, former State Department official George Kenney traced its origin to the Bosnian information minister, Senada Krešo, who in late June 1993 "told journalists that 200,000 had died. Knowing her from her service as my translator and guide around Sarajevo, I believe that this was an outburst of naive zeal. Nevertheless, the major newspapers and wire services quickly began using these numbers, unsourced and unsupported."

On 28 June, the *Christian Science Monitor* quoted Senada Krešo, "a government official", as declaring that: "Two hundred thousand people died for Bosnia." The same article also quoted Bosnian foreign minister Haris Siljadžić as deploring "ten months of war and 100,000 killed".[55] Of these two suspiciously round and equally unverified figures, Western media henceforth chose to take the larger one as authoritative.

Kenney, with the extremely rare courage to admit having been wrong, recalled that he himself had used the figure of 200,000 dead in articles and speeches for a while in 1993. But unlike the press, which "simply never bothered to learn the origins of the numbers it reported", Kenney began to inquire. His findings:[56]

The Red Cross has confirmed well under 20,000 fatalities on all sides. Extrapolating from that and from the observations of experienced investigators in Bosnia, its analysts estimate total fatalities at 20,000 to 30,000, with a small chance that they may exceed 35,000.

Analysts at the C.I.A. and the State Department's Bureau of Intelligence and Research put fatalities in the tens of thousands but hesitate to give a more precise range until the war is over. European military intelligence officers with extensive experience in Bosnia estimate fatalities in the mid tens of thousands. From these and other estimates by generally reliable relief workers, and given the arguments about the physical impossibility of high numbers, I arrived at the range of 25,000 to 60,000 fatalities.

Kenney concluded that "counts count", because the big numbers were deliberately used to urge the United States to take measures (arming the Muslims) that would result in many more deaths.

A decade later, it is still impossible to say exactly how many people were killed in the 1992–95 war in Bosnia-Herzegovina (just as it was impossible to determine how many people were killed in the war half a century earlier). The 1996 *SIPRI Yearbook*, an authoritative source, estimated the number killed at between 30,000 and 50,000 *on all sides*.[57] But the media continued to circulate the figure of 200,000, or 250,000, implying they were all Muslims, and without giving any source. Kenney at least tried to research the question, which Rieff did not. Those who wrote about Bosnia in those years did not consider it appropriate to regard the propaganda of both sides with equal skepticism, or to check sources of allegations against the Serbs. Large casualty figures and horror stories were deemed helpful to the cause.

Kenney concluded:[58]

In the words of the writer David Rieff, "Bosnia became our Spain", though not for political reasons, which is what he meant, but rather because too many journalists dreamed self-aggrandizing dreams of becoming Hemingway.

What was being destroyed in this "genocide" was not the Bosnian people, who despite undeniable hardships and heartaches – yes, and despite Srebrenica – have survived, although widely dispersed.[59] What was being destroyed was the Western intellectuals' multicultural dream. Meanwhile, by readily believing the worst horror stories, they exacerbated hatred on all sides and helped to destroy the Yugoslavs' multicultural reality.

Izetbegović: Islamic hero of the Western world

Of the separatist leaders who tore apart Yugoslavia in the early 1990s, the president of Bosnia-Herzegovina, Alija Izetbegović, was the only one to be seen as a hero in the world outside, notably in Muslim countries, France, and the United States.[60] His Western supporters venerated him as a martyr, but took no serious interest in his ideas or political program. Perhaps they considered his ideas of as little consequence as the "ideas" expressed in contemporary Western political platforms. Yet they were the foundation of his Party of Democratic Action (SDA), the Muslim political movement in control of the Sarajevo government, and a key to understanding the civil war. Bosnian Serbs openly, and Croats more discreetly, considered him an Islamic fundamentalist. This was dismissed in the West with total incredulity and outrage as blatant Serb propaganda, invented to justify aggression and ethnic cleansing. How could the leader of the Bosnian Muslims be an "Islamic fundamentalist" when the Bosnian Muslims were obviously such a model of modern tolerance?

In reality, Izetbegović not only failed utterly to represent the population of Bosnia-Herzegovina in its multicultural variety, he did not even represent all the Muslims. In the 1990 election, the former head of the republic's important agro-industrial company, Fikret Abdić, received 1,010,618 votes, compared to 847,386 for Izetbegović. As president of Bosnia, the pragmatic Abdić could have been acceptable to the non-Muslim populations. But in a deal that remains mysterious, Abdić stepped aside in favor of Izetbegović.[61] This was supposed to be a shared presidency, to be rotated annually between a Muslim, a Serb, and a Croat. But Izetbegović proved unmoveable.

Politics and religion

That Izetbegović could not be considered the uncontested leader of a unanimous Muslim community, much less of "multi-ethnic Bosnia", is clear from his own published writings, the "Islamic Declaration", and a full-length book, *Islam Between East and West*.[62] First distributed in 1970 and republished 20 years later, precisely at the time of his bid for the presidency, the "Islamic Declaration" was a manifesto addressed to Bosnian Muslims who, according to Izetbegović, could not be satisfied in a secular order.

> Islamic society without an Islamic government is incomplete and impotent ... A Muslim, in general, does not exist as an individual ... to live and exist as a Muslim, he must create an environment, a community, a social order ... History does not know of a single truly Islamic movement which was not simultaneously a political movement.

This Declaration reflected a global revival of the Muslim world, "made up of 700 million people possessing enormous natural resources and occupying a geographical area of the first importance". Among the "enormous natural resources", first place was of course occupied by petroleum, whose revenues at this time were beginning to finance heavily the global awakening hailed by Izetbegović. "The time of passivity and peace is gone forever", he declared. The time had come for "the rebirth of Islamic religious thinking and creation of an Islamic community from Morocco to Indonesia".

The deliberately political nature of Izetbegović's Islam is evident in his attack on two currents within the Muslim community, accused of blocking the political renewal of Islam: the "conservatives" on the one hand, and the "modernists" on the other. By "conservatives" he meant those linked to the Sufi tradition of mystical Islam. They were sharply criticized for neglecting politics for spiritual concerns, thereby going along with a secular regime which he condemned as incompatible with genuine Islamic life.

As for the "modernists", who unlike the mystics were often influential in public life, Izetbegović viewed them as a veritable disaster for Islam throughout the Muslim world. They too considered Islam merely a religion that need not or could not order the external world. Like the mystics, they accommodated secularism and prevented Islam from exerting its proper role in ordering all aspects of life. The "Islamic Declaration" thus very explicitly rejected the intellectual currents which, notably in Arab countries, were attempting to build modern secular nation-states on the Western model of separation between government and religion.

Izetbegović illustrated this condemnation with the example of Turkey, a Muslim country ruined, in his view, by secularism and nationalism. "Turkey as an Islamic country ruled the world. Turkey as a copy of Europe is a third-rate country like a hundred others around the world." This is particularly significant, inasmuch as he himself is an heir to a Muslim elite which bitterly opposed attempts by the later Turkish Sultans to make concessions to Balkan Christians in order to preserve Ottoman rule in the Balkans. When the Ottoman Empire collapsed, a number of Balkan Muslims emigrated to Turkey, where even today they may constitute a lobby favorable to Islamic political restoration within Turkey itself.

The country Izetbegović singled out in his "Declaration" as an example and inspiration, as "our great hope", was Pakistan.

"Pakistan constitutes the rehearsal for introduction of Islamic order in contemporary conditions and at the present level of development." For secular society, Pakistan as an example is hardly reassuring, considering its longstanding support to armed Islamic groups in neighboring countries, notably Afghanistan. Izetbegović's repeated message was that the Koran calls for unification of religious faith and politics. Separation of church and state is explicitly rejected as a Christian division totally unacceptable to Muslims. "The first and most important" conclusion to be drawn from the Koran is "the impossibility of any connection between Islam and other non-Islamic systems. There is neither peace nor coexistence between the 'Islamic religion' and non-Islamic social and political institutions."

> Having the right to govern its own world, Islam clearly excludes the right and possibility of putting a foreign ideology into practice on its territory. There is thus no principle of secular government and the State must express and support the moral principles of religion.

Izetbegović's immediate concern in writing the 1970 "Islamic Declaration" was not in combating the communist regime in Yugoslavia, which by recognizing a "Muslim nationality" had greatly facilitated the revival of a Muslim consciousness and community. Rather, he was calling for an awakening of an Islamic consciousness as the first necessary step toward eventual restoration of international Islamic unity and Islamic government wherever Muslims would constitute a majority, regardless of the nature of the existing government. The first step was education. "We must be preachers first and soldiers later", he wrote. The moment to conquer power must be carefully chosen.

> One can however establish a general rule: the Islamic movement can and must take power as soon as it is normally and numerically strong enough not only to destroy the existing non-Islamic government, but also to construct a new Islamic government ... Acting too soon is as dangerous as acting too late! Seizing power ... without adequate moral and psychological preparation and the indispensable minimum of strong and well-trained cadre means making a coup d'état, not an Islamic revolution ...

If "fundamentalism" can be defined as basing an entire social and political order on religion, then Izetbegović was indeed a "fundamentalist". Izetbegović's demand for an Islamic state *once Muslims are a majority of the population* deserves attention, since demographic changes in Bosnia-Herzegovina were moving toward a Muslim majority. Did fear of this prospect help drive non-Muslim citizens of Bosnia-Herzegovina into the arms of nationalist Serb and Croat parties? Whether or not such fears were groundless, the question needs to be raised.

The Islamic Revolution in Iran opened new prospects. Notably, a sort of competition between Shi'ite Iran and Sunni Saudi Arabia provided Islamic movements everywhere with a lucrative rivalry for influence between oil-rich sponsors. Izetbegović's party was notably successful in winning important political and material support from all Muslim countries, regardless of differences between them. Izetbegović had been a militant supporter of conservative Islam all his life. In 1943, at age 18, he headed the Muslim Youth organization in Sarajevo, which opposed modernizing trends. His ideas became notorious locally when, along with a dozen co-religionists, he was arrested and sentenced to prison in 1983 for seeking to transform Bosnia-Herzegovina into an "ethnically pure Islamic state". (All were freed by a general amnesty in 1988.)[63] The very fact that such charges were brought by a communist state, and again reiterated by "nationalist" Serbs, has protected Izetbegović's writings from critical examination.

Sacrificing peace

Izetbegović was a man with a cause he considered sacred. He used his election to what was supposed to be a three-man rotating presidency to secure the lasting power of his own Islamic party, the SDA, over the government of Bosnia-Herzegovina. There was never any rotation: Izetbegović remained the sole president, presented to the outside world as representative of "the Bosnian people". In a strange confusion, "Bosnian" became synonymous with "Muslim", and with "multicultural" at the same time. Had Izetbegović sought peace for his people, he would have stepped aside for a less contested figure. He did not step aside, and he was ready to accept the possibility of war.

"I would sacrifice peace for a sovereign Bosnia-Herzegovina, but for that peace in Bosnia-Herzegovina I would not sacrifice sovereignty", Izetbegović declared on 27 February 1991.[64] At the time of that statement, Bosnia-Herzegovina was at peace but was not "sovereign". A year later, over protests from the Serb population, Izetbegović's government held a referendum in which a majority of voters casting ballots – but only 39 per cent of the electorate – voted for independence. On that same day, 1 March 1992, the split between communities was underscored when Muslim paramilitaries fired on a Serb wedding procession in Sarajevo, killing the father of the bridegroom.[65]

Izetbegović expected this war and had been actively preparing for it. At a February 1991 meeting of the SDA, his close associate Hasan Čengić proposed a strategy to prepare for the future independent state.[66] This strategy was in three parts: (1) international public relations in favor of Bosnia-Herzegovina, an endeavor entrusted to handsome, English-speaking Haris Siljadžić; (2) Muslim control of the Interior Ministry, meaning the police; and (3) a Muslim military organization. Čengić, the imam of the Zagreb mosque who was to become a general and Izetbegović's deputy defense minister, took charge of the military part. This involved obtaining money, arms, and volunteers from Muslim countries. In May 1991, ten months *before* the proclamation of independence that set off civil war in Bosnia-Herzegovina, Čengić gave written instructions to SDA party faithful from all over the Republic to form Muslim brigades under the command of General Sulejman Vranja, a Yugoslav army officer still on active duty. Needless to say, this clearly treasonable activity was kept secret at the time.

Thus Izetbegović's Islamic party, the SDA, had its own armed forces, which went into action to secure Muslim areas at the same time and in much the same way as the Bosnian Serb party, the SDS, in the spring of 1992. The Croatian nationalist party did the same, backed openly by the Croatian army.

The prospect of war never deterred Izetbegović. Once the war began, he wanted to keep it going, and even after Dayton, he continued to arm in order to be able to resume it. But there has never been the slightest suggestion by the International Criminal Tribunal that Izetbegović's declared readiness to sacrifice peace might imply any responsibility whatsoever for the ensuing war.

At Dayton, however, eager to secure a settlement, U.S. diplomat Richard Holbrooke finally lost patience with Izetbegović. "If you want to let the fighting go on, that is your right," he told the

Muslim leader, "but Washington does not want you to expect the United States to be your air force. If you continue the war, you will be shooting craps with your nation's destiny."[67] Aside from the inappropriate nature of the metaphor (one cannot imagine the austere Izetbegović "shooting craps" or having any familiarity with such an activity), Holbrooke's warning ironically echoed an earlier warning to Izetbegović voiced by none other than the Bosnian Serb leader, Radovan Karadžić – the very warning that was cited by the International Criminal Tribunal as the main evidence of Karadžić's intention to commit "genocide" (see Chapter 3).

According to the first commander of the army of Bosnia-Herzegovina, Šefer Halilović, this public struggle for multi-ethnic Bosnia was a sham: "Izetbegović and the people around him have been working on an ethnic division of Bosnia-Herzegovina ever since they came to power."[68] To a certain number of indigenous Muslims, it was clear that Izetbegović's SDA was using outside forces, primarily the international Islamic network but also naive Western supporters, to solidify his control over Bosnian Muslims who, without the war, would never have accepted the leadership of a religious party.

In 1992, several thousand Islamic "holy warriors" entered Bosnia, mostly with accreditation to humanitarian organizations based in Kuwait, Saudi Arabia, Egypt, and other Muslim countries. A principal channel for illegal arms smuggling into Bosnia was the Third World Relief Agency (TWRA), founded in 1987 by Elfatih Hassanein, to encourage the rebirth of Islam in Eastern Europe and the USSR. Hassanein belonged to Sudan's ruling National Islamic Front and was an old friend of Izetbegović. "Bosnia, in the end, must be Muslim Bosnia. Otherwise everything has lost its meaning and this war was for nothing", he declared in a 1994 interview.[69] In August 1996, the Sarajevo government awarded a gold medal to TWRA, and Hassanein hosted Izetbegović in Istanbul, where he had transferred his operations in 1994 after his Vienna headquarters were closed down as Austrian police began to investigate arms smuggling. The Islamic recruits included veterans of the wars in Afghanistan and members of the Algerian *Groupe Islamique Armée* (GIA), held responsible for massive massacres of Algerian civilians. Described as "pretty good fighters and certainly ruthless" by U.S. officials, some 4,000 of these volunteers were assigned to the Bosnian army's 3rd Corps with headquarters in

Zenica. A special "Al Mujahed" unit was registered in August 1993 under direct command of Izetbegović himself. The best-armed unit in the 3rd Corps, Al Mujahed was credited with the Muslims' greatest victories against the Serbs in the spring of 1995, as well as with the habit of beheading Serbian soldiers. The emir, or commander, of Al Mujahed during the successful 1995 campaign was an Algerian member of the GIA close to Osama bin Laden.[70]

Thousands of Islamic supporters were granted Bosnian citizenship and passports under the loose wartime Law on Citizenship. Izetbegović gave orders to issue passports to "everyone who has helped our cause". Allies of Osama bin Laden were given boxes of blank passports to distribute as they saw fit. All that seems to have been missing was bin Laden himself, although that is not certain. "If bin Laden does not have a Bosnia-Herzegovina passport, then he has only himself to blame", commented a Bosnian newspaper editor. "He should have asked for it in time."[71]

Only after the Dayton Accords, fear for the safety of U.S. forces moved the Clinton administration to put pressure on Izetbegović to sack Čengić as deputy defense minister and to expel the Islamic mujahidin, whose presence had been studiously ignored throughout the conflict. Not surprisingly, Izetbegović was more loyal to his Muslim friends than to Washington. The Čengić family is one of the powerful semi-feudal clans dividing up power in Izetbegović's Bosnia, with control over the Goražde enclave and a major share in trafficking. Although the December 1995 Dayton Accord ordered all foreign forces to be repatriated by 19 January, mujahidin settled in villages north of the Islamic stronghold of Zenica, barred outside visitors and imposed strict Islamic law.[72] In February 1996, NATO occupation forces announced the discovery of an Islamic "terror arsenal", including fragmentation bombs disguised as children's toys. Subsequently, occasional incidents indicated that the hard core continued to prepare car bombs and other attacks. After the September 2001 World Trade Center bombing, U.S. attention was finally drawn to the bin Laden connection in Bosnia which had been there all the time. The U.S. and British embassies in Sarajevo were closed in fear of terror attacks from their Muslim "allies" in Bosnia.

The United States and Britain have a long tradition of supporting Islamic obscurantists in preference to secular leftists or nationalists in the Middle East. One reason for this is certainly the observation that Islamists never allow their religious convictions to conflict with business interests – starting with their own. In August 1999, the *New York Times* reported that Bosnia's leaders had outfoxed the close scrutiny of the International Community running the Bosnian protectorate to steal as much as $1 billion from public funds or international aid projects.[73] Since almost all the aid went to the Muslim part of Bosnia, that is where it disappeared. "Rampant corruption has discouraged foreign investment", the *Times* noted, citing various examples, including the theft of $450,000 in relief aid from Saudi Arabia by the mayor of Sanski Most, Mehmed Alagić. The Bosnia-Herzegovina Bank in Sarajevo managed to lose track of tens of millions of dollars deposited by international agencies and ten foreign embassies. The president's son, Bakir Izetbegović, was allotted a prime source of bribery money: control of the City Development Institute, which decides who has a right to live in 80,000 publicly owned apartments in Sarajevo, many of which were expropriated from Serbs or Croats and were turned over to members of the SDA. Bakir's assets included 15 per cent of the state airline, Bosnia Air, and he reportedly took a cut of the extortion money paid out by local shopkeepers to Sarajevo gangsters.[74]

In January 2002, Bosnian authorities asked the United States to extradite the ardent young former Bosnian ambassador to the United Nations, Mohammed Sacirbey, to face criminal charges.[75] Sacirbey, a U.S. citizen, was charged with embezzling $610,980 from Bosnia's UN mission, including over $90,000 earmarked for the US-run program to "Train and Equip" Bosnia's Muslim forces. Sacirbey defended his "convoluted" bookkeeping as necessary to mislead Croat and Serb officials imposed by international administrators on Bosnia's Muslim government.[76]

The impact of Saudi money and nepotism encouraged the age-old symbiosis of religious bigotry and corruption in Sarajevo. When Izetbegović retired in October 2000, the Western enthusiasts had gone home. The internationals still paying attention welcomed his departure. James Lyon of the International Crisis Group blamed Izetbegović for having allowed the SDA "to participate in the massive corruption at the highest level".

Violence, intolerance, and corruption marked all three nationalist parties that fought each other in Bosnia-Herzegovina. Each had its own objectives, and "multiculturalism" was not among them. The longer the war went on, the more the many ordinary citizens who wanted to live in a peaceful, mixed society were isolated, discouraged, and driven out. Far from saving the people of Bosnia-Herzegovina, insistence on holding out for a mythical "multicultural Bosnia" led by Izetbegović merely prolonged the agony and increased the heritage of bitterness.

2 Moral Dualism in a Multicultural World

The break-up of Yugoslavia was increasingly represented by the mass media and Western political leaders as a struggle between good and evil. This Manichean approach was suited to mass media simplification. But it also fitted into a disturbing tendency in the United States first of all, increasingly followed by Western Europe, to reduce social and political problems to criminal cases and courtroom disputes.

1. MANICHEAN MEDIA

The easiest way to describe a totally unfamiliar situation in a short time is by analogy to a familiar one. Nothing was more familiar to the Western public of the late twentieth century than Hitler and the Holocaust. Describing an event in these terms could arouse interest and an impression of understanding. It "sells" on news desks. Once the mass media began to treat the Yugoslav conflicts in these terms, likening the Serbs to "the new Nazis", the dynamic became irresistible. Serbs as Nazis, with Milošević as Hitler, was "the story" that reporters were sent to look for. To succeed, they (or their desk editors) as often as not poured whatever they found into that mould.

When in doubt, atrocities were attributed to the Serbs. Once launched, unproven accusations were repeated so often that they became obviously true, because familiar. A particularly significant instance of this mechanism concerned the three market massacres in Sarajevo. The three atrocities were strikingly similar. All three involved explosions of uncertain origin which killed and maimed defenseless civilians within a small area of central Sarajevo under Muslim control. In all three cases, the timing ensured that blaming the Serbs for such atrocities would have a decisive impact on the war.

- On 27 May 1992, an explosion mowed down Sarajevo citizens attracted to a bakery by an announcement of the distribution of free bread. Cameras were already set up at the scene. Images of carnage were broadcast to the world. Ballistics experts were unable to conclude what caused the explosion. Despite denials, the Serbs were officially blamed. The timing was crucial, as the Security Council was about to vote on sanctions against Serbia. Indeed, three days later, the UN adopted Resolution 757 decreeing a total trade embargo on Belgrade, followed by what the *New York Times* called "the most sweeping sanctions in history". The timing of the "breadline massacre" certainly clinched adoption of these extraordinary punitive measures.
- On 5 February 1994, a mortar shell struck the Sarajevo market, killing 58 people outright and wounding about 200, a dozen of whom died later. There was no conclusive finding as to who fired the shell. The market bombing was immediately used to back demands for air strikes on Bosnian Serb forces and withdrawal of Serb heavy weapons.
- On 28 August 1995, another ghastly market massacre ripped people to bits in a busy shopping area of Sarajevo. The Bosnian Serb government in Pale had just accepted Washington's terms for peace talks. British and French ballistics experts found no evidence that Bosnian Serbs fired the mortars, and suspected that the Izetbegović government was behind the massacre in order to produce the very result that was indeed produced: less than 48 hours later, NATO began massive air strikes on Bosnian Serb positions, effectively entering the war on the side of the Muslims.

The media rushed to blame the Serbs, echoing the rapid judgment of U.S. officials already eager to punish the Serbian side. A few reports indicated that British and French ballistic experts had concluded that the explosions were not of Serb origin, and officers serving in the UN-sponsored force suggested that the Muslims had caused the explosions to gain international sympathy. In retaliation, Muslim public relations effectively focused criticism on the UN force itself. Blaming the United Nations was a way for the media to strike a posture of underdogs criticizing the powerful.

While serious independent *investigation* of such incidents was beyond the capacity of journalists in war conditions, critical *analysis* is always possible. An unbiased analysis should take into account these considerations:

1. Each of these atrocities was committed at a crucial moment for the future of the conflict: on the eve of an international decision to take punitive measures against the Bosnian Serbs. In each case the atrocity became a clinching argument for such measures. The timing could not have been worse for the Serb side, or better for the Muslim side.
2. One element in deciding who may have committed an anonymous crime is motive. The Muslim motive would have been to trigger international action on their side. The Bosnian Serbs had nothing to gain and much to lose from those particular attacks at those particular times.
3. Staging attacks on one's own side for propaganda purposes is an aspect of psychological war familiar to specialists. It is called "black propaganda".
4. It may be hard to imagine that the Muslims would kill "their own people". However, in Bosnia there were several thousand mujahidin from Muslim countries, including veterans of the war in Afghanistan and Algerian Islamic terrorists, for whom Sarajevo's fun-loving, often hard-drinking inhabitants were not exactly "their own people". For the sake of the cause, such foreign fighters might have few qualms about killing a number of Sarajevo civilians, few of whom were likely to be devout Muslims.
5. The Izetbegović government, throughout the war, refused proposals to make Sarajevo a genuinely open, that is a demilitarized, city. "Besieged Sarajevo" was a key asset in the Muslim strategy of winning foreign sympathy and support. It diverted attention from other fronts where Muslims were fighting more aggressively and with success.

Black propaganda does exist. A relatively harmless but fully acknowledged instance occurred in Croatia on 6 February 1993, when the Croatian army staged a fake "Serbian" artillery attack on the Croatian Adriatic port city of Šibenik in front of television cameras, which relayed the "Serbian atrocity" to credulous viewers.[1] The deception was later exposed and even admitted. The officer credited with ordering the feigned attack, Davor Škugor, Chief of General Staff of the 113th Brigade of the Croatian Army, scornfully shrugged off the uproar with this observation: "There is no city in Croatia in which such tactical tricks were not used. After all, they are an integral part of strategic plans. They are only one in a series of stratagems we have resorted to during the war."

While the general public in the West is unaware of this sort of thing, their governments are not so naive. But neither governments nor media would care to suggest the possibility of such cynical behavior, least of all on the part of the side already designated as "the victim of aggression". Moral dualism is necessary to keep the public from awareness of a more troubling reality.

2. CREATING PUBLIC OPINION

On 7 July 1991, under the auspices of the European Community, the leaders of Slovenia and Croatia agreed (in the so-called "Brioni Declaration") to suspend their declarations of independence for three months to allow negotiations toward a peaceful solution. However, during this supposed cooling-off period a major unilateral step was taken in the most decisive of all the wars in Yugoslavia: the public relations war. On 12 August 1991, the Croatian government hired the American public relations firm Ruder Finn Global Public Affairs to "develop and carry out strategies and tactics for communication with members of the U.S. House of Representatives and the Senate as well as with officials of the U.S. government including the State Department, the National Security Council and other relevant agencies and departments of the U.S. government as well as with American and international news media".[2] On 12 November 1991, Ruder Finn's contract was renewed to include lobbying in relation to diplomatic recognition, sanctions, and embargoes, as well as briefings for officials of the first Bush administration and preparation of special background material, press releases, both reactive and proactive articles and letters to the editors to appear in major newspapers, briefings for journalists, columnists, and commentators.[3] In January and February 1992, Ruder Finn organized trips to Croatia for U.S. Congressmen. The United States recognized Croatia as an independent state on 7 April 1992.

Many people's first impressions of the conflict were influenced by the deluge of press releases sent to Congressmen and media. Video clips with frightful images of death and destruction were distributed worldwide with commentaries designed to support the idea that the fighting taking place in Croatia was part of a deliberate plan to create "Greater Serbia" by conquering Croatia.

On 23 June 1992, Izetbegović's government in Sarajevo in turn signed a contract with Ruder Finn in order to promote a stronger leadership role for the United States in the Balkans. To this end, the agency undertook an impressive array of actions, notably setting up a "Bosnia Crisis Communication Center" in contact with American, British, and French media; media appearance coaching for Bosnian foreign minister Haris Silajdžić; sending press releases to U.S. Congressmen and "Fax Updates" on developments in Bosnia-Herzegovina to over 300 addresses, including the most important world media and parliamentarians; writing 17 letters to be signed by Izetbegović and Silajdžić and addressed to top world officials; setting up press conferences and interviews with Bosnian representatives at international conferences; organizing personal contacts between Silajdžić and Al Gore, Margaret Thatcher, and other influential personalities, including 17 U.S. Senators; placing articles on the editorial pages of the *New York Times*, the *Washington Post*, *USA Today*, the *Wall Street Journal*, and so on.[4]

Silajdžić revealed the effects of his Ruder Finn training in subsequent conversation with the French writer Bernard-Henri Lévy, who had undertaken volunteer public relations for Izetbegović in Paris. Silajdžić boasted naively of being a "star" in the United States, and claimed that he was able to change millions of votes by merely appearing on television. Silajdžić startled Lévy by reproaching him for failing to exploit sufficiently the "propaganda" theme of "genocide". This showed his "American side", commented Lévy.[5]

Eighteen months after taking the Croatian contract, Ruder Finn was able to boast of having "developed a reputation as the international public relations agency with the greatest experience and involvement with the crisis in the Balkans. Our work has helped put Ruder Finn on the map in Washington, DC, and internationally." The agency claimed to have gained "dozens of close contacts in Congress and among the news media".[6]

In October 1992, Ruder Finn took up the job of public relations for the ethnic Albanian separatists in the Serbian province of Kosovo.

In March 1993, as hostilities sharpened between Croatian and

Muslim forces disputing territory in Bosnia-Herzegovina, the Croatian government turned to another American agency, Waterman and Associates, to stave off eventual Muslim accusations that Croatia shared equal responsibility with Serbia.[7] The campaigns on behalf of Tudjman's Croatia enjoyed financial and political support from Croatian émigré organizations in the United States and Canada.

In April 1993, French television journalist Jacques Merlino visited the Washington headquarters of Ruder Finn Global Public Affairs to interview the man in charge of the Balkan contracts, James Harff. Merlino asked Harff what he considered his proudest achievement in this operation. The answer: "Having succeeded in putting Jewish opinion on our side." The image of both Croats and Bosnian Muslims risked being tarnished by their involvement in the persecution of Jews during World War II. "Our challenge was to turn that around", Harff told Merlino, and this had been done thanks to the "camps" story.

In the first days of August 1992, the Long Island newspaper *Newsday* published reports by its Bonn correspondent Roy Gutman, based on interviews in Zagreb, telling of horrendous conditions in Serb-run internment camps in Bosnia. Seeing the potential impact of comparison with Nazi "death camps", Ruder Finn immediately contacted three major Jewish organizations, the B'nai B'rith Anti-Defamation League, the American Jewish Committee, and the American Jewish Congress, suggesting they publicly protest. They did. This launched the demonization of Serbs as the new Nazis.[8] In 1993, Ruder Finn was awarded the Silver Medal of the Public Relations Society of America in the category "crisis communication".

The Nazi equation

Most of the nastiest fighting in Bosnia-Herzegovina took place in the *de facto* partitioning, which immediately followed Western diplomatic recognition in April 1992. The Bosnian Serbs moved to seize control of contiguous territory encompassing majority Serb areas, the Croats more discreetly did the same in Herzegovina, while the central government of Izetbegović tried to hold as much territory as possible. Members of ethnic minorities presumed to be a threat to any of these arrangements were brutally expelled. In this period, the term "ethnic cleansing" first came into widespread use, and was applied exclusively to the Serbs. Presented as a new form of racist extermination, like the Nazi Holocaust, it was incomparably more compelling to news media and politicians than the brutal scramble for control of Bosnian arms factories and mountain passes.

In the early summer of 1992, Serb, Muslim, and Croat forces all set up improvised prison camps for people they considered threatening to their respective territorial control. Most were men of military age, but prisoners included some women and community leaders. According to International Red Cross data, in the autumn of 1992 a total of 2,692 civilians were being held in 25 detention centers. Of these, 1,203 detainees were held by Bosnian Serbs in eight camps; 1,061 by Muslim forces in twelve camps; and 428 by Croats in five camps. These makeshift detention centers were set up hastily in such sinister locales as abandoned factories – Omarska (reportedly the worst Serb camp) was in an abandoned iron mine. Prisoners are always more or less at the mercy of their guards, but all the more so in conditions of chaotic civil war where legal surveillance has collapsed and the worst impulses can be satisfied with relative impunity. In the improvised camps at the start of the war in Bosnia-Herzegovina, defenseless citizens were exposed to all sorts of abuse.

What made the camps run by the Bosnian Serbs different from those run by the Muslims and Croats? The quick answer is, "Ruder Finn". In the summer of 1992, Western media began picking up reports from Zagreb suggesting that the Serbs were herding the Muslim population into the equivalent of Nazi concentration camps. To quash the rumors, which he insisted were false, Bosnian Serb president, Radovan Karadžić, who was *not* being advised by Ruder Finn, invited a British television team, Independent Television News, to visit the Serb camps. What he failed to appreciate was that news photographers were bound to be looking for "the big story", the pictures that could confirm the reappearance in Europe of "Nazi death camps". The Muslims and Croats did not make such a mistake, and no photographs of their camps ever reached the public.[9]

Much later, in 1996, the Tribunal actually indicted four men for crimes including torture and rape perpetrated against Bosnian Serb prisoners at the Čelebići camp in the central Bosnian town of Konjic. This camp was run by Muslim forces who had "ethnically cleansed" Serb villages in the area between Mostar and Sarajevo in May 1992. At the time, it was ignored by the media. Four years later, the belated Tribunal conviction of Muslim guards attracted scant media attention and failed to make a dent in the solid impression that only Muslims were abused in camps and only Serbs did such things.

That impression had been fixed in the public mind in August 1992 by a series of photographs taken by the British ITN team at Trnopolje, where a large number of men were standing around shirtless in the sun. ITN filmed them through a barbed wire fence, focusing in particular on a very thin young man named Fikret Alić. As a result, on 6 August 1992, virtually all the leading television stations and newspaper in the West received and ran the henceforth emblematic photograph of a thin Muslim behind barbed wire. The image was instantly interpreted by headline writers and editorialists as "proof" that the Serbs had set up Nazi-style "death camps" to exterminate the Muslim population of Bosnia.[10]

A picture may be better than words in telling a story, but the story it can be made to tell is not necessarily true. One thin man in a group is not proof of mass starvation, and the presence of barbed wire is not even proof of confinement. The stunning success of the equation, Bosnian Serbs = Nazis, depended on the focus of the contemporary political culture, steeped in stories of Nazi death camps and with a unique fixation on the Holocaust. By free association, mention "camp", "barbed wire", and "thin", and the words that come up will be "Bergen-Belsen" and "Auschwitz". Still, anyone who attentively compared the Trnopolje pictures with photographs of Nazi concentration camps could not seriously consider them equivalent. The extraordinary impact of these pictures depended on the hyped headlines and commentaries that were added by editors who, for all the protests that "it mustn't happen again!", seemed eager to announce that indeed it *was* happening again.

Years later, after the "thin man behind barbed wire" photo had been printed in thousands of periodicals and engraved in millions of memories, the background of this famous image was described by German journalist Thomas Deichmann:[11]

The fact is that Fikret Alić and his fellow Bosnian Muslims were not imprisoned behind a barbed wire fence. There was no barbed wire fence surrounding Trnopolje camp. It was not a prison, and certainly not a "concentration camp", but a collection centre for refugees, many of whom went there seeking safety and could leave again if they wished.

The barbed wire in the picture is not around the Bosnian Muslims; it is around the cameraman and the journalists. It formed part of a broken-down barbed wire fence encircling a small compound that was next to Trnopolje camp. The British news team filmed from inside this compound.

In August 1992, the "thin man behind barbed wire" photos made the tour of the front pages of virtually every tabloid newspaper in the Western world and appeared on the covers of *Time, Newsweek,* and other mass circulation magazines. On 12 August, the United States proposed to the Committee for the Protection of Human Rights in Geneva that the United Nations should consider setting up an international tribunal to prosecute war crimes in Yugoslavia and Iraq. On 19 August, German foreign minister Klaus Kinkel raised the rhetorical level by declaring: "The attempt of the Serbian aggressors to carry out an ethnic cleansing action aimed at other population groups in order to achieve their national goals in Bosnia-Herzegovina is genocide." At the London conference the following week, Kinkel made clear his intention to press for the establishment of an international court to prosecute leading Serbs for crimes against humanity and genocide, and also for strengthening the UN embargo against Serbia.

The context makes it very clear that the International Criminal Tribunal for former Yugoslavia was conceived from the start as a means to prosecute *Serbian* leaders, not to enforce humanitarian law in general. The "thin man behind barbed wire" photographs were the backdrop to the whole operation. On 6 October, Security Council Resolution 780 called on the Secretary General to set up a Commission of impartial experts to analyse reports of grave violations of the Geneva Conventions and humanitarian law in ex-Yugoslavia. The Commission oriented its investigations against the Serbs. In December 1992, the acting U.S. secretary of state, Lawrence Eagleburger, caused something of a sensation at a Geneva meeting by issuing a list of people he described as war criminals. The list included a couple of Croat paramilitary leaders who had massacred Serb women and children and the Muslim commander of a Croat-run camp where Serbs had been beaten to death. But these small fry went unnoticed next to the big name Serb leaders on Eagleburger's list: Milošević, Karadžić, and Mladić. Here lay the constant bias: although Croats, Serbs, and Muslims were all accused of criminal acts, only the Serb leadership was considered responsible for what was done by subordinates. The bias was political: only the Serb crimes were judged *a priori* to be part of a deliberate policy, and thus qualitatively different from crimes committed by others.

This political bias was evident from the start and remained constant, despite the occasional arrest and prosecution of a few Croats and fewer Muslims. In light of the fact that, from the start, the Tribunal was clearly aimed at discrediting and prosecuting the Serb leadership, it is scarcely surprising that the Serb leadership did not rush to support the Tribunal or recognize its jurisdiction.

In January and February 1993, the French humanitarian organization Médecins du Monde (Doctors of the World, separate from the better-known Médecins sans Frontières, Doctors without Borders) used the Trnopolje photos in a montage suggesting a Nazi camp for an extraordinary publicity campaign, "Stop ethnic cleansing in ex-Yugoslavia". Three hundred thousand posters, measuring 3 × 4 meters, were posted on walls in major French cities. Half of them showed Milošević and Hitler side by side, with the caption, "Speeches about ethnic cleansing, does that remind you of anything?"[12] The general public had no way of knowing that far from giving "speeches about ethnic cleansing", Milošević continued to advocate harmony between Yugoslavia's peoples.

A second poster showed the thin man, Fikret Alic, behind barbed wire, with the caption, "A camp where they purify ethnic groups, does that remind you of anything?"[13] The text read: "Ethnic cleansing means camps, rapes, murders, executions and mass deportation of the non-Serb populations of Bosnia-Herzegovina and Sarajevo. The Serb nationalists will go all the way with their murderous ideology ..." Médecins du Monde also sponsored three weeks of TV spots denouncing "Serb crimes against humanity", featuring film stars Jane Birkin and Michel Piccoli. The whole campaign cost over FF11 million (some $2 million).

This advertising campaign was riddled with factual lies. But the most fundamental lie was to present the Serb campaign to secure a swath of defendable territory as a matter of "ideology" and "genocide". It was the emphasis on a supposed "ideology" that excited intellectuals into taking sides in a brutal little war between Bosnians, on the mistaken impression that they were heroically opposing the equivalent of Hitler's project to conquer Europe in the name of German racial superiority.

If justice is the goal, those who advocate an international criminal court should be equally determined to establish an international court where parties considering themselves defamed can bring charges of libel. As it is, there is no recourse for political defamation of foreign leaders or nations. Lawyers representing members of the Serbian émigré community in France tried in vain to sue Médecins du Monde on the grounds that the association's publicity campaign incited hatred against Serbs, in violation of a French law against inciting hatred of an ethnic, national, racial, or religious group. The plaintiffs discovered an interesting aspect of this law: it cannot be invoked by the people considering themselves injured, but only by the State Prosecutor or by a regularly declared association already existing for at least five years at the time of the facts whose purpose, according to its statutes, are to combat racism.[14] No such established association was interested in defending the Serbs once they were stigmatized as racist.

The state of war is a state of crime. Killing people in peacetime, the worst of crimes, becomes a laudable act of civic courage and may be rewarded with medals and public esteem. Destruction of public and private property that would be considered vandalism and arson is encouraged and carried out systematically. On the sidelines of this massive and official criminal activity, war provides an opportunity for a multitude of more or less surreptitious private crimes, notably pillage and rape. Civil war may be the worst in this respect.

When, in the early months of the war which raged across Bosnia-Herzegovina in 1992, agencies in Sarajevo and Zagreb presented Western media with reports accusing the Serbs of pursuing a deliberate policy of genocide, a basic principle of caution, essential to justice, was rapidly abandoned. That is the principle that the more serious the accusation, the greater the need for proof, since otherwise accusations will become an instrument of the lynch mob. Most in need of proof is the fact that the crime in question was actually committed.

On the contrary, from that point on, the principle that has prevailed in Western media and public discussion has been quite the opposite, namely that the more grave the accusation, the less the need for solid proof. Simply demanding evidence may be stigmatized as disrespect for the victims. Between the error of jumping to the conclusion that a holocaust took place when it did not and the error of dismissing a holocaust that might later turn out to have been real, the first error was felt to carry the smaller risk. Nobody wanted to be equated with the infamous "good Germans" who claimed "not to have known" what was happening to the Jews.

Believing the worst

It is sometimes assumed that particular courage is required to tell a terrible story and expose a frightful crime. The opposite assumption would be just as well founded: it may take particular courage to deny a terrible story. The observable fact is that there is a large and avid public for horror stories, as popular fiction and cinema attest. Newspaper editors are aware of this public and cater to it. There is apparently a cathartic function in "believing the worst" so long as the believer is not directly affected. In regard to fiction and entertainment, this is harmless and may even be beneficial. It is hard to draw a clear line between the inadvertent distortion of news reports to fit standards of popular entertainment and deliberate politically motivated propaganda.

In any case, the preference of editors for horror stories from Bosnia can be shown by the facts of professional reward. Three times, the most famous U.S. journalism award, the Pulitzer prize, was awarded to correspondents whose reports from Yugoslavia were weak on documentary proofs but strong on condemnation of the Serbs. In 1993, the Pulitzer prize for international reporting was shared between the two authors of the most sensational "Serb atrocity stories" of the year: Roy Gutman of *Newsday* and John Burns of the *New York Times*. Gutman's first sensational reports based on interviews with Muslim refugees in the Croatian capital, Zagreb, announced that the Serbs were running "death camps". Burns' story was no more than an interview with Borislav Herak, a mentally deranged Bosnian Serb prisoner in a Sarajevo jail, who readily confessed to a stream of crimes, some imaginary.[15] It is quite likely that the reporters did not find these stories for themselves, but were "put on to" them by spokesmen for governments involved in the conflict. These stories were the sort of war propaganda that goes looking for a journalist. They are scarcely models for the highest standards of skeptical journalism. However, they are stories that cause a sensation and perhaps influence events. Thus in selecting these stories for awards, the U.S. journalism profession was honoring not the journalists' *professional methods* and *procedures*, but rather, quite simply, the *power of the press* to influence opinion and events.

In April 1996, *Christian Science Monitor* correspondent David Rohde was awarded the Pulitzer prize for an October 1995 report in which he said he had visited the site of the suspected "mass grave" near Srebrenica which Madeleine Albright had designated on the basis of U.S. satellite photos showing "recently moved earth". Rohde, who does not speak Serbo-Croat, claimed to have found the exact site within Serb-held territory and to have seen exactly what the aerial photograph showed: "what appeared to be a human femur and tibia surrounded by bits of tattered fabric jutted from rich brown dirt". How did he find this nondescript patch of dirt in an unfamiliar war-torn country? "I had the locations of the graves marked on a map ... which I got from a U.S. intelligence source". he told *Newsweek* later. In fact, his trip did not establish the presence of "graves", since all he saw, by his own account, was exactly what the aerial intelligence photo had already shown: something that "appeared to be a human" leg. Since he was there, couldn't he at least make sure what it was? Why didn't he take close-up photographs that would show more detail than the satellite photo? But in the same *Newsweek* interview, he indicated that on that trip, he did not even bother to take a camera. And for this amazing reporting, he won a Pulitzer prize. Not only that, he went on to write a book, *Endgame*, about the Srebrenica massacre in semi-fictional style, where known fact cannot be separated from the author's imagination, inasmuch as the book presumed to tell the story from inside the minds of its Muslim characters. The result is neither a good novel nor good journalism. On the jacket of this book is a statement by Bill Moyers claiming that: "David Rohde broke the story the old-fashioned way. He followed some rumors, he followed some trails until he came to a leg protruding from the ground. He wrote the story of Srebrenica and the nation suddenly knew of the largest single killing in Europe since Jews were murdered wholesale in the Second World War." This blurb contradicts Rohde's own account of the way he "broke the story" – unless the "old-fashioned way" is indeed to follow a U.S. intelligence trail in order to confirm a public accusation made by the United States government representative at the United Nations.[16]

Once the accusation of genocide was widely accepted, it became a matter of honor not even to listen to the other side. A circular process developed in which the very horror of the alleged crime protected the allegation from the need for proof. The most horrible crimes had to be believed because they were so horrible.

3. THE USES OF RAPE

Nowhere is this circular process more evident than concerning the issue of rape. If the accusation of "death camps" was well calculated to mobilize Jewish organizations, as Ruder Finn claimed to have done, the accusation of "rape camps" was certain to arouse indignation within influential women's movements in key Western countries such as the United States and Germany. The stigmatization of Serbs as "Nazi rapists" was an extremely effective way to win over to the side of their enemies two constituencies with enormous influence in the liberal mainstream of Western society.

Accusations of genocide and of rape are most fearful, as displaying skepticism toward either can raise suspicion of undue indulgence or even passive complicity. Doubting accusations of genocide can be condemned as "revisionism" or even "Holocaust denial". As for rape, the women's movement of the last three decades of the twentieth century raised awareness of the fact that, in ordinary life, rape has traditionally been hard to prove (DNA tests are changing that), and that most women never report rapes, or when they do, very often face insult and humiliation. People who have been sensitized to this problem can be expected to object strenuously to any doubt cast on allegations of rape.

Women are raped every day in peacetime in the most "advanced" societies.[17] There is no reason to doubt that in wartime, especially during civil war, rape is even more common. But aside from the matter of believing or doubting the word of the women themselves, in wartime there is the additional problem of whether or not to believe allegations made in the context of war propaganda. This distinction was generally overlooked in regard to the reports of rape of Bosnian Muslim women by Serbs in Bosnia in 1992 and 1993.

The same journalist who launched the "death camps" story, Roy Gutman, also played a major role in the rape story. His 9 August 1992, *Newsday* article, headlined "Bosnia Rape Horror", began with a vivid description of the rape of a 16-year-old girl by three Serb guards. The account was drawn from an interview with a refugee girl and her mother who had been persuaded by a doctor in Croatia to tell the story to the *Newsday* journalist. Gutman added a multiplier drawn from politically interested sources:[18]

The triple rape of the Muslim teenager in June was only one

among thousands, maybe tens of thousands, of assaults that officials of Bosnia-Herzegovina fear have been carried out against Muslim and Croat women in the Serb prison camps of northern Bosnia.

Reports of rape have been so extensive that some analysts think it was systematic. Ševko Omerbašić, leader of the Muslim community in Croatia and Slovenia, who is in direct touch with hundreds of refugees every week, has reached that conclusion. "There is more and more evidence that all the young woman have been raped," he told *Newsday* in a recent interview.

This "evidence" was not produced. Meanwhile, Western media showed no interest in evidence that Serb women refugees had also been raped. The Serb women refugees were not in Croatia, and the journalists were.

Gutman, who was Bonn bureau chief for *Newsday* from 1990 to 1994, left the German capital from time to time to report on the Bosnian war from Croatia, where government public relations provided stories damaging to the Serbs. One of his sources was Jadranka Cigelj, who combined the roles of rape victim and Croatian nationalist propagandist with considerable success.

In a 21 February 1993 story for *Newsday* titled "One By One", Gutman reported from the Croatian capital on what he called the "gulag of Serb detention camps in Bosnia", and particularly Omarska, which he called a "death camp". The terms "gulag" and "death camp" grossly exaggerate the function and duration of Omarska, which was shut down in August 1992, shortly after the first reports of its existence, and whose prisoners were mostly expelled. In this article, Gutman recounted one woman's version of the ordeal in Omarska:[19]

In the same rooms where the men were interrogated and beaten by day, women allegedly were molested by night. "The first thing we had to do each evening was clean up the blood and the mess of those who had been tortured during the day," recalled Jadranka Cigelj, 45, an ethnic Croat from the north Bosnian city of Prijedor. Cigelj, a lawyer and political activist, said she was held in Omarska for seven weeks, from June 14 to Aug. 3.

"They took the women one by one," she said, describing the nightly beatings and rapes. "Not every one every day. They had a timetable. I was taken out four nights. Every night, a different one." She alleged that one of the men who raped her was Zeliko Mejahic, the commander of the guards at the camp.[20]

Gutman's other source was "a Western diplomat, who asked not to be identified by name or country", who confirmed that women were raped and men were killed at Omarska. How are readers to evaluate the credibility of a source who refuses to be identified "by name or country"?

Cigelj herself, added Gutman, "has become a leading activist in a growing effort to document alleged war crimes in Bosnia". This was something of an understatement. Cigelj was a vice president of Croatian president Franjo Tudjman's ruling nationalist party, the Croatian Democratic Community (HDZ) and was in charge of the Zagreb office of the Croatia Information Center (CIC), a wartime propaganda agency funded by the same right-wing Croatian émigré groups that backed Tudjman. The primary source for reports of rape in Bosnia was Cigelj's CIC and associated women's groups, which sent "piles of testimony to Western women and to the press".[21]

The CIC benefited from a close connection with the "International Gesellschaft für Menschenrechte" (International Association for Human Rights, IGfM), a far right propaganda institute set up in 1981 as a continuation of the Association of Russian Solidarists, an expatriate group which worked for the Nazis and the Croatian fascist Ustashe regime during World War II. In the 1980s, this organization led a propaganda campaign against the Sandinistas in Nicaragua, accusing them of running camps where opponents were tortured, raped, and murdered on a massive scale. "The Nicaraguan campaign was a market testing exercise for the offensive which the IGfM, together with the CIC, started in 1991", according to Dutch journalist Aart Brouwer.[22] The CIC ran all the wartime "foreign press centers" in Croatia, primarily in Zagreb and Split, and also had branches in Canada and the United States. Thanks to the strong North American connection, the large staff spoke fluent English and provided visiting Western journalists with information and interviews. CIC director Ante Beljo had formed branches of Tudjman's HDZ in Canada and the United States prior to Croatian independence.[23] Cigelj was featured as victim and witness in numerous IGfM publications, as Jadranka Cigelj, but also as Jadranka C., Jadranka Cigev, Jadranka Cigay, or simply Mrs Jadranka. Whereas she told Gutman she had been raped by camp commander Mejakic and three other men, in the IGfM brochure, "God's

Forgotten Children", she told of being repeatedly raped by only one man, named Grabovac, and in a long interview in the *Frankfurter Allgemeine Zeitung* of 5 April 1993, Cigelj denied that Mejakic had raped her.

Regardless of such discrepancies, Cigelj became a feminist heroine. In June 1993, she was honored by the Minnesota Advocates for Human Rights "for outstanding contributions to international women's rights" and the *Minneapolis Star Tribune* identified her as a "Bosnian Muslim victim". In 1996, she was featured in a documentary film, "Calling the Ghosts: A Story of Rape, War and Women", launched by Human Rights Watch in June 1996 at its annual film festival and distributed by Women Make Movies. Amnesty International thereafter sponsored a 25-city U.S. tour. The promotional blurb stated that "Jadranka Cigelj and Nusreta Sivac, childhood friends and legal professionals, lived the lives of ordinary women in Bosnia-Herzegovina, until one day their neighbors became their tormentors. This film documents mass rapes as a wartime tactic, focusing on these two survivors, whose personal struggles transform into a larger fight for justice against the backdrop of the International War Crimes Tribunal in The Hague." Two women, one of them a professional propagandist for the Tudjman regime, became documentary evidence for "mass rapes as a wartime tactic". The film was shown on university campuses as part of programs on Yugoslavia with such celebrities as NATO Commander General Wesley K. Clark, Bosnian ambassador to the UN Muhamed Sacirbey, and Bianca Jagger.

A political activist such as Cigelj, working for the propaganda agency of one of the parties to the conflict, and who tells an inconsistent story, cannot be considered the most reliable witness. There was naiveté on the part of women's groups, and sloppiness on the part of journalists, to accept without question such a partisan source.

Another main source was the State Commission for War Crimes in Sarajevo, which claimed to have 20,000 well-documented cases of rape intended to conceive "Serb children". The women were allegedly held captive until too late for abortion. Adoption offers poured in for the unwanted babies. Neither the documentation nor the babies ever materialized.[24]

After Gutman's report, every editor wanted a "Serb rape" story for his own paper. Pursuing the search in Bosnia-Herzegovina, a fledgling feminist journalist named Alexandra Stiglmayer complained to a German colleague, Martin Lettmayer, that it was "damned hard" to find a victim to interview.[25] When she finally found one, a 40-year-old Bosnian Muslim identified as "Besima", Stiglmayer had the basis for the articles that propelled her to fame in early November 1992. Her first rape story was published in a left-wing weekly in early November.[26] It was then reprinted or cited in all Germany's mass circulation newspapers and magazines. Although based on only one victim, Stiglmayer's story magnified this single case by giving it a broad political interpretation in terms familiar to the women's movement. She denounced "humiliation as a weapon: in Bosnia-Herzegovina rape is systematic, in order to destroy the enemy's morale; the total degradation of woman to merchandise". Stiglmayer appeared on German television and instantly became the authority on politically purposeful Serbian rape. This was the beginning of a highly successful career in journalism.

As a freelance TV journalist, Lettmayer went looking for visual evidence. His search took him to a private home in Doboj, which had been described by Ragib Hadžić, director of the "Center for War Crimes Investigation" in Zenica (the stronghold of Islamic fundamentalism in Bosnia), as a brothel where Muslim women were held prisoner by Serbs.[27] All he found was a small residence inhabited by the Muslim widow of a Serb policeman, whose Muslim neighbors expressed indignant astonishment at the wild tale. In Manjača, where a woman had told German television of being raped before 1,500 spectators in the stadium, there turned out to be no stadium. Back in Zagreb, asked to supply video coverage of a radio report that a clinic there was overflowing with women pregnant from having been raped in Serb camps, Lettmayer found the clinic largely deserted. Medical staff said that only three raped women had been treated there in the past seven months. Lettmayer had nothing to sell. A rape story is a rape story, even if unverified. A no rape story is no story at all.

Rape and politics

Both rape and propaganda accusations of rape are standard aspects of wars. It is a crime that armies have tended to condemn formally but often to treat with indulgence, as a sort of bonus for the belligerent virility required for hand-to-hand combat. There is not the slightest reason to doubt that a large number of women were raped and otherwise abused during the Yugoslav conflicts, just as there is no reason to be surprised that rapes were exaggerated and exploited for propaganda purposes. Muslim, Serbian, and Croatian women all reported having been raped. The mainstream media chose to play up stories involving Muslim victims, while ignoring the rape of Serbian women. To this bias was added a political twist: rape was "promoted" from a sordid personal crime to a central feature of the strategy of one of the warring parties.

The idea that the Serbs were using rape as a strategic weapon mobilized a number of women's groups and women politicians. Although the evidence was slight, it seemed that exaggerated numbers and excessive indignation could do no harm and might help put an end to such abuses. By accident, a group of basically uninformed European women politicians became the main source for a figure, which was thereafter repeated as authoritative. In February 1993, Gutman reported:

> A probe authorized by the European Community came to the conclusion that at least 20,000 Muslim women had been raped during the Serb conquest. Some of the rapes occurred in special detention centers set up for women and children.

This was a reference to the "Warburton Report", which, in the absence of serious sources, became the available and thus favorite "official source" for countless politicians and journalists. It so happens that the European Community, ever anxious to seem at the forefront of events over which it had no control, sent an observation mission headed by Anne Warburton (UK) to report on treatment of Muslim women in ex-Yugoslavia.

At this time, the European Community was insisting that Bosnia-Herzegovina must be preserved at all costs as a *multicultural* country. The basic premise of cultural equality underlying this position might seem to imply equal concern for *all* the women of Bosnia-Herzegovina exposed to the dangers of war, including the Serbs, who made up a third of the population. But the Warburton mission's mandate covered only *Muslim* women.

In December 1992 and January 1993, the mission sought information from Red Cross, UN High Commission for Refugees, and UN human rights center officials in Geneva before going on to Zagreb in search of victims. The delegation soon noted the discrepancy between the huge number of presumed rape victims reported by the media and the absence of concrete evidence. Despite the limits of its mandate, the mission took note of disturbing reports of sexual abuse of Serb or Croat woman, as well as of male prisoners, by all three groups. The report acknowledged the intrinsic difficulty of collecting statistics on rape in the prevailing chaotic conditions. In Zagreb, the delegation was largely frustrated in its attempt to find either victims or solid data. Nevertheless, in an attempt to snatch success from the jaws of defeat, it concluded with the one statement that would make it famous: namely, that "although the exact number of victims cannot be fixed, it is possible to speak of several thousand. The most reasonable estimate given the delegation indicated a figure of twenty thousand victims in the Zagreb region."

Now in reality, this proves only that "less reasonable" estimates were given the delegation. What were they? 50,000? 100,000? And what was the criterion for a "reasonable" estimate? The Warburton mission lacked the means to carry out a serious, scientific investigation. Formed under pressure to "do something", it could only repeat the accusations it heard in Zagreb, capital of a country at war with the Serbs. There, the delegation had "often heard" that rape or threat of rape had been used by Serbs as a weapon of war to make people flee. Seen from that angle, it concluded that "rape is part of a strategic design". All this was hearsay in wartime. The Warburton mission's mixture of hasty amateurism and political credentials made it an ideal, because unwitting, channel of propaganda. Its impressionistic, undocumented statements were treated as more authoritative than the more cautious conclusions drawn, for instance, by Amnesty International.[28]

The Warburton mission was followed by a public hearing on the rape of women in former Yugoslavia held in the European Parliament in Brussels on 18 February 1993. The most prestigious member of the delegation was Simone Veil, a former French minister of health who had served as president of the European Parliament. Having been sent to Auschwitz with her mother during World War II, and having introduced the first law to legalize abortion in France, Mme Veil had no need to prove her credentials either as victim or as feminist. She withdrew from the Warburton delegation after its first mission and refused to estimate the number of rapes. She stressed the need to be extremely rigorous in gathering documentation and complained that the working conditions of the delegation in Croatia were "abominable": no vehicles, no interpreters, no direct contacts, and so on. Mme Veil criticized the EU governments for having instructed the Warburton delegation to investigate the rape of *Muslim* women only (without specifying whether, as reported, it was the German government that eliminated Serb rape victims from the mandate).[29]

While Mme Veil stepped back, others stepped forward, especially Mrs Doris Pack, a German Christian Democrat who first as vice chairman and later as chairwoman of the European Parliament (EP) delegation for relations with the republics of former Yugoslavia found a mission as one of the chief demonizers of the Serbs. This "war of Serbian aggression was based on a diabolical plan" in which "rape of women and castration of men were part of the arsenal of war of the Serbian aggressors", she declared at the EP hearing. If Croat and Muslim men raped Serbian women, for Mrs Pack that was only a matter of an "isolated reaction" to having seen Serbs commit mass rapes or behead and burn children alive in front of their mothers. To Mrs Pack, the absence of proof was no obstacle to repeating such horrendous tales. A Zagreb activist claimed that Serbs, following a "fascist ideology", were carrying out "systematic genocide" of non-Serb people in Croatia and Bosnia-Herzegovina, exterminating people daily and using rape as a genocidal tool.[30] This seemingly contradictory project was carried out, she claimed, by raping women and then killing them for purposes of extermination, and by letting them live to bear "Serbian babies". Serbian systematic rape, she declared, extended to everybody in the country – men, women, children, "even our rivers!"

A Serbian spokeswoman, Dr. Ljubica Toholj, claimed that almost all the Serbian women in northern Bosnia had been raped by Muslim mercenaries, who had come from all around the world in order to kill non-Muslims. The expert international organizations, which had actually attempted to collect serious data, were cautious. Thierry Germond, of the International Committee of the Red Cross (ICRC), said abuses had been committed by all sides and there was not enough evidence to describe rapes as "systematic". Yet the only conclusion drawn by the European Parliamentarians was expressed in a resolution adopted on 11 March 1993, demanding that "systematic rape of women be considered a war crime and a crime against humanity" and calling for rapid establishment of the International Criminal Tribunal for former Yugoslavia (ICTY). The crime, it should be noted, was not simply rape but "*systematic*" rape. Yet "systematic" rape was a mere assumption.

Numbers and patterns

The only international body to pursue a thorough investigation of rape accusations was the Commission set up by the Security Council to prepare the documentary basis for the ICTY. It began work in October 1992 under the presidency of Frits Kalshoven, professor of humanitarian international law at the University of Leiden. At the February 1993 European Parliamentary hearing, Professor Kalshoven pointed out that rape had been considered a war crime since time immemorial and was, moreover, always deemed to be a crime in legal terms. This was not particularly welcome news to politicians, who were clamoring to accomplish an historic advance for women by recognizing rape as a war crime. Professor Kalshoven also reported that many victims of abuses, including rape, described the aggressor as being "paramilitary" which, he noted, "could mean many things in the present situation, as everyone had uniforms and arms at home".

In the summer of 1993, Professor Kalshoven resigned and was succeeded by Professor Mahmoud Cherif Bassiouni. An American of Egyptian origin, Professor Bassiouni was an author of books and essays on Islam. His sympathy for the Muslims of Bosnia was manifest. The first arrests and prosecutions were prepared on the basis of a war crimes "database" which he prepared with a group of volunteers at DePaul University Law School in Chicago.

This Commission received reports of over 1,600 cases of rape, and interviewed 223 victims who reported up to 4,500 cases. But at the conclusion of its work in May 1994, the Commission had gathered just 575 affidavits with precise identifications. The actual number of documented rape victims in the Commission's files was 105.

It is entirely reasonable to assume there were many more rapes than those documented, although the full extent is impossible to evaluate. This was the first conflict in which investigators searched actively for instances of rape and encouraged women to overcome their reluctance to report it. In the absence of comparative studies, it is impossible to know whether what was unusual about the war in Bosnia-Herzegovina was the frequency of rape or the attention focused on it.

Despite the small number of confirmed cases, in testimony before a U.S. Senate committee in August 1995, Professor Bassiouni replied to questions by calling the figure of 20,000 rapes a "sustainable projection". The significant fact is that all the larger figures were *projections*, based on multiplying approximate estimates by arbitrary factors. In a conflict where vivid accusations were certainly every bit as much a "weapon of war" as was rape, there was an obvious intent to inflate the figures.

Professor Bassiouni took personal charge of the Commission's investigations of sexual assault reports in an effort to prove that rape was part of a Serb strategy. Only in this way could the accusation of rape be used not merely against the rapists – unsavory characters of no political interest – but against the *political leadership* of the Serbs. This would "promote" rape to a higher level and enhance its prosecution. In the absence of large, verifiable figures, Professor Bassiouni sought to base the case less on the clearly inadequate number of proven cases than on what he considered "patterns", from which he deduced a "policy". The search for "patterns" became a regular substitute for either numbers or documentary evidence.

Reports of rape were classified into five "patterns": 1) sexual violence with looting and intimidation; 2) sexual violence during fighting; 3) sexual violence in detention facilities; 4) sexual violence in special rape camps; and 5) sexual violence in brothels. In presenting these Commission "patterns" to a July 1996 ICTY hearing, Dutch criminologist Tineke Christine Cleiren stressed that the "reliability and the credibility of reports and testimonies could not be verified" and that "individuals, as well as groups, may be driven by political or personal revenge or by encouraging groups to report sexual violence ... some people identified themselves so much with victims of sexual violence that they state hearsay stories as their own experience. There are indications that sexual violence was reported by the parties in the conflict as an element of propaganda. The information in the reports was second or third hand, and much of this was very general." Do five different "patterns" of alleged rape prove a "pattern" that in turn proves a "policy"; or do they simply indicate that the crime of rape, like any other action, can be put in different categories?

The projected numbers and supposed patterns acted in a reinforcing circle. The initial impression that rapes were "massive" suggested a deliberate policy and thus a pattern. When, later, there was a lack of evidence of such large numbers, then the "pattern" implied a "policy" which in turn implied that the numbers must have been massive.

Five years after resigning from the UN commission, Professor Kalshoven told Dutch journalist Aart Brouwer:

> Terms like "genocide" came all too easily from the mouths of people like Bassiouni, an American professor of law, who had to establish a reputation and to work on fund-raising. In my opinion these terms were way out of line. "Genocidal rape" is utter nonsense. "Genocide" means extermination, and it is of course impossible to exterminate people and make them pregnant at the same time. It is a propaganda term which was used against the Serbs right from the start, but I have never found any indication that rape was committed systematically by any of the parties – and I understand by "systematically", on orders from the top.

Professor Kalshoven added that the Croats and the Muslims "had by far the best public relations, much better than the Serbs had. I had tremendous problems in obtaining evidence from the Serbs though they sometimes held clear testimony with lots of photographs. They were completely convinced that the whole world was against them."

Finally, it was. The accusation that the Serbs initiated a deliberate policy of mass rape has never been substantiated. But the belief that this happened is widespread and persistent. This belief is certainly a major factor in the extraordinary, almost unique absence of public sympathy for the Serbian people when they were being bombed, sanctioned, and ethnically cleansed.

In May 1997, a group of nine U.S. women senators sent a letter to President Clinton demanding tougher prosecution of Serbian war criminals and claiming that "investigators have documented rapes of over 50,000 women and girls and the use of rape as a weapon in a brutal campaign of ethnic cleansing". This was simply untrue. The desire to believe the worst, or the fear of *not* believing it, is stronger than the simple need to know and speak the truth.[31]

Imaginary rapes in Kosovo

In April 1999, as NATO bombing of Yugoslavia was heading into its second month, anti-Serb propaganda was enriched by the addition of "rape" charges, considered effective for their "resonance".[32]

"It's a war being fought by polls", a Senate source said, explaining that the Clinton administration was racheting up the U.S. war effort only incrementally as daily polls provided hints about how to proceed. Almost minute verbal changes reflect the process, he said, citing the way in which charges of rape have become more prominent in U.S. rhetoric after polls showed its resonance. "Ethnic cleansing", now deemed too "sanitary sounding", has started giving way to terms such as ethnic gutting and ethnic brutality.

On 10 May 1999, the U.S. State Department issued a report entitled "Erasing History: Ethnic Cleansing in Kosovo" which, based on refugee accounts and aerial photos, estimated that 90 per cent of Kosovo Albanians had been driven from their homes. This was wildly inaccurate, as it later turned out, but in unveiling the report Albright said the report "makes clear beyond any doubt" the existence of "horrific patterns of war crimes and crimes against humanity", including "systematic executions" and "organized rape", and that the "evil" could turn out to be even greater.

These allegations echoed others drawn from the copious annals of war propaganda, and notably the report by Lord Bryce, whose wild tales of German atrocities did so much to help the British hate the "Huns" during World War I. The Bryce Report concluded that German soldiers in Belgium had engaged in "murder, lust and pillage" on a scale "unparalleled in any war between civilised nations during the last three centuries".[33] A classic in its genre, the Report included an exciting piece of fiction about how German officers and men had raped 20 Belgian girls in the market square at Liége.

The "town square mass rape" story was recycled during the Kosovo bombing and ended up in the *Philadelphia Inquirer* under the headline "Serb's system of rape" which gave this vivid description of life in Kosovo under NATO bombing: "In other cases, mass rapes are organized in town squares. Townspeople are assembled to observe these horrific events; the fear and revulsion sometimes spur residents to flee voluntarily."[34] The more preposterous the tale, the more fiendish the enemy. Moreover, editors know that sex crime stories attract readers. During the Kosovo bombing and refugee crisis, the insatiable demand of journalists for "rape stories" irritated some aid workers. Dr. Richard Munz, a German surgeon working with humanitarian aid in Macedonia, complained to the daily *Die Welt* about the inability of most reporters to accept the fact that among the 60,000 Kosovo Albanian refugees in their camp, medical aid workers had not encountered a single case of rape.

In one of his many bursts of wartime hyperbole, British foreign secretary Robin Cook claimed: "Young women are being separated from the refugee columns, and forced to undergo systematic rape in an army camp. We have evidence from many refugees who have managed to escape that others were taken to rape camps." This set off a rush of reporters to "get the story" by harassing Kosovo Albanian women as they arrived in refugee camps along the Macedonian border. *Guardian* reporter Audrey Gillan later reported that she knew of "several tabloid reporters who were dispatched to Macedonia and Albania with the sole purpose of finding a rape victim". Chatting together in the bar of Skopje's Hotel Continental, reporters rehearsed the "notorious" question: "Is there anyone here who's been raped and speaks English?" Benedicte Giaever, the coordinator for OSCE's field office in Skopje, complained that almost every journalist who came to see her asked one thing: could she give them a rape victim to interview.[35] Despite this feverish search, there was never any evidence to confirm Robin Cook's accusation. However, the story continued to be repeated by the Kosovo Liberation Army spokesman in London, who used it to back his demand that NATO send ground troops into Kosovo to fight the Serbs.[36]

The final OSCE Kosovo Verification Mission report on refugee testimony, intended for the Hague Tribunal, demonstrated a willingness, even an eagerness, to believe the worst. Noting that "very little" had been documented on the subject of rape, the KVM hastened to explain that this did not prove anything. "A woman who admits having been raped can be rejected or expelled by her husband, her family or her husband's family." Yet, the report continued, interviewers "received the support of the men in trying to make the women feel secure enough to talk ... and often they would encourage the women to tell the whole story with all details". While the absence of accusation aroused skepticism, there was no skepticism regarding accusations made under conditions perhaps contrary to Albanian customs, but certainly not contrary to the interests of anti-Serb propaganda. No news was never good news. "The actual number of women who were raped before they were killed can be expected to be significantly higher than is indicated by the reports", the KVM reported, without giving any reasons for this "expectation".

4. CRIMINALIZING THE ROGUES

Opportunistic criminal activities, such as rape, pillage, and acts of personal vengeance, have flourished in wars throughout history. In a mountainous country whose inhabitants had been trained to wage a guerrilla war of resistance, the universal possession of firearms and old uniforms meant that the opportunities afforded by the breakdown of law and order accompanying the disintegration of the recognized central state could be seized easily and violently. Virtually every male citizen with a firearm at home could suddenly become a "paramilitary". On the other hand, a large part of the young male population of Yugoslavia was far from eager to take part in a civil war against fellow Yugoslavs. In Serbia, an estimated 200,000 youths went abroad to escape military service. Many thousands of young Bosnian Muslims sought asylum elsewhere, probably for similar reasons. The reluctance of very many Yugoslavs to participate in a fratricidal war created an opportunity for more combative individuals – including foreigners – to offer their services to the various nationalist causes as irregular paramilitaries, while compensating themselves through pillage.

Crime flourishes in civil war. So do rumors, lies, and propaganda. In the confusion of suffering, destruction, and conflicting accusations, it is extremely difficult for outsiders to sort out exactly who did what to whom. Never before, however, have the international media given remote observers such a vivid impression of knowing what was going on. To do so, they often relayed the readily available propaganda of the anti-Serb side, but this bias was rarely clear to distant viewers. The illusion of knowing created an illusion of responsibility, fuelling the growing demand from the opinion-makers to *do* something. In the United States, politicians called for "lifting the arms embargo" to aid the Muslims – an embargo which in fact was non-functional. To many more cautious observers, an *ad hoc* criminal Tribunal to sort it all out seemed a more peaceful solution. The creation of the International Criminal Tribunal to judge crimes in the former Yugoslavia thus initially encountered scant criticism. An *ad hoc* tribunal set up for one or two situations (the Tribunal was also given the mandate to judge crimes in Rwanda) was by no means the institution envisaged by advocates of an international criminal court with universal jurisdiction. Its legal basis was shaky. Nevertheless, it was widely welcomed as "better than nothing" and a "step in the right direction" toward a world legal order.

Great powers judge small ones

There are two kinds of international criminal courts, one that has always existed and one that is an ideal. The one that has always existed is the court of the victors who judge the vanquished. The Versailles Treaty called for the prosecution of Kaiser Wilhelm II by the victorious powers for his responsibility in the First World War, but the Netherlands refused to extradite the exiled king and the trial never took place. Ironically, it was the 1934 assassination of King Alexander I of Yugoslavia in Marseilles by Croatian fascists that led the League of Nations to adopt a convention on the creation of an international penal tribunal; it came to nothing. After World War II, the victorious powers set up tribunals at Nuremberg and Tokyo. Nuremberg, if not Tokyo, was widely accepted as just because of the horrendous nature of Hitler Germany's gratuitous aggression and racist mass murder. But the fact remains that here too it was a matter of "victors' justice": the tribunals were *ad hoc* rather than universal, and proposals to include judges from countries other than the victorious Allied Powers were rejected. The promise of chief Nuremberg prosecutor Robert Jackson that the United States would not establish rules without being willing to have them applied to itself was never kept.

In the early 1950s, the United Nations General Assembly took initial steps toward codification of crimes against peace and the establishment of a permanent international penal tribunal. It was always understood that the legal basis for such a tribunal would be an international treaty. By signing such a treaty, states would transfer part of their sovereign rights to the tribunal. The principle of *nullum crimen sine lege*, according to which the law must be precisely defined before it can be applied, would be upheld. The establishment of such a tribunal was blocked by refusal of the Great Powers to grant such a tribunal jurisdiction over their own citizens.

This refusal was still blocking the work of the International Law Commission (the body working on the project) in the early 1990s, when the conflict in Yugoslavia broke out. The United States, still unwilling to support a universal tribunal, proved willing and even eager to set up *ad hoc* tribunals to try not only Yugoslavs, but also Rwandans, as well as Saddam Hussein and Pol Pot. This means in effect a series of Great Power tribunals to judge small countries.

A democratic court is set up by a community to judge its own members. Theoretically, this can apply to any community, including the world community of nations. After World War II, the United Nations, as a community of nations, established the International Court of Justice (ICJ). The ICJ adjudicates disputes between member states, as a sort of higher court of appeal for the interpretation of international law. It rules on legal issues on the basis of briefs presented on behalf of contending states. Even though some states are in fact much more powerful than others, and ignore adverse court rulings (the attitude of the United States in particular), there is a certain equality before the law among states which corresponds to normal standards of democratic justice.

The ICTY, in contrast, was set up in defiance of such principles. It was a top-down, totally undemocratic institution set up by the Great Powers, using the UN Security Council, in order to judge citizens of smaller, weaker countries which were excluded from making the rules or interpreting them. From the very start, the Tribunal was intended not as an instrument of unbiased justice, but as a way to punish a particular national group, the Serbs. As early as August 1992, German foreign minister Klaus Kinkel, whose government led the drive to fragment Yugoslavia at the expense of its Serb and Yugoslav citizens, called for the creation of an international court to prosecute leading Serbs for "genocide". Kinkel was "the father of the Tribunal", according to its first president, Italian jurist Antonio Cassese, who declared that "This Tribunal is Kinkel's spiritual child."[37] Later on, Cassese's American successor identified Madeleine Albright as its mother. In remarks to the U.S. Supreme Court on 5 April 1999, presiding judge Gabrielle Kirk McDonald recalled that as permanent U.S. representative to the United Nations, Albright had "worked with unceasing resolve to establish the Tribunal. Indeed, we often refer to her as the 'mother of the Tribunal'". The *political* parentage of the Tribunal was clear. *Legally,* however, its antecedents were extremely dubious.

When the Security Council first expressed the intention to found an international tribunal for Yugoslavia in February 1993, the legal basis for such a creation was a complete mystery. By the time it adopted Resolution 827 of 25 May 1993 which established the ICTY, an expedient solution had been found: the Security Council gave itself the right to set up a judicial body thanks to a broad interpretation of Chapter VII of the UN Charter, whereby it had to right to "take measures" and "set up subsidiary bodies" to maintain or restore international peace and security. This was an ingenious usurpation of judicial authority, which clearly overstepped the Security Council's mandate as envisaged by the authors of the Charter. However, said the UN Secretary General, it was an "approach" which had "the advantage of being expeditious and immediately effective", because all UN member states are "under a binding obligation to take whatever action is required" to carry out decisions taken under Chapter VII.[38] No need to waste time negotiating and ratifying a treaty, when it was so much faster simply to impose a Security Council decision on governments which had no say in the matter.

The fact that the ICTY set up its operations in The Hague led many people to assume it was somehow related to the International Court of Justice in the same town. The two are entirely separate, in origins and in function. The ICJ rules on issues of international law, a matter clearly within the competence of distinguished jurists. The ICTY is called upon to judge disputed facts in distant places, a far more problematic task.

The purposes of law

The purpose of judicial process in criminal matters is not solely to avenge victims and punish wrong-doers. A civilized judicial process is also a way to protect the innocent from the dangers of false accusation. This requires basing judgments heavily on material evidence, able to save an innocent person from malicious accusations. Any proper criminal court must require the prosecution and enable the defense to gather and present exhaustive material evidence. This is expensive and difficult in any case, doubly so dealing with crimes committed in another country. The ICTY has not met this criterion. Its proceedings have often rested essentially on verbal testimony. Moreover, the Tribunal has been heavily dependent on the government of the United States, which sponsored its creation and provided it with personnel, resources, and information needed to formulate indictments. These material and political assets went to strengthen the prosecution. Individuals convicted by the Tribunal have no recourse to any other court of appeal than the Tribunal itself, according to procedures which it adjusts as it goes along.

The most enlightened political argument in favor of the Tribunal was that individual responsibility needed to be established in order to replace the notion of collective guilt.[39] This laudable ambition has not been realized. By setting out from the very start to build a case against the political leadership of the Serbs and only the

Serbs, the notion of collective Serb guilt has been bolstered. Only Serb political leaders have been indicted for crimes attributed to subordinates, crimes no different in nature from those committed by subordinates of the opposing sides, whose political leaders have not been charged. Rather than individualizing guilt, this has made a powerful contribution toward comforting notions of the collective guilt of the Serbs.

ICTY apologists sometimes claim that prosecution of a leader such as Milošević is necessary to "deter" any future "dictator". It is hard to believe that those who espouse this notion have thought it through. It assumes that a political leader in a uniquely complex and dramatic situation sees his choice as between being "good" or "bad", and that if he sees a tribunal looming, he will be "good". This infantile notion is suitable for children in a candy shop, where the prospect of "getting caught" can weigh more heavily than the fun of grabbing the goodies. It is totally irrelevant to unforeseeable historic dramas, such as the disintegration of an established country.

All in all, the declaratory purposes of the ICTY are extremely dubious. The official purpose of maintaining "international peace and security" was essentially a verbal trick to enable the Security Council to set up a tribunal and thereby forgo proper diplomatic procedure. In practice, the Tribunal has been used for *political* purposes that have to do with power, not justice. For political purposes, mere indictment has proved to be a powerful weapon. It is enough to describe somebody as an "indicted war criminal" to stigmatize that person and ban him from the international political scene. This stigmatizing function of indictment was first used most effectively against the president of the Bosnian Serbs, Radovan Karadžić. On 24 July 1995, the Tribunal indicted Karadžić for "genocide". The accusation immediately served to ban the Bosnian Serb leader from the world stage. "Let us see who will sit down at the negotiating table now with a man accused of genocide", was the comment of Antonio Cassese, at the time the Presiding Judge at the Tribunal, "That gentleman will not be able to take part in peace negotiations."[40] Disqualifying Karadžić forced the Bosnian Serbs to be represented at the Dayton negotiations by the Serbian president, Slobodan Milošević, who – as the United States knew full well – was ready and eager to make concessions in order to get the United States to lift sanctions against Serbia. The Tribunal went on to indict other Bosnian Serb political leaders, before indicting Milošević himself and four other senior Yugoslav officials for "crimes against humanity" on 27 May 1999, in the midst of NATO bombing of Yugoslavia. This was the most blatantly political indictment of all, clearly serving as propaganda for NATO's war. By stigmatizing the Serb leadership as "indicted war criminals", the Tribunal served the constant U.S. policy of treating its chosen adversaries as mere criminals with whom negotiation is not appropriate, but who must be forced to accept some form of unconditional surrender.

Victims' justice

Collective guilt can imply collective innocence. Whitewashed by the indictment of their Serbian counterparts and convinced that the Tribunal was on their side, the Bosnian Muslim leaders were encouraged to seek not compromise but institutionalized vengeance. Ironically, the institution set up on the pretext of promoting "international peace and security" relegated peace to second place after a "justice" it was incapable of providing. In the early days of Tribunal activity, around the time of the Dayton Accords, the common slogan of Tribunal advocates was that there can be "no peace without justice".[41] This slogan may well be a formula for eternal war when justice on one side of the mountains is injustice on the other. The Muslims' insistence that "there can be no real peace until Karadzic is sent to The Hague" was a demand for vengeance and exoneration, not for peace.

The Tribunal's first Chief Prosecutor, Richard Goldstone, explicitly gave precedence to the desire for vengeance on the part of the pre-judged victims over all other possible purposes. "The victims of the Yugoslav war want legal vengeance", he declared in mid-1996. "For us the victims are the most important." The victims "should decide what is appropriate". Goldstone compared Bosnian victims, who wanted revenge, with South African blacks who were satisfied with a truth commission.[42] He attributed this contrast to a "big difference between apartheid and genocide in the extent of the crime". Apartheid in South Africa wasn't so bad, because "there were never systematic mass rapes, people there were not killed in order to get rid of an entire people, but for political motives".[43]

This surprising comparison reveals that Goldstone, for all his talk of establishing individual responsibility, had prejudged the Bosnia conflict in terms of group guilt and group victims. In his mind, the Muslims were victims of "genocide", all of them, and as "victims" had the right to demand vengeance.

In South Africa, Goldstone had presided over investigation of police and army abuses for the Truth Commission; there he was not a prosecutor. In The Hague he was. A "victim-centered" justice is extremely favorable to the prosecution and unfavorable to the defense. In the name of "the victims" the ICTY has limited the rights of the defense to a degree that would not be possible in any of the democratic countries that support it. If taken as a precedent, ICTY practice would represent a dangerous trend for courts following the Anglo-Saxon common law tradition. In reality, a victim-centered justice creates its own victims: those who are unjustly accused and who cannot be properly defended because fair and thorough defense may be rejected as offensive to the presumed victims.

But finally, who were "the victims"? And were they really demanding legal vengeance? The ordinary citizens of Bosnia-Herzegovina, whether Muslim, Serb, or Croat, show little enthusiasm for the Tribunal.[44] Justice "for the victims" is above all a justice that works to the benefit of the self-appointed defenders of "the victims". In this case, the Muslim party in Sarajevo is counting on ICTY conviction of Serb leaders to strengthen its suit filed against the Belgrade government at the International Court of Justice for "genocide". If it wins, the way will be open to demand massive financial reparations from Serbia. Like most lawsuits, this is finally about money.

Undue process

Tribunal indictments being the equivalent of conviction in the court of public opinion, with guilt taken for granted, actual prosecution and conviction are scarcely necessary, and the next step can be execution. Out of deference to its European supporters, the ICTY can inflict long prison sentences, but not capital punishment. However, the number of unconvicted defendants who have died while in custody of the ICTY or its agents ought to have caused a major scandal in any proper criminal jurisdiction. Defendants appear to run a strong statistical risk of a *de facto* death penalty before being put on trial. Here are some examples:

1. *Simo Drljača.*[45] In 1993, as police chief of Prijedor, Drljača was a member of the Crisis Group formed by the local Serbian

government to take emergency measures, including setting up temporary prison camps. Drljača escorted and briefed outside visitors, but was not accused of personally abusing prisoners. However, based on the hypothetical allegation that Omarska and Keraterm camps were intended "to destroy, in part, the Bosnian Muslim and Bosnian Croat people as national, ethnic or religious groups", the Tribunal indicted Drljača for "genocide". On 10 July 1997, Drljača, 49, his son Siniša, 17, and his brother-in-law, Špiro Milanović, were having breakfast while on a camping trip before taking a swim in the nearby lake. Suddenly three helicopters and four tanks manned by British Special Air Service (SAS) commandos swooped down on them. Drljača ran toward the lake. The soldiers ran after him, caught him, and shot him dead. The soldiers then loaded the body and the dead man's two family members onto a helicopter and flew them to The Hague. There was no investigation to confirm the claim, denied by the two witnesses, that the shooting was in "self-defense". This raid, code-named "Operation Tango", had been approved in advance by Bill Clinton and British prime minister Tony Blair. Afterwards, with its "indicted war criminal" dead on arrival at The Hague, Clinton commented that "it was the right thing to do".

2. *Dragan Gagović*. Gagović was also a chief of police, in the town of Foča. Prosecutors in The Hague proudly pointed to Gagović's 1996 indictment as the first time that rape was treated as a war crime. He was charged with raping a woman in a local detention center for which he was responsible in July 1992. This accusation could never be proved or disproved in court because Gagović too was dead on arrival. On 9 January 1999, French SFOR troops set up a road block to arrest Gagović as he drove five children aged between eight and twelve home in his van from a karate training session. He too was shot dead "in self-defense" by SFOR soldiers, who said they felt threatened. Local residents were furious that SFOR had chosen to arrest the karate coach in circumstances that endangered the lives of children.

3. *Djordje Djukić*. Bosnian Serb General Djukić was never indicted. However, in February 1996, when he was on his way to negotiate arrangements to carry out the Dayton Accords, he was taken prisoner by Bosnian Muslims and subsequently shipped to The Hague for intensive questioning of the "fishing expedition" sort, hoping to get him to incriminate his colleagues. This failed and

he was sent home three months later, just in time to die of untreated cancer at home rather than in a cell in The Hague.

4. *Slavko Dokmanović.* A Serb, Dokmanović was elected mayor of Vukovar, in eastern Slavonia, in Croatia's first multiparty elections in the spring of 1990. As the Tudjman government prepared to secede from Yugoslavia, the longstanding good relations between Serbs and Croats collapsed and Dokmanović was drawn to the Serb side in the brutal civil war, which destroyed his city and ended in Serb control of eastern Slavonia. Dokmanović took part in negotiating the "Erdut agreement" by which the Serbs gave eastern Slavonia back to Croatia, before moving to Serbia. Later, on 26 March 1997, under urging from Croatian authorities, Dokmanović's name was secretly added to the "Vukovar indictment" – accusing him of complicity in the November 1991 abduction and execution of 250 soldiers from a hospital in Vukovar. Dokmanović was unaware of this "sealed indictment" when on 27 June 1997 he responded to an invitation by U.S. diplomat Jacques Klein, the head of the United Nations authority policing eastern Slavonia. It was an ambush. As he crossed the Danube from Serbia, Dokmanović was seized by a score of masked gunmen and shipped to The Hague. At his trial, Dokmanović pleaded innocent. Defense witnesses testified he was elsewhere at the time of the Vukovar hospital massacre. Observers predicted that he would have to be acquitted.[46] However, in the early hours of 29 June 1998, Dokmanović was found hanged in his cell.

5. *Milan Kovačević.* An anesthetist by profession, Dr. Kovačević was director of the Prijedor hospital and a leading figure in the town. During the 1992 civil war, he was second only to the mayor and a member of the Crisis Staff. Because of these responsibilities, he was secretly indicted for "genocide" along with Simo Drljača. On the day Drljača was killed, 10 July 1997, four British soldiers arrived at Prijedor hospital to "deliver a parcel". They arrested Dr. Kovačević, who was unaware of the "sealed indictment" against him, and whisked him to The Hague. Despite having meanwhile suffered a stroke and a heart attack, Dr. Kovačević was ruled fit to go on trial on 7 July 1998. On 1 August, at age 57, Dr. Kovačević died in his Tribunal cell in the Hague suburb of Scheveningen. For several hours before his death, other inmates (there were 26 at the time) banged on their cell doors and shouted to the guards to bring help to the dying man.

Embarrassed Tribunal spokesmen first said that Dr. Kovačević had died of a heart attack, but his lawyer and other witnesses said he had bled to death from a ruptured aorta in his abdomen which could have been repaired surgically.[47]

These deaths are the most dramatic indication of the lack of concern for the rights or even the lives of the defendants that prevails at the Hague Tribunal. But many aspects of procedure exhibit the same assumption of guilt that comes from giving top priority to "the rights of the victims". Representing the interests of presumed victims, there are active lobbies, human rights organizations, and women's groups with ready access to both the Tribunal and the media. Defenders of the minority of Croat and Muslim defendants also have friends in the media and in the courts. But when it comes to Serbs accused of terrible crimes, no powerful human rights groups and no mainstream media are interested in seeing that they get fair treatment.

Aspects of Tribunal procedures that ensure *unfair* treatment are numerous.

The methods of arrest are so spectacular as to convey the impression that the suspect is a wild beast who must be grabbed with all the delicacy of hounds tearing apart a wild boar. The public has been indoctrinated to accept with satisfaction that "indicted war criminals" are put behind bars, never mind how. Brutal arrest simply serves to demonstrate the criminal nature of the indicted person.

For example, on 3 April 2000, French-led NATO troops arrested one of the most prominent leaders of the Bosnian Serbs, Momčilo Krajišnik, a signatory of the Dayton Accords who had succeeded Karadžić as the Serbian member of the joint three-man Bosnia-Herzegovina presidency. On the urging of Bosnian Muslim leaders, the Tribunal on 21 February 2000 raised a secret "sealed" indictment against Krajišnik for "genocide" on grounds of his political leadership role during the civil war. This was a purely political case, designed to convict the Serb side in the Bosnian war of deliberate "genocide". Krajišnik was clearly being arrested as a substitute for Karadžić: "The case we'll be presenting against Krajišnik is effectively the case we'd be presenting against Karadžić", announced deputy ICTY prosecutor Graham Blewitt.[48] The method of arrest of this ex-president was worthy of an escaped serial killer. Early in the morning, NATO troops surrounded his home in Pale, blasted open the door with explosives, and dragged the 54-year-old out of his bed while his two sons, aged 21 and 19, were tied up and held face down on the floor. Instead of allowing Krajišnik to get dressed, the humanitarian soldiery dragged him off barefooted, in his pyjamas.

On 25 August 1999, General Momir Talić, chief of staff of the army of Republika Srpska, was seized in Vienna by Austrian security forces and shipped to The Hague on a sealed indictment. General Talić was in Vienna on official invitation from the OSCE and the Austrian Defense Ministry to take part in an international defense policy seminar on the Dayton peace process. Several international Conventions signed precisely in Vienna guarantee the inviolability of official representatives to such international meetings. So much for respect of international conventions.

The huge rewards offered by the United States for capture of "Serbian war criminals" led mercenaries and extreme right commandos to infiltrate Serbia itself as bounty hunters.[49]

A July 1998 article in *U.S. News and World Report* described a new adventure sport for the men of SEAL, the U.S. Navy's special counter-terrorism unit: hunting beasts of prey called PIFWCS, pronounced "Pifwix". Capturing these "Persons Indicted for War Crimes" has led to "one of the broadest covert operations since the Vietnam War". The intensity of the hunt "reflects the intense interest among some of America's top decision makers", the magazine reported. "Secretary of State Madeleine Albright is well known as an advocate of aggressive efforts to arrest PIFWCS. General [Wesley] Clark also 'is passionate about getting these guys,' says a NATO staffer – 'either seeing them killed or [delivered to] the Hague'..." In September 1997, more than 100 people involved in the Pifwix chase met at Fort Bragg, North Carolina, to draw up plans for capturing Karadžić, but "some analysts suspect that members of Karadžić's security detail may have orders to kill their charge instead of letting him be taken alive in a raid ..." This looks ominously like an advance excuse for bringing in the top Pifwix too dead to stand trial and defend himself. As a "successful" effort, the magazine cited these: "British troops seized one PIFWC and killed another in a shootout last July, and got two more this April." In short: *Wanted, dead or alive.*[50]

Who would dare object that "Pifwix" are human beings, and innocent until proven guilty?

The practice of "sealed indictments" was openly designed to

destabilize virtually all Serbs who have held any position of responsibility and prevent them from normal life and travel. Without warning, anyone can be brutally arrested by a group of armed commandos, who may blow down the door and drag the accused person from his bed. Trial may take place many months or even years later. Far from home, in a hostile environment, the defendants attract no attention from the human rights activists who concern themselves with the fate of accused criminals in the United States or European countries. They are pariahs, doomed to rot in prison. If convicted, the only appeal is to the same Tribunal, which may decide to inflict a penalty far more severe than the first time around.

In addition to killing defendants or virtually burying them alive without hope, the Tribunal disregards the rights of the defense in many other, less dramatic ways.

The Tribunal makes its own rules and privileges the Prosecution. Article 15 of the ICTY Statute authorized its judges to adopt Rules of Procedure and Evidence, which they have repeatedly amended – very confusing for any defense, but not for the Prosecutor, who is "an organ of the Tribunal", with extraordinarily extensive rights including the right to propose amendments to the Rules. The Prosecutor dominates the court, whose judges, as one observer has noted, "are drawn from the second tier of courts around the world" and "whatever their individual merits ... rarely seem in charge of the court".[51] Certainly it has been each of the Chief Prosecutors – Richard Goldstone, Louise Arbour, Carla Del Ponte – who has been the uncontested media "star" of the Tribunal.[52] Until Milošević defied the Tribunal's exhortations to take charge of his own defense, the defense was invisible and inaudible. His skill in cross-examining witnesses and exposing glaring contradictions in the Prosecution's case soon caused the media spotlights to be turned off.

Anonymous testimony and secret documentation handicap the defense. The Tribunal uses methods similar to the most questionable practices of Western mass media, notably reliance on "unidentified sources". The defense may be barred from access to documents or information that "may be contrary to public interest or affect the security interests of any state" – a provision apparently designed to protect the cover of CIA operatives or other friendly government intelligence services providing information to the prosecution. (This recalls the Dreyfus case in France, when official documents that would have proved the innocence of Captain Dreyfus were withheld from the defense on spurious grounds of French national security.)

Moreover, Tribunal rules allow a judge or trial chamber to take measures to prevent disclosure of the identity or whereabouts of a victim or witness, on the pretext that they must be protected from reprisals. Witnesses may testify through closed circuit television using image-distorting or voice-altering devices and use of a pseudonym to conceal identity – a practice reminiscent of the hooded witnesses of the Inquisition. This anonymity is particularly grave in proceedings where verbal testimony rather than material proof constitutes the principal basis for conviction.

The unreliability of oral testimony in Bosnia was illustrated by the first case of alleged Serbian "genocide". In March 1993, a Muslim court in Sarajevo convicted a Serb, Srećko Damjanović, of murdering two Muslim brothers, Kasim and Asim Blekić, on the basis of verbal testimony. This included his own confession, which he retracted in court, saying he had been tortured into signing it by Muslim jailers. Four years later, the *New York Times* found the two "victims of genocide" alive and well, at home in a Sarajevo suburb. This incident illustrated a fact well known to experts: that witnesses' statements and even confessions are the least reliable proof of guilt. But they are the mainstay of the ICTY.

Some pay the bills, others pay the price. Originally, it was stipulated that the expenses of the International Criminal Tribunal were to be covered by the regular UN budget. But this was changed almost immediately, and a special fund was set up for the Tribunal, which could receive specific contributions from governments or non-governmental benefactors to supplement its budget. The U.S. government, while notoriously failing to pay its UN dues, chipped in along with private donors to pay for the Tribunal. This is a step toward the "privatization" of both the United Nations and justice itself. Rich countries and organizations finance the activities they like, while others dry up for lack of funding.

The preparation of the ICTY war crimes "database" supervised by Professor Bassiouni was paid for by international financier George Soros, who by his various philanthropic donations appears to have launched a hostile takeover of what is left of Yugoslavia.[53] In addition to Soros' "Open Society Institute", private donors to the ICTY include the Rockefeller Foundation and the "United States Institute for Peace" created by the Reagan administration as a way of funneling Congressional appropriations to international projects deemed in the U.S. national interest.

Part of Louise Arbour's job as Chief Prosecutor was fund-raising in the "international community", notably among the governments of NATO member states. An example: on 18 April 1997, Arbour called a meeting at ICTY headquarters in The Hague to raise volunteer contributions to pay for the exhumations in Bosnia. "International Community" diplomats were treated to coffee and cakes and a rundown on exhumations from Arbour and her chief expert, Bill Haglund. It was emphasized that this activity was financed by volunteer contributions. Contributors might even choose how the money was spent: a particular site was being exhumed at the request of Swiss donors.

Not only funding but also personnel for this *ad hoc* Tribunal are decided in an *ad hoc* way. Since the budget is tight, the Tribunal, rather than hiring its own staff members, can accept "seconded" personnel from member states. It is the rich ones that can afford to provide equipment and personnel. As of mid-1996, six countries and the European Union had seconded 52 staff members, 23 of them from the United States Departments of State, Defense, and Justice. The Tribunal can blackball unwanted secondings to this tight club. The working language is English. The other two official languages, French and Serbo-Croatian (the latter artificially split into "Serbian", "Croatian", and "Bosnian") are largely hypothetical, as documents are often available only in English.

On 12 May 1999, during the NATO bombing of Yugoslavia, in a speech to the Council on Foreign Relations, chief ICTY Judge Gabrielle Kirk McDonald praised the U.S. government and "the corporate sector" for responding to the "moral imperative" of contributing to the Tribunal. The Tribunal does not yet interrupt its deliberations for a message from our sponsor. But the message comes through nevertheless. With her fulsome praise for Albright, and her condemnation of Yugoslavia as "a rogue state", Kirk McDonald sounded more like a U.S. government spokesperson than the chief magistrate of an unbiased international court.[54] During the NATO bombing, Clinton obtained a special $27 million appropriation to help the ICTY, largely earmarked for collecting testimony from ethnic Albanian refugees to incriminate the Serbs.

When asked on 17 May 1999 what would happen if NATO itself were brought before the Tribunal, NATO spokesman Jamie Shea dismissed such a notion by pointing out that without NATO countries there would be no Tribunal, since it was the NATO countries which had been in the forefront of getting it set up and which funded and supported its activity on a daily basis. He knew what he was talking about.

Although the jurists who set up the Tribunal were overwhelmingly drawn from the Anglo-Saxon tradition of common law, one of that tradition's historic principles, the right to be judged by one's peers, has been totally ignored. This principle, from its initial class implications, has evolved over time to have a broader significance. It can be understood to ensure that an individual is judged by persons who are not prejudiced against him for reasons of social category (race, nationality, religion, etc.) and are socially close enough to be able to evaluate such intangible factors as motivation. In the United States, the principle is applied in the demand that members of racial minorities be included in juries judging matters involving other members of racial minorities.

In the United States, another practice that has developed in favor of the defense is to demand that jurors be without prejudice toward the defendant. This may mean seeking jurors who have not followed media coverage of a case. In comparison to such scruples, what can one say of judging – without any jury whatsoever – citizens of Balkan states by judges from distant continents with no understanding whatsoever of the complicated background of Balkan conflicts beyond what they have gleaned from the media?

At certain hearings of the ICTY, a single "expert" designated by the court is supposed to inform judges from distant continents of the historic background of the conflict they are called upon to judge. Leaving aside personal bias, a single viewpoint is quite inadequate for initiating a panel of ignorant foreigners into the complexities of Yugoslav politics, marked by contrary interpretations of the same history. There is no adversary relationship in the choice of experts; there is no confrontation between experts of the prosecution and experts of the defense, for instance, in the matter of historic and political background. A debate between Yugoslav historians would be far more enlightening – so enlightening, perhaps, that the international jurists might recognize their incapacity to judge these matters correctly.

5. PRESUMED GUILTY UNTIL PROVEN INNOCENT

The presumption that a defendant is "innocent until proven guilty" has been cast aside by the ICTY. The presumption of guilt is blatant in regard to Serb political leaders, starting with the president

of the "Serb Republic of Bosnia-Herzegovina", or Republika Srpska,
Dr. Radovan Karadžić. After years of hearing commentators rail
against the occupation forces in Bosnia for failing to arrest "the
indicted war criminal Radovan Karadžić", the Western public must
be convinced that the case against him is overwhelming. This
impression, based on media uproar, is not borne out by close
examination.

The Karadžić case

On 24 July 1995, and again on 14 November 1995, the ICTY indicted
Karadžić on 16 counts of genocide, various crimes against humanity,
violation of the laws or customs of war, unlawful confinement of
civilians, the shelling of a civilian gathering, destruction of sacred
sites, extensive destruction of property, appropriation and plunder
of property, sniping against civilian targets, and other grave
breaches of the laws or customs of war. This is a compendium of
all the crimes that may or may not have been committed in the
course of the war. But guilt depends on personal responsibility.
The grave accusations against the Bosnian Serb leader were based
on the following factors:

1. An *a priori* judgment that the war aim of the Bosnian Serbs was
   "genocide".
2. A statement made by Karadžić during a parliamentary debate,
   which was interpreted by his adversaries as a "threat".
3. Attribution of "command responsibility" to Karadžić for all crimes
   allegedly committed by Serbs in Bosnia during the civil war.
4. Specific responsibility for the "Srebrenica massacre" – a charge
   added in the 14 November 1995 indictment.

In late June and early July 1996, the case against Karadžić was
laid out in a novel ICTY exercise called a Rule 61 Hearing. Invented
by the Tribunal judges, "Rule 61 of the Rules of Procedure and
Evidence" allows the Prosecution to present all the charges against
an accused person in his absence after indictment. This "Rule 61
Hearing" is just one of the innovations made by the ICTY drastically
reducing the rights of the defense. At the opening of the 27 June
1996 hearing, the French presiding judge, Claude Jorda, author
of Rule 61, refused to allow Karadžić's defense attorney, Igor
Pantelić, to represent his client during the hearing. He was merely
permitted to observe proceedings from the public gallery. In short,

this was a public ceremony of uncontested accusation, in which the indicted man's attorney was banned from cross-examining witnesses or offering rebuttals. Three attorneys for the prosecution presented the case, based on the four factors mentioned above.

1. The charge of "genocide"

The term "genocide" tends to be used increasingly for crimes that fall far short of the literal meaning: the annihilation of a people. Already, the definition of the term in the 1948 Convention on Genocide was extremely broad and included "causing serious bodily or mental harm to members of [a] group", if committed "with intent to destroy, in whole or in part, a national, racial or religious group".[55] There is a marked tendency in war to harm or kill people along lines of "national", ethnic, or religious identity. This was clearly the case in Bosnia-Herzegovina. Therefore, technically, all sides might be charged with "genocide". However, although the Hague Tribunal has occasionally accused Croats and Muslims of "war crimes", the "genocide" accusation has been reserved for Serbs. The key word seems to be "intent". It has simply been assumed from the start that the intention of the Serbs was more "genocidal" than the intentions of the others.

Even at the Rule 61 hearing, where all the witnesses were called by and for the Prosecution, such intent was assumed or inferred, but never demonstrated. An Australian police officer named John Hunter Ralston was called to explain the political program of Karadžić's Serbian Democratic Party (SDS). The party was founded in Sarajevo in July 1990 and went on to win an overwhelming majority of Serb votes in the November 1990 elections in Bosnia-Herzegovina. Ralston acknowledged that the main goal of the SDS was "the complete and unconditional civil, national, cultural, religious and economic equality of the Serbs in Bosnia-Herzegovina. Its most important political goal was a federal Yugoslavia and within it a federal Bosnia-Herzegovina." This does not sound much like "genocide".

2. Karadžić's threat

The main "evidence" of genocidal intent produced at the Rule 61 hearing was a statement by Karadžić uttered during a heated exchange in the parliament of Bosnia-Herzegovina during the night of 14-15 October 1991. Karadžić's Serb Democratic Party wanted to keep Bosnia-Herzegovina within Yugoslavia or, short of that, create autonomous Serb regions. Izetbegović's Democratic Action Party totally rejected such suggestions. Calling on Izetbegović to recognize the Serbian people's desire to remain in Yugoslavia, Karadžić declared: "You want to take Bosnia-Herzegovina down the same highway of hell and suffering that Slovenia and Croatia are travelling. Do not think that you will not lead Bosnia-Herzegovina into hell, and do not think that you will not perhaps make the Muslim people disappear, because the Muslims cannot defend themselves if there is war – How will you prevent everyone from being killed in Bosnia-Herzegovina?"[56]

Despite the double negatives, these are strong words, uttered in the heat of debate. They are certainly no more warlike than Izetbegović's statement months before, in February 1991, that he "would sacrifice peace for a sovereign Bosnia-Herzegovina, but for that peace in Bosnia-Herzegovina ... would not sacrifice sovereignty". Karadžić's statement could be interpreted as a warning to Izetbegović of the dangers of war and an invitation to compromise to save the peace. Izetbegović, who had chosen war, described the Serb leader's statement as a threat, in an obvious move to shift blame. Accepting this interpretation, the Tribunal presented the citation as proof of Karadžić's intent to commit "genocide".

3. Attribution of command responsibility for all crimes committed by Serbs in Bosnia-Herzegovina

Had Karadžić been defended at the Rule 61 hearing, his attorney could have presented documents indicating that Karadžić not only did not order the crimes enumerated, he also did not (as accused) "fail to take the necessary and reasonable measures to prevent such acts or to punish the perpetrators". His very first directive issued as president of Republika Srpska, on 13 May 1992, was an order to the armed forces to respect international conventions of war. To this end, he reminded officers of their "duty to initiate prosecution invoking the full sanctions of the law against individuals under their command who offend against the international conventions of war", and also to "hold regular training sessions" to make sure the conventions are understood. A month later, he issued an order outlawing paramilitary groups and another giving detailed instructions for humane treatment of prisoners of war. Subsequent directives stressed the need for "proper conduct towards the civilian population of other nationalities in our Republic". On 19 August 1992, Karadžić issued an order reiterating the need for "compliance with international humanitarian law and particularly the 3rd and 4th Geneva conventions", and ordering a "stop to forced movement and other illegal measures against the civilian population". (This order was clearly directed against "ethnic cleansing".) And so on.[57]

This may prove nothing to those whose minds are made up. But in the absence of presidential orders to commit crimes, the hypothesis can at least be advanced that whatever crimes were committed by Serb forces were in violation of Karadžić's orders and without his consent.

The Tribunal's application of the principle of "command responsibility" was blatantly selective. For example, in May 1995, violating a UN-sponsored truce, Tudjman sent his forces to recapture western Slavonia from Serb rebels, driving tens of thousands of Serbs from the region and killing hundreds of civilians who were too old, weak or sick to flee.[58] In retaliation, and to get the Croats to stop attacking Serb civilians, Krajina Serbs lobbed two Orkan rockets into central Zagreb, killing seven people. For this, the ICTY indicted the president of the Serbian Krajina, Milan Martić. Three months later, the Croatian army, strengthened by illegal arms shipments and U.S. advisors, swept through the Krajina, driving out some 200,000 Serbs, destroying homes, and killing civilians. In a rare moment of boldness, EU envoy Carl Bildt suggested that if ordering shelling was a war crime, Croatian president Franjo Tudjman might deserve an ICTY indictment as much as Martić. The only result was that Bildt himself was declared *persona non grata* in Croatia.[59] Supported by the United States and Germany, Tudjman never needed to fear indictment for his command responsibility. He remained above criticism until safely dead (he died on 10 December 1999).

Srebrenica

However, for public opinion, all of this seems like quibbling. The case against Karadžić, and indeed against "the Serbs" in general, can be reduced to a single word: "Srebrenica". The difficulty in knowing the truth about Srebrenica began with the fact that before any solid information was available, Srebrenica had already become an important symbol and overwhelming political weapon. Uncertainty has persisted concerning the actual number of people killed, the circumstances and motives involved, and the political significance of the real or assumed killing that took place. In trying to understand what happened at Srebrenica, a number of factors should be taken into account.

The "safe areas" in Bosnia-Herzegovina were not demilitarized, and thus served as Muslim military bases under UN protection

Six so-called "safe areas" were set up by the United Nations in April and May 1993: Bihać (200,000 inhabitants), Goražde (60,000 inhabitants), Sarajevo (380,000 inhabitants), Tuzla (130,000 inhabitants, swollen by refugees), Žepa (12,000 inhabitants), and Srebrenica (an enclave with 44,000 Muslims, the Serb inhabitants having fled in 1992). Common sense would suggest that a "safe area" in wartime must be demilitarized. In reality, these were all Muslim-held towns and the Muslims refused to demilitarize them. All were used by Muslim forces as safe *bases*, from which to attack the Serbs. The UN protection force (UNPROFOR) ensured safe transit to the "safe areas" of food shipments and other provisions from international charitable organizations. The Serbs suspected – correctly – that these shipments were also used to smuggle weapons.[60] From the Serb viewpoint, the "safe areas" were a fraud, a disguised form of aid to the Muslim side.

In April 1993, the Bosnian Serbs had given in to international pressure not to capture the enclave on condition that Srebrenica be demilitarized. On 21 April, UNPROFOR announced that "demilitarization of Srebrenica was a success". This was deceptive. The Muslims "handed over approximately 300 weapons, a large number of which were non-serviceable".[61] Only the central urban area of the "safe" zone was demilitarized, while the Muslim forces in the outskirts kept their weapons and continued to make forays into Serb territory, attacking civilians as well as Serb soldiers. By taking up positions close to the Dutch UN troops and opening fire on the Serbs, Muslim units tried to provoke a fight between Serbs and UNPROFOR, which had neither the mandate nor the forces to stop them.[62]

The Muslim military force stationed in Srebrenica—some 5,000 men under the command of Naser Orić, had carried out murderous raids against nearby Serb villages

Serbs fled Srebrenica in May 1992, after the murder of a prominent Serb judge. Srebrenica thus became a Muslim enclave. The Muslim National Council gave command of the area to Naser Orić, who set about attacking surrounding Serb villages with remarkable brutality. Orić's raiders chose the Orthodox Christmas day, 7 January 1993, to attack the village of Kravica, slaughtering villagers and burning homes. Forty-six Serbs were killed outright, some as they left church after Christmas services. The Western media almost entirely ignored the Christmas massacre at Kravica.[63] Between May 1992 and January 1994, some 192 Serb villages were pillaged and burnt, and over 1,300 villagers were killed, while many more fled.[64] In 1994 and 1995, as Muslim commander in Srebrenica, Orić actually invited foreign reporters to his comfortable apartment to show off his "war trophies": videocassette tapes of his exploits displaying severed heads and dead bodies of Serbs, burning houses, and heaps of corpses.[65] These grisly images exist, but have never been seen by millions of people, who vividly recall the picture of a thin Bosnian Muslim man behind barbed wire. To become a determining factor in public opinion, an event needs to be recalled repeatedly in reports, articles, and editorial comment. Analogies thrive on specific historical memories. In the West, a thin man behind barbed wire can signify "Auschwitz". Among Bosnian Serbs, decapitation signifies "the Turks".[66] Serbs were reminded of the centuries of Ottoman rule when the Turkish method of repression featured decapitating rebels and displaying their heads to the public.[67]

In one of their raids, on 26 June 1995, Srebrenica-based Muslim units penetrated behind Serb lines to burn down the village of Visnjica, and reported killing 40 "Chetniks" (meaning Serbs). To put a stop to these raids, the regional command of the Serb army hastily planned "Operation Krivaja 95", initially aimed only at the non-demilitarized surroundings of Srebrenica municipality.[68]

Izetbegović pulled Naser Orić out of Srebrenica prior to the anticipated Serb offensive, deliberately leaving the enclave undefended

The Serb offensive changed its objective when it encountered no resistance, whether from the Muslims or from UNPROFOR. Finding Srebrenica undefended and in chaos, General Ratko Mladić abruptly ordered the Bosnian Serb forces to occupy the entire enclave, including the center.[69]

Various explanations have been offered for the Muslim command's decision to abandon Srebrenica to Serb forces. Some observers have suggested that the Serb takeover was part of a secret or tacit trade-off meant to simplify the forthcoming Dayton peace deal. Letting the Serbs overrun two of the Muslim enclaves in Serb-controlled eastern Bosnia could satisfy the demand of U.S. diplomats for a simpler territorial division between the opposing parties.[70] While gaining the enclaves of Srebrenica and Žepa, the Serbs were soon driven out of large stretches of solidly Serb-inhabited territory in western Bosnia (the Bosnian Krajina). This reduced the percentage of territory held by the Bosnian Serbs from almost 70 per cent to approximately 49 per cent, making it easier for Holbrooke to get the Muslims to accept a peace deal. Another suggestion is that Izetbegović had agreed to give up Srebrenica in exchange for the Serb-inhabited suburbs of Sarajevo, but preferred to let the enclave be captured by force.

The fact that the Izetbegović government did nothing to defend Srebrenica suggests not only a tacit deal, but also has aroused the strong suspicion of a calculated sacrifice. Offering the Bosnian Serbs an opportunity (likely to be seized) to carry out revenge killings could be more valuable to the cause than holding onto an impoverished enclave. The November 1999 UN Report on Srebrenica notes the following:

> Some surviving members of the Srebrenica delegation have stated that President Izetbegović also told them he had learned that a NATO intervention in Bosnia and Herzegovina was possible, but could occur only if the Serbs were to break into Srebrenica, killing at least 5,000 of its people.

Recriminations between Muslims have never ceased regarding the attitude of the leadership in Sarajevo. With their commanding officers pulled out to safety, thousands of Muslim soldiers manning the enclave were left without clear command or orders. Abandoned by Sarajevo, and knowing that the approaching Serbs were enraged by Orić's attacks on villagers, the soldiers were terrified. They quarreled among themselves over whether to resist or to give up the town without a fight and flee through Serb lines to Tuzla. Muslim officers still in Srebrenica could not agree on what to do. Things were so chaotic that "Muslim commanders shot at their own people. When the Serbs marched in, there were already some bodies lying in the streets."[71] Some wanted to surrender, but most decided to try to break through Serb lines and flee. By all accounts, this chaos deepened during the long retreat. Wild scenes occurred, as confused soldiers fell into Serb ambushes, sometimes fighting back, sometimes shooting each other or even committing suicide.

Ibran Mustafić, a member of the Bosnian parliament and founder and former president of the Srebrenica branch of Izetbegović's party, accused the Sarajevo leadership of "consciously premeditating the scenario of the betrayal of Srebrenica". In an interview with the Sarajevo newspaper *Slobodna Bosna* in July 1996, Mustafić said that the orders came from Sarajevo for the Muslim army in Srebrenica to attack outside the safe area in order to provoke Serb forces to attack the safe area. Srebrenica, he said, was meant to be the "lamb sacrificed on the foundations of the state". Mustafić insisted that many more Srebrenicans had survived than were acknowledged. The Sarajevo government's attitude, he said, "persuades me simply that the government hoped not to see so many people survive, that for them there are so to speak too many survivors from Srebrenica".[72]

The United States used the inevitable failure of the ambiguous "UN safe area" concept to discredit the United Nations as a peacekeeping force, thus promoting NATO to that role

The non-demilitarized, or only partially demilitarized, "safe areas" put UNPROFOR in the impossible position of a formally neutral force "protecting" the military bases of one side in the conflict. But the force was never granted the military means necessary even to defend itself, much less anybody else. The UNPROFOR mission was a planned failure. For the advocates of armed "humanitarian intervention", the fall of Srebrenica was used as proof of the failure of the United Nations. More than that, it was used to discredit the whole tradition of neutral diplomacy in favor of the moral absolutist approach of "identifying and destroying the enemy". Thus, in November 1999, Washington's choice as Secretary General, Kofi Annan, duly issued a sweeping *mea culpa* on behalf of the United Nations. His report on Srebrenica claimed that "the tragedy of Srebrenica will haunt our history forever". The report condemned "an institutional ideology of impartiality even when confronted with attempted genocide" and lauded the role of air power. The report concluded that "the cardinal lesson of Srebrenica is that deliberate and systematic attempts to terrorize, expel or murder an entire people must be met decisively with all necessary means". The United Nations thereby renounced the role of impartial diplomacy and endorsed U.S. military might as the best means to deal with civil conflicts.

The number of Muslims killed or missing after the fall of Srebrenica is uncertain, and more effort has been made to inflate the figures than to identify and count the real victims

After Bosnian Serb troops captured the town on 11 July 1995, women and children were evacuated. Of military-age men, many were detained and many more fled. Two months later, the International Committee of the Red Cross (ICRC) announced that it was trying to obtain information from Bosnian Serb authorities about 3,000 persons who witnesses said had been detained, and from Sarajevo authorities about some 5,000 individuals "who fled Srebrenica, some of whom reached central Bosnia". The total of these two figures was the original source of the oft-repeated estimate that 8,000 Muslims had been massacred.[73] However, from the start, it was understood that the missing 5,000 had not all been killed. On 18 July, the *New York Times* had reported that "some 3,000 to 4,000 Bosnian Muslims who were considered by UN officials to be missing after the fall of Srebrenica have made their way through enemy lines to Bosnian government territory. The group, which included wounded refugees, sneaked past Serb lines under fire and crossed some 30 miles through forests to safety."[74]

So, when the Red Cross announced it was asking Sarajevo what happened to some 5,000 individuals who fled Srebrenica, it was asking about Muslims, most of whom were presumed to have made it to safety in Muslim territory. The problem was that Bosnian government authorities were not cooperative in revealing the names and number of these survivors. The Sarajevo authorities *never* chose to answer questions from the Red Cross or even to inform next of kin as to precisely what happened to those men. The London *Times* reported on 2 August that thousands of "missing" Bosnian Muslim soldiers from Srebrenica at the center of reports of mass executions had been regrouped in Muslim territory. The Red Cross in Geneva said it had heard from sources in Bosnia that "up to 2,000 Bosnian Government troops were in an area north of Tuzla. They had made their way there from Srebrenica 'without their families being informed', a spokesman said, adding that it had not been possible to verify the reports because the Bosnian Government refused to allow the Red Cross into the area."[75]

The ICRC continued to post a list of "missing" that its own officials knew was not accurate, because the Bosnian government refused to provide information, holding back the names of the survivors not only from the Red Cross, but even from the men's own families.[76]

Six years after the summer of 1995, ICTY forensic teams had exhumed 2,361 bodies in the region, and identified fewer than 50. In an area where fighting had raged for years, some of the bodies were certainly of Serbs as well as of Muslims. Of those bodies, 199 were found to have been bound or blindfolded, and must reasonably be presumed on the basis of the material evidence to have been executed.

There is still no clear way to account for the fate of all the Muslim men reported missing in Srebrenica. There is no record of how many prisoners, such as Ibran Mustafić, the political leader of Srebrenica's Muslim party already quoted, were released in exchanges. An undetermined number of prisoners were even dispersed abroad.[77]

The initial accusation against the Bosnian Serbs was politically motivated

The accusation of a "Srebrenica massacre" was used by the Clinton administration to focus world attention on Serb misdeeds at precisely the moment when some 200,000 Serbs were being driven out of the Krajina by the Croatian army, supported by the United States. At a closed session of the Security Council on 10 August 1995, U.S. Ambassador Albright displayed U.S. spy satellite photographs, dramatically claiming that pictures of an empty field showed evidence that the Bosnian Serbs had "committed wide-scale atrocities against Muslim civilians". This successfully diverted attention from the main business on the agenda that day: the drafting of Security Council Resolution 1000 on the Croatian "Operation Storm", which was then "ethnically cleansing" the Krajina of its large Serb population. The Security Council resolution politely invited the Croats to stop and respect international law, but did not condemn their violation of the cease-fire or Croatian massacres of helpless, elderly Serb civilians.

Most of Albright's satellite photographs were classified "for security reasons". They could not be critically examined by the public. The meaning of these unseen photos was "spun" for the media by the habitual American official who did not wish to be identified:[78]

According to one American official who has seen the photographs, one shows hundreds and perhaps thousands of Muslim men and boys in a field near a soccer stadium about 5 miles north of Srebrenica. Another photo taken several days later shows a large area of freshly dug earth, consistent with the appearance of known mass graves, near the stadium, which is empty.

Waving her pictures at the 14 members of the Security Council, Albright excused any future failure to find the "hundreds and perhaps thousands of Muslim men and boys" in the "mass grave" by warning ominously: "We will keep watching to see if the Bosnian Serbs try to erase the evidence of what they have done."[79]

If the United States was really able to watch everything the Bosnian Serbs were doing, and the massacres took place on the scale alleged, questions arise. Why were no photos displayed showing the massacres? More troubling still, if U.S. satellites observed the Serbs carrying out massacres in July, why did the United States wait until August to denounce the crime? If the U.S. government was aware at the time that thousands of men were being executed, why did it make no move to prevent it?

And apparently, although they presumably "kept watching", the U.S. spy satellites never did manage to observe the Serbs erasing that supposed "evidence".

The image of an empty field that "might contain victims of Serb genocide" completely obliterated images of the huge exodus of Serbs caused by the Croatian offensive. *Christian Science Monitor* reporter David Rohde, although based in Zagreb, ignored the Croatian "Operation Storm" against the Serbs. Instead, armed with the famous photograph of the dirt field, he rushed to the spot and rushed backed to write that yes, the field was there. But even Rohde, a couple of years and a Pulitzer prize later, had no clear idea how many people were killed in Srebrenica. At the end of his 1997 book, *Endgame: The Betrayal and Fall of Srebrenica, Europe's Worst Massacre Since World War II*, he concluded:

> Barring secret labor camps and the Bosnian government massively inflating the ICRC missing figure, Bosnian Serb Soldiers systematically slaughtered 7,079 mostly unarmed Muslim men in ambushes and mass executions between July 12 and July 16, 1995.
>
> ... But even if the number of victims proves to be no higher than the roughly 500 found so far at four execution sites and 150 found to date at one ambush site, what occurred in Srebrenica

was unprecedented in postwar Europe. Srebrenica is unique because of the international community's role in the tragedy.

The international community partially disarmed thousands of men, promised them they would be safeguarded and then delivered them to their sworn enemies. Srebrenica was not simply a case of the international community standing by as a far-off atrocity was committed. The actions of the international community encouraged, aided and emboldened the executioners.

Significantly, Rohde rests his case not on the 7,000 figure whose fragility he must know, but on the political argument, which can be valid even if the number of victims proves no higher than roughly 500 or 600. What matters, finally, is that the "International Community" must in the future intervene more vigorously on the "right" side. The point is to discredit neutrality in favor of aggressive military "humanitarian intervention".

Insofar as Muslims were actually executed following the fall of Srebrenica, such crimes bear all the signs of spontaneous acts of revenge rather than a project of "genocide"

Much is made of the fact that when they captured Srebrenica, the Serb forces filtered the men of military age from women and children, who were offered safe passage. This was often mentioned as something particularly sinister. However, one thing should be obvious: one does not commit "genocide" by sparing women and children.

The men were singled out partly because the Serbs could exchange Muslim POWs for Serb POWs. More relevant to the accusations, Serbs were looking for Muslim fighters who took part in Naser Orić's raids, starting with Orić himself. The unexpectedly easy and rapid capture of Srebrenica, with Muslim forces in total disarray, presented the Bosnian Serbs with an opportunity to exact revenge. It was even a chance to eliminate easily a part of the enemy's army. War crimes? The Serbs themselves do not deny that crimes were committed.[80] Part of a plan of genocide? For this there is no evidence whatsoever.

Some observers consider that Srebrenica was a "trap" for the Serbs who stupidly fell into it.

Testifying to a French parliamentary inquiry, General Philippe Morillon declared that Mladić had fallen into a deliberate "trap". This was the "only way Izetbegović could get what he wanted –

for the International Community to take his side", said Morillon, insisting: "I'm not afraid to say that it is Sarajevo that deliberately provoked the dramatic events. It was the presidency, it was Izetbegović."[81]

The rage of Bosnian Serbs at Orić and his men was no secret. One man who wanted to keep Bosnian Serb forces away from Srebrenica was Slobodan Milošević. In April 1993, he had helped forestall Bosnian Serb capture of Srebrenica because he feared that "the tremendous bad blood that existed" between Serb and Muslim fighters in the region might result in a bloodbath.[82] Nevertheless, the accusation of "genocide" in Srebrenica was used to construct the presumption that Milošević must be plotting to commit genocide in Kosovo and finally to accuse him of responsibility for the Bosnian disaster he had sought to avert.

Selective justice: NATO and Milošević

The NATO air strikes against Yugoslavia, initiated on 24 March 1999, were in flagrant violation of international law on numerous counts. Yugoslavia was attacked, without any mandate from the UN Security Council, although it had not committed any act of aggression against any other country. As the bombing continued, civilian targets were increasingly hit in an open effort to demoralize the population. The NATO action violated virtually every relevant international convention and treaty, as well as several national Constitutions.

On 7 May, a team of lawyers from Canada and Europe submitted a brief to Louise Arbour, the Canadian Chief Prosecutor at the International Criminal Tribunal for former Yugoslavia, accusing U.S. and other NATO officials of war crimes, including "wanton destruction of cities, towns, or villages, or devastation not justified by military necessity, attack, or bombardment, by whatever means, of undefended towns, villages, dwellings, or buildings". One of the lawyers, Professor Michael Mandel of Osgoode Hall Law School of York University in Toronto, where Arbour herself once taught, argued that "charging the war's victors, and not only the losers, would be a watershed in international criminal law, showing the world that no one is above the law". This and a number of other initiatives by international jurists pointing to the illegality of the NATO action were widely ignored by mainstream media. Mainstream media almost entirely ignored the legal objections to the NATO bombing, mentioning these initiatives only to refute them, blocking meaningful public debate on this important issue.[83]

Instead, on 27 May, Arbour formally charged Milošević and other senior officials in the Yugoslav and Serbian governments of crimes against humanity and war crimes allegedly committed in Kosovo. Arbour's indictment was based on material she had received from the U.S. government only one day earlier. The charges against the Yugoslav leaders were provided by a special U.S. intelligence unit called the "Interagency Balkan Task Force", housed at the CIA with input from the Defense Intelligence Agency, the National Security Agency, and the State Department.[84] Some of the charges were substantially identical to those filed earlier against the officials responsible for the NATO bombing: "the widespread shelling of towns and villages; the burning of homes, farms and businesses, and the destruction of personal property". NATO accomplished these acts on a larger scale and with far bigger weapons.

The U.S. government was naturally extremely interested in obtaining this indictment as a justification of its own bombing campaign, which at that very moment was causing increased civilian casualties and public misgivings at home. "The indictment confirms that our war is just", Clinton commented. That was, of course, the whole point and purpose.

The Yugoslav government itself tried on 29 April 1999, to institute proceedings at the International Court of Justice in The Hague against NATO governments for a broad range of war crimes and crimes against humanity. The Western media, in brief reports, let it be known that such an initiative was "not serious". The case was in fact stalled because the Genocide Convention, the legal basis for Belgrade's suit, has never been recognized by the United States as applying to itself, although Washington is willing to let it apply to others.[85]

After the electoral defeat of Milošević in October 2000 pressure mounted to sacrifice the defeated president as scapegoat. The newly elected president of Yugoslavia, Vojislav Koštunica, insisted that Milošević should not be tried outside Yugoslavia, and the highest court ruled that his extradition would violate the Serbian Constitution. However, the Serbian government headed by the unpopular Zoran Djindjic, which had ridden to power on Kostunica's coat-tails with much financial backing from the United States and Germany, on 28 June 2001, took up the task of bounty hunter by whisking Milošević off to The Hague in the vain hope that this would bring big international investment into Serbia. This was a fool's bargain. Serbia got virtually nothing for selling its former president. Rather, the planned conviction of Milošević by the ICTY was designed not only to justify NATO bombing, but also to establish Serbia's guilt for all the wars of Yugoslav disintegration. This could complete the destruction of the country by burdening ruined Serbia with endless reparation payments to its neighbors – an outcome eagerly sought by the Izetbegović regime in Sarajevo.

6. THE LONG ARM OF GLOBALIZATION

Since war is itself the breakdown of law, order and justice, stopping war would seem to be more important than attempting to turn it into yet another object of courtroom proceedings. It is remarkable how certain ICTY jurists take it for granted that there will be more and more wars, and are comforted by the prospect of regulating these wars by judicial institutions. The aspiration seems to be to make war more sporting, a game to be played within rules. This is grotesquely inappropriate for modern warfare, which has been transformed by technology into a merciless slaughter of innocent bystanders.

The experience of the ICTY should give pause even to those who are enthusiastic about the project for an International Criminal Court (ICC). Unlike the *ad hoc* tribunals, the ICC is intended to be universal. But is this possible? In reality the project raises problems that have yet to be solved satisfactorily.

There is no authentic justice that is not applied equally to all. The Hague Tribunal has already shown that selective justice results from the political bias of the most influential powers, the prejudices created by mass media and finally from budgetary constraints. An international tribunal simply lacks the means to judge equitably all the various crimes that may be committed in the course of violent civil strife or war. Serious detective work at a long distance, sifting truth from lies in distant countries torn by civil conflict is a mammoth, not to say impossible, task. It is neither politically nor financially feasible for an international court to prosecute all the dreadful human rights violations that take place around the world. Inevitably, a few spectacular cases will be singled out by the interests of Great Powers, media attention and financial support. In short, an international *criminal* tribunal is almost certain to turn into an international *political* tribunal that stages show trials of scapegoats.

Two aspects of the ICC statutes directly continue the practice of the ICTY. For one, according to Article 16, the UN Security Council will have the power to impede or suspend initiatives by the Prosecution. In practice, this will ensure the ongoing impunity of the Great Powers, as well as of their most favored clients. Secondly, according to Article 116, the ICC can be financed by voluntary contributions from governments, international organizations, private individuals, companies, and so on.[86] Those with the means to pay will tend to determine the choice of cases brought before court.

Furthermore, no court can function without a police force. This also will make the ICC dependent on the powerful. The ICTY's police force is NATO, since on 9 May 1996, the ICTY prosecution signed a memorandum of understanding with the NATO supreme command in Europe covering practical aspects of NATO assistance and delivery of suspects. Now, if a criminal court requires a police force to arrest suspects and provide material evidence, a police force requires a criminal court to legitimatize its repressive activities. Thus, if the Tribunal needed NATO, NATO needed the Tribunal in order to complete its transformation from a traditional military alliance into a "humanitarian" world police. The May 1996 agreement made the Tribunal dependent on NATO to fill its docks. And if NATO were ever to commit war crimes, who could the Tribunal send to arrest NATO? Nobody, obviously. The Tribunal mandate promoted NATO troops into policemen of a new type, enjoying a special impunity.

And here we approach a conundrum, which it is dangerous to evade: how can the law judging war crimes ever be other than the law of the victor? Now, it well may be that the vanquished are more criminal than the victors, as in World War II. But is superior military force always and forever the proof of virtue? To believe this is to accept that "might is right". If Hitler had won the war, who would have judged the Nazis at Nuremberg? Many in the West consider the Soviet Union under Stalin guilty of appalling crimes: would the Soviet Union have sent judges to Nuremberg without the victory of the Red Army? The tribunals at Nuremberg and Tokyo were obviously victors' tribunals, even though the former was considered legitimate by public opinion. Supporters of the ICTY can claim that it overcomes this difficulty, since it was set up toward the start of a conflict, by outside powers that were not themselves involved. This is not wholly true, inasmuch as the outside powers who sponsored the creation of the ICTY had already chosen "their sides" in the Yugoslav civil wars, and later actually did get involved as belligerents. In this case, the ICTY has been applying, so to speak, a *future* victor's justice, inasmuch as the need to enforce the Tribunal and arrest the persons it has indicted becomes an incitement and a *raison d'être* for the victorious military action of the powers who sponsored it.

Absolute unchallenged power creates absolute impunity, and the current imbalance of power in favor of the United States is not a favorable environment for the establishment of a balanced system of international justice. In a more balanced world, an international criminal court could be the appropriate jurisdiction for clearly international crimes, such as, for example, the alleged involvement of Osama bin Laden in the World Trade Center suicide bombings. Assuming it was planned abroad, that was indeed an international crime. So was the U.S. sabotage of Sandinista Nicaragua, the U.S. invasion of Grenada, the clandestine U.S. encouragement of drugs for arms deals in various parts of the world, and so on. Thus it is significant that up to now the call for *ad hoc* "international criminal tribunals", and even the arguments in favor of an international criminal court, have focused primarily on the prospect of punishing famous perpetrators of essentially *internal* crimes (General Pinochet, Pol Pot), described as "crimes against humanity". This focus on "evil dictators" conveys the message that they can be stopped, judged, and punished by the benevolent outside intervention of the "International Community". It enforces the dualistic view of an essentially good Western imperial condominium obliged to punish "bad" men who trouble the moral order.

If presidents are to be tried in criminal court for acts committed during wars, incidents immediately come to mind that could justify putting U.S. presidents on trial. What about the responsibility of the U.S. president for the My Lai massacre in Vietnam? Or more recently, who should be considered responsible for the gratuitous massacre by U.S. forces of surrendering Iraqis at the end of the Gulf War?[87] Of course, the very idea of indicting the president of the world's greatest military power seems utterly preposterous. It is indeed preposterous because of the relationship of forces.

A major obstacle to any universal justice at present is the obvious fact that the prime suspect in truly international crimes is likely to be the U.S. government, which understandably refuses to submit to any international jurisdiction. Nor can it be forced to do so, given the present totally lopsided relationship of forces. Sincere champions of international justice should be aware of the danger that under these circumstances, any international criminal court is likely to become an instrument to break down the sovereignty of weak states and thus to further the aims of an inequitable process of globalization.

3 Comparative Nationalisms

Throughout the 1990s, "nationalism" was widely denounced, with theYugoslav disaster given as the prime illustration of where it could lead. However, the condemnation of Serbian nationalism as the arch villain supposedly opposing "multiculturalism" led to tacit endorsement of the separatist nationalisms that were tearing apart the multinational state of Yugoslavia. Anti-nationalism in theory became pro-nationalism in practice.

1. FROM STATE-BUILDING TO STATE-BREAKING

The principal difference between the Serbs and the others was their attitude toward the preservation or destruction of Yugoslavia. The leaders of each of the other nationalist movements needed to break up Yugoslavia in order to create an independent state apparatus of their own. Serb opposition to dismantling Yugoslavia was inevitable considering the Serbs' population distribution and political history. However, by portraying Serb attachment to Yugoslavia as an aggressive nationalist plot to create "Greater Serbia", the secessionists transformed this obstacle into an asset. Serbs' desire to stay in Yugoslavia was transformed into the main argument for destroying it.

Different historical experiences have indeed created differences in national consciousness between Yugoslavia's peoples. The current caricature of archaic Serbs obsessed with the 1389 Battle of Kosovo has served to obscure the importance of a less distant past. Two historical factors had a major impact on Serb national consciousness. The first was the long struggle to liberate their people from centuries of subjugation and build a viable state. The second was the brutal destruction of the Yugoslav state by the Nazi invasion of 1941 and the massacres that followed.

The Serbian national movement emerged in the early years of the nineteenth century as the liberation struggle of an oppressed people. In the Ottoman Empire, political and economic privileges were reserved for Muslims. While the mosques called the Islamic faithful to prayer several times a day, the Sultan's law banned Orthodox Christian Serbs from marking their celebrations by ringing church bells.[1] However, the fundamental problem was not religion itself, but the social hierarchy imposed by religion. Christians were an inferior caste, the *Rayah*, obliged to pay taxes and provide labor in order to support the caste of spahis (cavalry) and janissaries (infantry) who served the Sultan. Their most promising sons could be taken from their families in childhood and abducted to Turkey to be converted to Islam, given new names, and trained to become members of the elite guards of the Sultan. Retrospective condemnation of Western Europe's own record of religious intolerance and persecution has shed a misleading if flattering light on the supposed "religious tolerance" of Ottoman rule. Ottoman "tolerance" of Christian peasants in the Balkans was a matter of economic self-interest. Laborious inferiors were a necessary source of income. The *Rayah* system, like black slavery and medieval serfdom, was ultimately intolerable. The Serbs were the first in the Balkans to rise up and defeat this unjust system.[2]

As is often the case, a belated effort at reform set off a series of events leading to revolution. As the janissaries increasingly abused their privileges, the Sultan in Istanbul tried to enact reforms to modernize the administration. But his attempt to improve the condition of his Christian subjects provoked revolt among the privileged Muslims. In the Belgrade *pashalik*, an administrative area including central Serbia south of the fortress city of Belgrade, four minor janissary chieftains seized power and imposed a reign of terror. In 1804, in order to prevent the Serbs from organizing armed resistance, they began to execute Serb village leaders. Within two months, 72 village leaders had been decapitated and their heads displayed on the wall of the Kalemegdan fortress in Belgrade.[3] Others escaped to the forested Šumadija region south of Belgrade to organize armed resistance. As their leader, they elected Djordje

Petrović, nicknamed Karadjordje, or "Black George", a pig dealer who had learned soldiering as a volunteer in the Austrian army. Forced to defend themselves, the Serbian peasants took up arms in what was eventually to become the liberation struggle of all the Christian peoples of the Balkans.

This small, emerging nation immediately found itself at the center of clashes between several powerful empires. Previously, the Serbs had looked toward Vienna, capital of the Christian empire of the Habsburgs, for support. Now other empires arrived on the scene. Tsarist Russia, whose cultivated classes were stirred by the plight of the Balkan Slavs, was assuming the role of protector of Orthodox Christians within the Ottoman Empire. The Habsburg Empire, in contrast, was the main protector of the Catholics. Little Serbia could no longer look for help to one Christian power without arousing the hostile suspicions of the others. All considered little nations pawns in the geostrategic game played out between the Great Powers.

While other states in the region that threw off "the Turkish yoke" were endowed in short order with a German prince sent by the Great Powers to provide a dynasty related to the other ruling houses of Europe, only Serbia chose its own princes from among its peasant warriors. Two rival dynasties came to symbolize, roughly, two different approaches to the dilemma of foreign relations, which continued to divide the Serbs themselves. The Obrenović princes tended to accept Serbia's place in the Habsburg sphere of influence, whereas the Karadjordjević approach was to seek more distant alliances, with Russia to the East and France to the West.

Balkan history cannot be untangled in a few pages. However, in relation to the events and allegations of the 1990s, mention should be made of Ilya Garašanin, foreign minister of the young Serbian principality and author of a confidential draft project (*Načertanije*) written in 1844, at a time when Serbia had its own government but was still part of the Ottoman Empire. Published only in 1906, this document is the origin of the "Greater Serbia" project, repeatedly blamed for all the woes of the 1990s.[4] The concern was to prevent a future independent Serbia from being swallowed up by Austria or Russia. To this end, Garašanin advised Serbia to champion the independence movements of neighboring Serb-inhabited lands to the southwest (Montenegro, Bosnia-Herzegovina, southern Dalmatia). Garašanin's project was more cautious than the policy urged on him by exiled Poles and Czechs, who at that time viewed the Serbs in the Balkans as natural allies who could help weaken their common enemies.[5] Their goal of dismantling the Habsburg Empire was too ambitious for Garašanin. The "Greater Serbia" project was limited to building a secure, viable Serbian state, with an outlet to the Adriatic that could end Austria's stranglehold on landlocked Serbia's trade routes.

The first Bosnian protectorate

At the 1878 Congress of Berlin, the Great Powers astounded the Serbs by assigning Bosnia-Herzegovina not to the Serb rebels who had fought to liberate it from the Turks, but to Austria-Hungary as a "protectorate". Bosnia-Herzegovina was the bone of contention that transformed Serbs and Austrians from allies against the Turks into bitter enemies. The Austro-Hungarian Empire henceforth had the support of the more dynamic, newly unified German Empire, in a joint *Drang nach Osten*, the effort to extend their hegemony eastwards.

The Habsburg Empire's foremost authority on Serbia and Bosnia was a Hungarian aristocrat, Benjamin von Kallay, who had written an authoritative history of the Serbs in which he stressed that: "Bosnia is a Serbian land, the people in it are of Serbian nationality, and even the Muslims themselves are Serbs."[6] Without outside interference, the merger of Bosnia and Serbia would have been only a matter of time. To prevent this unwanted outcome, in 1882 Kallay himself was put in charge of running the Protectorate. His job was to exacerbate the social and religious divisions introduced by the Turks, the better to divide and rule. His method was to invent and encourage a separate "Bosnian" or "*bošnjak*" national identity for the Muslim aristocracy. To drive a wedge between Bosnia and Serbia, the local Serbo-Croatian was proclaimed to be a separate "Bosnian" language, the Cyrillic alphabet was suppressed, and Serbian books and newspapers were prohibited. Kallay even banned the book on Serbian history he had written himself.

Meanwhile, in 1908, a group of Turkish officers led a coup to modernize the troubled Ottoman Empire. Vienna used the "Young Turk" revolt as a pretext unilaterally (and illegally) to annex its protectorate in Bosnia-Herzegovina. These events created the crisis that led to two Balkan wars and the assassination of the Archduke Franz Ferdinand in Sarajevo in 1914. In those days, assassinations of leaders were regular events, which did not lead to world war.[7] On that fateful day in June 1914 when Franz Ferdinand made his state visit to Sarajevo, the route was lined with a half dozen aspiring young assassins, each more incompetent than the next. One lobbed a bomb at the back of the imperial automobile. In a moment of confusion over which way to turn, the chauffeur stopped the open car in front of young Gavrilo Princip, who managed to strike the easy target afforded him, killing Franz Ferdinand and then, by mistake, the Archduke's wife. The assassination was seized upon by the war party in Vienna to present Serbia with a 48-hour ultimatum designed to be rejected, allowing the Austrian army to carry out its long-prepared plans to strike Belgrade from across the Sava river and bring Serbia to its knees. This supposedly rapid operation led to four years of merciless slaughter, which bled Europe and ended in the defeat and destruction of the Austro-Hungarian Empire itself.

In the early years of the twentieth century, the Serbs were admired in the West for their patriotism, stoic courage, love of poetry, and laconic sense of humor. A century later, the West despised what it once admired. In the 1990s, the dominant Western power was more favorably inclined toward state demolition than state-building.

Compared to the other Yugoslavs, the significant distinction of the Serbian nation was to have been the "state-builders" who made the greatest effort to establish a modern nation-state in the Western Balkans. The Serbian national movement belonged to the liberal period of early nineteenth-century popular emancipation, based on establishing the sovereignty of the people as equal citizens of a particular territory. Eric Hobsbawm distinguishes the inclusive and unifying "territory-oriented movements for liberation" from the later separatist and exclusionist nationalist movements, such as that of the Basques.[8] Opposed to the "state-builders", such as the Serbs, who necessarily promoted the ideal of territorial citizenship, the subsequent "state-splitters", such as the Croats, stressed "identity" and differences, tending toward exclusion of those not like themselves.

For state-building, timing and neighbors are decisive. The most powerful nation-states have been built on bloody wars and ruthless suppression of rebellious minorities. Once the national unification is complete, the successful states can vigorously condemn others for practices no longer useful to themselves. In the 1990s, the US-led International Community was no longer interested in promoting state-building. Nation-state deconstruction was more compatible with economic globalization measures. Recalling that the unswerving goal of U.S. policy is to keep Europe "open to trade", Madeleine Albright has stressed that, with communism defeated, "The struggle now is between democracy and extreme forms of nationalism".[9] The "extreme" nationalism is likely to be the one thought to be least likely to fall in line with International Community economic dictates. Yugoslavia's traditional "state-builders" drew less sympathy than the splitters. Held together, Yugoslavia might have been a potential source of independent policy. Fragmented, it could easily be subdued or marginalized.

Bureaucratic decentralism

In the twentieth century, the Serbian elite transferred its state-building ethos from Serbia to Yugoslavia. While the "first Yugoslavia" between the two world wars was a continuation of the Karadjordjević kingdom of the Serbs, the "second Yugoslavia" under Tito deliberately played down the role of Serbs and Serbia in an effort to placate the nationalist feelings of the Croats and Albanians, exploited by Nazi Germany and Fascist Italy to dismember the country during World War II. "Brotherhood and unity" was the watchword of the "second" Yugoslavia. It expressed the official doctrine that all the country's peoples had been united in a fraternal class struggle first against fascism and then against the bourgeoisie. Posts were allotted by a system of national "keys", or quotas, to ensure proportional distribution of top positions in government administration and the army between the various nationalities. To prevent any return to Serbian predominance, the country was divided administratively along geographic lines into republics that enlarged the "home republics" of the non-Serb nationalities while reducing the Republic of Serbia, notably by creating the Republic of Macedonia in what had been southern Serbia and recognizing a new "nationality", the Macedonians, whose Slavic language resembles both Bulgarian and Serbian.

Whatever one can say for or against the Yugoslav communist system, it was certainly not designed to oppress national minorities, nor did it have that effect. On the contrary. Nowhere, perhaps, did national minorities enjoy such extensive cultural rights, including schooling in their own languages, as in Yugoslavia. Moreover, decentralization had been the trend in Yugoslavia since at least the mid-1960s. In sharp contrast to the notion of communism as "bureaucratic centralism", Yugoslavia developed its own "bureaucratic decentralism". Against movements of opposition,

Tito repeatedly resorted to methods of decentralization. The most famous of these was "workers' self-management" under which workers had the right to elect management of big enterprises defined as "social property". Self-management was the innovation designed to distinguish Tito's Yugoslavia from the Soviet Bloc and its centralized planning. It was theoretically justified as a step toward the "withering away of the state" which would characterize true communism.

Tito's closest collaborator, the Slovenian communist Edvard Kardelj, was the theoretician of Yugoslav self-management. A fatal flaw in Kardelj's approach was its concentration on the local or enterprise level. Workers were encouraged to identify with the competitiveness of their enterprise and the preservation of their own jobs. This tended to give priority to local self-interest. Already in 1947, another Slovenian and a close collaborator of Kardelj, Boris Kidrič, warned that the "bureaucratic centralism" which the new system was meant to combat risked emerging within each of the various Yugoslav republics, "with the same or in even greater measure, with the same or worse effects". Kidrič recommended giving self-management a vertical dimension, by electing workers from the various republics to make global economic decisions in the best interests of all. Without this, he predicted, decentralized workers' self-management along the lines of the republics would "inevitably lead back into state capitalism – in fact, several state capitalisms, particularistic towards the whole, bureaucratic-centralist towards workers' collectives".[10] No "vertical dimension" was established and Kidrič's prediction came true.

The other decentralizing method was to strengthen the powers of the constituent republics and autonomous regions against the central Federal government. Both of these apparently "left" methods of softening communist rule ended up contributing to the rise of nationalism in Yugoslavia. In practice, Yugoslav self-management increased the power of local managers and party leaders, pitting each of the six republics and two autonomous regions against the others. This tendency was enforced by Tito's habitual means of dealing with opposition movements: avoid democracy by making concessions to nationalists ready to settle for more power at home. The party, or League of Communists, supposedly the unifying political force, itself was fragmented between local party machines wielding power in each of the constituent republics. This centrifugal movement culminated in the 1974 Constitution, whose transfer of power to the local party leaders running the republics and autonomous regions created a permanent deadlock that could be broken only by the president-for-life, Tito himself.

The death of Tito in 1980 literally decapitated Yugoslavia. Without its prestigious leader, Yugoslavia was theoretically run by a collective nine-man annually rotating presidency, whose need for consensus led to paralysis. The governments of the six republics and two autonomous regions grew in power as the center sunk into insignificance. Naturally enough, each of these local bureaucracies sought ideological justifications for its growing power. Thus the heritage of decentralized single-party rule fostered a new sort of *bureaucratic nationalism*, as the success of local party officials depended increasingly on seeking advantage for their own particular republic at the expense of the others.[11] Those who rose to power as "communists" were soon motivated to maintain and enforce that power by dropping "brotherhood and unity" the better to flatter the local "national identity" by reviving or inventing grievances against other national groups and blaming them for whatever went wrong.

Under these circumstances, secession of the various republics did not signify a democratic revolt against a dictatorial centralized regime, so much as the acceleration of a process well underway in the final years of Tito's system. A socialist democratization would have extended workers' self-management to central political decision-making. A liberal, Western-style democratization would have involved multiparty elections at various levels, not least the election of a Federal Yugoslav government. No Federal elections were held. For the bureaucratic nationalists who stood to make fortunes by controlling privatization at the republic level, the devolution of power to the republics turned out to be the easiest way to turn themselves into capitalists by taking over social property and bid for early entry into the club of rich capitalist countries.

The power of attraction of the European Community, soon to be the European Union, was enormous in this period. Throughout East-Central Europe, the light at the end of the tunnel of the Soviet Bloc was the prospect of membership of the European Union. Far from contributing to a sense of solidarity in the region, this shared ambition often took the form of a race between leaders of East-Central European countries to win the favor of the Brussels institutions by demonstrating that they were more "Western" and

"European" than the others. As the richest, most northern and most western of the federated republics, ambitious Slovenians (with encouragement from Austria in particular) saw their republic as most eligible to jump the Yugoslav ship and get aboard "Europe". This prospect was by far the most powerful incentive to Slovenia's political class to secede. Slovenia's declaration of independence in June 1991 was the immediate trigger for the disintegration of Yugoslavia.

2. SLOVENIA: THE END OF SOLIDARITY

In the 1980s, the ferment for post-Titoist reform was greatest in the two republics whose political leaders had traditionally been considered the most liberal and the most inclined to cooperate with each other: Serbia and Slovenia. In both, there was sharp criticism of both the political restraints and the economic mismanagement characterizing the single-party system. In both, there were mounting demands for change. But the intellectuals who defined the terms of post-Tito political debate took opposite directions in the two republics. The political polarization between Serbs and Slovenes which dominated Yugoslav politics throughout the 1980s may be considered the most lethal blow dealt to Yugoslav unity from within.[12]

The tension between Serbs and Slovenes came to a head in 1988, leading up to the latest revision of the Yugoslav Constitution. Revision of the Constitution was a periodic exercise in Titoist Yugoslavia. Following the principles adopted by the partisan-organized "Antifascist Council of National Liberation of Yugoslavia" (AVNOJ) in November 1943, Constitutions were adopted or extensively amended in 1946, 1953, 1963, 1967, 1968, 1971, 1974, 1981, and 1988. In Marxist terms, revision of the Constitution after the break with Stalin was presented as an aspect of "permanent revolution" leading to "the withering away of the state". Indeed, the trend of constitutional reform, culminating in the virtually inapplicable 1974 version, was the withering away of the *central*, Federal state, and the progressive strengthening of the powers of the republics – in effect, of the local League of Communists organization in each of the republics and autonomous regions. In 1956, the Slovene Kardelj, principal author of the 1974 Constitution and all those that preceded it, had described Yugoslavia itself as "an historic transition" rather than a permanent nation-state.[13]

The 1974 Constitution had increased the independent decision-making powers of all the republics except Serbia. Because of the veto powers of its two autonomous regions, Serbia was almost as hamstrung as the Federal government, also located in the Serbian capital, Belgrade. The Serbs sought a constitutional revision that would reverse the trend and enable Belgrade to carry out policy in an effective way.

As Federal authority declined, however, Slovenia had been increasingly pulled into the orbit of a revived *Mitteleuropa*. Located on the rich northwestern rim of the Federation, experiencing the strong attraction of their still richer neighbors, Italy and Austria, the Slovenes in the 1980s became the champions of the centrifugal forces leading to the break-up of the Federation. Yugoslavia's open borders posed no obstacle to the development of trade and cultural exchanges with its capitalist neighbors. In 1978, neutral Austria sponsored the foundation of an association called *Alpen-Adria*[14] to foster such exchanges between provinces within Italy, Yugoslavia, and Austria, which had all formerly belonged to the Austro-Hungarian Empire. Cross-border regional groupings were promoted as a way of overcoming outdated nationalisms and ideological differences in the interests of the environment, trade, and cultural exchange. In theory, they were apolitical; in reality, with the benevolent encouragement of Otto von Habsburg, heir to the throne of the defunct empire, and the blessings of the Catholic Church, *Alpen-Adria* promoted a strong sense of the superiority of "civilized" *Mitteleuropa* over the "backward, barbarous" Balkans.

In the 1980s, Western leftists increasingly turned their attention from the working class and Third World to disarmament, feminism, human rights, and the environment. Interest faded in "workers' self-management" as an alternative to Soviet-style, state-controlled socialism. Instead, the fashionable political concept of the 1980s was "civil society". This coincided with the decline of political parties and the growth of international "networking". By the end of the decade, people who came from socialist countries as representatives of a renewed "civil society" were welcomed as the vanguard of democratic progress.

In the late 1980s, attractive young Slovenian intellectuals toured Western European capitals to alert human rights activists and anti-militarist journalists to the dangers of Yugoslav militarism. These youthful Slovenes spoke in terms of the values shared notably by German Greens, such as pacifism and human rights.

The center of this Slovenian movement was the magazine *Mladina* (Youth). As part of a "civil society" developing in the more prosperous northern parts of Yugoslavia, the *Mladina* people were easily recognized as "our kind" throughout the human rights and peace networks that grew up in the wake of the Helsinki Accords and during the movement against nuclear missiles in Europe. They supported conscientious objection, opposed the death penalty and nuclear power, and expressed concern for the environment. They explained that the main obstacle to civil society was the military.

Originally the organ of Slovenian Socialist Youth, *Mladina* developed in the 1980s into a center of criticism of the existing system. A prime target was the Yugoslav People's Army. The *Mladina* people warned that the postwar Yugoslav defense concept, "socialized defense", was leading to the militarization of society and would be used to suppress democratic civil society. This concept had emerged from the partisar. struggle against Nazi occupation and was designed to prepare the whole population to resist an invasion, from whatever quarter. The armed forces were divided between the regular army, supposed to defend the borders, and the territorial defense forces, which could mobilize the local population for guerrilla resistance if border defense failed.

In Yugoslavia, anti-militarism had implications not necessarily obvious to foreigners, since it was aimed at an army that was the last strong Federal institution holding the country together, as the Communist Party fragmented along the lines of the republics and autonomous regions. Universal military service was the principal "melting pot" in multinational Yugoslavia, the guardian of the spirit of "brotherhood and unity", the repository of the anti-fascist tradition going back to the wartime partisan struggle. But as the Cold War came to an end, the notion of defense against invasion seemed absurd to more and more young people, and the saga of the anti-fascist struggle was ancient history and regarded with skepticism.

The hero of the anti-army movement was Janez Janša, a defense consultant to the Slovenian assembly and a member of the presidium of the official "Alliance of Socialist Youth of Slovenia". By 1988, Janša was campaigning to "modernize" the organization by removing the word "socialist" from its name.

In the spring of 1988, a young officer, Janša, and two other *Mladina* staff members were arrested for theft of a secret military document allegedly concerning plans to deal with domestic uprising. A large human rights organization was founded to defend Janša and his colleagues.[15] It was as representatives of the Janša defense that several young Slovenian intellectuals[16] toured the Western networks. In the atmosphere created by Germany's big 1980s peace movement, anyone who was jailed for anti-militarism was certain to attract widespread sympathy at that time.

Janša's emissaries described the case as symptomatic of a broader conflict between two opposing political tendencies: democratic modernization championed by the rich northwestern parts of Yugoslavia and conservative, repressive centralization in the southeast. By modernization, they meant free competition, the market as an unhindered distributive mechanism, and promotion of highly qualified labor over the low productivity needed to sustain employment. Slovenia's young urban professionals were naturally concerned to improve what they considered inadequate job opportunities for intellectuals. The main obstacle to innovations in Slovenian production benefiting the better educated, in their view, was the priority given to development of the backward southern regions: Macedonia, Montenegro, and the Serbian province of Kosovo. They claimed that centralization was destroying the country by draining the wealth of the north toward the poor south.

The Slovenes pointed out that their republic, with only 8 per cent of the population, contributed 20 per cent of the Federal budget. Much of this was earmarked for "development funds" supposed to help more backward regions catch up. Slovenes complained that these funds in reality served mainly to benefit the local power elite, while draining Slovenia of its own capacity for self-development.

In fact, this complaint applied primarily to Kosovo, which absorbed the lion's share of development funds, managed by local party leaders, predominantly Albanian. However, for strategic political reasons, the Slovenian modernizers avoided criticism of the Kosovo Albanians. Indeed, they supported Kosovo separatism as an objective ally against Serbian centralization. Kosovo was the bone of contention that created the greatest suspicion and resentment between Serbs and Slovenes. Throughout the 1980s, the Serb minority in Kosovo had been complaining of discrimination, intimidation, and mistreatment by the Albanian majority in the autonomous province, whose ruling party apparatus was dominated by Albanians. The Slovenes' political support to the Albanians appeared to the Serbs to be insincere in light of Slovenia's refusal to contribute to the Federal Aid Fund for underdeveloped regions, which provided roughly half of investment in Kosovo. From the Serb viewpoint, the Slovenian support to people in a region they would not even deign to visit on account of its "backwardness" was nothing but a totally hypocritical way to promote Yugoslav disintegration in pursuit of their own narrow interests, which had nothing to do with Kosovo Albanians. For their part, the Slovenes chose to interpret the Serbian movement to regain control over Kosovo as a threat to Slovenia itself, a "first step" toward trying to control Slovenia too. Serbs were accused of "provocations" intended to justify a military takeover of Slovenia by the army in order to liquidate the liberal reformist movement.

While the young Slovene liberal reformers used the contemporary political means of NGO networking, described as "civil society", in Serbia the reform movement went into the streets in mass demonstrations supporting Milošević's program of constitutional reform. Self-styled as an "anti-bureaucratic revolution", the Serbian movement was portrayed by the Slovenes as the harbinger of a "mobilization dictatorship" similar to that of Hitler or Mao. Networking appeared much more civilized and modern than mass demonstrations. The Slovenes showed a marked tendency to interpret everything that happened in Serbia as evidence of a basic insurmountable cultural difference between "Europe" (including Slovenia and Croatia) and "the Balkans", meaning the rest. Serbian complaints about Kosovo were dismissed out of hand as a symptom of negative cultural traits. This attitude toward the Serbs flowed through the NGO networks into the West European human rights and peace movements.

The Slovenes also held demonstrations. On 27 February 1989 a major rally was called in Ljubljana to support the strike of Albanian miners protesting against constitutional changes reducing Kosovo's autonomy. On this occasion, Slovenian Communist Party leader Milan Kučan sealed his alliance with the young nationalists – an alliance that prepared his long term in office as president of anti-communist independent Slovenia – by characterizing Serbia's reduction of Kosovo autonomy as a human rights issue and a threat to Slovenia's own democracy. A subsequent Slovenian foreign minister, Dimitrij Rupel, admitted in March 1992 that Slovene nationalists had "used Kosovo" to achieve their own goal of independence.[17] Thus it did not matter that the Kosovo Albanian miners were striking partly to defend precisely the sort of communist, labor-intensive, full employment policy that the Slovenian reformers were determined to get rid of – in Slovenia.

Slovenian nationalism grew up as such a civilized, modern, continental European variety that it was never even perceived as nationalism. It was indeed a new sort of nationalism: the exaltation of EU membership over national sovereignty, expressed in terms of self-glorification as anti-nationalist, devoted to human rights, ecologically sensitive, industrious, deservedly prosperous, and suitable to join "the club". Joining the club was indeed the overriding motive of Slovenian separatism: leaving Yugoslavia was the way to join the rich man's club ahead of the others. But putting this separatism in terms of escaping from Serbian "oppression" gave it a more appealing political dimension. Because it was simply a variant of EU chauvinism, Slovenian nationalism was invisible in Europe.

Slovenians portrayed themselves to the West as a civilized barrier against dangerous neighbors further to the southeast. In June 1991, the Slovenian minister of science, Dr. Petar Tancig, sent an e-mail to world scientists explaining the "mess" in Yugoslavia by the "incompatibility of two main frames of reference/civilization".[18] On one side, he said, was a "typical violent and crooked oriental-bizantine [sic] heritage, best exemplified by Serbia and Montenegro". On the other side, stood "a more humble and diligent western-catholic tradition", exemplified by Slovenia and Croatia. These "humble" Catholics "could and would act as a 'cordon sanitaire' against the eastern tide of chaos", the Slovenian cabinet minister promised.

On 25 June 1991, Slovenia unilaterally declared its independence and a Territorial Defense squad lowered the Yugoslav flag and raised the flag of Slovenia in Ljubljana.

The U.S. ambassador at the time of the disintegration, Warren Zimmermann, wrote of the Slovenes: "Their virtue was democracy and their vice was selfishness. In their drive to separate from Yugoslavia they simply ignored the 22 million Yugoslavs who were not Slovenes. They bear considerable responsibility for the bloodbath that followed their secession."[19]

Contrary to the general view, it was the Slovenes who started the war. Their independence declaration, which had not been preceded by even the most token effort to negotiate, effectively put under their control all the border and customs posts between Slovenia and its two neighbors, Italy and Austria. This meant that Slovenia, the only international gateway between the West and Yugoslavia, had unilaterally appropriated the right to goods destined for other republics, as well as customs revenues estimated at some 75 per cent of the Yugoslav federal budget. Even an army less primitive than the [Yugoslav national army] would have reacted.

In fact, it didn't react very much. In ten days of greatly publicized "hostilities", during which Slovene spokesmen provided credulous world media with fictional battle reports, a dozen Slovenes and about 40 Yugoslav soldiers were killed. Ambassador Zimmermann concluded that "in provoking war, the Slovenes won the support of the world's television viewers and consolidated their entire population behind independence ... It was the most brilliant public relations coup in the history of Yugoslavia."

At the time, the Western media reported the show as presented by the Slovenian propagandists. Amid condemnations of the Yugoslav People's Army presence as a "Serb invasion", it went unnoticed that the officer in command of the JNA forces along Slovenia's international border crossings was himself a Slovenian, General Konrad Kolšek. A decade later, Kolšek described the ten-day public relations war: "Forces belonging to the Republic of Slovenia assaulted all 35 border crossings and certain smaller units in 87 watch towers and 40 other facilities."[20] The 2,000 JNA personnel were easily outnumbered by the Slovenian Territorial Defense and police units, illegally armed from abroad in preparation for secession, with the ratio in some locations at 10 or 20:1. Subsequent testimony indicated the Slovenian forces had raised the number of casualties by continuing to fire on soldiers of the Yugoslav People's Army who had already surrendered. In any case, there never was an "invasion" of Slovenia by the Yugoslav army, but only a half-hearted, quickly abandoned self-defense by army units trapped on the territory which they were legally pledged to defend.

Slovenia's unilateral secession was characteristic of the late twentieth-century tendency of the rich to secede from the poor, both socially and even geographically. The Slovenian haste to cut itself off from poorer Yugoslavia has its parallels in the growth of the Northern League in Italy, based on resentment of "paying for" the "poor, shiftless, criminal South". In Belgium, Flemish nationalism thrives on the notion that prosperous Flanders is "paying for" the depressed old industrial regions of Wallonia, and calls for splitting the country's social security system. In short, the desire for autonomy can no longer be considered the product of poverty and oppression. It may just as well be the expression of the unwillingness of the "winners" in the competitive market game to be burdened with the cost of solidarity with the losers.

Success stories

If, ideologically, Slovenian nationalism was a form of European nationalism, structurally it was a bureaucratic nationalism, whereby an existing power elite was able to strengthen its dominance and increase its wealth by creating its own, independent state. Remarkably little attention has been paid to one of the most compelling motives for the leaders of a small community of under two million to create their own independent state: the huge increase of prestige, power, and income it affords those who occupy the top positions in the new government. Editors of small journals may suddenly become cabinet ministers and ambassadors, not to mention arms dealers and import/export tycoons. The smaller the community, the bigger the leap from the small pond of provincial politics to the big pond of international relations.[21]

Despite the emphasis on differences, Slovenia's transition to "democracy" had much in common with that of Serbia. Like Serbia, Slovenia adopted free, multiparty elections in 1990, leading to coalition governments headed by former Communist Party leaders, joined by nationalist dissidents who had been jailed under Tito (Vojislav Šešelj in Serbia; Janez Janša in Slovenia). As in Serbia, the top positions in the Slovenian state continued to be held by former Communist Party leaders who changed political affiliation, but in regard to Slovenia, this was politely ignored by the West. The career of Milan Kučan resembled that of Milošević, but with greater success. At the end of the 1980s, Kučan was his republic's top communist leader as president of the Central Committee of the League of Communists of Slovenia. His discreet alliance with the nationalists enabled him to be elected president of Slovenia in 1990 and to remain in office longer than Milošević, without ever being described as "the last communist leader in Europe".

A former president of the rotating Socialist Yugoslav Federal presidency, Janez Drnovšek, opportunely converted into leader of the Slovenian Liberal Democratic Party, the LDS, and spent most of the 1990s as prime minister. Nobody in the West has complained about that either.

As in Serbia, an occasional surprising newcomer appeared on

the political scene. In 1992, Milan Panić, who had left Yugoslavia as a young man to make his fortune in California, returned as prime minister of Yugoslavia in an unsuccessful bid to overcome Belgrade's isolation. Something similar but even more bizarre occurred in the spring of 2000 when a US-educated Argentinian economist named Andrej Bajuk was shipped into Ljubljana to take over as prime minister of a right-wing government. Andrej was only two years old in 1945 when the Third Reich collapsed and the Bajuk family left Slovenia for refugee camps in Austria before emigrating to Argentina. After studying at the University of Chicago and Berkeley, Andrej Bajuk worked for international banking institutions and supported the economic policy of the notorious Argentine junta. At the time he was nominated to become prime minister, Bajuk was staying in a Ljubljana hotel waiting to be granted permanent resident status. Bajuk's right-wing program included introducing the Catholic catechism into public schools, a measure strongly supported by Archbishop Franc Rode (also an Argentine) against the majority of Slovenians who, according to opinion surveys, are not particularly devout (polls indicate that only 19 per cent of Slovenians actually believe the doctrine of the Catholic Church).[22] Before he could accomplish all this, his "New Slovenia" Party was decisively defeated and Drnovšek returned to office. Bajuk had had time only to effect an extraordinary purge of the administration, dismissing countless officials and replacing them with less qualified but more "politically correct" friends.

However amazing the career of Bajuk, little Slovenia's most remarkable success story is undoubtedly that of Janez Janša, the former martyr of anti-militarism who rapidly went on to become defense minister. In 1984, writing for *Mladina*, Janša had criticized the militaristic appetites of nation-states, concluding that "never before have so many people lived on war only because war brings high profits". As Slovenian defense minister, Janša put his ideas into practice. Having demoralized the Yugoslav People's Army with accusations of "militarization of society" and involvement in the "death trade" of arms exports, Janša organized a largely clandestine import of weapons into Slovenia, most of which were illegally re-exported to Croatia.

The arms embargo on Yugoslavia was to the arms trade what prohibition was to bootlegging: the opportunity for enormously lucrative deals. On 25 October 1991, the UN Security Council adopted Resolution 713 establishing an immediate and total embargo on export of arms and military equipment to Yugoslavia, an embargo which was lifted only after the Dayton Accords in late 1995. The embargo increased the risks, and the profits, of weapons dealers. The enthusiasm of Slovenian leaders for the embargo against their erstwhile compatriots made sense in business terms. It applied in fact to all parts of former Yugoslavia, but Slovenia could count on the discreet indulgence of the NATO countries.

Janša, the former hero of conscientious objectors, claimed that Slovenia had to violate the embargo to import war equipment needed for its new compulsory military training program. According to the well-informed local journalists of the news agency AIM, "little Switzerland" (as the Western press called Slovenia) succeeded in smuggling far more military equipment than its small army could possibly absorb, most of it being resold, at double the price, to the Croats or the Bosnian Muslims.

In 1995, Izetbegović's top arms procurer, Hasan Čengić, disclosed that he had bought weapons from Slovenia in March 1992 – just before the Bosnian civil war broke out, although after the arms embargo was decreed. For a package of arms worth about $30 million, the dealer's commission was said to be $15 million – but since nothing was in writing, evidence is only hearsay. Čengić said that in handling such deals, "some of Janša's very close associates became greedy" and the commission charges got out of hand. So Izetbegović turned to Kučan to work out something more reasonable.[23] A business rivalry seems to have developed between Janša's clan and that of prime minister Drnovšek, accused of making a secret arms deal with Israel in 1993. AIM suggests that Israel was chosen to be the main supplier of the Slovenian army because "only Israel was ready to actually violate the embargo and sell Slovenia the desired types of arms".[24] This seems exaggerated. The Israelis were certainly not the only ones ready to violate the embargo. On 28 May 2000, the *Guardian* reported that in 1991, *before* Slovenia seceded from Yugoslavia, Britain had secretly sold millions of pounds worth of military communications equipment to Ljubljana to be used against the Yugoslav army, at a time when the British government was officially opposing secession and supporting Yugoslavia's territorial integrity. Needless to say, Austria and Germany, both of which had encouraged secession, never had any qualms about shipping arms to Slovenia, embargo or no embargo.

Slovenia, reported the *New York Times* in March 2000, is described by experts as "a jewel", "a chocolate box", or "Eastern Europe's best-kept secret". Indeed, Slovenia has its secrets, and if they are the best kept, it may be that interest is widespread in keeping them.

What armies are for

There was an extra bonus in attacking the Yugoslav People's Army in Slovenia. The career officers and veterans had something that other people could acquire: apartments and houses. The officers and their families did not possess their homes, but were housed by the state, as is the case with many armies. With secession, they lost all their rights, including their right to lodgings and often their pensions. Others profited. The victory of the "human rights activists" had shattering effects on the human rights of certain others. The International Community and its civil society have shown no particular interest, even though the Slovenian government has been condemned by the European Human Rights court for its tardiness in dealing with cases filed by the dispossessed.

It was easy in the climate of the 1980s and 1990s to be cynical about devotion to ideals of "brotherhood and unity". And yet in Yugoslavia, many men and women had taken those ideals seriously since the terrible conflicts of World War II had made them seem absolutely necessary. The Yugoslav People's Army was never trained for aggressive operations and was easily demoralized when the "people" whose "brotherhood and unity" it was pledged to defend turned against it. The demoralization was complete when Yugoslav officers heeded the warning by the United States that Washington would not tolerate the use of force to preserve the Federation – which in effect meant tolerating the use of force to tear it apart.

The Yugoslav People's Army "was not in the service of a party. It was truly the guardian of freedom and peace", according to Slovenian novelist Marija Vogrič. "It was neither founded nor trained to turn against the people on Yugoslav soil. The nationalists knew that very well ... The fate of Yugoslavia could have been decided peacefully following a parliamentary debate. Such a conclusion was however unacceptable for certain members of the collegial presidency and especially for the representatives of the republics which already had both feet in secession. The spokesmen of violence were recruited first of all in the defense ministries [of the Republics] and the leaders of political parties. They did everything to compromise the army, and then to break it."[25]

That is only one person's analysis, which could be debated. But it is the kind of opinion that was never echoed by Western media, and there was no debate. Instead, the world has accepted the big lie of Slovenia's heroic "liberation" from an alleged "invading army" sent by Milošević. Taken up with enthusiasm by Western media, the big lie about Slovenia was the basis for subsequent interpretation of every phase of the Yugoslav crisis as a result of "Greater Serbian" aggression against oppressed minority nations, justifying their secession.

Slovenia itself has not been exactly the ideal democracy imagined by the prophets of "civil society". Thus on 30 June 2000, prime minister Bajuk, defense minister Janša, foreign minister Lojze Peterle, and the Catholic Archbishop Franc Rode attended a commemoration for the "victims of communism" at which speakers ridiculed the anti-Nazi resistance and glorified Slovenians who had collaborated with the Nazi occupation. A certain Justin Stanovnik declared that "the civil war in Slovenia still continues" led by "post-communists" and called the People's Liberation struggle a "fraud". The new Slovenia wants nothing to do with "brotherhood and unity" – it wants its place in the rich men's club. The long march against militarism has led through the institutions to ... the new NATO.

The priority given to joining NATO by Slovenia's new "liberal" elite provides another motive for getting rid of the Yugoslav People's Army, whose priority was defense. To join NATO, Slovenia (like other candidates for membership) must abandon territorial defense, scrap its air force, and halve the number of its soldiers, in order to "modernize". This means creating a single brigade to be used by NATO for "out of area" missions. Territorial defense, like "national consciousness", is considered hopelessly old-fashioned for small countries.[26] The Ljubljana government has shown its good intentions by promising to increase its military budget from 1.87 to 2.3 per cent of GNP by the end of the decade and by ordering 30 U.S. Humvee all-terrain vehicles which are, in reality, too cumbersome for Slovenia's mountainous terrain, but may be useful to the Slovenian brigade when it tags along on a NATO intervention in, let us say, Central Asia. Slovenia's political elite has remained the same throughout these events; only their convictions have changed. "Once they were all for socialism and Yugoslavia, and today for Euro-Atlantic integration", observed a Slovenian author, adding that then as now anyone who disagrees with them is denounced as an enemy of the state.[27] In his 2002 New Year's address, Slovenia's durably flexible president, Milan Kučan, vowed to continue to press for Slovenia's admission to the EU and NATO, for the first time equating the two policy goals. At the same time, Slovenian media were complaining that the government was paying hundreds of thousands of dollars to former Senator Bob Dole to lobby Capitol Hill in favor of admitting Slovenia to NATO, without any tangible results.[28]

The Slovenian "success story" and its deceptions set the stage for the disasters that followed, starting with a secession that was certain to be far more bloody and destructive: that of Croatia.

3. CROATIAN NATIONALISM: THE END OF YUGOSLAVISM

Croatian and Serbian nationalist aspirations both took shape in the nineteenth century, but in totally contrasting circumstances. Unlike the revolt of the *Rayah* forced to take up arms to gain their most basic rights, Croatian nationalism developed in the prosperous environment of the Austro-Hungarian Empire essentially as a movement for cultural recognition and status. The Serbs were intent on breaking away from their oppressors, which led them to seek full independence in a state of their own. The final goal of Croatian nationalism was not as clear. Recognition and status depend on maintaining a connection with those whose recognition is sought.

If in the 1990s Croatian secessionists dismissed Yugoslavia as "an artificial creation", the irony is that it was primarily a Croatian artifice. The Yugoslav idea was born in the course of the effort to improve the status of Croatia within the Austro-Hungarian Empire. It suffered from the ambiguity of that struggle. After seven centuries of submission to Budapest, the awareness of a "Croatian" identity was uncertain. Only the area around Zagreb was known as Hrvatska, or Croatia. Like the Serbs, the Croats spoke a language derived from Slavonic, but whereas the Serbs had a Church that used and enhanced their language, the Catholic clergy suppressed the vernacular in favor of Latin. As a result, Croatian drifted into divergent regional dialects. Unification of the Croatian literary language was accomplished by choosing to favor the dialect that coincided with literary Serbian as it had been standardized by the poet and scholar Vuk Karadžić (1787–1864) in the first half of the nineteenth century. Just as modern Italian was based on the Tuscan dialect to facilitate Italian unification, modern Serbo-Croatian provided the southwestern Slavs with a single common language. This helped to unify Croats themselves, before turning into a source of resentment on the part of the Croats who wished to distinguish themselves from the Serbs.

Since language had prevailed over religion in unifying Germans in a single state, why couldn't a single language unify Catholics and Orthodox who, unlike the German Catholics and Protestants, had no history of bitter religious wars to put behind them? However, unification around Serbo-Croat could mean two very different things, depending on whether it took place within the Habsburg Empire or outside it. This was the problem that seems not to have been clearly defined and faced, leading to tragic confusion between the idea of unifying Serbs and Croats in order to secure a better place for the Slavs within a strengthened Habsburg Empire, and those who saw this same unification as the nucleus of a new independent nation.

The Croatian nationalist movement centered on demanding recognition of the "rights" of the medieval kingdom of Croatia, which in 1102 had ceded its crown to the kingdom of Hungary, in turn absorbed into the Habsburg Empire in 1527. Croatian nationalists argued that the "historic rights" of twelfth-century Croatia had been merely lent, and not ceded, to the Hungarian Crown. The political and religious conservativism of the Croatian national movement centered on legalistic insistence on the inherited "rights" of the medieval Croatian kingdom, along with rigid adherence to the Roman Catholic Church, was a recurring source of conflict with the essentially egalitarian and more secular Serbian outlook. In the decades leading up to the war of 1914–18, Croatian national ambitions were torn between the attraction exercised by Serbia's emergence as a vigorous, modernizing state and the prospect of serving as nucleus for an expanding Slavic component within the Habsburg Empire. The outcome of World War I seemed to resolve this conflict. The defeat of the Austro-Hungarian Empire put an end to the second option and delivered leadership of the Croatian national movement to a group of émigrés in Paris who, in April 1915, formed a "Yugoslav Committee". While the Serbian government preferred to speak of "Serbs, Croats, and Slovenes", the term "Yugoslav" seems to have been coined largely for the benefit of Western public opinion. The word itself was artificial, mixing the Serbo-Croatian for "south" (*Jugo*, or Yugo) with the French and English word "Slav" (the Serbo-Croatian word being "sloven").[29] On 20 July 1917, the Yugoslav Committee and the Serbian government issued the "Corfu Declaration" calling for the creation of a constitutional monarchy, based on parliamentary democracy, called the "Kingdom of the Serbs, Croats, and Slovenes, also known as Yugoslavs". The Kingdom of the Serbs, Croats, and Slovenes was officially proclaimed on 1 December 1918 and accorded diplomatic recognition by the United States the following February.

With the Austro-Hungarian Empire facing defeat, assertion of a common identity with the victorious Serbs enabled the Croats (and Slovenes) to emerge on the winning side as part of a new kingdom sponsored by the Western Allied Powers, Britain and France. Far from being forced on reluctant Croats by expansionist Serbs, leading Serb politicians had doubts about unification of Serbia and Croatia in a single Yugoslav kingdom.[30] The material advantages to Slovenia and Croatia were considerable. They avoided the heavy reparations imposed on the losers at Versailles. Moreover, they obtained important territories, notably a large part of the Dalmatian coast, which had been secretly promised to Italy by the British. Had they not merged with Serbia, Croatia and Slovenia would surely have lost their present valuable coastal territories to Italy, probably definitively. Italian resentment at being deprived of Adriatic coastal towns and islands was a major stimulus to the nationalist fervor that favored the rise of Benito Mussolini's Fascists.

The fatal misunderstanding was that the Serbs, whose leaders had been reluctant to form Yugoslavia to begin with, took seriously the project of building the unified state once it was established, while the Croats, whose leaders had promoted the idea, saw it as only a temporary expedient and subsequently tore it down. Croatian politicians had honed a formidable skill in obstructionism as their main political weapon in defending their "rights" against the Hungarians and the Austrians. While resented for its institutional continuity with the Serbian kingdom, the Karadjordjević monarchy that ruled Yugoslavia between World Wars I and II made more concessions to the demands of Croatian politicians for autonomy than to the Serbian parties' demands for greater democracy.[31] This concession to decentralization at the expense of democracy can be seen as an early version of the policy later adopted by Tito.

An obscure fratricide

On 27 March 1941, Serb officers overthrew the government in Belgrade for having signed a pact with Hitler. In retaliation, on 6 April, the *Luftwaffe* bombed Belgrade. The *Wehrmacht* invaded Yugoslavia in rapid *blitzkrieg* fashion. Only slightly more than 20 years after leaving the defeated Habsburg Empire to form Yugoslavia, Croatia was detached from Yugoslavia by Fascist Italy and Nazi Germany. The Italians helped themselves to the coveted Adriatic coast, but Croatia was compensated by being enlarged inland to include Bosnia-Herzegovina. The "Independent State of Croatia" (NDH) was proclaimed and turned over to the fascist Ustashe leader Ante Pavelić, who had enjoyed Mussolini's protection after plotting the assassination of King Alexander of Yugoslavia in Marseilles in 1934. That set the stage for one of the most horrendous, as well as most forgotten, of twentieth-century genocides.

Pavelić immediately set out to achieve the Ustashe goal of a pure Croatian state. At the time, Serbs made up over a quarter of the population.[32] A new law restricted citizenship to "persons of Aryan race". In Ustashe racist ideology, "Aryans" included both Germans and Croats, but also Bosnian Muslims, considered to be an aristocracy of the purest Croatian race. It excluded Jews, Serbs, and Gypsies. A series of decrees deprived the non-Aryans of all imaginable rights and special emergency courts were set up to judge "high treason", defined as "any offense whatever to the honor or interests of the Croatian people", which was punishable by death.

Amid inflammatory speeches, massacres spread through the countryside.[33] On 14 May 1941, over 700 Serbs were assembled in the town of Glina, in the Krajina, and led to the local Orthodox church to celebrate the Croatian state. The church was locked and Ustashe killers proceeded to slaughter the Orthodox priest Bogdan Opačić and all his parishioners. Others were sent to camps such as Jasenovac where they died by the thousand. The total number of victims of these savage massacres was never determined and thus remains open to controversy. The "official" figure of 700,000 Serbs murdered is an estimate, as are other figures, some higher, some lower. What is undisputed is the extraordinary ferocity of these killings, as confirmed by numerous witnesses, in particular Italian and German observers who were ostensibly the allies and protectors of the Ustashe killers. Atrocity stories abound, notably concerning mutilations, especially the practice of gouging out the eyes of murdered Serbs.[34] Such horror stories may be exaggerated, but the massacres were committed openly and reported by diplomats stationed in Zagreb, as well as by the Italian press at the time.

The Catholic Bishop of Sarajevo, Monseigneur Šarić, declared that "the descendants of those who hated Jesus" [meaning the Jews] "are even more guilty than their ancestors ... Satan has helped them create socialism and communism ... The movement aimed at freeing the world from the Jews is a movement that will lead to the rebirth of human dignity." By the end of the war, most of Croatia's Jewish population had perished, except those who managed to find protection in Italian-occupied Dalmatia. The number of Gypsies exterminated is estimated at 28,000, close to the entire Gypsy population of the NDH.

What distinguished Croatia from other countries under Nazi occupation was that the genocidal massacres committed there aimed not only at exterminating Jews and Gypsies, but were voluntarily and enthusiastically extended to target Serbs. Serbs were seen as the main enemy, in cahoots with the Jews. Hitler blamed the Jews for both capitalism and communism, and saw their elimination as necessary to rid the world of those evils. The Croatian Ustashe readily endorsed that view, but added their own twist by accusing the Serbs too of being both "communists" and "the tools of British and French imperialism". A senior government official, Professor Aleksander Zajc, declared that "the Jewish-Serbian capitalist-democratic front must disappear from the entire world for ever".[35]

While subsequently blame for the horrendous crimes in Croatia was readily shifted to the Nazis, it was not the Axis occupying powers that ordered the slaughter of the Serbs. The massacres of the Serbian inhabitants of Croatia were not only carried out independently of orders from the Nazi or Fascist occupiers, but actually aroused their shocked reprobation, as expressed in a considerable body of documents, newspaper reports, letters written home by soldiers, official diplomatic reports, and memoirs.[36] The Germans, who preferred to do even the nastiest business in an orderly way, criticized the NDH especially on grounds that it was failing to establish order and that the massacres of peasants were disrupting agriculture (needed to feed the *Wehrmacht*) and preventing pacification by driving Serbs into armed rebellion. Italian soldiers stationed in Croatia and Dalmatia often sympathized with the victims and took them under their protection.

Half a century later, the genocidal assault on the Serbs of Croatia remained one of the most obscure episodes of World War II. For political reasons, it was swept under the rug by the victorious Allied Powers, both East and West. In Yugoslavia itself, Tito's policy was to promote reconciliation around the myth of "brotherhood and unity", burying national and religious antagonisms by reference to class war. The Yugoslav Communist Party itself preferred to forget its efforts between the world wars to ally with the Ustashe movement "against the hegemony of the Serbian bourgeoisie".

In the West, little attention was paid to the pogroms directed against Serbs. A number of former Ustashe escaped to the West, where they presented themselves as freedom-loving Catholics fleeing communism. To combat communism, Washington was indulgent toward "nationalists" from the East and readily overlooked their criminal past.

There was another aspect of the Croatian events so unique as to be nearly incredible and which may help to explain that the subject was taboo: the extraordinary involvement of Catholic clergy in the massacres of the Serbs.

The spirit of the Crusades

In a speech delivered on 3 August 1941, the Ustashe minister of public education, Mile Budak, recalled the Crusades mounted by the Catholic Church. "If that is what happened in the 11th and 12th centuries, we are sure the Church will have understanding for the Ustashe struggle", he claimed. He was not altogether wrong. Strangely enough, in twentieth-century Europe, Pavelić revived not only the long-dead medieval Croatia but also, and especially, the fanatical spirit of the medieval Crusades. The call to arms by Budak and his comrades echoed the thirteenth-century Crusade against the Albigensian heretics of southwestern France, the Cathars, ordered by Innocent III, when Simon de Montfort justified indiscriminate massacres with the slogan, "Kill them all; God will recognize his own." In medieval Bosnia, the ideological cousins of the Cathars were the Bogomil heretics. The Catholic Church sent Franciscan friars to combat the heresy. Elsewhere esteemed for their unworldly pacifism, the Franciscans of Bosnia-Herzegovina (whose stronghold is in the district of the recent "miracles" of Medjugorje in western Herzegovina) acted as a virtual military order to propagate the official doctrine of the Church against both the heretics (Bogomils) and the "schismatics" (Greek Orthodox, that is, Serbs). In those border territories of the faith, along the East–West border with Orthodoxy, the Catholic Church sponsored a militant aggression in total contrast to the meek, ecumenical attitudes displayed in other times and places.

When Pavelić took power in Zagreb, he was hailed by Monseigneur Alojzije Stepinac, Archbishop of Zagreb, as "the great man" who had arrived to accomplish changes in which Stepinac perceived "the hand of God". He was made chaplain of the NDH army. Catholicism was proclaimed the state religion. On 19 May 1941, at the height of the persecution of Jews and Serbs, Pavelić was described by the Vatican newspaper *L'Osservatore Romano* as a "great statesman" and was received in audience by Pius XII.

The Vatican never condemned the Ustashe crimes against the Serbs. The Ustashe were perceived as "a bulwark against Bolshevism" (as was Nazism, for that matter). They were also carrying out a centuries-old program to replace the "schismatic" Orthodox Church with Roman Catholicism. In May 1941, a "law concerning conversion from one religion to the other" was promulgated by Pavelić and his education minister, Mile Budak. This amounted to an ultimatum to Serbs to convert to Catholicism or die. Stepinac's office in Zagreb defined Serbs as "renegades from the Catholic Church" and approved the government's plans to convert them. In a notorious sermon to his parishioners in Udbina, Father Mate Mugoša declared that up to now:[37]

> we have worked for the Catholic faith with the missal and the cross. Now the time has come to act with the rifle and the pistol. We will drive them out of Croatia or we will exterminate the Serb population in Croatia. And I will be happy when we can distribute Serbs' lands to Croats. The Ustashe will fight without mercy and will exterminate all those who are not faithful to the NDH and its Leader and founder. Look, people, at these 16 Ustashe standing at my side. They have 16 thousand cartridges and they will kill 16 thousand Serbs ...

The general policy of Budak and Pavelić was to convert the poor and ignorant Serbs, after giving them religious instruction, but to reject the intelligentsia and the well-to-do merchants and artisans, whose sincerity would be dubious and whose property could be confiscated. Serbs were not allowed to evade these measures by converting to Protestantism, considered by the Croat clergy a German religion, to be respected because of its influence in "rich advanced countries" but open only to "Aryans".[38]

A tentative explanation for the Church's attitude is offered by a Serbian scholar, Dr. Smilja Avramov, in terms of the Vatican's insecurity following the loss of its Italian territories (the Papal States became part of modern Italy in 1871), and then the disappearance of the Habsburg Empire – the Vatican's most reliable ally in all of

Europe. Henceforth, she suggests, the Vatican sought at all costs to construct a new political bulwark against its three ideological adversaries: Protestantism, bolshevism, and the Greek Orthodox "schismatics".[39]

After the war, in late 1946, Stepinac was put on trial for his support to the Ustashe regime. It is noteworthy that while the leader of the first armed resistance movement against Nazi occupation in all of Europe, Draža Mihailović, head of the royalist Yugoslav forces (called Chetniks), was sentenced to death and executed for alleged treason and collaboration, Stepinac was sentenced to 16 years in prison and released four years later. Refusing the offer to emigrate, he was kept under house arrest. Despite this relatively mild treatment, the Vatican promoted him to cardinal and elevated the former Ustashe chaplain into a hero and martyr of "human rights". Visiting Zagreb on 2 October 1998, amid NATO threats to bomb Serbia, the Polish Pope Karol Wojtyla, John Paul II, beatified Stepinac, praising him for his resistance to communism. Sainthood is expected to be the next step. The Vatican showed no such reverence for the martyrdom of Mihailović, executed by the same communist courts that let off Stepinac relatively easily. Mihailović was a Serb who belonged to the Orthodox Christian Church.

Why such hatred?

The events of 1941 raise the most difficult question of all: why such hatred? A common hypothesis rests on the notion that people "hate each other because they are different". But there may be cases of hatred that arise not because "people are different", but because they are *both* different *and* very much alike.

A clue may be found in the original nature of the Croatian national movement. Rather than a broad liberation movement like that of the Serbs, it began as a fairly narrow effort to gain prestige within a hierarchical order. The deep underlying ambition of the leaders of Croatian nationalism was to be recognized as equals of the Austrians and Hungarians in the cultural sphere. Croatian leaders who had been moved by the outcome of World War I to ally with the victors found themselves no longer tied to the dazzling cultural life of Vienna, but harnessed to their poor cousins in Belgrade, heroic pig farmers, whose habits and religion they had been conditioned to despise as inferior to the refinements of the Habsburg Empire. This unexpected transfer from being "the poorest of the rich" to being "the richest among the poor" set off a reaction of total rejection, with emphasis on the great cultural superiority of the Croats.[40] Real and imagined grievances found an ideological justification in the racist fantasies of the founder of the "Croatian Party of Rights", Ante Starčević (1823–96). Drawing on nineteenth-century European racist ideology, Starčević proclaimed the Croats to be a superior race, responsible for all the cultural and political achievements of the medieval Western Balkan kingdoms. He blamed their decline and fall on the mongrelization of the pure Croatian race with inferior stock such as Shqiptars (Albanians) and Vlachs, which had produced what were called "Serbs", not a real people at all, according to him. This racist megalomania went so far as to claim that "not a single other living nation in Europe has a more glorious past than the Croatian nation". The Croatian race, he asserted, was "the oldest and purest nobility that Europe has", whose renaissance depended on eliminating the non-people responsible for their decline, the so-called Serbs.

Pavelić was a direct disciple of Starčević. As secretary general of the Croatian Party of Rights, Pavelić opposed the Kingdom of Serbs, Croats, and Slovenes from its inception, before going on to found the Ustashe ten years later as the military wing of a broader movement to destroy the Yugoslav state. The Principles of the Croatian Ustashe movement proclaimed the Croatian people to be "a nation apart, not similar to any other nation". The future Croatian state would be "governed only by the Croatian people", who alone would exercise the rights of a "political people" on their territory. Never seriously studied or condemned by the outside world, this semi-delirious racist Croatian nationalism simply went into exile after World War II and reorganized, waiting for better days.

Tudjman's historic compromise

When the Axis Powers were defeated, Hitler committed suicide, Mussolini was executed, and both Nazism and Fascism were definitively disgraced in their countries of origin. But Pavelić escaped to an Austrian monastery along with several hundred Catholic clergymen, headed by Archbishop Šarić of Sarajevo. Pavelić went on to another monastery in Rome, then to Argentina, and finally to Madrid where he died peacefully in a German hospital in 1954, having received the personal blessing of Pius XII. Meanwhile, he had formed a new "Croatian Liberation Movement" (HOP), which in 1967 was reorganized by his successor, Stjepan Hefer. For the next several years, the HOP carried out a series of assassinations and bomb attacks against Yugoslav diplomats and embassies, notably in Sweden and Australia, where Croatian émigré communities were particularly strong. The purpose of these attacks was totally baffling to outsiders, but they served as publicity for an obstinate determination to carry out the goal proclaimed by one of the several émigré organizations formed by Ustashe veterans, the Croatian National Resistance:[41]

> Yugoslavia must be destroyed, either with the help of the Russians or with the help of the Americans, with the help of communists, non-communists, or anti-communists, with the help of anyone who is willing to destroy Yugoslavia, to destroy it by dialectics or dynamite – but destroy it at all costs.

With this common goal and no ideological prejudice as to how to achieve it, eight nationalist organizations, three political parties and the Washington-based newspaper *Hrvatska Borba* (Croatian Struggle) got together in Toronto in 1974 to form a coalition under the umbrella of the Croatian National Council (Hrvatsko Narodno Vijece, HNV).[42] Whereas in the past Croatian separatism had won its greatest support first from the Soviet Union and then from the Axis Powers, while the Western allies had favored Yugoslavia, the strategy henceforth was to seek support from the West by uniting various Croat political tendencies and forging tactical alliances with Bulgarian irredentists in Macedonia and Albanian irredentists in Kosovo. Whereas toward Moscow, the Croatian separatist line had stressed oppression of the Croatian people at the hands of the "Serbian bourgeoisie", toward the West the line was to identify the Serbs with communism ... and with the Russians.[43]

Croatian nationalism reappeared in Croatia in the "mass movement" (*maspokret*) of 1970–71. The 1974 Constitution was promulgated in part to assuage the Croats. The next step was to unify the anti-Yugoslav Croatian diaspora, largely linked to Ustashe exiles, with nationalists who had stayed in Croatia as communists. A key figure and the main winner in this crucial merger was Franjo Tudjman (1922–99). At the age of 19, Tudjman had joined the partisans and after the war rose to Tito's general staff in Belgrade. Retiring early with the rank of major general in 1960, Tudjman returned to his native Croatia and took up a second career as scholar. His writings increasingly glorified Croatian cultural particularism.

Accused of encouraging nationalist revival, he was expelled from the League of Communists (the Party) and jailed for several months in 1972. He was jailed again in the early 1980s. This only enhanced his credibility as nationalist leader.

Tudjman's trump card, and the key to his subsequent dazzling success, was the knowledge he had gained, apparently from his longstanding connections with Yugoslav intelligence services, of the anti-Yugoslav Croatian nationalist diaspora. Intimately involved with nationalists at home and closely acquainted with the rich, politically active émigré communities in Australia, South America, and especially North America, Tudjman was ideally placed to engineer their fusion into a political movement capable of leading Croatia out of the Yugoslav Federation. The diaspora was ready and able to bankroll such a project, which would enable many an exile to return home comfortably, some even to positions of power in a new independent state.

Tudjman's most notorious ideological contribution to the cause was a long treatise, entitled *Bespuca Povjesne Zbiljnosti*, published in Zagreb in 1989.[44] In this book, he maintained that genocide was a constant and natural occurrence in human history, which was wrong but not exceptional. Tudjman questioned the number of victims, both of the Holocaust, and of the Jasenovac camp, suggesting that the figures usually cited were impossible to verify and highly exaggerated. He concluded that only 2,000–3,000 prisoners, mostly Gypsies, had perished at Jasenovac, described as a work camp administered by "free prisoners" who were Jews.[45] This led to the conclusion that the Ustashe were not anti-Semitic, but even pro-Jewish. The daring novelty of this argument was to minimize Ustashe crimes and, at the same time, lay the groundwork for Croatia's good relations and trade with Israel in the military field.[46] The readiness of a former notable of the communist regime such as Tudjman to relativize the Ustashe's massacres signaled the prospect of an "historic compromise" between the extreme nationalist right and part of the Communist Party apparatus. This could bring together sufficient forces to found the second independent Croatian state.

Tudjman's acts were consistent with his writings. In his speech to the first convention of his new political party, the Croatian Democratic Community (Hrvatska Demokratska Zajednica, HDZ), in February 1990, he officially proclaimed the historical compromise: "The Independent State of Croatia was not a mere Quisling creation, but was also an expression of the historic aspirations of the Croatian people for an independent state of their own and recognition of international factors – the government of Hitler's Germany in this case." This announced the rehabilitation of Ustashe émigrés, who were already present at the HDZ convention. In the first multiparty elections on 22 April and 7 May, the HDZ won 42 per cent of the vote, giving it a large enough relative majority to elect Tudjman president of Croatia on 30 May 990.

All this had been prepared in advance. In three trips in the summers of 1987, 1988, and 1989, Tudjman held key meeting at a farm in Norval, near Toronto, with a group of far right Herzegovina exiles in Canada headed by the Franciscan friar Ljubo Krasić and pizza magnate Gojko Šušak. There, it was decided (1) that the future Croatia must be an independent state; (2) that Croatia's Serbs should be reduced to minority status with a view to expelling them in the event of conflict with Serbia; (3) that the struggle in Croatia should be pursued against the Serbs as the main enemy, not against the communists – or not at first; and (4) policy toward Bosnia-Herzegovina must be conducted so as to include western Herzegovina in the Croatian state.[47] Šušak had useful Washington connections and would later become Tudjman's defense minister in the civil wars that followed the proclamation of independence. Far more intransigent in its drive for "Greater Croatia" than Croats in Croatia itself, the Herzegovina lobby was essential to Tudjman's power system, just as he was essential to the realization of their project, a "Greater Croatia" including the western part of Herzegovina. That was the region of the most militant Franciscan crusaders and many of the bloodiest massacres of World War II. This project to change borders was called "stuffing the Croatian croissant".

Even though the study of genocide became a rather macabre fashion in the 1990s, the 1941 Ustashe genocide of Serbs aroused little interest. At the opening of the Holocaust museum in Washington, the Croats as U.S. allies were invited, the Serbs were not.

Dwelling on past crimes does not necessarily promote reconciliation. In Yugoslavia, although Tito's ostrich policy was no doubt in part self-serving, the hope surely existed that it would favor a healing process through forgetfulness. To some extent it worked. Serbs and Croats lived and worked together after the war, befriended and married each other. But out of sight and ignored, old hatreds and fears went underground – or into exile. When they emerged half a century after the unacknowledged genocide, the outside world had no idea what was going on. And yet it was clearly impossible to grasp the reaction of Yugoslavia's Serbs to the events of the early 1990s without taking into account what had happened half a century earlier. The return to power of Ustashe symbols, ideas, and methods was certain to arouse Serb fears of a repetition of the events of 1941. These fears were ignored or dismissed, and Serb hostility to a revived "independent state of Croatia" was attributed to an aggressive "Greater Serbia" project. Finally, the NATO powers supported Croatian nationalism and, in 1995, Tudjman's army, trained by U.S. officers and armed illegally by the "International Community", successfully completed the ethnic cleansing of the Krajina Serbs begun with Nazi backing in 1941.

The second Bosnian protectorate

Everything that happens in the Balkans echoes previous events. The Krajina conflict awakened memories of the terrible killing that took place in Bosnia-Herzegovina when it was part of the "Independent State of Croatia" during World War II. At that time, the Muslims of Bosnia were invited by the new Croatian Ustashe rulers to consider themselves Croats and combat the Serbs. In July 1941, the Muslim beys tried to use the situation to reverse the Yugoslav agrarian reform and recover their old privileges.[48] A Bosnian Muslim branch of the Ustashe party headed by school teacher Hakija Hadžić advocated cleansing Bosnia of its Serb population. A current of ultra-right-wing Muslims refused to be identified as Croats and sought to have Bosnia placed directly under a German Protectorate. A letter to Hitler dated 1 November 1942, claimed that the Bosnian Muslims were "an integral part of the Islamic people of the Orient, who amount to 300 million souls, and who cannot forge their liberation other than against British imperialism, Jewry, Free Masonry and bolshevism, and by following the German people led by their Führer".[49] The Mufti of Jerusalem, Emin el Husseini, gave his blessing to the establishment of the 13th division of the SS, called the "Handžar (dagger) division", composed exclusively of 12,000 Bosnian Muslims. On the other side, Muslims were also recruited by the communist-led partisans, mainly based in Bosnia throughout the war.

Bosnia-Herzegovina was the scene of a merciless civil war between not two but several parties: Ustashe, partisans, Chetniks, the *Wehrmacht*, Italian occupation forces, and even militia such as the

Muslim units from the Serbian region of Sandžak who attacked Serb villages in eastern Bosnia, setting off a terrible cycle of reprisals and revenge.[50] Precisely because Bosnia-Herzegovina had experienced the most massive killing and worst atrocities during the war, the official version, glorifying mass support for the partisans, brotherhood and unity, was imposed with special rigor. The regime in that republic won the reputation as the most repressive in Yugoslavia. This seems to have been tacitly accepted by many as the lesser evil by far, compared to the bloodshed of the early 1940s.

Initially, Bosnia-Herzegovina, unlike the other republics in Tito's "second Yugoslavia", did not rank as the "homeland" of any particular "nationality". Official recognition in 1971 of yet another Yugoslav *narod*, the "Muslim" nationality (with a capital letter, in contrast to "muslims", referring to religious affiliation), was meant to satisfy Muslims by giving them a place in the "key" or quota system domestically, while giving Yugoslavia an advantage on the international level. An official "Muslim" nationality in Yugoslavia was a diplomatic asset designed to increase Yugoslav influence in Muslim countries. In the long run, however, it had the opposite effect of giving Islamic countries an unexpectedly strong influence over internal Yugoslav affairs.

During the early years of the Cold War, when leaders of Muslim countries such as Egypt joined Tito in founding the Non-Aligned Movement as an alternative to the United States or the Soviet "camp", national independence was far more important than Islam as a political orientation. In this context, recognition of a "Muslim nationality" within Yugoslavia seemed an innocuous way of improving cooperation with Muslim countries. Yugoslav Muslims were welcome emissaries and helped close deals with important trade partners. However, the increase in oil revenues in the 1970s led directly to an international Islamic revival lavishly financed first by Saudi Arabia, followed by Iran and other oil-rich Muslim states. Support for an Islamist such as Izetbegović was yet another form of divisive outside interference in domestic Yugoslav affairs.

There were very many people with no religion at all in Bosnia-Herzegovina, a small number of Jews and even Protestants, not to mention many families whose members were of different religious affiliation. Intermarriage was frequent, and a growing number of Bosnians considered themselves "Yugoslavs". However, the system discouraged people from identifying themselves as "Yugoslav" – an identity without a quota – and instead encouraged them to stress community identity as a way of gaining privileges. Only those who identified themselves as "Muslims" could claim membership in the leading community. The number of Bosnians identifying themselves as "Muslims" rose with recognition of the new "nationality".

The identification of a religion with nationality, and that nationality with the territory of Bosnia-Herzegovina, was bound to cause confusion. While most "Muslims" of Bosnia were not particularly devout, more fundamentalist Muslims could be found in the southwestern part of Serbia known as the Sandžak of Novi Pazar, where Turkish rule had lasted into the twentieth century. Some of these Muslims joined Izetbegović's party and began to consider that they were, in some way, "Bosnians" or "Bosniaks", even though they had never lived there. In the 1990s, a decisive public relations success of the Izetbegović party was to identify "Muslim" with "Bosnian", so much so that many people in the West had the impression that the real "Bosnians" were Muslims who had been invaded by Serbs from Serbia. U.S. officials took to referring to the Muslims as "Bosnians": in his book *To End a War*, Richard Holbrooke consistently used the term "Bosnian" to refer solely to the Muslims. In reality, the United States was not supporting "the Bosnians", but Izetbegović as leader of the Party of Democratic Action (SDA), which was not so much a "Bosnian" party as a Muslim party, with an important and particularly militant branch outside Bosnia, in the Novi Pazar region of southwestern Serbia.

Moreover, as mentioned previously, in the 1990 presidential election in Bosnia-Herzegovina, the most popular Muslim proved to be not Izetbegović, but Fikret Abdić, who won over one million votes but stepped aside for Izetbegović. While Izetbegović enjoyed political and financial support from many Muslim governments and won decisive backing from the United States, Abdić owed his popularity only to his own practical achievements on behalf of his people. Abdić was famous for having transformed the Bihać pocket, the heavily Muslim-inhabited western region of Bosnia, from total backwardness into a thriving area of prosperity. In the late 1960s, without paved roads or electricity, the inhabitants survived by seeking work as hired laborers in Croatia and Slovenia. Abdić managed to transform a backward agricultural cooperative into a modern business called *Agrokomerc* (Agrocommerce), with headquarters in Velika Kladuša. Over 13,000 jobs were created. Roads were paved for the first time, people were provided with electricity and running water, poultry farms and factories sprung up.[51] Abdić was celebrated throughout Bosnia for this economic miracle.

Economic miracles often involve cheating. In September 1987, the newspaper *Borba* accused Agrocommerce of financing its growth by issuing unsupported promissory notes worth a total of over $800 million to at least 57 banks in four republics, countersigned by the Bank of Bihać. This was a standard response of Yugoslav businesses when Federal investment funds were cut, but this time Abdić was caught in an anti-corruption campaign.[52] His subsequent trial and conviction disrupted the Bosnian political scene, weakening the pro-Yugoslav business elite and favoring the Islamists. Nevertheless, Abdić was still popular in 1990, and had Western powers really been so much in favor of the "ethnic coexistence" they kept proclaiming as their ideal, he should have been their man. However, he spoke no English and had no American partisans working for him in Washington. Abdić withdrew to the Bihać pocket where he presided as benevolent patriarch, nicknamed "Babo" or Daddy. At the end of 1992, on the eve of civil war, Abdić "was in favour of negotiating and compromising with Croats and Serbs to achieve a settlement, and scathing about those Muslims who wanted to block any such settlement", David Owen recalled.[53] Concerned about his people in the Bihać pocket, wedged between Croatia and the heavily Serb parts of Bosnia, Abdić wanted above all to avoid war. The way to do so, he saw, was to accept a decentralized constitution for Bosnia-Herzegovina, allowing considerable autonomy to different regions. This was fiercely opposed by Izetbegović, whose followers succeeded in convincing the Western media that any decentralization would be a "betrayal of multi-ethnic society". After Izetbegović, with U.S. encouragement, had ruined the last chance for peace by rejecting the March 1992 EU cantonization plan, Abdić broke with Sarajevo and undertook to make his own deals with surrounding Croats and Serbs in order to keep the Bihać pocket out of war. On 14 September 1993, Abdić made a deal with Bosnian Croat leader Mate Boban for mutual recognition of their separate "republics" within a decentralized Bosnia-Herzegovina. A month later, on 22 October, he made a similar deal with the Serbs. From then on, his main enemies were the followers of Izetbegović. Western media, still portraying Izetbegović as unarmed victim of Serb aggression, failed to report the war that finally raged around Bihać in 1995 as an attack by Muslims against fellow Muslims. With help from foreign mujahidin and the US-backed Croatian offensive that emptied the neighboring Bosnian Krajina of its solidly Serb population, Izetbegović's forces put an end to the heresy in the Bihać pocket. Abdić fled to Croatia, where he was put on trial in Karlovac in October 2001. The man who wanted peace was accused of war crimes and crimes against humanity during defense of the Bihać pocket.

Inside and outside intervention

The story of Abdić illustrates the fact that the International Community rejected all forms of administrative division of Bosnia-Herzegovina – if worked out between local leaders themselves. In contrast, administrative divisions sponsored by the United States had to be accepted. In March 1994, the United States put pressure on the Bosnian Muslims and the Croat nationalists to form a "Federation" of Bosnian Croats and Muslims, which in turn was to be linked in some unspecified manner to Croatia. The agreement on federation was signed at the White House on 18 March 1994 in the presence of President Clinton. At the same time, a declaration linking the Federation to Croatia was signed by Izetbegović and Tudjman. In reality, this forced marriage created no love between the two parties. The Croats and Muslims were fighting each other at the time over possession of villages in Bosnia-Herzegovina, and the main Herzegovina city of Mostar has remained sharply and bitterly divided. There was no democratic consultation of the peoples involved. The "Federation" was an imperial diktat from Washington, accepted by Tudjman and Izetbegović for the material advantages they expected to reap: U.S. military aid, first of all. The Croat leaders were willing to go along in the short run, in bad faith, since they continued to run "Herceg-Bosna" as a purely Croat entity, with Croatian currency, flags, and stamps. In 2001, the leaders of this totally Croatian enclave in Herzegovina openly announced their refusal to continue to participate in the "Federation". In reality, the "Muslim-Croatian" Federation was simply a way of isolating the Bosnian Serbs. It made it easier for the United States to provide military support to both the Croats and the Muslims, despite the hostility between them.

Contrary to the image presented by the Western media of a war between "multicultural Sarajevo" and Serb aggressors, the civil war in Bosnia-Herzegovina was primarily a war between nationalist *parties:* the Party of Democratic Action (SDA) led by Izetbegović, the Serbian

Democratic Party (SDS) led by Karadžić and the Croatian Democratic Union (HDZ) led by Tudjman, through his local Bosnian followers. It was the parties who scrawled their initials on the walls and roads of conquered villages. Sponsoring the Muslim and Croat nationalist parties by way of a largely fictional "Federation" inevitably strengthened all three nationalist parties: the first two directly and the Serb nationalists indirectly, by confirming their interpretation of the conflict as a foreign-sponsored assault against the Serbs.

Dismissing history as of no importance, United States diplomats created a "Federation" that was inevitably reminiscent of the Nazi-backed Independent State of Croatia set up in 1941. The enforced public suppression under Tito of a bloody past convinced a certain number of foreign observers that Bosnia was a "healed society", whose serene multicultural cohabitation was disrupted by the aggression of an evil Serb nationalist leader, Milošević.[54] Identification of Belgrade as the malevolent "outsider" stirring trouble in the Bosnian "multicultural paradise" served to justify the intervention of the traditional outsiders – the Great Powers – in their new guise as the "International Community". It also both justified and obscured the intervention of the Islamic outsiders who provided strong political backing, financial support and armed fighters to Izetbegović's Muslim party.

In reality, on its own, Bosnia-Herzegovina had never thoroughly healed the many social fractures caused by its complex history. An accommodation had been reached within the framework of Yugoslavia. Without the larger framework of Yugoslavia, the balance was broken.

In this situation, there were two dimensions of "outside" interference: interference from other parts of disintegrating Yugoslavia, and interference from further away. The interference from Yugoslavia had been benign and unifying. As Yugoslavia disintegrated, the conflict pitting Croats against Serbs immediately affected Bosnia in a negative way. The Serbs of the Croatian Krajina were politically close to the Serbs of the Bosnian Krajina, forming a single nationalist political party to the right of the Serbian Socialist Party of Milošević in Serbia itself. Rejecting the break-up of Yugoslavia as illegal, Serbs saw nothing wrong with aiding fellow Serbs within Yugoslavia. Croats openly sought to enlarge Croatia at the expense of Bosnia-Herzegovina. Some of the Slavic Muslims within Serbia itself identified with Izetbegović's Islamic party and rushed to offer their support. This layer of "outside" interference from Yugoslavia itself was simply an inevitable result of suddenly creating an "independent" country on a territory belonging to a larger country, and whose mixed population was linked to the mixed population of that larger country.

The second layer of outside interference came from Europe, the United States, and Muslim countries that chose sides between these contending parties. This shifted the internal balance of power not only between, but also within, identity communities. Among the population of Muslim origin, it was Izetbegović's Islamic party that clearly benefited the most from aid provided by Muslim countries. Thanks to skillful lobbying, the Izetbegović party also benefited from U.S. support, which was faltering but decisive. The most peculiar form of foreign interference was the demand, voiced especially in the United States, to "create an even playing field" by lifting the arms embargo (which was being systematically violated, in fact) in order to arm the Muslims. The notion of an "even playing field" equated civil war with a sporting event, which should be allowed to go on into more innings.

Whatever the declared or real motives of outside intervention, they are likely to diverge considerably from the interests of the populations affected. If a local war is a playing field, the game of outside powers uses local combatants as pawns. In 1942, Hitler sought to extend the power of the Third Reich eastward to the oilfields of Baku and the Middle East by exploiting Arab Muslim resentment of British imperialism in the Middle East, which had favored Jewish settlement in Palestine. The Bosnian Muslims appeared to be a useful pawn in the game of gaining Muslim support for Hitler's war aims. In 1992, U.S. support to the Bosnian Muslims helped solidify Washington's geostrategic alliance with rich oil-producing Muslim states. The U.S. alliance with Muslim states was not anti-Jewish, but on the contrary was meant to illustrate that support to Israel was compatible with support to Muslims elsewhere. The creation of a "Muslim" state could even help break Israel's relative isolation as a religiously defined state.

Champions of Bosnia could occasionally be heard to lament that their cause lacked support from Western powers because Bosnia had no oil. In reality, Bosnia's friends had lots of oil and lots of dollars. As a result, the cause never lacked support. While officially enforcing the arms embargo, the Pentagon in reality ensured the regular flow of arms to the Bosnian Muslims by turning a blind Awacs eye to clandestine flights of a fleet of black C-130 Hercules transport aircraft delivering military equipment into the "safe area" at Tuzla.

In both Afghanistan and the Gulf, the Pentagon had incurred debts to Islamist groups and their Middle Eastern sponsors. By 1993 these groups, many supported by Iran and Saudi Arabia, were anxious to help Bosnian Muslims fighting in the former Yugoslavia and called in their debts with the Americans. Bill Clinton and the Pentagon were keen to be seen as creditworthy and repaid in the form of an Iran-Contra style operation – in flagrant violation of the UN security council arms embargo against all combatants in the former Yugoslavia.

The result was a vast secret conduit of weapons smuggling through Croatia. This was arranged by the clandestine agencies of the U.S., Turkey, and Iran, together with a range of radical Islamist groups, including Afghan mujahidin and the pro-Iranian Hizbullah.[55]

Saudi Arabia openly linked its business deals to support for the Bosnian Muslims. In April 1994, Reuters reported that Saudi Arabia's "anger over Europe's reluctance to move against Serbs in Bosnia" was a "crucial factor" in preferring the United States over France as supplier for a $6 billion aircraft deal. French prime minister Edouard Balladur had received a "taste of Saudi anger" when Crown Prince Abdullah "told him to his face that Europe's behaviour in Bosnia was shameful and made clear it was a tall order for it to expect a share of the aircraft deal". Unidentified diplomats told Reuters that "it was natural that Saudi Arabia, a champion of Islamic causes, would see Bosnia as a key element when studying offers by the European consortium Airbus Industrie and by Boeing Co. and McDonnell Douglas of the United States. Saudi Arabia, home to Islam's holiest shrines, is a strong financial backer of Bosnian Moslems."[56]

The second Bosnian Protectorate was designed by the United States at Dayton in late 1995. It included a division between the fictional "Federation" (in fact divided sharply between Muslim and Croatian territories) and the "Serbian Republic of Bosnia" or *Republika Srpska*. An equally good, or bad, solution could have been found four years earlier, before the war that devastated the region. But such a solution would have been found under European, or even UN, auspices, whereas the clearly stated purpose of U.S.

policy was to demonstrate that only the United States had the power and influence to force a solution. Second, the American-sponsored Bosnia solidified the strategic alliance with Turkey (Israel's main partner in the eastern Mediterranean) and with the oil-rich Muslim states. Finally, the Bosnian settlement was the first experiment in a new model of non-sovereign statelet, run essentially by the new globalization instruments: official organizations such as the International Monetary Fund (with total authority over the Bosnian economy) and the OSCE (with massive administrative powers) aided by a vast panoply of semi-governmental "non-governmental organizations" which absorb most of the "donations" and constitute a permanent lobby within the Western countries from which they come for the continuation of such arrangements.

4 The Making of Empires

1. GERMANY IS BORN AGAIN

With the Yugoslav crisis of the 1990s, newly reunified Germany abruptly emerged on the international scene as the major power wielder in Europe. It was the foreign minister, Hans-Dietrich Genscher, who successfully put pressure on his country's West European partners to dismantle Yugoslavia by recognizing Slovenia and Croatia as independent states. Which Germany was this? Was it the old Germany of Kaiser Wilhelm and the Third Reich pursuing its centuries-old *Drang nach Osten*? Or was this a new Germany, purified by penitence for the Holocaust, henceforth devoted solely to the universal promotion of democracy, civil society, and human rights? Or was it, in some very odd way, a combination of both?

German policy toward the Balkans in the early 1990s emerged as a singular blend of "ideals and interests". For Germans, assertion of humanitarian ideals as justification for foreign intervention was widely understood as a form of compensation for their Nazi past. And yet, ironically, this intervention can be shown to have marked a return (consciously or, more often, unconsciously) to precisely the forms of foreign intervention characteristic of traditional German power politics, notably as pursued by the Nazis. On the left, the ideals; on the right, the corresponding interests.

This moralized power politics was embraced with striking unanimity by German politicians. The few dissenting voices were quickly marginalized. The crisis in Yugoslavia enabled German leaders

165

to proclaim a new Germany, not only innocent of the *realpolitik* sins of the past, but moved by a special responsibility born of the Holocaust to play a prominent role in the crusade for universal human rights. This justified abandoning Germany's pledge to renounce forever the use of military intervention abroad. It united the two contrary tendencies in German foreign policy – traditional German expansionism to the East, and the more recent rejection of German militarism expressed by the emergence of the Greens as a political force. This paradoxical merger was perfected with the rise of the prominent Green, Joschka Fischer, to the key post of foreign minister just in time to justify German participation in NATO's devastating air strikes against Yugoslavia. The presence of Fischer as wartime foreign minister served to conceal the fundamental secret of this new military humanitarianism: its perfect continuity with the most aggressive traditions of German policy toward the Balkans as practiced by Berlin in two world wars.

Why "Serbia must die"

German public opinion was prepared to blame the Serbs for everything by a vehement press campaign at the start of the decade. Croats in Yugoslavia were portrayed as abused prisoners held captive against their will by barbarous Serbs. In July 1991, a virulent barrage of articles appeared in the German press, led by the influential conservative newspaper, the *Frankfurter Allgemeine Zeitung* (FAZ). Day after day, FAZ editor Johann Georg Reissmüller denounced the "Serbo-communist power called Yugoslavia", "Belgrade Serbo-communism" that held a "Greater Serbian-communist knife at the throat" of the Slovenes and Croats. Reissmüller described "the Yugo-Serbs" as essentially oriental "militarist Bolsheviks" who had "no place in the European Community". For Reissmüller, the Serbs combined the faults of the Jews as portrayed in Nazi propaganda (essentially "Bolsheviks", who had no place in Europe) with the faults of the Nazis themselves: "The civilized world must ... warn the Serbian nation to abandon its master race madness [*Herrenvolk-Wahn*]." This German press campaign had an influence in Croatia itself. In July 1991, Reissmüller's reports to the FAZ from Croatia were reproduced in the leading Croatian daily *Vjesnik*, where, understood as the voice of Europe's most powerful country, they served to silence opposition to President Tudjman's secessionist policy which was leading Yugoslavia into civil war.[1]

While the anti-Serb press campaign was initiated by the *Frankfurter Allgemeine Zeitung* and the right-wing *Die Welt*, Germany's left-of-center press followed suit. The influential weekly *Der Spiegel* devoted its 8 July 1991 cover article to "Serb Terror", depicting Yugoslavia as a "prison of peoples" clamoring to escape. Everywhere, Serbs were stigmatized as "non-European" barbarians intruding into civilized Europe. Nineteen months after German reunification, and for the first time since Hitler's defeat in 1945, the German media resounded with condemnation of an entire ethnic group reminiscent of the pre-war propaganda against the Jews.[2]

This German propaganda onslaught was the signal that times had changed fundamentally. In the 1980s, under the perceived threat of nuclear war between the two superpowers, a new generation of Germans had preached reconciliation with the peoples who had suffered from Nazi aggression. Activists had stressed the need to put an end to "enemy stereotypes" (*Feindbilder*). This laudable effort stopped short when it came to the Serbs. Scarcely anyone seemed to be shocked by the ferocious emergence of the enemy stereotype of "the Serbs".

Yet the demonization of Serbia in 1991 echoed Nazi propaganda in 1941, which in turned echoed 1914, when Germany and Austria launched World War I by invading Serbia. On both occasions, the little Balkan country was stigmatized as a troublemaker that must be eliminated. The attitude was summed up in the 1914 slogan "*Serbien muss sterbien*" (a play on the word *sterben*, to die), meaning "Serbia must die".[3]

In 1991, hardly anybody in Germany seemed to remember how the Third Reich had treated the Serbs half a century earlier. In 1941, after bombing Belgrade, Germany invaded Yugoslavia and began to carve it up. Pieces of Serbia itself were distributed to surrounding allies of Hitler. Serb guerrillas were the first to combat the Nazi occupation.[4] On 16 September 1941, the supreme German occupation commander, Field Marshal Wilhelm Keitel, announced that for every German killed, 50 Serb hostages would be executed. Guerrilla attacks continued. On 6 October 1941, Keitel issued a warning notice, posted in German and Serbian, announcing that German "patience is finally at an end". Henceforth, he decreed, for every German soldier killed in ambush, 100 Serbs would be shot dead. Any family giving aid or information to the guerrillas would be shot, their property confiscated, and their house burned to the ground. Any explosion or planned explosion would be punished with the execution of 50 Serbs. Any locality from which unknown fire would be directed at German soldiers would be burned down, the male population would be captured, and every other one would be executed. On 20 October, all the male inhabitants of Kragujevac, in central Serbia, were dragged from their homes and herded into the German barracks. The night before, a German convoy had been ambushed, killing ten soldiers. In retaliation, the Wehrmacht slaughtered 7,000 civilian hostages, between the ages of 14 and 80, including ten priests, 300 schoolboys and 20 teachers. The principal of the boys' school, Lazar Pantelić, chose to die with his students when the soldiers ignored his pleas to spare them.[5] This was the worst but by no means the only such slaughter of civilian hostages. In the city of Kraljevo, 5,700 Serb hostages, again including schoolboys and a few women, were executed. Altogether some 44,000 Serbian men, women, and children were killed in this way, including some Jews and Gypsies.

A few observations: these hostages were all civilians, in no way linked to the acts being punished. The policy of retaliation was carried out not by the SS, usually held responsible for all the criminal acts of Nazi occuption, but by the *Wehrmacht*, the regular army. Nobody was punished. And this bloody retaliation was clearly directed not at "Yugoslavs" in general, much less at Croats, Bosnians, or Albanians, but precisely and openly at Serbs, considered the basic enemy.

One might have expected the younger generation of Germans, seemingly so sensitive to the suffering of Hitler's victims, to object to a policy toward Yugoslavia eerily reminiscent of the past. Very few did.

Nation-state versus volk-state

After the reunification of Germany, the rehabilitation of Germany. This was the agenda of the Bonn government. The identification of Serbia as the quintessential demon of war was a step toward a revisionist interpretation of Germany as innocent victim of the two world wars. If elsewhere the question of guilt for launching war in 1914 seemed a moot point in 1990, for some members of the German foreign policy community it never ceased to be a burning issue. "Overcoming the consequences of the *First* World War" was rapidly set as a policy goal of unified Germany in a significant speech by a leading policy-maker, Rupert Scholz, deputy chairman of the CDU/CSU faction in the German *Bundestag*.

In September 1991, Scholz gave a talk on "the security policy role of the Germans in Europe" to a forum of business leaders and army officers in which he stressed the "basically new tasks and orientation" of German foreign and security policy that came with "German reunification and the recovered full sovereignty".[6] As a former defense minister, Scholz was an important figure among Chancellor Helmut Kohl's military policy-makers. The conflict in Yugoslavia had a "fundamental, unquestionable significance" for all of Europe, he said, because after overcoming the division of Germany, the next task was "to overcome the consequences of World War I". Far from feeling restrained by Germany's aggressive role in the Balkans in two world wars, Scholz maintained that this "historic experience" gave Germans a special mandate to show solidarity ... with Croats and Slovenians. He called for immediate international recognition of Croatia and Slovenia. "Once such a recognition is carried out, then the Yugoslav conflict is no longer a matter of an internal political problem of Yugoslavia, in which there should be no international intervention," he pointed out. Once Croatia and Slovenia were recognized as independent states, it would be possible, by obtaining a UN Security Council mandate, to exercise "international security responsibility" by means of military intervention.

Scholz's meaning was clear: rapid recognition of Croatia and Slovenia was designed *not* – as was officially claimed by the German government – to *prevent* military conflict, but to *internationalize* it, in order to justify outside military intervention, *with German participation*, under the auspices of either the UN or the OSCE. This would be a way of completing the transformation of a united, sovereign Germany back into a "normal" power again.

In December 1991, Scholz denounced calls for "stability" in Europe as a huge danger, "for when individual nations are held fast in unwanted, unnatural or forced State organizations, this creates everything but real stability".[7] The clear implication was that European boundaries should not be considered inviolable if they were the boundaries of "unwanted" states ("unwanted" by whom and why?) or "unnatural" (*widernatürlich*) states. The concept of "unnatural states" was an implicit reversion to the notion that "natural" states are expressions of ethnic homogeneity, and that ethnically mixed states are contrary to "nature" and thus need not be respected. This is a traditional feature of German foreign policy at its most aggressive. In this traditional German view, "self-determination" is above all an *ethnic* – or *völkisch*, from the German word for ethnic or national group, *Volk* – rather than a *political* principle, a matter not of the political rights (such as equality before the law, free elections, and other civil rights) of people sharing a particular territory, but rather of the collective right of a racially and culturally homogeneous population to assert its identity as the basic principle of political organization.

Adolf Hitler expressed this clearly in his 1924 manifesto, *Mein Kampf*, which provided the basis for the policies he pursued as *Führer* of the Third Reich. The state was not an end in itself, he insisted, but only a means to an end, and that end was "the preservation and promotion of a community of physically and spiritually identical creatures". In terms reminiscent of Scholz's, Hitler declared that "states that do not serve this end, are illusions if not abortions".[8]

Hitler advocated, and for a time achieved, what he called the *völkische Staat*. This differed drastically from the nation-state. Full citizenship depended on blood or race. Only Aryans could be citizens of the German *völkische Staat*. In between citizens and foreign residents, a third category of inhabitants, *Staatsgehöriger* (subjects), consisted of people born in the country but not of the dominant race and therefore deprived of political rights. The final goal of Hitler was the Third Reich, or the revived German Empire. With its base in the German *völkische Staat*, the new empire would extend the hegemony of the German master race over most of Europe, notably Eastern Europe, whose Slavic populations were considered lesser breeds. Hitler's project was based on the essentially racist view that the members of each and every *Volk* share a specific common and permanent nature.

In contrast to Hitler's racialist concept, the political nation-state can be considered the result of a social revolution that overthrew a hereditary class of rulers and bestowed "sovereignty" on the nation, understood as the general population (starting with male property owners and extending to the entire citizenry). Over time, this concept has favored the development of democratic institutions and acceptance of the principle that the state exists in order to further the well-being of all its citizens. At the same time, the nation-state proved to be a most effective framework for a remarkable burst of economic, scientific, and technological progress. The developed European nation-states used their enormous advantage in these fields to subjugate distant peoples, *preventing* them from developing their own political and economic defense mechanisms. Their geographic position gave the Atlantic nation-states an insuperable advantage in the creation of empires. Trying to compete, Germany developed its own rationale for expanding within Europe itself, toward the East. This rationale involved creating an ideology of racial hierarchy essentially the same as that of the Atlantic imperialist powers during the nineteenth century, but applied to Europeans. The notion that different peoples are permanently, because racially, suited to particular forms of social organization is expressed in the concept of the "folk-state" as opposed to the (often racially mixed) nation-state. Progressive liberalism saw different political forms as products of stages of material and intellectual development, and therefore both potentially applicable to everybody and subject to change. The folk-state concept accepts the perpetuation of hierarchic and patriarchal social forms which in practice keep their populations weak and easily dominated by large modern nations.

Ethnic imperialism as ethical imperialism[9]

The concept of stressing ethnic identity as a means of "ethical imperialism" was first made explicit toward the end of World War I, at a moment when the German Empire had not lost hope of winning the war. On the eve of being named Chancellor, Prince Max von Baden addressed a paper on "Thoughts on Ethical Imperialism" to the Kaiser in which he stressed that in order to gain worldwide acceptance, Germany's imperialist aims must be stated in terms of ideals and not simply of interests. "If German imperialism is to stand up to the onslaught of democracy with its claim to improve the world, it must be ethically grounded. Democracy can easily dismiss a sheer claim to power ... Therefore we must incorporate general human goals into our national will." The basis for an ethical purpose and human goals was to be found in the existence, all around Germany itself, of a large number of small nationalities that were intermingled as minorities, without independent nation-states of their own. These *Randvölker* (peripheral peoples) were the key to Germany's expansion in Europe, since support to their ethnic claims would weaken neighboring nation-states and facilitate the spread of German influence. "We must make it clear that we want to deal honestly as protectors of the rights of all *Randvölker*."[10]

Even before Prince von Baden's explicit recommendation, Berlin and especially Vienna had been following such a policy in the

Balkans, discovering and promoting *Randvölker* (Albanians in particular) whose claims could potentially weaken Serbia, seen as the strongest independent state-builder obstructing the *Drang nach Osten* in the direction of the Middle East. Germany's defeat at the end of World War I, and the revision of boundaries that ensued, gave a new impetus and significance to Germany's ethnic foreign policy.

National minorities within the Austro-Hungarian Empire, especially the Czechs, had lobbied the Western allies during the war in favor of splitting the Habsburg lands into new nation-states. President Woodrow Wilson sought to provide a moral justification for the boundary changes based on the principle of "self-determination" of peoples. As a result, the Western allies sponsored the creation of succession states built on the ethnic/linguistic/national principle, even though they theoretically adhered mainly to the Franco-American political tradition, which identifies self-determination with popular sovereignty through the equal exercise of political rights, regardless of race, religion, or national origin. Wilsonian self-determination suffered from a fatal ambiguity: was political democracy or ethnic identity the guiding principle? In practice, neither functioned very well. In East-Central Europe, ethnic or linguistic identities were more often than not mixed and overlapping. Historical factors created loyalties and aspirations that sometimes conflicted with these "identities", as illustrated in some referendums which were ignored when the result would have restored to Germany territories awarded to Poland. The borders of states also had to take into consideration practical material factors such as reasonable size, economic coherence, and natural boundaries (mountains, rivers), more permanent than the ethnic composition of populations. Supposedly to enhance their national defense and economic viability, the boundaries of Poland and Czechoslovakia were drawn to include large German minorities whose discontent was a destabilizing factor. The Succession States (Poland, Czechoslovakia, Romania, Yugoslavia) remained dependent on their unreliable Western sponsors, mainly interested in using them as a *cordon sanitaire* to isolate the Soviet Union.

The Versailles Treaty gave a new impulse and meaning to Germany's already existing policy of emphasizing ethnic identity. Forced to accept what it considered unjust loss of territory to Poland, the Weimar Republic doggedly pursued a policy aimed at getting it back by peaceful means. Championing the rights of ethnic minorities could be a way to justify recovering lost German territory. Gustav Stresemann, the Weimar Republic's Chancellor from 1923 to 1929, pursued a policy of championing cultural freedom for minorities first within Germany itself (where scarcely any were left). This aimed at reassuring non-German populations that their cultural identities would be preserved in the event that the territories where they lived were returned to Germany.[11] In a January 1925 paper, Stresemann proposed "as a lasting means of influencing world opinion", to seek to use the "right of self-determination of peoples" to solve the "problem" of German minorities.[12] In the early 1920s, the Foreign Ministry of the Weimar Republic began to provide discreet support to the *Verband der deutschen Volksgruppen in Europa* (League of German Folk Groups in Europe) to the tune of 30 million Reichsmarks.[13] In neighboring countries such as Poland and Denmark, real estate and businesses were bought out in order to enlarge and solidify areas settled by German *Volksgruppen*, a procedure described by the Foreign Ministry as the "struggle for land" (*Kampf um den Boden*).[14]

The grievances of German ethnic minorities provided the pretexts for both the occupation of Czechoslovakia and the invasion of Poland. After the fall of France in 1940, Alsace, historically rooted in German culture, was (as after the Franco-Prussian war of 1870–71) detached from France and attached to the Third Reich. But the Nazi policy was not concerned only with German minorities. Nazi geopolitician Karl Haushofer pointed to the "tremendous possibilities" offered by a far-seeing policy attentive to "the self-determination of big and small *Völker*, under the slogan 'Dignity, Freedom and Equal Rights'".[15] Commenting on this, Franz Neumann concluded:[16]

Nothing could be more frank. Self-determination is merely a weapon. Take advantage of every friction growing out of the minority problem. Stir up national and racial conflicts where you can. Every conflict will play into the hands of Germany, the new self-appointed guardian of honor, freedom, and equality all over the world.

Volksgruppen-Commandos sought out small national minorities within countries conquered by the *Wehrmacht*, in order to "help" them toward autonomy and thereby weaken the occupied state: the Flemish in Belgium, as a "Germanic" people, for example; but attention was also paid to the Bretons in Brittany and other regional populations that could be considered "oppressed minorities" and thus "helped" to gain autonomy from France.[17] As a long-established, rich world power to which citizens were proud to belong, France was clearly harder to fragment than the much younger and more fragile states to the east, with their very mixed populations. SS and Gestapo leader Heinrich Himmler's advice to Hitler on the "handling of foreign peoples in the East" was explicit: "we have the greatest interest not only in not unifying the population of the East, but in actually dividing them into as many parts and splinters as possible". Alongside Jews and Poles, Himmler recommended recognizing not only the Ukrainians and the White Russians but also other peoples whose very existence was unknown to the outside world: Gorals, Lemkens and Kashubs. But, he added, Germany's interest was not to lead even these smaller peoples to unity and eventual national consciousness, but rather to "dissolve them into countless little splinters and particles".[18]

The return of the *vertriebene*

Precisely because the supposed "protection" of German minorities had been the *casus belli* for Hitler's invasion of Eastern European countries, and the German minorities had frequently acted as a "fifth column" facilitating Nazi conquest, after World War II, those countries undertook to protect themselves by expelling their ethnic German minorities. The largest of these population shifts concerned some two and a half million Germans expelled from the Czech Sudetenland and some three and a half million Germans expelled from Poland. Once in Germany, these expelled Germans, or *Vertriebene* (literally, "driven out"), formed large and politically powerful associations, whose lobbies gained strong influence in political parties, notably the right-wing Christian Social Union Party (CSU) in Bavaria, where many resettled.

The problem of the expelled Germans gave a fresh impetus to German *Volkspolitik*. Discreetly, the Bonn government resumed Berlin's pre-war practice of subsidizing an impressive array of international federations devoted to the defense of ethnic minorities or *Volksgruppen*, to promotion of regional autonomy, and defense of minority languages. As often happens, those with the greatest interest in a problem end up defining the solutions. So it is that the German-sponsored array of organizations devoted to the rights of minorities have succeeded in exerting a decisive influence over perceptions of ethnic conflicts in Yugoslavia and elsewhere, and even over international legislation.

In 1945, the plight of the expelled Germans elicited little sympathy among Europeans largely persuaded that Germans deserved whatever happened to them. The conflicts in Yugoslavia created a new context by focusing international attention on the expulsion of populations, described by a shocking new term, "ethnic cleansing". The outrage aroused by "ethnic cleansing" set the stage for a shift in both public sympathy and international law favorable to the demands of the *Vertriebene* to recover the rights and property they had lost in their former homelands.

In the autumn of 1992, the impact in Germany of the first reports of rapes of Muslim women by Serbs was magnified by the analogy with German women who had been raped by soldiers of the Red Army at the end of World War II. The women's movement had recently begun to sensitize opinion to this theme. Rupert Neudeck, himself a *Vertriebener*, stressed the analogy in his reports on Bosnia-Herzegovina for the German medical aid association Komitee Cap Anamur. In testimony to the Bundestag committee on women and youth, as well as in articles and television appearances, Neudeck made it clear that his emotional response to Bosnia-Herzegovina was strongly influenced by his experience as a child of six in the spring of 1945, when he fled from Danzig "with the permanent fear of mass rapes perpetrated here and there, with a grandmother still at an age to be raped, with an aunt, with my mother, with a big sister age eleven, all of them equally threatened with being raped".[19] Neudeck readily identified the Serbs with the Russians, but claimed the Serbs were even worse. Neudeck's emotional identification with "the victims of the Serbs" seems to have simultaneously distorted his accuracy and enhanced his credibility, a paradox that may be frequent in such circumstances.[20]

For the German *Vertriebene*, the greatest achievement was the recognition of the "right to a homeland" (*Heimat* in German) by the United Nations Human Rights Commission on 17 April 1998. Major credit for this achievement goes to a Harvard-educated jurist, Alfred-Maurice de Zayas, who based his UN report on a 1995 article entitled "The Right to One's Homeland, Ethnic Cleansing and the International Criminal Tribunal for the former Yugoslavia".[21] Zayas was awarded the highest honor bestowed by the *Bund der Vertriebene* in grateful recognition of his lifelong work on their behalf. Two elements contributed to Zayas' success. One was the strong network of German organizations supporting his efforts; the other was the parallel with events in Yugoslavia interpreted as a one-sided abuse of minorities perpetrated by Orthodox Slavs. Zayas made the parallel explicit by adopting the term "ethnic cleansing" for the English language version of an earlier German work on the subject: *A Terrible Revenge: The Ethnic Cleansing of the East European Germans 1944–1950.*[22]

The condemnation of "Serbian ethnic cleansing" has constituted an enormous moral victory for the postwar German expellees. For the Germans themselves, the identification of the Serbs with the Russians has added an irrational but emotionally powerful element of "poetic justice". This emotion, mobilizing people of considerable ability and influence, has provided a strong, invisible support to the enemies of the Serbs within Yugoslavia.

While material compensation to *Volksdeutsche* is clearly beyond the present means of the economically strapped East European countries, the right to return is most likely to be granted in the context of European unification. Even a small number of German returnees, "on account of their high level of intellectual training in all fields (scientific, industrial, agricultural, etc.), will provide leadership and expertise to all the countries of Eastern Europe eager to conform to Western standards". In this way, German influence is likely to be significantly extended eastward.[23]

The new Utopia: peoples without borders

Aside from the effective lobbying of the *Vertriebene*, German *Volkspolitik* seems to have a momentum of its own. In a new "Europe of peoples" rather than states, the Germans would play the dominant role thanks to their greater numbers, economic strength, and recognized competence in many fields. German influence could dominate a Europe dotted with grateful little folk-states or autonomous minorities owing their recognition to Germany, while such an "ethnically impure" nation-state as France is torn between Corsicans, Bretons, Alsatians, Basques, etc.

The German and Austrian governments have persistently financed the promotion of small nationalities (*Völker*) through an impressive array of specialized organizations, starting with the European Congress of Nationalities which met between 1925 and 1938. Its revival in 1949 led to the foundation of the most tenacious and influential of the *Volkspolitik* institutions, the *Föderalistiche Union Europäischer Volksgruppen* (FUEV). According to its statutes, FUEV sets out to "preserve ethnic particularities" and achieve "autonomy" for ethnic groups. Its leading founders included veterans of Nazi *Volkspolitik* in occupied Europe.[24]

Similar aims are pursued by a network of like-minded and sometimes overlapping organizations: the International Association for the Defense of Threatened Languages and Cultures, founded in 1963; the International Scientific Conference Minorities for Europe of Tomorrow (ISCOMET), focused on southeastern Europe; the European Bureau for Lesser Used Languages (EBLUL); the Minority Rights Group (MRG); the *Gesellschaft für Bedrohte Völker* headed by Tilman Zülch; the Association of European Border Regions, founded on 18 June 1971 in Germany and led by such important German politicians as the former leader of the Christian Democratic Party, Wolfgang Schäuble. The Charter of this organization declares its objective as overcoming national boundaries or at least to reducing them to mere "administrative borders". Thus, German organizations worked both to reduce certain national frontiers to administrative borders, and – in Yugoslavia – to transform administrative borders into national frontiers. The apparent contradiction is explained by the fact that in both cases German influence increased.

A most significant role in reshaping Europe was played by a subsidiary of the Association of European Border Regions: the *Alpen-Adria Arbeitsgemeinschaft*, founded in November 1978 to bring together the German state of Bavaria and territories once ruled by the Habsburg Empire: most of Austria, parts of northern Italy and Hungary, and both Slovenia and Croatia. *Alpen-Adria* played an important role in persuading Slovenian and Croatian politicians that they were genuine "Europeans" belonging to the more prosperous West, and culturally and even racially superior to "Balkan barbarians". The secession of Slovenia and Croatia was openly encouraged by *Alpen-Adria* which at its 3 July 1991 assembly in Klagenfurt adopted a resolution supporting the "right to independence" of the two Yugoslav republics.[25]

Reshaping Europe is not likely to end with Yugoslavia. In December 1996, in the keynote speech inaugurating yet another such organization, the European Center for Minority Issues (ECMI), its director Anton Troebst said: "The modern history of Europe teaches us that the process of nation-building has not – as we in the West tend to assume – come to an end. To the contrary, it is going on and on, and the emergence of additional actors is highly likely." The "results of Soviet and Yugoslav nation-building from above", having been judged "artificial and thus not viable", today the "new nations of, say, the Bosnians, the Moldovans, or the Macedonians are consolidated – not least by crises, conflicts and wars" and should be treated as equal members of the family of European nations. "But if *they* have built their nations, other ethnic groups might do so as well", Troebst continued, citing social scientist Ernest Gellner's reference to "Sleeping Beauty Nations" that "can wake up almost any minute". Troebst speculated that "let's say, the Karelians in the very northwest of the Russian Federation, the Pomaks in the Greek–Bulgarian border area, or the Occitanians of Southern France will or will not put forward a national program, organize a national movement and ultimately demand or even fight for their own nation-state"; in such cases, he claimed, "no minority should be at the mercy of a repressive central government" and "even sovereign states have to accept intervention by the international community. In cases like Kosovo, only in that way can the escalation of inter-ethnic tension be prevented."[26] ECMI was an offshoot of FUEV and was founded with German government support.

Troebst's call for international intervention in Kosovo was based on the constant assumption that centralist governments are to blame for crises stemming from demands such as those of Corsican nationalists. This can only encourage ambitious separatist movements to intensify their demands in expectation of support from the network of influential lobbies supported by the powerful German government. ECMI, said Troebst, would identify crisis zones and measure the "degree of ethnic tension". ECMI, along with FUEV and other such organizations, also undertook to lobby the European Union to "introduc[e] new elements into international law which will allow the international community directly to interfere in situations of escalating conflict". With a major contribution from the international law faculty of the University of Innsbruck, these lobbies have indeed succeeded in creating a new international legal framework to which self-styled oppressed minorities (self-styled because no clear legal definition exists) can appeal against their governments. Offering support to minorities as such, without examining the merits of each case, can invite self-proclaimed leaders of minorities to defy democratic majorities in order to carve out fiefdoms for themselves.

In 1993, the founding declaration in Munich of yet another organization, the International Institute for the Rights of Ethic

Groups and for Regionalism (INTEREG), had dramatized the problem.[27] Noting the increase and intensification of minority conflicts, the declaration judged that the "nation-state" and the "automatic rule of the majority" were increasingly inadequate. The solution it proposed was "regionalism" and a Charter of the Rights of Minorities, which would lead to "relativising" the nation-state. The starting point of all these organizations is hostility to both the nation-state and its forms of majority rule. The belief in the essentially distinct nature of each *"Volk"* leads to the view that the nation-state is "an oppressive organization ensuring the crushing hegemony of a single ethnic component of the nation".[28] For former FUEV president Christoph Pan, the nation-state is a thing of the past, in both theory and practice. In his welcoming address to the 1996 FUEV congress at Timisoara, Romania, Pan declared that "the problem of nationalities is caused by democracy. Without democracy, there is no nationalities problem." For Pan and his colleagues, the objective is not the rule of the majority by elections, but exemption from majority rule for ethnic minorities. On the assumption that different ethnic groups will by their nature be opposed, minorities are certain to be oppressed by majorities simply because they are minorities. *Ergo*, majority rule is oppression – always on the assumption, of course, that people function primarily according to ethnic identity. This implies a radical denial of both individual choice as the basis of democratic life and of differences in outlook or interests which cut across the "ethnic" boundaries and determine political choices. By this logic, any nation-state that is not "ethnically pure" must be an oppressive structure. Moreover, according to the FUEV ideology, the majority (or relative majority) is automatically guilty of any conflict with a minority.

The case of Yugoslavia has already illustrated the functioning of this ideology, with its inherent bias in favor of "nation-splitting" versus "nation-building" peoples. In the FUEV perspective, the Serbs were necessarily the villains in Yugoslavia, because they were the relative majority and preferred a multinational nation-state to ethnic separatism. One of FUEV's member organizations is the Union of Kosovo Albanians which, until recently at least, had two headquarters, both in the United States: one in Aurora, Illinois and the other in Howard Beach, New York. The resolutions introduced at FUEV congresses in 1996 and 1997 by the US-based Kosovo Albanians demanded the "right of self-determination" for Albanians not only in Kosovo but also in Macedonia, Montenegro, and eastern Serbia. In 1998, the congress of FUEV called for putting "stronger pressure" on the Yugoslav and Serb governments and for the immediate stationing of NATO troops in Kosovo.

Once a "minority" gains its autonomy, it ceases to be a minority in its autonomous region. Somebody else may become a minority ... the whole notion of "majority" and "minority" peoples is too precarious and flexible to serve as a stable political principle. The Serbs were a majority in Serbia but a minority in the province of Kosovo, where in the 1980s they complained of being persecuted by the Albanian majority. After the NATO occupation, the Serbian minority was harassed, murdered, and driven out, without arousing the indignation of organizations like FUEV, supposed to be defender of minorities. These organizations claim that their goal is to prevent conflict. However, their biased emphasis on "the rights of minorities" is undermining the universalist concept of equal rights which constitutes the basis of the democratic compromise. It tends to empower patriarchal leaders. The interpretation of the right to self-determination as the right to separate from others abandons the progressive goal of equal rights in a society open to all people regardless of religion or national origin.

Self-determination as ethnic determination

Officially, in order to achieve reunification – which meant a unilateral takeover of the German Democratic Republic in the East by the Federal Republic of Germany – German leaders had solemnly acknowledged their obligation to reassure the rest of Europe that their nation would never again revert to the aggressive policies of the Third Reich. On 12 September 1990, less than a month before the official unification of the two German states, their two foreign ministers, along with the foreign ministers of the four Allied Occupation Powers – the Soviet Union, the United States, the United Kingdom, and France – signed the treaty for the final settlement of the German question, known as the "Two Plus Four" Treaty. In particular, the treaty included a binding commitment never again to export war from German soil. Henceforth, the Germans vowed, the German Constitution barred any disturbance of peaceful coexistence between peoples. On the day of reunification, 3 October 1990, Chancellor Helmut Kohl sent a message to all the world's governments, including that of Yugoslavia, declaring that: "With its national unity restored, our country will serve peace in the world."[29]

In the future, Germany will send only peace out into the world. We are well aware that the intangibility of borders and respect for the territorial integrity and the sovereignty of all States in Europe is a basic condition for peace.

He added: "At the same time, we stand by the moral and legal obligations resulting from German history."

The Chancellor spoke with a forked tongue. To the people of the European nations that had suffered from the Third Reich's contempt for "territorial integrity" and "sovereignty" of other European states, whose lands had been devastated, and whose populations had suffered in the war sent out into the world by Germany in two world wars, such words would be taken as an assurance that the future German government would restrain itself from any intervention, let alone any military intervention, disturbing their sovereignty or territorial integrity. Nowhere in Europe would such restraint seem more obligatory than in Yugoslavia, a country attacked, invaded, occupied, and fragmented by Hitler's *Wehrmacht*.

But it was soon to emerge that the "moral and legal obligations resulting from German history" could be – and would be – interpreted in an altogether different way: as an obligation to destroy the territorial integrity of Yugoslavia by hasty recognition of illegal nationalist secessions, destroy its sovereignty by transforming pieces of the destroyed country into protectorates, and finally attacking and invading it militarily.

The old tradition of ethnic or linguistic determination of state boundaries was given a fresh emotional charge by the 1989 slogan *"Wir sind ein Volk"* justifying the rapid unification of the two German states. The celebration of a single German identity (somewhat overblown, as ongoing tensions between "Ossies" and "Wessies" soon demonstrated) set the stage for revival of "ethnic imperialism" in the guise of "ethical imperialism", identifying the ethical value of self-determination with the primacy of ethnic identity in determining political boundaries and organization.

The German political class as a whole interpreted German reunification almost as a sacred anointing of the German nation to champion "self-determination", as interpreted in the traditional German way. In a 1995 article[30] on "The Right to Self-Determination and German Policy", Rupert Scholz declared that its recent history made Germany particularly attached to the right of self-determination, in the form of the "self-determination of the single, indivisible German nation". After this right was reasserted with German reunification, "many parties to international self-determination or minority conflicts naturally turn to Germany in expectation of support". They will not be disappointed, because "German foreign policy is consistently and actively committed to the universal application of the right to self-determination". Scholz observed that this "raised the question of the possibilities and limits of so-called humanitarian intervention", by which he meant eventually "military operations on behalf of oppressed minorities".

The enthusiasm of politicians and the media for Germany's special mission to defend "self-determination" moved Genscher, the main architect of the successful reunification policy, to overrule the warnings of the German diplomatic corps, including Bonn's own ambassador in Belgrade, and force through immediate recognition of Slovenia and Croatia. Such recognition was certain to give Serbs the impression that they were facing a repetition of 1941, when Germany backed the establishment of the murderous "Independent State of Croatia". This would convince many Serbs that they must set up their own autonomous regions in self-defense, thus confronting Croatia with partition or civil war. That such recognition was almost certain to provoke a bloody conflict in Bosnia-Herzegovina was obvious at the time to all diplomats and independent observers, including the Secretary General of the United Nations. Recognizing unnegotiated secessions was a flagrant violation of the pledge to respect "intangibility of borders and territorial integrity", as Yugoslavia's territory was suddenly stripped of its two richest territories. Yet the German public apparently believed that this was merely a virtuous support for "self-determination", not realizing that the political purpose was to transform Yugoslavia's internal problems into an international conflict that would enable foreign intervention.

It took heavy pressure from the Bonn government to persuade the member states of the European Community to disregard the advice of their own diplomats and recognize Slovenia and Croatia as independent states. Germany blatantly used the heavy hand of its economic power to force its EC partner governments to do what they knew was wrong.[31] Once they had done so, however reluctantly, they were caught in the escalating process of justifying their own error after the fact, by shifting the blame to the designated scapegoat: the fictional "Milošević" and "Serbian nationalism".

Having achieved European unanimity by pressure, German political leaders were free to pursue reinterpretation of their obligations to peace undisturbed by criticism, whether at home or elsewhere in the European Union. A high point of this transformation was the debate in the *Bundestag* on 6 December 1995, culminating in the vote to send 4,000 *Bundeswehr* soldiers to former Yugoslavia.[32] Chancellor Kohl emphasized the need for "fair burden-sharing" and hailed the Bosnian mission as a "wonderful experience"; since Russia was also taking part, Kohl claimed that "old enemy stereotypes are being overcome" (except, of course, the old enemy stereotype of the Serbs). Wolfgang Schäuble, at the time Kohl's heir apparent to leadership of the ruling Christian Democratic Union (CDU), defined the "lesson from Bosnia-Herzegovina" as "whoever is not ready to fight will not ensure peace". In the future, said Schäuble, "we – the Europeans, NATO, and the international community as a whole – must go into action sooner, more resolutely and more clearly", since "the real heart of peace-keeping" is being "in a position to show that the use of military force does not pay". In short, for Germany to send peace into the world, it would have to send military forces – the traditional way that Germany and all Great Powers have "kept the peace", ending in war.

Although Germany's support to the breakaway republics dealt a fatal blow to the peaceful life together enjoyed by Yugoslavia's peoples, Schäuble actually proposed that Germans could help Croats, Serbs, and Muslims "learn to live together" during their stay in Germany as refugees. That, he claimed, would be a special contribution to reconstructing Bosnia, in addition to the "great service that our country has rendered by taking in so many refugees".

In reality, the life of Croats, Serbs, and Muslims seeking refuge in Germany took a bitter turn. Croats and Muslims found sympathy and support; Bosnian Serbs risked being convicted for war crimes by German courts.

- On 23 May 1997, the Bavarian high court sentenced Bosnian Serb Novislav Džajić, aged 35, to five years in prison for abetting the murder and attempted murder of 15 Bosnian Muslims. An original charge of genocide was dropped when all that could be established was that Džajić was present when Serb soldiers shot at 15 Muslim prisoners who escaped, or tried to escape, by jumping from a bridge into the Drina. Džajić himself had not fired a shot.

- On 26 September 1997, a Düsseldorf court sentenced 50-year-old Bosnian Serb Nikola Jorgić to life imprisonment on eleven counts of genocide and 30 counts of murder for allegedly masterminding a unit that killed Muslims. He was the first person ever convicted by a German court of genocidal acts. (That is to say, no German was ever convicted for "genocide" by a German court for acts committed during the Nazi period.)

- On 29 November 1999, a Düsseldorf court sentenced Bosnian Serb Maksim Sokolović, age 58, to nine years in prison for "abetting genocide" by inflicting bodily harm on Muslims and depriving them of their liberty while driving them out of the surroundings of his home village of Osmaci in Bosnia.

In all these cases, the International Criminal Tribunal for former Yugoslavia asked German courts to try these suspects, arrested in Germany, on the grounds that its own case-load was too overwhelming. The implications are troubling. In the case of Jorgić, if his crime was so grave as to merit a life sentence – harsher than any sentence actually pronounced by The Hague Tribunal – it is hard to understand why the ICTY refused to take responsibility for his trial. In the case of Džajić, the evidence was very flimsy and the charges retained hardly seem to merit such an extraordinary procedure as trial, conviction, and imprisonment in a foreign country. Either way, the German sentences were severe in comparison to both the ICTY and the German courts' treatment of their own nationals. The overall impression is of a questionable eagerness to convict Serb soldiers of the sorts of crimes committed by Germans during World War II. The exceptional readiness of German courts to condemn Serbs contrasts disturbingly with the absence of any proceedings against *Wehrmacht* officers who massacred thousands of hostages in occupied Serbia in 1941.

Old friends and old enemies

Reunified Germany's forceful backing of its World War II clients, the Croatian and Albanian nationalists, may have seemed startling to those who accepted the postwar description of the Federal Republic of Germany as an "economic giant and a political dwarf". In reality, Germany's absence from international politics was largely an illusion fostered by the Bonn government's discretion in the face of the widespread hostility left from the war. The foreign minister was always drawn from the small, liberal, elite Free Democratic Party, ideologically closest to the victorious Western allies. Until Hans-Dietrich Genscher's final push for reunification, the foreign minister worked closely with his counterparts in the West, pursuing projects of European unification in close cooperation with France, always tactfully allowed to take center stage. However, thanks to its federal structure and to the government-endowed foundations of the major political parties, the Federal Republic had several parallel foreign policies. Each political party, through its foundation, was able to strengthen German presence abroad, according to its own political shading. At one end of the spectrum, the Social Democratic Party (SPD), through its Friedrich Ebert Stiftung, offered friendly counsel to Third World liberation movements, while at the other end, the Christian Social Union (CSU) boss of Bavaria, Franz Josef Strauss, facilitated profitable contacts with dictators such as General Pinochet of Chile and with the apartheid regime in South Africa. Strauss was also the first Western statesman to pay a formal visit to Enver Hoxha's Albania. Thanks to this multifaceted informal diplomacy, the postwar Federal Republic of Germany was not really the "political dwarf" it pretended to be.[33]

In addition, there were the undercover operations of the *Bundesnachrichtendienst* (BND), the German equivalent of the CIA. The rapid shift of the United States under President Truman to an anti-Soviet "Cold War" adopted features of the defeated Nazis' anti-Bolshevik campaign. This enabled the BND, founded in 1949 by General Reinhard Gehlen, to keep working with many of the same agents and the same focus as the Nazi secret services. Dismissing Yugoslavia's non-alignment as temporary, Gehlen prepared to counter a hypothetical Russian influence in Belgrade by playing the Croatian card.[34] Once Khrushchev had restored "peaceful coexistence" with Tito in the late 1950s, the BND intensified contacts with militant Croatian nationalist exiles.[35]

Intelligence agents proliferate in border areas such as Yugoslavia, strategically and politically situated between East and West, North and South. Vulnerable to plots from all sides, Belgrade's State Security Directorate UDBA (*Uprava Državne Bezbednosti*) needed to be on constant alert and use whatever contacts it could – including the BND, which, during the heat of the Stalin–Tito feud, is said to have warned of a plot (real or invented) to assassinate Tito.[36]

One of the fatal consequences of the disastrous 1974 Yugoslav Constitution was that it enabled each of the republics to set up its own clandestine intelligence service. Such a parallel service, directed by people with experience and contacts drawn from Yugoslavia, was an ideal instrument for preparing secession, arranging clandestine arms imports, and ensuring diplomatic, political, and financial support from abroad. Initially, since Tito himself was a Croat, Croats had a prominent place within Yugoslav intelligence services. One of these was Ivan Krajačić, who had been Tito's main Comintern agent during World War II. Despite – or because of – his Comintern experience, Krajačić was entrusted by Tito after the 1948 break with Stalin to run the ruthless repression of alleged Stalinists which sent over 50,000 Yugoslav communists to Tito's island gulag, Goli Otok – the most severe repression of his entire regime. Krajačić reverted to Croatian nationalism and in the 1970s his circle of "national communists" pursued contacts with a BND agent in Yugoslavia, Klaus Dörner, who organized numerous secret meetings in Germany, Austria, and Croatia itself designed to forge an effective alliance between the national communists and the Ustashe emigration.[37]

From the mid-1970s, Dörner's prize contact was Bruno Busić, author of a manifesto for the reconciliation of all Croatian forces regardless of political past with a view to an independent Greater Croatia. Well connected with the Ustashe emigration in Europe, Busić appeared to be the rising star of Croatian nationalism until he was murdered in Paris in 1979.[38] His unsolved assassination opened the way for General Franjo Tudjman to take over the leadership of the Croatian nationalist revival, using Busić's ideas.

Between 1979 and 1982, the head of the *Bundesnachrichtendienst* was none other than Klaus Kinkel, who emerged in May 1992 as Genscher's successor as foreign minister. "We must force Serbia to its knees", declared Kinkel on 24 May 1992, only six days after taking office.[39]

It was years before the German public received any hint of its government's role in preparing the disintegration of Yugoslavia. In January 1995 journalist Andreas Zumach disclosed reports indicating that[40]

since the 1980s, in cooperation with the Croatian secret service, the BND systematically worked to aggravate conflicts between Zagreb and Belgrade. Partly using channels and individuals who had already played a role in cooperation between the Nazis and the fascist Ustashe and with whom the BND kept up intensive contact. In addition there are indications of massive deliveries of weapons to Croat destinations from German sources during the 1980s. The question remains whether the BND activity and the arms deliveries were carried out with support from the Bonn government. Finally, it is said that Genscher, in telephone conversations with President Tudjman (which U.S. intelligence would have overheard), repeatedly urged the latter to declare Croatia's independence.

These connections were recounted in detail in intelligence analyst Erich Schmidt-Eenboom's 1995 book on Kinkel, *Die Schattenkrieger*. As is frequently the case in our modern free societies, the truth, or part of the truth, finally comes out (if at all) at a time when it can no longer change public opinion or the course of events.

By this time, Croatia was independent and grateful. "Danke Deutschland!" was the kitsch hit song of the winter of 1991–92 in Zagreb. By a mixture of undercover intrigue, arms smuggling, and unstinting political support, Germany recovered a sphere of influence with a magnificent coastline much appreciated by German tourists. Visiting German politicians went home from closing business deals in the Croatian capital decorated with "the order of Tomislav" or some such pseudo-medieval trinket. The only problem for German influence was that the Americans were also moving in, offering military assistance and making deals.

In the case of the Albanians, it seems there was not so much continuity as a resumption of relations between the German secret services and Albanian secessionists in Kosovo. The enthusiasm of the armed Kosovo Albanian rebels for NATO has a clear precedent in the enthusiasm of their fathers and grandfathers for the German *Wehrmacht* 50 years earlier.

When the Nazi armies invaded and broke up Yugoslavia in 1941, most of what is now Kosovo was incorporated into the "Greater Albania" run by Fascist Italy. The Germans helped themselves to the northern part of the province in order to control the important Trepča mining complex. Hitler was enchanted by the wildness of Albania, which he called "the last romantic spot left in Europe", and by the Albanians, "this proud, arms-bearing mountain people". He aspired to create an independent Albania under German domination. When Italy capitulated to the Allies in September 1943, the Germans proclaimed themselves the "protectors" of the Albanians. Through sponsorship of a so-called "Second Prizren League" and the formation of an all-Albanian SS Division named for the Albanian national hero Skanderbeg, the Nazi occupiers actively encouraged their proud, gun-toting mountaineer allies to create a "racially pure Greater Albania" (including Kosovo) by massacring Serbs, Greeks, and other non-Albanians. The Nazis held on to Kosovo until the end of the war, aided by their Albanian allies in the extreme right-wing organization *Balli Kombetar* (National Front), which spread terror among the remaining Serbian population. Through family ties and memories, the heritage of *Balli Kombetar* has been continued by the "Kosovo Liberation Army" (UÇK).[41] For nostalgic Albanian nationalists, the return of the Germans to Kosovo in 1999 was the signal that the time had truly come to accomplish the old dream of an ethnically pure Greater Albania.

The pied pipers of Frankfurt

To pursue a Balkan policy so similar to that of the Third Reich, Germany had to convince itself and others that it was doing quite the contrary. Nobody was better suited to this task than certain former militants of the famous 1968 generation, historically innocent and sure of their own virtue, whose self-taught power politics sent them scrambling up the improvised ladder of radical politics. Such were the leaders of the "Rose-Green" coalition that won the German elections in September 1998, in time to take the helm and lead Germany into war over Kosovo. Social Democratic Chancellor Gerhard Schröder and his government turned out to be ideal salesmen for a remilitarized Germany. The champion in this exercise was without doubt the Green foreign minister, Joschka Fischer.

In response to the nuclear missile crisis of the early 1980s, Germans built a peace movement that spectacularly transformed the country's image from the bastion of aggressive Prussian militarism to the green garden of the flower children. Generational change and the lessons of defeat in the war appeared to have transformed Germany into a nation devoted to peace and disarmament. This altered perception may well have made it easier for the Russians and other victims of Nazi aggression to agree to German reunification and to the dismantling of the Warsaw Pact.

The political expression of this apparent generational mutation was a rapidly rising new party, *die Grünen*. The Greens' program was dedicated to the values of peace, ecology, feminism, and grassroots democracy. None of these values could be said to be embodied by Fischer, who began his career as revolutionary street fighter and was always more macho than ecolo. The German Greens were not only a party of environmentalists, pacifists, and feminists, but also the lifeboat which picked up a quarrelsome band of stranded revolutionaries-without-a-revolution, veterans of the several Maoist "K-groups".[42] Fischer joined the Greens after the wreck of "Revolutionary Struggle", an ultra-left group in Frankfurt closer to the Italian "Lotta Continua" than to the K-groups in its belief in triggering "spontaneous" revolt among the masses. As "war minister" of his organization's combat unit, the *Putzgruppe* or "cleansing group", Fischer systematically trained his fighters for well-coordinated street battles with the Frankfurt police in the early 1970s, primarily in defense of leftist squats. As the not-so-spontaneous violence began to veer into outright terrorism, Fischer gave it up.[43] The Greens eventually offered a new leaf to his political career. His strong personality and oratorical skill singled him out for favored media attention among the first batch of Greens elected to the *Bundestag* in 1983. Thanks in large part to the media, Fischer was able to become the informal leader of a party that did not want a leader.

In his battle to win leadership of the Greens, Fischer was allied with his long-time Frankfurt friend and co-tactician Daniel Cohn-Bendit, another media favorite, since his spectacular emergence as symbol of the May'68 student uprising in Paris. After acquiring fame in Paris, "Dany the Red" settled in Frankfurt where he ran a "Sponti" movement newspaper before belatedly joining the Greens in time to be elected to be in charge of "multiculturalism" in Frankfurt. There he joined Fischer in combating the more committed ecological, pacifist, and feminist tendencies within the Greens, derisively dubbed "Fundis" (fundamentalists). The media overwhelmingly preferred the supposed "Realos" (realists), Fischer and Cohn-Bendit, who showed a readiness to compromise with the demands of political office.

Yugoslavia provided the opportunity for Fischer to prove the practical value of such self-proclaimed "realism". The challenge was to come up with a rhetorical formula able to transform "peace" into war and a peace movement into a cheering section for military intervention.

In 1994, the conflict in Bosnia took a new turn. Secretly armed by Islamic countries and supported diplomatically by the United States, the Bosnian Muslims were on the offensive in Bosnia itself, although the media studiously ignored Muslim attacks or military advances. The "story" could only be the martyrdom of unarmed Muslims and of Sarajevo under siege. The fact that the Muslim party was maintaining the "siege of Sarajevo" (occasionally shelling the Sarajevo airport, for instance, to block relief flights) in order to win foreign support, was too cynical a reality to serve up to Western consumers of mediated wars.[44] It was precisely in 1994, when the Bosnian Serbs were on the defensive and more disposed than the Muslims to make peace, that the portrayal of the Muslims as helpless victims abandoned by a heartless world to Serbian "genocide" reached a peak. This was the year when a group of French intellectuals, propelled by fashionable opinion writer Bernard-Henri Lévy, launched a "Sarajevo list" for the European Parliament elections, with the slogan "Europe lives or dies in Sarajevo". The list flopped, but in Germany, Cohn-Bendit won a seat in the European Parliament on the Green list and promptly departed from the majority Green position by calling for German participation in military intervention in Bosnia. In this way, he played the useful role of Joschka's "trial balloon", repeatedly taking strong positions in favor of military intervention enabling Fischer to move in that direction in the name of party unification and moderation.

The highly controversial question of German participation in military intervention against Bosnian Serbs was a burning issue in December 1994. At that time, Chancellor Kohl was arguing that, on the one hand, because of the suffering caused to the people of Yugoslavia in World War II by the *Wehrmacht*, Germany should stay out; but, on the other hand, "precisely because of German history we cannot evade our responsibility" to contribute German Tornado fighter planes to "humanitarian intervention". At that time, the Social Democrats and Greens were overwhelmingly against such intervention. The exception was Cohn-Bendit, who dismissed Green objections as "ridiculous" and found original arguments to support Kohl's position. He claimed that the peoples of the world would revert to nationalism if they saw that the international community was failing to defend the "little multicultural *Volk*" in Bosnia – overlooking the regrettable fact that the "multicultural *Volk*" was split into warring factions unlikely to be reunited by Tornados flying to the aid of one against another.

At that time, Fischer was still arguing that Germany should stay out. But by the following August, Cohn-Bendit was able to announce that his friend Joschka was "on the right path", even though he still opposed sending in German soldiers. But, predicted Cohn-Bendit with remarkable clairvoyance, "Once Fischer is foreign minister, he won't be able to maintain this position."[45] Ambition was having its effect. On 6 December 1995, the historic question of sending German armed forces to intervene outside the NATO area came before the *Bundestag*. By then, the Green parliamentary group was split on the question of sending troops into Bosnia. As Green spokesman, Fischer was in the early stages of the transformation that would make Cohn-Bendit's prediction come true. The rhetorical hinge by which Fischer led the gradual swing from one "moral obligation" to its opposite was a profound moral dilemma allegedly afflicting the Green conscience: a "genuine conflict of basic values". On the one hand, "non-violence"; on the other, the need to help people survive. Over several years, Fischer developed variations on this theme of a dilemma between "values". In a sharper version, the value of "non-violence", or "pacifism", was pitted against the need to "combat Auschwitz", or "genocide", posited as a special German obligation.

This supposed "value dilemma" enabled Fischer to abandon his original position that the Germans of all people should stay out of a country they had devastated half a century earlier. Ironically, this triumph of *realpolitik* allowing Germany to become a "normal" military power again was accomplished by ignoring realistic questions in the name of purely idealistic, abstract weighing of "values". Realistically, one could have asked whether air power was the most appropriate means of "saving women and children", and if it were, why it must be German air power; how the uncertain military results compared to the negative psychological results of sending German war planes back to Yugoslav skies; and above all, whether this was merely a first public relations step toward the remilitarization of German foreign policy. Instead of centering on such questions, the debate on Yugoslavia became a matter of *German conscience* first and foremost, encouraging self-absorbed moralistic poses favored by self-styled "realists". Together, Cohn-Bendit and Fischer had succeeded in playing the role of pied pipers of Frankfurt, leading the Green children over the brink into support of German participation in NATO's war against the Serbs.

The ideological domination of this moralistic approach was

achieved by constant analogy with "Auschwitz" and "the Holocaust", equating the Serbs with the Nazis. In a heady mood of self-righteous indignation, German politicians across the board joined in using Germany's past guilt as a reason, not for restraint, but for "bearing their share of the military burden". In the name of human rights, the Federal Republic lifted its ban on military operations outside the NATO defensive area. Germany could once again be a "normal" military power – thanks to the "Serb threat".

What occurred in Germany was a strange sort of mass transfer of Nazi identity, and guilt, to the Serbs. Perhaps this provided the Germans with a comforting sense of relief to be innocent, and even heroes, faced with a new "criminal" people, the Serbs. Condemning "Serb genocide" seemed to provide the psychological key to overcoming Germany's Nazi past in order to become a "normal" Great Power again, able to project military power abroad.

In the final analysis, the "realism" of the *Realos* applied primarily to their own political careers. With every move toward endorsement of out-of-area military intervention, the Green Party lost more supporters, but Joschka moved closer to the big job. From self-taught revolutionary street fighter to foreign minister of Europe's most powerful nation – this was an amazing success story. Strangely enough, the appointment of this upstart, who in the 1970s had hung around with the ultra-leftists who bombed the U.S. army headquarters in Frankfurt, aroused not the slightest qualm in Washington, usually deeply suspicious of far more respectable European leftists. Even before Fischer took office, Richard Holbrooke had predicted that the formerly Red, then Green firebrand would make "a great foreign minister". Somehow or other, in spite of – or perhaps, in some way that is still obscure, because of – a past that could normally be used against him, Fischer had managed to reassure the kingmakers in Germany and Washington that here was a man they could trust.

Within less than a decade, "sending out peace from German soil" turned out to mean "sending out peace-keepers", which in turn meant sending out war planes and *Luftwaffe* bombing raids in order to prepare the terrain to receive the peace-keepers, who turned out to be German soldiers who, in their very first days in Kosovo, became heroes to their comrades when they shot and killed a few Serbs. The Germans' arrival in Kosovo in 1999 was reminiscent of the time when the *Wehrmacht* and SS had helped Albanian fascists extend their "Greater Albania" to Kosovo by driving out Serb civilians. In October 1999, *Der Spiegel* reported that "The Germans were received as old friends. Children enthusiastically extended their arms in the Hitler 'Heil' greeting. And old men recollected the common Indo-Germanic roots and shouted in a brotherly manner, 'We are all Aryans!' The Albanian soldiers, now 32,000 of them, all want to become like the spiffy Germans."[46]

Far from being embarrassed by this echo of a not so distant past, many Germans reveled in it. Returning from his visit to German troops in Kosovo, Chancellor Schröder declared: "It is already impressive and moved me deeply, when in Prizren I saw on the one hand German tanks and German soldiers with machine guns, and on the other hand I could share the experience of the extraordinary euphoric jubilation with which a German Chancellor was welcomed. I find that in the context of the specific German history in this region, really anyone must be moved by this."[47]

This is an astonishing statement, although whether for its ignorance or its cynicism is hard to decide. It would seem at first glance that Schröder was moved because, knowing that Nazi Germany had brutally occupied Yugoslavia during World War II, he interpreted the enthusiasm in Prizren as a sign of forgiveness by former victims and welcome to the "new" Germany. But is it credible that the German Chancellor, however ignorant of history, was not informed by his advisors of the fact that the enthusiasm came from the same Albanians, or their descendants, whose terror against Serbian inhabitants was encouraged by the Nazi occupiers? Was the Chancellor ignorant, or was he counting on the ignorance of his compatriots? Or was this a deliberate amnesia affecting a whole new generation?

In January 2002, after early resignations of the Frenchman Bernard Kouchner followed by the Dane, Hans Haekkerup, the post of UN administrator of the Kosovo protectorate went to a German, Michael Steiner, Chancellor Schröder's former foreign policy advisor. Many things had changed in 50 years, not least the fact that Germany and the United States were now on the same side.

2. RECLAIMING THE HABSBURG HERITAGE

For over 1,000 years, the political pattern that dominated Germany was the Holy Roman Empire. Today, many Germans consider they have rejected the nation-state in favor of regionalism and European federalism as a form of national modesty and proof that they have abandoned the aggressive nationalism of Hitler. However, this preference echoes the old imperial pattern of an ethnically variegated Europe ruled from a German imperial center. Such an idea continues to enjoy active support from a class of wealthy and well-connected Europeans unknown to most of the public, except through the glossy picture magazines found in waiting rooms: the European royal families, overwhelmingly German in origin. Of all these families, the most devoted to shaping the future of Europe is the most illustrious of all, the Habsburg dynasty. After centuries of ruling the Holy Roman Empire, Spain, and Flanders, the Habsburgs were forced into exile by the dismantling of the Austro-Hungarian Empire at the end of World War I. But in a period of historical defeat and confusion on the left, nobody can rule out the possibility that the fragmentation of East-Central Europe into patriarchal folk-states may prepare the ground for a return of the traditional political summit of patriarchal society: monarchy.

To much of the public, especially in the United States, the Habsburg Empire is a phantom from history. In reality, the Habsburg dynasty lives on, vigorously adapting to the opportunities of a changing Europe, under the leadership of the heir to the abolished throne of the Austro-Hungarian Empire, Otto von Habsburg, born in 1912. The uncrowned emperor is arguably the most able individual ever produced by the Habsburg family as well as the most effective prince of twentieth-century Europe. With none of the restraints of a reigning constitutional monarch, but all the vast network of relationships afforded by his rank as head of Europe's most durably successful royal family, he has exercised a discreet influence on events perhaps greater than that of today's reigning royals.[48] For Yugoslavia, and in particular for the Serbs, he has proved a tenacious and skillful adversary.

Von Habsburg found a congenial political haven near his native Austria in the highly conservative state of Bavaria, long ruled by his close friend, the late Franz-Josef Strauss, who as minister-president of Bavaria was the uncontested leader of the most conservative sector of the German right. As plain Otto Habsburg, he was elected to the European Parliament in 1979 on the list of the Strauss's Christian Social Party (CSU). Highly intelligent, fluent in several languages, elegant and hard-working, von Habsburg has been described as "the most influential authority on all problems of foreign policy in that young institution".[49] In particular, throughout the crisis in Yugoslavia, von Habsburg was the most influential single member of the European Parliament when it came to interpreting events in southeastern Europe. Unconcerned at the possible bias or dynastic projects of the deposed heir to the Austro-Hungarian Empire, the European Parliament named von Habsburg as its *rapporteur* on relations with Hungary and, subsequently, as chairman of the joint parliamentary commission with Hungary.

"If Germany recognized Slovenia and Croatia so rapidly," von Habsburg recalled later, "even against the will of Hans-Dietrich Genscher who did not want to take that step, it's because the Bonn government was subjected to an almost irresistible pressure of public opinion. In this regard, the German press rendered a very great service, in particular the *Frankfurter Allgemeine Zeitung* and Carl Gustav Ströhm, that great German journalist who works for *Die Welt*."[50] This suggests that von Habsburg had more to do with making Germany's foreign policy than Genscher, since he could be counted among those who created that "public opinion". In January 1988, von Habsburg had invited spokesmen for Slovenian, Croatian, and Albanian national viewpoints to testify at European Parliament hearings in Strasbourg on the crisis in Yugoslavia. A frequent contributor to debates in the European Parliament as well as to various journals, von Habsburg consistently promoted a version of the Yugoslav crisis as a characteristic aggression by Serb barbarians against the Croats, representatives of Western civilization. To defend Croatian secession in 1991, he repeatedly described the Croats as "a civilized part of Europe, who have nothing in common with Serb primitivism". This was the favorite theme of Croatian nationalists, who in the 1990s were still cornering Germans at press gatherings to impress on them the unique "Aryan" origins of the Croats, in contrast to the "oriental" Serbs.[51] In his regular column in Spanish, von Habsburg drew a precise geographic line separating Croatian civilization from Balkan barbarism. It is "totally clear", he wrote, that "the frontier between the Balkans and the West runs to the east of Croatia and Bosnia".[52]

During World War II, Otto von Habsburg took refuge in the United States where he cooperated with U.S. intelligence. From the 1950s on he worked tirelessly to oppose the Soviet Bloc. As president of the Pan-European Union, a right-wing European federalist organization close to the Catholic Church, von Habsburg has long advocated eastward expansion of the European Community up to, but not including, Orthodox Christian Russia. In Bavaria, he cooperated with the powerful association of Germans expelled from

Czechoslovakia after World War II, notably in backing various regionalist initiatives that helped revive the concept of a *Mitteleuropa* largely coinciding with the former territories of the Austro-Hungarian Empire.

Otto's marriage to Regina von Saxe-Meiningen produced two sons and five daughters, prepared to ensure the ongoing influence of the dynasty. In Belgium, where he has many supporters, Princess Astrid is married to a Habsburg. Otto's eldest son, Karl, was elected to the European Parliament in 1996 as an independent in second place on the list of the conservative Austrian People's Party (a public dispute ensued as to whether or not he had unsuccessfully sought nomination on the list of Jörg Haider's Freedom Party). Active in his father's Pan-European Union, president of *Alpen-Adria Arbeitkreis*, the young Archduke envisages the European Union primarily as a "security community" that will extend to the Russian border.[53] Before being elected to the European Parliament, he had worked there as a technical advisor on the question of special rights for national minorities (*Volksgruppenrecht*). In 1993, Karl married Baroness Francesca Thyssen-Bornemisza, daughter of the billionaire steel magnate.

On 20 September 1997, in Zagreb Cathedral, Cardinal Franjo Kuharić, primate of Croatia, baptised the couple's three-month-old son his Imperial and Royal Highness the Archduke Ferdinand Zvonimir. The name Zvonimir was explained as "an homage to the Croatian people"; it is the name of the monarch who unified the country in the eleventh century. With such a name, the infant is on his way to qualify as King of Croatia, should the job ever be open. The Archduchess Francesca explained that they had chosen to celebrate the baptism in Zagreb because the couple had met there in October 1991. "Since our marriage, we have both worked for this country – for my part through my foundation for the preservation of its artistic heritage, and Karl in the European Parliament in order to facilitate Croatia's integration into the EEC."[54]

Otto's second son, Georg, took up residence in Budapest in 1993, obtained Hungarian citizenship as György, and says he looks forward to representing Hungary in the European Parliament once that country in turn joins the European Union. Meanwhile, the young Habsburg sits on the board of the National Museum (site of his royal wedding reception) and directs programming for a popular Hungarian radio station.

Between Karl, György, and Zvonimir, three former Habsburg lands
– Austria, Hungary, and Croatia – can easily be equipped with princes,
on the offchance that future political stalemate provides the sort
of opportunity that led to the successful restoration of Juan Carlos
to the Spanish throne. Unlikely as it seems, a European swing to
the right might offer surprising opportunities for an enterprising
imperial family business.

The disintegration of Yugoslavia was encouraging to this
hypothetical restoration in a number of ways. By confirming the
notion that Yugoslavia was not viable, it tended to credit the idea
that the Serbs were to blame for World War I and that the forced
abdication of the Habsburgs was a tragic historical error. The
detachment of Croatia created a conservative Catholic state with
strong royalist currents linked to nostalgia for the medieval Croatian
kingdom. Since devotion to the Habsburgs is part of the Croatian
conservative tradition, a restoration of Habsburg rule is more
probable there than in any other part of what was once the Austro-
Hungarian Empire. In a more general way, the death of Yugoslavia
brought a reversion to the type of deeply conservative ethnic
consciousness favorable to paternalistic monarchy.

Between the Vatican and the Comintern

The Yugoslav Kingdom of the Serbs, Croats, and Slovenians, which
emerged from World War I, was surrounded by powerful enemies.
Hungary and Austria had fallen from their imperial status to the
condition of small countries that hoped to regain territory they
had lost to the succession states. Italian nationalists were furious
at losing Adriatic coastal areas, secretly promised by the Western
allies, who later reneged.

Another formidable enemy was the Vatican. The fall of the
Habsburg Empire was perceived as a calamity by the Catholic Church,
which deplored the spectacle of Catholic lands falling under the
rule of an Orthodox Christian king. The Vatican's militant thrust
against the Orthodox "schismatics" found a natural ally in the
Habsburg monarchy's own *Drang nach Osten*. The coordination was
such that for a long time the Vatican shared the Austrian Embassy
in many capitals.

The initial reaction of the Vatican was to treat the Kingdom of
the Serbs, Croats, and Slovenes as temporary and to continue to
organize the Catholic Church as if the Habsburg Empire still
existed. Thus the Vatican refused to alter the territories of Catholic

bishoprics to fit the new national boundaries. The old dioceses of the Habsburg era were retained intact. Knin in Croatia continued to depend on Kalocsa in Hungary, and the church in the Slovenian capital of Ljubljana was dependent on the diocese of Gorizia in Italy. Moreover, the Vatican continued to retain German, Hungarian, or Italian bishops rather than name Slavic (Croatian or Slovenian) prelates, preferred to recruit members of international orders rather than local Slavs for the lower clergy, and kept the Institute of Saint Jerome, the main theological foundation in Rome for training Yugoslav clergy, under the control of Italian clergy hostile to the very existence of Yugoslavia and favorable to Italian takeover of the Yugoslav Adriatic coast.[55] As of 1920, the only Catholic bishop who was not attached to the territory of Austro-Hungary was Monseigneur Miedia, bishop of Skopje, an Austrian-educated Albanian who continued to offer prayers for the deposed Habsburg emperor and blocked Belgrade's efforts to provide financial aid to Albanian Catholics. As for Bosnia, the choice of Johannes Šarić, leader of the most extreme anti-Serb current, as bishop of Sarajevo was a virtual "declaration of war" against the Orthodox and designed to foster antagonism between Serbs and Croats, the better to destroy Yugoslavia and allow reconstitution of the Habsburg Empire.[56]

There was a division in the Catholic Church between the prelates and the poor local priests, who, influenced by the example of their Serbian Orthodox counterparts, were calling for liberal reforms to benefit local parishes and the lower clergy.[57] In response, the Vatican recruited more compliant members of the Franciscan Order to take over local clerical duties in Yugoslavia.

For over a decade, the Vatican refused to respond to Belgrade's overtures to extend to Yugoslavia the Concordat it had signed with Serbia on the eve of war in 1914. The Orthodox Serb King Alexander was eager to make whatever concessions were necessary to placate his restive Croatian subjects and get the Vatican to accept Yugoslavia. Finally, Belgrade entrusted negotiations with the Vatican to Catholics, who brought back a Concordat granting the Catholic Church complete economic autonomy, exemption from agrarian reform, special ecclesiastic tribunals for clergy, and religious education for Catholic pupils in public schools. But when these concessions were disclosed in 1936, the Orthodox clergy interpreted the accord as an invitation to the Catholic Church to treat Yugoslavia as a missionary territory and threatened to excommunicate parliamentarians who voted for ratification. In July 1937, street demonstrations against the Concordat were brutally repressed by the police under the command of the powerful interior minister, Monseigneur Anton Korošec, a Slovenian Catholic clergyman.[58] The project was abandoned. Two decades of Vatican challenge to the very existence of multicultural Yugoslavia set the stage for the otherwise inexplicable participation of the Catholic clergy, notably Franciscans, in the Ustashe campaign to rid Croatia of Orthodox Serbs.

The attitude toward Yugoslavia was no friendlier at the other end of the ideological spectrum, in the international communist movement. After the 1917 revolution, a number of anti-communist Russian Orthodox clergy emigrated to Yugoslavia and found refuge in the Serbian Orthodox Church. Moscow considered Belgrade a haven for counter-revolutionaries as well as a pawn of British and French imperialism. Yugoslavia was part of the "cordon sanitaire" isolating the Soviet Union. The weakness of the industrial working class made proletarian revolution or even agitation an unlikely means to break up the country, but nationalism could be a potent force. In the 1920s, the Communist International branded Yugoslavia a "prison of peoples" (the same label earlier applied to the Austro-Hungarian Empire) and encouraged all the country's "oppressed peoples" to struggle against the "Serbian bourgeoisie". The so-called "Serbian bourgeoisie", made up of fairly small-scale merchants, army officers, government functionaries, and intellectuals, had little in common with the powerful bourgeoisies of the major imperialist countries which, incidentally, controlled most of the major assets of the Yugoslav economy.[59] While the Serbs indeed made up the bulk of civil servants, top positions were distributed to non-Serbs, broad autonomy was granted the Croats, and the economy continued to be far more developed in Slovenia and Croatia than in the rest of Yugoslavia. Serbia remained economically under-developed between the two world wars. The distinction between "oppressed" and "oppressor" peoples, drawn by Lenin to distinguish between the European imperialist nations and their overseas colonies, as applied to Yugoslavia, served only to blur class distinctions and exacerbate ethnic conflict.

After World War II, in a totally different context, Tito's Yugoslavia again found itself between a hostile Vatican and a hostile Soviet bloc, but managed to draw advantages from the Non-Aligned Movement and the opportunities afforded by the Cold War to use adversaries in one bloc to gain support from the other. The end of the Cold War removed such possibilities. With a virtual vacuum to the East, Yugoslavia was still confronted with powerful enemies in the West. When the Federal Republic of Germany defied European objections to back Slovenian and Croatian secession, it was immediately joined by the Vatican (and by the right wing of the Austrian coalition government). The strongest impetus for this policy came from traditional forces in German Catholicism, which is particularly strong in Bavaria, whose wealth and influence played the key role in ensuring the election of Karol Wojtyla as Pope John Paul II. The Polish pope was the ideal figure to lead the successful ideological crusade against communist rule in East-Central Europe. The reunification of Germany in the form of a takeover of the Democratic Republic by the Federal Republic marked the victory of this strategy. With the collapse of the Warsaw Pact, the Catholic lands of Central Europe moved clearly into the German sphere of influence. The only remaining exceptions were the Catholic parts of Yugoslavia. Many Yugoslavs considered themselves far ahead of the Soviet Bloc, and therefore scarcely affected by the changes there. But from the viewpoint of the Catholic German rollback, Yugoslavia was not ahead but behind, a bit of unfinished business.

5 The New Imperial Model

1. ALBANIANS: A PEOPLE IN SEARCH OF AN EMPIRE

Albanians have inhabited the Western Balkans since time immemorial, without organizing an Albanian state until less than a century ago. Calling themselves "Shqiptars", they were distinguished from their neighbors by language and customs. Their distinctive language is divided into two main dialects, the Gheg in the north and the Tosk in the south. Especially in the northern mountainous areas of Albania and in Kosovo, Albanian clans have continued to live according to their own orally transmitted code, the *Kanun*. The *Kanun* sets out elaborate rules concerning such matters as hospitality, marriage, and revenge, designed to preserve the honor of the "blood", the paternal family line. If an Albanian is killed, deliberately or accidentally, by another, the lost "blood" must be paid by another "blood". The male members of the victim's family are under obligation to kill the person responsible, or any male member of his family. To escape revenge, the men in a family caught in a blood feud may remain housebound for years, while their women carry out the tasks necessary for survival. This custom is reflected in the form of the typical Albanian rural home – a wall-enclosed compound, which can serve as a defensive fortress.[1]

Although Albanian Christian knights fought alongside Serbs against the Turks at the famous battle of Kosovo in 1389, under Turkish rule the majority gradually converted to Islam. A Catholic minority remained in the north and an Orthodox minority in the south. After Serbs sided with the Habsburgs in their seventeenth-century wars against the Ottoman Empire, the Turks turned to Albanian converts to Islam to suppress the Serbs in Kosovo. From then on, the Albanians became the fiercest oppressors of the Christian *Rayah*. The attitude of the Albanians toward religion has often been characterized as both flexible and credulous. According to the Albanian Orthodox Christian bishop Fan Noli, "the Albanian is heathen and honors every God whose name he ever heard".[2] Muslim Albanians have tended toward a mystical and pantheistic version of Islam, the Dervish order of the Bektashis. An oft-quoted statement dating back to the late nineteenth century claimed that "The religion of the Albanians is Albanianism".[3]

Be that as it may, since Albanian Muslims in Kosovo enjoyed privileges due to their religion, they fiercely defended both. At a time when both Balkan Christian and Arab Muslim peoples were inspired by revolutionary ideas to free themselves from the Ottomans, the vast majority of Albanians remained under the domination of feudal chieftains, keen to preserve the privileges they had gained under Turkish rule by converting to Islam. The Albanian *pashas* did not want a modern state. They wanted to continue to run things their own way, according to their own ancient traditions.

The predominantly Albanian town of Prizren in southwestern Kosovo was the site chosen by some 300 Albanian Muslim leaders to meet on the eve of the June 1878 Congress of Berlin where the Great Powers decided the future of the Balkans. Prizren then had the reputation of being the "most dangerous spot" in the whole Muslim world for a Christian, a town where Islamic zealots were "actively encouraging a policy akin to ethnic cleansing".[4] The newly formed "Prizren League" called for the preservation of Ottoman rule and of Islam. This made a negative impression in Berlin, although for the moment, the Great Powers left most of the southern Balkans, including present-day Albania, Kosovo, and Macedonia, under Ottoman rule.

It was only as they saw that the Turks were no longer determined to preserve the old order that the Prizren League tried to expel them and take over. Armed rebellion erupted over efforts of Ottoman rulers to modernize fiscal policy. Albanians were enraged at being ordered to pay taxes, like the Christian *Rayah*.[5] In the years that followed, the Turks never succeeded in restoring order, least of all in protecting Serb peasants from robbery, harassment, and intimidation.[6]

The fact that toward the end of the Ottoman Empire the Albanian leadership had more to lose than to gain from the creation of new modern states, whereas the Serbs had everything to gain and little to lose, confirmed the deep cleavage between the two communities. After the collapse of the Ottoman Empire, Albanian leaders looked to whatever alternative empire they might serve in return for being left alone to pursue their ancient ways, rather than be obliged to reach accommodation with their nearest neighbors. This has made them attractive clients for empires attempting to gain a foothold in the Balkans by using the classic methods of divide and rule.

The crowded "cradle of civilization"

In October 1912, the Balkan League of Orthodox Christian nations went to war in the final drive to end Ottoman rule. As Turkish rule crumbled, Ismail Kemal, a prominent Albanian statesman who had served the Sultan in Istanbul, returned to the Albanian port of Vlora and, on 28 November 1912, encouraged by Austria, proclaimed: "From today on Albania is free and independent." Less than a week later, on 3 December, Turkey capitulated. Kosovo was triumphantly occupied by Serbs, exalted by the recovery of what they called "Old Serbia".

Decades later, the agreement of the Great Powers to allow Serbia to incorporate Kosovo into its own territory was portrayed by Albanian nationalists as an enormous injustice. However, at the time, there was no viable alternative. Despite the Vlora declaration, there was no coherent national movement that could claim to represent the core of a representative Albanian state. There was an ill-defined "Albania", in the sense of a region known to be populated by people speaking the Albanian language, and a Great Power meeting in London in December 1912 agreed that an "Albania" should be recognized among the successors to the Ottoman Empire. On 29 July 1913, the Great Powers (Austria-Hungary, France, Britain, Russia, Germany, and Italy) officially recognized independent Albania. But the country had no clearly defined borders, proper roads, currency, industry, hospitals, or schools. At least seven local "governments" vied for power. The main rivals were Ismail Kemal, supported by Austria, and Essad Pasha Toptani, a Muslim feudal landlord who was supported by Serbia. Unable to impose order, Kemal asked the Great Powers to send in a German prince. The European powers sent a German general staff officer, Wilhelm von Wied, who as a Protestant was supposed to deal even-handedly with Catholics, Muslims, and Orthodox. Von Wied arrived in Durrës in March 1914 to endure six months of endless intrigue and deception before being obliged to return home. During World War I, Albania was once again plunged into civil war, anarchy, and foreign invasion. With the defeat of Austria, Italy was in the strongest position to take control of Albania, judged by the Great Powers to be unprepared for self-government. Allied with Essad Pasha Toptani until his assassination in Paris in June 1920, the Belgrade government did what it could to champion an independent Albania in opposition to Italy. Italy in turn sought to gain support among Albanians by advocating a "Greater Albania", including Kosovo and other parts of Serbia. After a brief and turbulent period of semi-independence, Albania was taken over by Fascist Italy, which went on to carve "Greater Albania" out of Yugoslav territory.[7]

The victorious Serbs who recovered "the cradle of their civilization" in Kosovo in 1912 considered that they were rescuing their people from brutal and lawless oppressors. Serb forces were ruthless in their annihilation of Albanian "bandits".[8] From the Albanian viewpoint, the Serbs were occupying the cradle of the Prizren League and of their own national movement. Each population was largely convinced that the other had "stolen" Kosovo. Monuments of the past were unquestionably Serbian, but by 1912 the Albanians were the most numerous group in a mixed population, including not only Orthodox Serbs and Montenegrins, but also a large number of Serbian Muslims (notably the Gorani in the mountainous southernmost tip of Kosovo), Turks, Gypsies, and even some Circassians brought in by the Turks. The dispute over exactly how many of the population were Albanian and how many Serb is endless, since the old censuses were counted by families, or family heads, and were quite unreliable. There were no doubt more Albanians than the Serbs cared to acknowledge, and more Serbs than the Albanians now recognize. By the same token, each side has remembered being massacred by the other, but forgotten times when it was the other way around.

Even the name of the region is disputed. For the Serbs, it was "Old Serbia". The term "Kosovo", meaning "of the blackbirds" in Serbian, is short for "Kosovo Polje", "the field of blackbirds", scene of the famous 1389 battle. The Albanians spell it "Kosova", which means nothing in Albanian, or use other terms of their own. The official Yugoslav name is Kosovo-Metohija, the second term coming from the Greek and designating the Orthodox Church domains in the western area close to Montenegro.

In the first Yugoslavia, Belgrade undertook an ambiguous land reform and colonization program in Kosovo-Metohija, which aimed at dispossessing large landholders in favor of smaller ones, as well as enabling poor peasants from rocky stretches of the Krajina and Montenegro to settle on vacant land in Kosovo. This combined agrarian reform with an effort to redress the population balance. Some Serb families who had fled Kosovo were able to return.

The "pacification" of Kosovo carried out by Belgrade did not shock the sensibilities of Western Europeans who in those days were still ready to employ whatever means were necessary to pacify their own colonial empires. In contrast, the Serbs did not cross oceans to conquer foreign lands. They were liberating the traditional heartland of their nation, still inhabited by Serb peasants who had been oppressed by Albanians. Ironically, Serbia's role in Kosovo probably benefited in the first half of the century from being likened to European colonialism, even to Zionism, just as it suffered from the comparison toward the end of the century, when attitudes had changed. But attitudes had changed among Serbs as well, and neither the majority nor the official view in 1990 was represented by a proposal written in 1937 by a prominent Belgrade intellectual, Vaso Čubrilović. Yet this proposal was repeatedly cited in the 1990s as the proof of the unbroken continuity of Serbian "ethnic cleansing".[9] Writing at a time when Yugoslavia felt threatened by the rise of Nazism, Čubrilović observed:

We have had no success to speak of in assimilating the Albanians into our nation. On the contrary, because they are based in Albania, their national awareness is awakened and if we do not settle accounts with them at the proper time, within 20 to 30 years we shall have to cope with a terrible irredentism, signs of which are already apparent and which will inevitably put all our southern territories in jeopardy.

Čubrilović concluded:

we have only one course to follow: that of their mass resettlement. In this case we must consider two states: Albania and Turkey. With its sparse population, its many undrained swamps and uncultivated river valleys, Albania would be in a position to admit some hundred thousand Albanians from our country. With its large uninhabited and uncultivated territories in Asia minor and Kurdistan, modern Turkey has almost boundless possibilities for internal colonisation.

The proposal was far less shocking in 1937 than it seems now because of the proximity in time to other population transfers that accompanied the reorganization of the Balkans following the demise of the Ottoman Empire. The greatest of these had occurred only 14 years earlier, following a long series of massacres in Asia Minor and the end of Greek hopes to recover Greek-populated territories there. In January 1923, an agreement signed in Lausanne between Greece and Turkey obliged 1,300,000 Greeks to abandon their age-old homes in Asia Minor and move to Greece itself, while in exchange 400,000 Turks moved in the other direction. This dramatic population exchange was designed to end Greek claims to Asia Minor and Turkish claims to Greek territory. It is not so surprising that a Serb nationalist envisaged a similar solution, on a much smaller scale, to end Albanian claims to Kosovo. In his policy paper, Čubrilović referred directly to the Turkish transfer:

> But in spite of all of Kemal Ataturk's efforts, the Turks have still not filled the vacuum left by the transfer of the Asia minor Greeks to Greece and of a part of the Kurds to Persia. That is why Turkey offers the greatest possibilities for taking in most of our transplanted Albanians.

Indeed, an agreement for the resettlement of some 200,000 ethnic Albanians, Turks, and Muslims was reached in 1938 between Belgrade and Turkey, which was eager to repopulate areas of Anatolia emptied by the Greek exodus and various previous massacres. World War II prevented the plan from being carried out.

Čubrilović was thinking primarily in strategic terms and saw future Albanian irredentism (whose rise he foresaw) as a threat to the viability of the Yugoslav state. This was cold *realpolitik* rather than emotional racism. The goal was not an "ethnically pure" Serbian Kosovo. Čubrilović recommended encouraging the emigration to Kosovo of ethnic Hungarians and Germans from Voivodina, partly because being "more advanced and having a higher cultural level than ours, they will provide examples for rational cultivation of the land". Showing an unembarrassed understanding of the way state power can work, Čubrilović recommended bribing Tirana politicians to get their consent, instructing the Yugoslav media to exalt the beauty of the Turkish countryside so as to inspire Albanians to move there, and finally, creating the "appropriate psychosis" among the Albanians by various forms of harassment, including fining people for failing to leash their dogs, banning polygamy, "and especially in pitilessly applying the law for obligatory enrollment of girls in primary school". Finally, violent treatment from poor Montenegrin immigrants, whose rough customs were similar to those of the Albanians, would help persuade Albanians to leave Kosovo, he suggested.

Those who cite Čubrilović fail to point out that his proposal was not a description of official Yugoslav policy, but on the contrary was part of a sharp criticism of the policy actually pursued by the Belgrade government. This is obvious from the text itself, which provides instructive comments on the Balkan context:

> The fundamental error of the authorities in this period was that, forgetting where they were, that is in the troubled and bloody Balkans, they sought to resolve major ethnic questions by means of Western methods. Turkey brought into the Balkans the custom borrowed from the Sharia by which victory in war and conquest of a country confers the right over the life and property of the defeated populations. The Christians of the Balkans also learned from the Turks that not only power and domination but also a house and belongings are won or lost by the sword ... Without having to go back very far in time, we'll only mention some recent cases: the transfer of the Greeks of Asia minor to Greece and that of the Turks of Greece to Asia minor, as well as the latest transfer of the Turks of Bulgaria and of Rumania to Turkey. While all the Balkan countries since 1912 have resolved or are resolving the question of their national minorities by population transfers, for our part we are still using the slow or clumsy methods of gradual colonization whose results have been negative ... Statistical data show that in these regions, the natural growth of the Albanian population is greater than ours ...

Čubrilović went on to complain that the government had left "the best land in the hands of the Albanians" and had granted certificates of ownership to Albanians who never had title to the property they had usurped in Turkish times. Altogether it is clear from Čubrilović's own words that the Belgrade government's policy, in contrast to the one he advocated, represented an effort, new and rare in the Balkans, to conform to Western European standards.

Much more attention has been given to Čubrilović's dead letter proposal than to the very real violence exercised for generations against Kosovo Serbs to abandon their land to Albanians, notably to newcomers. When, in September 1943, the Nazi occupation army took over from Italy and gave free rein to Albanian nationalist violence, Serb and Montenegrin settlers were driven out of Kosovo. As the war drew to an end, in an effort to appease the Albanians, Tito's partisans issued decrees banning expelled Serb and Montenegrin settlers from returning to Kosovo.[10] This prevented some 60,000 Serbs from recovering their homesteads.[11]

Problems of education, language, and truth

For Tito, an "Albanian" Kosovo was initially perceived as an asset toward incorporating Albania itself into Yugoslavia on the way to creation of a broader Balkan federation (an ambition rapidly quashed by Moscow). In communist Yugoslavia, the different national characteristics of the population, including the Albanians, were celebrated rather than repressed. In general, the communist approach to ethnic conflict was scarcely different from that of development liberals in the capitalist world: give people economic progress and a higher standard of living, let them express their cultural peculiarities, and traditional enmities will gradually vanish. The communist government brought in electrification, paved roads, and built sewage systems which had never existed before in Kosovo. The Albanians fully enjoyed whatever political rights there were in the communist system, through representation in the ruling Communist Party of Kosovo. Development aid poured in.

However, the birthrate among Kosovo Albanians – Europe's highest by far – kept per capita income low.[12] The Albanian population kept growing by leaps and bounds, nearly doubling in the 20 years between 1960 and 1980, with its percentage rising from roughly two-thirds in 1961 to a claimed, but unverified, 90 per cent in the 1990s.[13] This demographic explosion contributed to incurable mass unemployment and to suspicion on the part of the Serbs that the Albanians were secretly pouring into the country from neighboring Albania, and that the baby boom was part of a policy designed by clan leaders to strengthen Albanian claims to the province by a demographic flood.[14] Such suspicions, readily condemned by outsiders as racist, were fed by the subservient role of women in Albanian society and by Albanians' capacity to act in unison following decisions of clan leaders – for instance, to boycott the census, claiming that it would undercount them. It was clearly part of the Albanian nationalist agenda to appear as numerous as possible.

Modern nations have usually been built around a single "official" language, sometimes largely invented for the purpose. The Turks notoriously ban languages, such as Kurdish, that could threaten the unity of the state. There was no schooling in Albanian while the Albanians were still within the confines of the Ottoman Empire. A first Albanian school was founded in Prizren in 1889, but in 1902 the Turkish authorities explicitly banned Albanian schools, Albanian books, and the use of the Albanian language even in private correspondence. Until the twentieth century, Albanian was essentially an oral, vernacular language. The Albanian elite were literate in other languages, notably Turkish. Nineteenth-century attempts to establish a standard written Albanian language were torn between the Latin, Arabic, Greek, and Cyrillic alphabets. In early 1912, on the eve of the first Balkan war, the Serbian government attempted to accommodate Albanian leaders in Kosovo by offering an accord guaranteeing freedom of religion, use of the Albanian language in schools and courts, and a separate Albanian assembly to legislate for the Albanian community.[15] The Albanian leaders rejected any such agreement. In 1912, there was no tradition of schooling in the Albanian language, whether in Kosovo or in Albania itself. The Albanian literary language, with a common Latin alphabet, was first standardized by a commission set up by the Austro-Hungarian government during its military occupation of northern Albania in 1916, as part of Vienna's promotion of Albanian nationalism in order to weaken Serbia.[16]

The poverty of the Albanian population in Kosovo in the twentieth century, in relation to the Serb population, was initially not to be measured in material wealth but in education. "The Albanian villages are much better, much richer than the Serbian ones", Leon Trotsky observed.[17] This was not surprising considering the relative status of the two communities under Turkish rule. Attached to their past way of life, the Albanians fell behind the Serbs in acquisition of modern skills and education. Albanian girls were kept out of school, contributing to a persistently high rate of illiteracy. Insofar as Albanians have been an oppressed population, they have been oppressed to a very large extent by their rigid patriarchal social system. This in turn put them at a disadvantage in relation to other national groups in Yugoslavia as education became the primary means of social advancement.

Immediately after World War II, in an effort to raise literacy levels, the communists opened schools for Albanian children and for adults. Despite a severe shortage of teachers able to provide instruction in Albanian, serious efforts were made to educate the Albanians of Kosovo, including girls and women, in their own language.[18] Education and economic development were expected to integrate Albanians into a modern progressive, multi-national society.

So what went wrong?

In reality, educating Albanians in their own language aggravated their cultural isolation and self-absorption. Since written Albanian was a relatively new language, there were no great libraries in the Albanian language treating all the various subjects required for a full modern education. Schooling in Serbian offered broader cultural resources, notably access to the modern scientific and technical culture greatly prized by the Serbs.

In November 1968, Albanian nationalism re-emerged when several hundred people demonstrated in Priština, chanting slogans in favor of Enver Hoxha's Albania. After violent police repression, concessions were made. In 1969 the University of Priština, until then a small provincial branch of the University of Belgrade, was converted into an independent university offering courses in Albanian as well as in Serbo-Croat. The most significant step came in 1970, when an agreement was signed with Tirana to import textbooks as well as over 200 teachers from Albania itself to set up courses in the Albanian language. This meant importing the peculiar worldview of Hoxha's isolated Albania. Another problem was that the official language of Albania was based on the southern Tosk dialect, mother tongue of Enver Hoxha, whereas the Albanian spoken in Kosovo was the northern Gheg dialect. This deepened the gap between Kosovo's Albanians and non-Albanians who had learned to speak Gheg with their neighbors, but had trouble understanding the Tosk-based standard language of Albania. The complaint was heard that Kosovo's Shqiptars were being "turned into Albanians".[19] The difference in dialect also contributed to a great imbalance between educated and uneducated Kosovo Albanians, noted by Arshi Pipa: on the one hand, the intelligentsia, "and on the other hand, you have just ignorance and illiteracy. And with ignorance comes fanaticism."[20]

In 1968, in an odd concession to Albanian nationalism, the Tito government banned use of the word Šiptar, the Serbo-Croatian version of Shqiptar, the name that the Albanians use for themselves. Claiming the term was pejorative, the authorities decreed that the proper term must be "Albanac" or Albanian. By outlawing the customary name, which nevertheless continued to be used by everyone, Albanians and Serbs, in private conversation, it became difficult to distinguish between citizens of Albania and ethnic Albanians in Kosovo. Subsequently, the insistence on being called "Kosovars" helped give the world the impression that the Shqiptars/Albanians were the only genuine inhabitants of Kosovo, just as calling Muslims "Bosniaks" or Bosnians suggested that Serbs and Croats were intruders in Bosnia.

Assuming that the Yugoslav authorities did not intend to prepare Kosovo Albanians for secession, which is a reasonable assumption, turning over responsibility for courses at Priština University to teachers from Tirana was a serious mistake. "An attempt by Albania to englobe Kosova would be a suicidal act, Albania's strategy has therefore taken the form of cultural politics, consisting of disseminating its ideology among the Kosovars. This has been done through cultural exchange, by exporting textbooks (history, language, and literature in particular) as well as by visiting professors", observed the Albanian-American scholar Arshi Pipa. "That the Yugoslav leaders have permitted the Albanian cultural invasion of Kosova can be seen as a compliment to their accommodating attitude, but not their Marxist wisdom", he added.[21]

After such a troubled history, there was an urgent need for young Serbs and Albanians to learn to understand and respect each other. Instead, each community went its own way. In the 1980s, when children entered first grade, their parents chose whether they were to be educated in Albanian, Serbian, or Turkish, and from then on, the children met only outside classes. With their schoolbooks imported from Tirana, Kosovo's Albanian children were being raised as citizens of a foreign state. Previously, although illiterate, many Serbs and Albanians were bilingual or trilingual (through Turkish) and could easily communicate with each other. This capacity to communicate with neighbors was reduced by the education policy adopted.

The question arises: how can any society survive when its children are educated in complete ignorance of each other and with no common language? Bilingualism can be a great cultural enrichment; parallel monolingualism is a recipe for disaster. In 1988, compulsory second-language classes were introduced in first grade, but true bilingualism never developed.

While Serbs continued to master technical and scientific subjects, the massive influx of first-generation Albanian students favored literary studies and courses in Albanian history which promoted exaltation of national feelings rather than serious scholarship. The desire to enhance group identity, especially in opposition to rival groups, is receptive to flattering but totally unverified myths, such as the claim that present-day Albanians are the descendents of the ancient Illyrians – a relatively recent assertion which may or may not be true, but which is widely taken by Albanians as proof of being the first – and therefore only legitimate – inhabitants of the region.

Studies in Albanology unfortunately prepared students to do little else but teach the same national culture to more young Albanians.[22] The University of Priština bred a generation of nationalist rebels, totally focused on their own national identity, with a bitter sense of grievance against "the Slavs". Yet in 1981, an Albanian professor at Priština University concluded from extensive travels abroad that "not a single national minority in the world has achieved the rights that the Albanian nationality enjoys in Socialist Yugoslavia". Only the Hungarians in Romania and the Swedes in Finland had their own universities, but without the full autonomy enjoyed by the Albanians at the University of Priština, he observed.[23] However, this autonomy did not ensure high standards. The quantity of education in Kosovo was enormous, but the quality was poor:[24]

Albanians now suffered from an explosion of education after having had none. The narrow cultural orientation of the new graduates inhibited the drive for development and isolated them from the rest of Yugoslav society ... Apart from the imbalance in the subjects studied, its hasty establishment had resulted in little or no academic criteria being applied to the employment of Albanian teaching staff, most of whom were semi-competent at best. Less than half of the professors possessed doctorates, and even those who did had generally published little and were not considered serious scholars by their peers in the rest of Yugoslavia. The academic environment was thus mediocre.

Despite spending more than any other part of Yugoslavia on education, Kosovo continued to have by far the highest rates of unemployment and illiteracy.[25] Although in the 1970s and 1980s, ethnic quotas (the "key" system) ensured Albanians an overwhelming majority of command posts in the Communist Party and administration of Kosovo, most Albanians angrily blamed the "Slavs" for their condition. "Among the many negative trends in the Province was a mentality of complacency among its leaders, who concentrated on asking for as much help as possible on the basis of Kosovo's underdeveloped status, but failed to strive for greater self-reliance."[26]

By early 1981, the University of Priština had 36,000 full-time students plus 18,000 in extension studies. A poor province of 1.5 million inhabitants could not support what amounted to the highest percentage of students in Yugoslavia, and the university relied on large subsidies from other parts of the country. Conditions were crowded and the free meals were not very good. For the Albanian students, indoctrinated in resentment, this had to be the fault of Serb persecution. Protests against the cafeteria food erupted on 11 March 1981, turning into full-scale riots in which Serb and Montenegrin citizens were beaten, their homes and businesses set on fire, their shops looted. This initiated a new generation of Albanian nationalist activists, leading directly to the "Kosovo Liberation Army" of the late 1990s. These troubles coincided with a period of grave economic stagnation. With the IMF demanding austerity and Slovenia and Croatia balking at contributing to Kosovo development, Yugoslavia was no longer able to use economic growth to solve its nationality problems. However, to see this movement as a mere revolt against socio-economic conditions would be to miss the point. The revolt was not even strictly speaking political, insofar as ethnic Albanians were in control of key positions in the autonomous province of Kosovo. It was an irredentist movement, seeking separation from Serbia through status as a republic, as a step on the way to secession from Yugoslavia.

The Western left often assumes that only socio-economic oppression leads to revolt; *ergo*, the Kosovo Albanians were oppressed.[27] This is precisely the assumption that led Yugoslav governments from Tito to Milošević to prescribe "economic and cultural development" as the cure for nationalist rebellion. It didn't work. "The nationalist movement gained momentum after the Constitution of 1974 promoted Kosovo to an autonomous unit of Federal Yugoslavia. Kosovars began acting as masters, making Serbs and Montenegrins feel like subjects."[28] By 1981 Albanians were running the party, the police, the administration, and the economy in Kosovo. Albanian was the predominant language. But this only fed nationalism rather than containing it. All the political and cultural demands that could possibly be met within the framework of Yugoslavia had been satisfied when students began to form illegal irredentist groups aimed at secession. "Albanian irredentism was inspired not by a lack of bread but by an excess of myths and nationalistically overloaded memories."[29]

2. VICTIMS AND VENGEANCE

In both reality and literature, vengeance plays a central role in human relations. This is especially true in traditional societies, not least in traditional Albanian culture, which places extraordinary emphasis on "blood", honor, and vengeance for affronts. This vendetta culture, which has been characterized as a "culture of hatred" or a "culture of spite", encourages its adherents to settle scores by bloodshed.[30] The self-justification of vengeance is that one is a victim and that there is a score that needs to be "evened". Breaking away from this vicious cycle is an important function of civilization, but the ubiquity of the theme of vengeance in both fact and fiction shows that the world still has a long way to go. In situations of longstanding conflict, such as Kosovo, persuading oneself and others that "we" are the victims is a key to successful vengeance.

The myth of the Serbian memorandum

In the five years after Tito's death in 1980, Yugoslavia stagnated economically and politically. The political system was blocked by an unworkable consensus system that had needed the arbitration of the "president for life" to function at all. Reforms were obviously needed. In June 1985, the Serbian Academy of Sciences and Arts (SANU) appointed a 16-man committee to draft a critical analysis of what had gone wrong. The academicians were not only intruding into the policy-making territory reserved for the League of Communists, they were openly critical of the party leadership, starting with Tito and his closest associate, Edvard Kardelj.

Before the memorandum was completed, excerpts of the draft version were leaked and published in the 24 September 1986 edition of *Večernje Novosti* (Evening News) and subjected to scathing criticism. This amounted to a pre-emptive strike. Under fierce attack, the Academy quickly dropped the project. Several years later, the attack on the memorandum was revived by Croatian secessionists as part of the international campaign against "Serbian nationalism". Before the text had been translated from Serbo-Croat, it was described repeatedly as a program to create a "Greater Serbia" by means of "ethnic cleansing". The "memorandum" became the most famous document of the entire Yugoslav drama, repeatedly cited as a blueprint for aggressive conquest, comparable to Hitler's *Mein Kampf*. This notion even showed up in a French textbook for advanced high school students:[31]

Ethnic cleansing: theory elaborated by members of the Serbian Academy of Sciences in Belgrade, which advocates ethnic homogenization of the territories of former Yugoslavia inhabited by Serbs, by using terror to drive out the other populations in order to enable the final annexation of these territories by Serbia.

None of this was true. Aside from the fact that "ethnic cleansing" is a practice rather than a "theory", there was no "theory" in the memorandum, whether of ethnic cleansing or anything else. There was no "advocacy" of "ethnic homogenization", and certainly nothing at all to suggest "driving out other populations" to annex territories. The authors of the textbook had clearly relied on erroneous newspaper articles rather than consulting the text itself.[32]

Looking at the document, it is easy to see why Serbian party leaders sought to discredit it. The memorandum was in two parts, different in tone and content. The first half, entitled "The Crisis in the Yugoslav Economy and Society", was a scathing critique of Yugoslavia's political and economic system. It described the official "consensus economy", supposed to replace both economic planning and the market, as "a complete fiasco". It denounced the authorities for secretly contracting foreign debt to subsidize domestic consumption, for fostering ethnic self-interest, for prosecuting alleged ideological offenses as "verbal crimes" while ignoring corruption and economic crime, for holding farcical elections, for restricting the independence of the judiciary as well as freedoms of speech and assembly and trade union rights; and so on. It included a devastating criticism of Yugoslav socialism's special pride, "workers' self-management". Political leaders had deliberately limited it to workplaces to keep control of the system themselves.

> The thesis that self-management is most fully exercised within basic organizations of associated labor is in fact just an excuse not to allow it access to that essential (macroeconomic) field of action in which decisions of vital importance for society are taken ... Consequently, self-management is mere window dressing and not the pillar of society. The system is totally inconsistent. There is no real plan, no real market, no real government, and no real self-management.

Any real debate over this section was precluded by the scandal concerning the second part. Entitled "The Status of Serbia and the Serbian Nation", this part focused on specifically Serbian grievances. Such a focus was in itself an offense against the unwritten code of conduct imposed by "brotherhood and unity". Drafted separately by Professor Vasilije Krestić, this section had yet to be approved by other members of the Academy when it was leaked to the press.[33] The author complained that throughout the postwar period, Serbia's economic development had been deliberately held back by the Yugoslav communist leadership, in keeping with the Comintern doctrine, dating from the 1920s, which stigmatized Serbia as the "oppressor nation" and considered all the others as "oppressed" nations. The author called this policy "a drastic example of how Marxist teachings about the class divisions in each nation were eclipsed by pragmatic considerations which, in an effort to take advantage of inter-communal friction, pushed class internationalism onto the sidelines".

This complaint was symptomatic of a backlash among Serb intellectuals against decades of national self-denial, at a time of sharp economic decline combined with a revival of Croatian and Albanian nationalist self-assertion. Inasmuch as the 1974 Constitution was proving unworkable, Yugoslavia was heading for yet another of its periodic constitutional revisions. Serb intellectuals feared that this could be the occasion for a shift to a Confederation and *de facto* dismemberment. The academician called on Serbia to stop the drift and to save Yugoslavia as a federal state. In this way, he said, Serbia could promote the equality of all national groups and help solve the political and economic crisis. Finally, no solutions were possible without constitutional changes to make Serbia itself governable. This was acknowledged even by the memorandum's fiercest critics.[34]

The memorandum certainly did not call for a "Greater Serbia". But for advocates of a looser confederation and possible secession, it was useful polemics to denounce the mere call for preservation of the Yugoslav Federation as an attempt to create "Greater Serbia".

As for "ethnic cleansing", the only mention in the memorandum was Krestić's dire warning concerning Albanian efforts to rid Kosovo of Serbs and other minorities:

> Unless things change radically, in less than ten years' time there will no longer be any Serbs left in Kosovo, and an "ethnically pure" Kosovo, that unambiguously stated goal of the Greater Albanian racists, already outlined in the programmes and actions of the Prizren League of 1878–1881, will be achieved.

The memorandum warned that:

> if genuine security and unambiguous equality for all peoples living in Kosovo and Metohija are not established; if objective and lasting conditions are not created for the return of the people driven out, that part of the Republic of Serbia will become a European issue, with the gravest possible unforeseeable consequences ... the demand for an ethnically pure Albanian Kosovo is not only a heavy and direct threat to all the peoples who are in a minority there but, if achieved, it will set off a wave of expansion threatening all the national groups in Yugoslavia.

Krestić went so far as to describe Albanian treatment of Serbs in Kosovo as "genocide", while putting the principal blame on Serbian communist officials.

> The physical, political, legal and cultural genocide of the Serbian population in Kosovo and Metohija is a worse defeat than any suffered in the liberation wars waged by Serbia from the First Serbian Uprising in 1804 to the uprising of 1941. The reasons for this defeat can primarily be laid at the door of the legacy of the Comintern ... but they also lie in ... the inveterate

opportunism of generations of Serbian politicians since World War II, who are always on the defensive and always worried more about what others think of them and their timid overtures at raising the issue of Serbia's status than about the objective facts affecting the future of the nation they lead.

Calling Albanian harassment of Serbs in Kosovo "genocide" was precisely the type of emotional overstatement that in the following decade would be used constantly against the Serbs themselves. The extent of that harassment was controversial because inadequately documented, with incidents that were firmly believed by Serbs dismissed as false by Albanian officials in Kosovo. The truth was hard to establish. In any case, the term "genocide" was dangerously excessive, as even Krestic himself acknowledged some years later.[35]

Whatever its faults, the memorandum clearly was not the elaboration of a "theory" advocating ethnic cleansing in order to create an "ethnically pure Greater Serbia". Yet this preposterous charge has continued to be repeated. In April 2001, an Albanian writer named Besnik Mustafaj had this to say to a Belgian magazine: "Let us never forget that the Belgrade Academy of Sciences drafted the first platform founding ethic cleansing in Kosovo. And that the famous Ivo Andric figured among the signatories." Here the usual falsehood was enhanced by additional untruths: there were no "signatories" to the memorandum, and had there been, the Yugoslav writer Ivo Andric, winner of the 1961 Nobel Prize for literature, could not have been among them for the simple reason that he died on 13 March 1975, eleven years before the memorandum was written.[36]

Perhaps the Albanian was simply misinformed. In any case, he illustrated the common tendency to tell outsiders whatever is thought to be good for one's own group. The notion that truth is a supreme value in itself is not universally self-evident. Lying to strangers is widely considered meritorious. And if what one says is believed by others, it becomes that much easier to believe that it may be true after all. In the decade leading up to the NATO bombing of Yugoslavia, the eager readiness of Westerners to believe the worst of the Serbs acted as an incitement to Kosovo Albanians to exaggerate the wrongs done them. Western credulity acted as a *de facto* confirmation, justifying and intensifying Albanian hatred of Serbs.

Politics and human rights

In the 1980s, Western journalists and diplomats had defended the Serb viewpoint. The *New York Times* published reports of the plight of Serbs being driven out of Kosovo by Albanian "ethnic cleansing".[37] Western governments supported modernizers (such as Milošević) who saw the need to reduce Kosovo's autonomy in order to enact economic reforms. When Milošević took over control of the Serbian League of Communists and roughly pushed through constitutional reform, he had reason to expect that he would enjoy Western support.

The 1989 constitutional changes retained Kosovo's status as an autonomous province, but blocked its transition to a "republic" theoretically able to secede from the Federation. During the 1980s, it was the Albanian communists under the leadership of Azem Vllasi who had repressed Kosovar nationalism, with a brutality that sometimes brought protests from Serb liberals in Belgrade. Now Vllasi was made a scapegoat for having failed to rein in the nationalism he had long denounced as the "reactionary dream of an ethnically cleansed Kosovo".[38] In defense of the deposed party leaders, thousands of workers in the Trepča mining complex – Kosovo's main industry – protested by marches, sit-ins, and even hunger strikes. The Kosovar miners' protests in the winter of 1988–89 have been described as "probably the last Titoist demonstrations in Yugoslavia".[39] This is perhaps the point where the political tragedy was sealed. The confrontation between reform socialism, represented by Milošević, and the last gasp of old-style communism, represented by the Albanian miners, devastated the Yugoslav left and presaged its ultimate debacle. The center of Milošević's program was to modernize socialism in opposition to communist "bureaucrats" and an inefficient economic system. The old-guard Titoists like Vllasi had squandered money and protected unproductive jobs without even beginning to overcome Kosovo's mammoth unemployment. Yet they were the modernizers in Kosovo and the only fragile barrier to unrestrained anti-Serb nationalism. Sweeping them aside left a vacuum that could be filled only by a combustible mix of conservative provincial nationalists and Marxist-Leninist followers of Enver Hoxha, whose leftist veneer barely concealed an even more violent nationalism. Although they were defending an economic system condemned by the West, the Trepča miners aroused international sympathy and the brutal repression of their movement was a fatal blow to the reputation of Milošević in such important sectors of the European left as the British labor movement.

Yet at the same time, Milošević was introducing political pluralism and had transformed the Serbian League of Communists into the Serbian Socialist Party, inviting ethnic Albanians to join. The new Constitution defined Serbia as "a democratic state of all its citizens", without ethnic distinctions. But Milošević and the Serbian leadership grievously underestimated the wound they had inflicted on Kosovo and the capacity for mobilization of the Albanian community. The formal equality offered by the new Constitution was of no interest to Albanian leaders who wanted nothing to do with Serbia.

The Milošević government's revision of the status of Kosovo coincided with the fall of the Berlin Wall and the defeat of communism in Eastern Europe. As Zimmermann had announced, Yugoslavia had lost its "geopolitical importance". Once Belgrade could no longer count on indulgent support from Washington as reward for standing up to Moscow, all of Yugoslavia's dissidents, by identifying their various nationalist causes with "human rights" and "market reforms", could hope to win support from Washington for standing up to Belgrade. At the end of this process, there might be no more Yugoslavia, but an undetermined number of new political entities in southeastern Europe, all of whose leaders would be grateful to Washington. The last traces of Tito's heretical communism would be swept away.

Milošević's crackdown on Kosovo was harsh, but no more so than Tito's style of governing, and it was accomplished for the sake of an economic reform program approved by the West. The Albanian protesters in Kosovo included a large contingent of dogmatic "Marxist-Leninists". Why should the United States support such people? The hostile Western reaction could only be baffling to Milošević and his advisors.

Massive arrests of Albanian nationalists and dismissal of Albanians who boycotted their workplace in protest were no longer regarded as regrettably harsh measures taken to preserve Yugoslavia's unity (acceptable when the goal was to maintain a bulwark against Soviet advance), but simply as "human rights abuses". The concentration on "human rights" blurred the basic political issue, which was always the status of the province, inside or outside of Serbia. To keep Kosovo inside Serbia, the Serbian authorities in 1989 and 1990 used strong arm tractics without regard for Albanian opinion and sensibilities. Subsequently, the repression was eased. The Western interpretation of the Kosovo conflict reversed cause and effect by presenting human rights violations as the *cause* of the problem. In this perspective, the issue was "violation of the human rights of the Kosovo Albanians". No other way of viewing the problem could capture the attention of the Western powers.

The entire strategy of the Albanian side in the 1990s was based on mobilizing international support, first political, later military, on behalf of Kosovo's secession from Serbia. This was vigorously promoted by Albania itself, and by the Albanian emigration, notably in Germany, the United States, and Turkey. The Serbian government, in contrast, had no visible strategy other than to keep the international community at bay by insisting that the Kosovo problem was an "internal affair".

The nature of these conflicting strategies produced a structural bias in favor of the ethnic Albanians on the part of the Great Powers, under their contemporary guise of the "International Community". The leading powers, the United States and Germany, were invited by Albanian leaders to come in and take over. The conflict provided an opportunity to demonstrate NATO's new mission, as well as an interesting field of operations for all the numerous governmental and non-governmental organizations which have found in Yugoslav troubles a perfect laboratory and justification for the extension of their own operations. Western opinion about Kosovo was heavily influenced by the bias of human rights organizations with government connections. The original human rights NGO, Amnesty International, was genuinely "non-governmental". It aimed at documenting and publicizing particular abuses, to save individuals and provide moral support to local forces engaged in trying to improve standards in their own countries. However, Amnesty has been increasingly upstaged by Human Rights Watch (HRW), which can scarcely be described as "non-governmental" given its close ties to the U.S. administration. Prominent HRW members include Morton Abramowitz, involved in using Islamists to wreck Afghanistan before going on to use the "Kosovars" to wreck Yugoslavia; former U.S. ambassador Warren Zimmerman; and Paul Goble, director of the U.S. propaganda news network Radio Free Europe, which for years displayed its bias by using only Albanian language names for towns in Kosovo. In regard to Yugoslavia, Human Rights Watch and above all its affiliate, the Vienna-based International Helsinki Federation for Human Rights, consistently worked to discredit and condemn the Belgrade government rather than encourage unbiased investigation or reform. Rather than report facts, HRW attacked complex and sensitive issues with broad generalizations and inflammatory rhetoric.

On 18 September 1997, HRW issued a long statement announcing in advance that the Serbian elections to be held three days later would be "neither free nor fair". This arrogant pre-judgment was accompanied by a long list of measures dictated to Belgrade on pain of being punished by the International Community. Among other things, the Serbian government was ordered to adopt new media laws drafted "in full consultation with the independent media in Yugoslavia" as well as permission meanwhile to all "unlicensed but currently operating radio and television stations to broadcast without interference".[40] Human Rights Watch/Helsinki concluded by calling on the OSCE to "deny Yugoslavia readmission ... until there are concrete improvements in the country's human rights record, including respect for freedom of the press, independence of the judiciary and minority rights, as well as cooperation with the International Criminal Tribunal for the former Yugoslavia".

No other OSCE member was subjected to such demands, much less excluded from membership. The constant demand to "respect freedom of the press" was a way of hiding the fact that press freedom already existed in Serbia, more so than in many other countries never served with such an ultimatum. At that time, Serbia had a broad range of media devoted to attacking the government, in both Serbo-Croat and in Albanian. As of June 1998, there were 2,319 print publications and 101 radio and television stations in Yugoslavia, over twice the number that existed in 1992. Belgrade alone had 14 daily newspapers. Six state-supported national dailies had a joint circulation of 180,000, compared to around 350,000 for seven leading opposition dailies.[41]

As for "minority rights", it would have been hard to find a country anywhere in the world where they were better protected than in Yugoslavia. The 1992 Constitutions of both Yugoslavia and Serbia guaranteed extensive rights to several national minorities, notably the right to education in their own mother tongue, the right to information media in their own language, and the right to use their own language in judicial or administrative proceedings. Friendly critics might urge more consistent application of these principles; hostile critics acted as if they did not exist.

In a March 1998 column, at a time when armed Albanian separatists were stepping up attacks on Serb policemen as part of the strategy of provoking retaliation that would bring in NATO support, Aaron Rhodes, executive director of the International Helsinki Federation for Human Rights, claimed that Albanians in Kosovo "have lived for years under conditions similar to those suffered by Jews in Nazi-controlled parts of Europe just before World War II. They have been ghettoized. They are not free, but politically disenfranchised and deprived of basic civil liberties."[42] This was as incendiary as it was untrue. Such blanket denunciation served not to promote democracy at the national level, but to assert the superior authority of the "International Community" as the only legitimate arbiter of democracy.

The Kosovo NGO

The authorities in Belgrade justified the harsh 1989 crackdown in Kosovo on the grounds that they were combating a violent secessionist movement. Those grounds were rapidly undermined by the unexpected decision of Kosovo Albanians to turn to something they had never tried before: non-violence. This sudden metamorphosis was described by the prominent Kosovo Albanian intellectual Shkelzen Maliqi "as a surprise not only to the Serbian militant top ranks, but also to Albanians who could have hardly imagined themselves in that particular role". Albanians had "never upheld such values as non-violence, patience, non-response to blows and insults". Until the end of 1989, "the feeling prevailing among the Albanians was one of revenge: they waited for a moment of maximum mobilization to start a massive armed uprising". In Maliqi's words:[43]

However, in winter and spring of 1990 there was a sudden and radical change. Warriors went out of fashion over night. The interesting thing is that there were no major theoretical disputes, nor organized campaigns propagating non-violence, nor was there even a specific personality to undertake the role of the Albanian Gandhi. Dr. Rugova became the most influential leader of the Albanians later on when the concept was already spontaneously formulated. The strategy of non-violence was somehow self-imposed as the best, most pragmatic and most efficient response to Serbian aggressive plans.

All at once, a people renowned for bloody clan feuds agreed to drop all internal quarrels and unite in non-violent resistance to the outside enemy. The clan leaders themselves, in a process invisible to the outside world, were behind this strategic change. Within a few months, about 2,000 families involved in blood feuds were reconciled and some 20,000 men were released from the "house arrest" imposed on targets of such vendettas. The event was impressive.

Albanians boycotted Serbian institutions, and refused to pay taxes or utility bills. Without public debate or charismatic leader, they proclaimed their own parallel state, which was immediately recognized by neighboring Albania (but by no one else). The mild-mannered literary critic Ibrahim Rugova was formally elected president in shadow elections, although it is unclear how he was chosen as sole candidate. His main function was to enhance the movement's international image by identifying it with pacifism. When not receiving foreign guests at the Albanian Writers Club in Priština, Rugova spent his shadow presidency traveling between crucial capitals such as Bonn, Brussels, and Washington, pleading the cause of Kosovo as an Albanian land oppressed by the Serbs.

Despite superficial resemblances, this Kosovo Albanian non-violent movement was essentially different from movements (such as the civil rights movement in the United States or the anti-apartheid movement in South Africa) aimed at obtaining equal rights and social integration. The Kosovo Albanians were not trying to gain improvements for Albanians within the framework of Yugoslav or Serbian institutions. They simply rejected those institutions totally. There was no non-violent campaign to gain equal access to education or other social benefits. The Kosovo Albanian movement boycotted them. A key non-violent political action is voting. The Kosovo Albanian movement boycotted elections, which its candidates would surely have won, because voting would imply recognition that they were citizens of Serbia.

Theoretically, it established parallel institutions. The first parallel elections were held in May 1992, but the parliament never passed a single piece of legislation. The effect of this "Kosovar democracy" was to draw ethnic Albanian voters away from official elections. Albanian abstention ensured President Milošević's party some 35 swing seats in parliament. If the Albanians had elected their own representatives instead of boycotting elections, they could have altered the political majority in Serbia. However, Albanian leaders preferred the "demonized" Milošević as an irreplaceable public relations asset to their cause.[44]

Much of the outside world was persuaded that Kosovo Albanians were "not allowed to use their own language". This was not true. After initial problems due to withdrawal of government subsidies,

Albanian language newspapers circulated freely, propagating the vision of a "Greater Albania" including parts of Serbia, Macedonia, and Montenegro. The right of Kosovo Albanians to education in their own language was never challenged. The bone of contention at first was the content of politically sensitive courses in history, geography, and Albanian literature. The Serbian authorities objected to primary school textbooks describing Kosovo as "occupied" by Serbia. In 1990, the Serbian parliament adopted a unified curriculum for the whole country. Refusing to accept the revised program, the Albanian community organized parallel schooling. By the end of 1992, the Serbian authorities had given in and accepted the principle that "leaders of each nation were responsible for the cultural development of their own people".[45] To get the children back in the official schools, Serbian officials told Albanian leaders during talks held in Switzerland that they could write their own program. But by that time, Albanian leaders were attached to their own system and saw its extraordinary value as a political weapon. They insisted not only on their own nationalist curriculum but also demanded that diplomas must be issued by the "Republic of Kosova". This was the sticking point. The quality of education was poor and the dropout rate rose.[46]

A similar power struggle between Albanian nationalists and the Serbian state tore apart the public health system in the province. In March 1990, during a regular official vaccination program, rumors were spread that Serb health workers had poisoned over 7,000 Albanian children by injection. No physical symptoms were confirmed.[47] This unsubstantiated rumor was the signal for a boycott of the Serbian public health system. Many ethnic Albanian doctors and other health workers left the official institutions to set up a parallel system, so inadequate that preventable childhood diseases reached epidemic proportions. In September 1996, WHO and UNICEF undertook to assist the "Mother Teresa" charity in vaccinating 300,000 children against polio. The worldwide publicity campaign around this program overlooked the fact that the same service was still provided by the official public health service of Serbia, systematically boycotted by Albanian parents. In 1998, the parallel "Kosovar" system was employing 239 general practitioners and 140 specialists, compared to around 2,000 physicians employed by the Serbian public health system in the province. In reality, many ethnic Albanians sensibly turned to the government health system when seriously ill. According to official figures in 1998, 64 per cent of the official Serbian system's health employees in Kosovo and 80 per cent of its patients were still ethnic Albanian.

While winning much admiration abroad, these parallel institutions remained rudimentary and failed to provide the benefits of the state institutions that were shunned. The weakness of the parallel structure was evident after NATO occupied Kosovo in June 1999 and drove out the Serbian authorities. Now freed from every trace of Serbian rule, the parallel institutions failed to emerge and provide basic services. The province sank into chaos and lawlessness, masked only by the complacent presence of the "international community".

Serbia was widely accused of practicing "apartheid" in Kosovo.[48] This likening of Kosovo to racist South Africa was a successful propaganda theme. But there was no state-decreed separation of populations in Kosovo. If "apartheid" is reduced to meaning a degree of separation between ethnic communities, in Kosovo it was organized by the very Kosovar Albanian nationalist leaders who denounced it in order to win support from international public opinion. The amazing strategy of "self-apartheid" was designed both to deepen the chasm between the Albanian majority in Kosovo and the dwindling Serbian minority, and to win international sympathy by posing as victims of "racism". It was successful thanks to the internal discipline of Albanian patriarchal society, which massively followed calls for boycott, and constant support from abroad. Western support took the form of readiness to believe – or seem to believe – that the Kosovo problem was a matter of human rights rather than a conflict between a recognized government and an irredentist movement seeking territorial secession.[49]

Since the ethnic Albanian movement in this phase was not demanding anything other than to be left alone, it remained essentially passive. It avoided open conflict with the government in Belgrade which, apart from occasional arrests of persons suspected of hoarding weapons and plotting armed resistance (which existed as well), allowed Rugova's shadow "Kosova" to continue its shadow existence. The impasse was total on both sides.

As early as 1992, officials in Belgrade recognized that concessions were necessary to restore some semblance of normal life to the province. In August 1992, the American businessman of Serb origin, Milan Panić, who had been made prime minister by Milošević in the hope that he could patch up relations with Washington, held secret talks in London with Rugova in search of a *modus vivendi*.[50] Belgrade sought to normalize the situation, hold new elections, and restore a working autonomy. The continuing refusal of Albanians to participate in elections pulled the political rug out from under Panić, who was sacked by Milošević as ineffective.

Some Serbs considered the Kosovo situation hopeless and would have welcomed any solution which could "save the monasteries" and cut losses. A number of prominent Serbian intellectuals sought to devise compromise solutions, using the examples of Finnish–Swedish accords or Sud Tirol/Alto Adige.[51] Various trial balloons were sent up, all studiously ignored by the "International Community". The idea of partitioning Kosovo between Serbs and Albanians was advocated by the novelist Dobrica Ćosić, considered the spiritual father of the Serbian national revival, during his short period as president of Yugoslavia in 1992 and 1993.[52] Ćosić warned that the Kosovo problem was destroying Serbia itself.[53]

> The human rights argument is no longer anything but an ideological weapon used by the secessionists and their foreign protectors in view of realizing their national ambition: the union of all Albanians in a single State. And so long as they will not have achieved that end, the question of human rights in Kosovo-Metohija will continue to be heated up and Serbia will remain indicted by the international community. It will not do us a bit of good to point out that the Albanians benefit from national and human rights such as no other national minority enjoys ... Kosovo will be Serbia's malignant tumor which will exhaust her economically, block her development and threaten her territorially by demographic expansion.

In such a dilemma, Ćosić concluded that it was necessary to satisfy the national aspirations of both the Serbian and Albanian peoples by a "peaceful and fair territorial division". In the summer of 1996, the president of the Serbian Academy of Sciences and Arts, Aleksandar Despić, again tried to stimulate discussion of a peaceful settlement based on secession and partition. The very suggestion has been dismissed out of hand by the West, either on dogmatic legal grounds of respecting internal borders of former Yugoslavia, or on supposedly humanitarian grounds that partition would involve population exchanges and thus a form of "ethnic cleansing". The fact that, without partition, Serbs are almost certain to be "ethnically cleansed" from all of Kosovo, including the northernmost region in the Ibar river valley which is overwhelmingly Serb, does not seem to matter. In view of the Western veto, Albanians had no reason to consider partition. Partition was a controversial idea for Serbs as well. Serbia is a multinational country, and the idea of changing borders every time the demographic balance shifts would be permanently destabilizing. Nevertheless, *a priori* dismissal of any suggestion does not help the search for peaceful resolution of a difficult problem.

In 1996, the radical Kosovo Albanian nationalist Adem Demaqi suggested a democratically re-federated Yugoslavia, with a new name such as "Balkania", including Kosovo. Some Albanian leaders proposed granting Kosovo the status of a third "republic" within Yugoslavia (alongside Serbia and Montenegro), without the right to secede.[54] Such ideas gained circulation at a time when the 1997 "pyramid scheme" collapse plunged Albania itself into lawlessness, which initially was understood as a blow to the political credibility of secession. This might have been the moment when unbiased outside mediation could have promoted efforts toward reconciliation and a peaceful compromise.[55] Instead, the breakdown of law and order in Albania led to pillaged armories and an unprecedented cross-border flow of weapons to Albanian rebels in Kosovo. In the months leading up to NATO intervention, Belgrade repeatedly sent high-ranking delegations to Priština with instructions to negotiate extensive self-government in Kosovo. Instead of encouraging such attempts at accommodation, the Western media and governments perpetuated the notion that "Milošević refused to negotiate".

Kosovo Albanians had no reason to negotiate when they could count on support from U.S. government-financed "NGOs". Through the National Endowment for Democracy (NED), set up by the Reagan administration to interfere in the internal affairs of other countries with U.S. taxpayers' money, the United States had a major influence on how Kosovo was seen by the world. Veton Surroi, the widely respected editor of Kosovo's main newspaper, *Koha Ditore* (Daily Times), subsidized by both the NED and the Soros foundation, caught the mood of the times neatly when he praised Kosovo itself as "the world's biggest non-governmental organization".[56] Aside from outside aid, the ability of Kosovo Albanians to live quite independently of their country's government depended heavily on the traditional archaic self-reliance of Albanian clans, which have never accepted the laws of any institutionalized government.

US aid to the Albanians was particularly significant in the crucial field of human rights information. The main source of all reports circulated worldwide concerning Serbian police brutality and other abuses originated with the Council for the Defense of Human Rights and Freedoms, founded in 1989 by militant Kosovo Albanian nationalists. Only alleged abuses of ethnic Albanians were of interest, and because the Council was a key instrument of propaganda for the secessionist cause, the objective was to make the situation sound as grim as possible. Even verbal slights were collated as "human rights violations". A NED grant "enabled the Council to hire a full-time director and set up field offices with fax machines and computers, improving its ability to monitor and report abuses quickly and systematically", the NED reported proudly in 1998. The Council maintained a network of 27 sub-councils comprising roughly 2,000 volunteers, present in almost every town in Kosovo. NED called the Council "the most important source of information on human rights in Kosovo. A wide variety of international human rights organizations and news agencies use its information, including the International Federation for Human Rights, the UN Commission for Human Rights, and the Associated Press."[57]

The implications of this are extraordinary. First of all, a province described as groaning under Nazi-like oppression was covered by a network of foreign-financed information offices staffed by militant opponents who were openly supplying international organizations and world media with the bulk of their reports on what was going on. Given the difficulty of penetrating Albanian society or even understanding its language, it can be assumed that foreign NGOs and news media could not easily verify the reports provided to them. Nevertheless, they accepted these reports and passed them along. This amounted to an open invitation to the 2,000 Albanians working in this network to report whatever they thought would best serve their cause, without regard to that abstract concept "truth". During the NATO bombing, this same US-financed Council continued to provide the West with horror stories of Serb atrocities – which subsequently proved to be unfounded.

Governments with their own intelligence systems must have been aware of the bias inherent in this system of reporting. In the months leading up to the NATO bombing, in response to demands for asylum lodged by Kosovo Albanians, the German Foreign Ministry and various regional German courts categorically denied that Kosovo Albanians were being persecuted or even that there was a "humanitarian catastrophe" resulting from Yugoslav security forces' repression of armed Albanian rebels. In late October 1998, the Bavarian administrative court, on the basis of intelligence reports from the German Foreign Ministry, concluded that the recent violence "was a selective use of force against the military underground movement (especially the UÇK – Ushtria Çlirimtare e Kosoves) ... A government program of persecution aimed at the whole ethnic group of Albanians has never existed either now or earlier."[58]

The ear of the Empire: the Albanian lobby in the United States

In the context of the eternal divide-and-rule strategy, a discontented ethnic minority is a potential key to weakening a stubbornly independent country.[59] Albanian separatists were able to capture the ear of the Empire because of their extraordinary eagerness to link their cause to the advance of NATO at the expense of a Yugoslav leadership still clinging to notions of national independence.

An influential Kosovo Albanian lobby emerged in the United States in the 1980s, at a time when Albanians were actually running Kosovo. The mainstream U.S. press was reporting that the Albanian majority were harassing Serbs in order to establish "an ethnically clean Albanian republic". The Albanian lobby in the United States sought to reverse the image and present Albanians as the victims of Serb persecution. The center of this lobby was New York Republican congressman Joseph DioGuardi, of Italian Albanian background. On 18 June 1986, Representative DioGuardi and Senator Bob Dole introduced Concurrent Resolution 150 "Expressing Concern over the Condition of Ethnic Albanians living in Yugoslavia". The resolution was not adopted, but it established Dole as the champion of the Albanians. In May 1987, Albanian-Americans held a fund-raiser for their two supporters in New York City, which raised $1.2 million for Dole's election campaign fund and $50,000 for DioGuardi's.[60] DioGuardi lost his seat, but went on to form the Albanian-American Civic League to pursue lobbying for the Albanian cause.

While strongly supporting Republican candidate Bob Dole, the Albanian lobbyists were also active in wooing the Democrats. For the 1996 elections, the Democrats set up nine steering committees to court the "ethnic" votes of Albanians, Arabs, Croatians, Greeks, Irish, Hungarians, Italians, Lithuanians, and Poles. "An energetic 31-year-old Albanian American, Ilir Zherka, was put in charge of the drive, which was called Ethnic Outreach."[61] In the past, ethnic lobbies were concerned with advancing the domestic condition of their constituents. As the United States has become more of an empire, the focus has shifted toward committing the American superpower to intervene on the side of exile groups with a political agenda to change things back home – possibly gaining a share of influence and power for themselves.

The leading role of the Albanian lobby in the Clinton campaign's "Ethnic Outreach" program is noteworthy, as is the absence of any Serbian lobby. Americans of Serbian descent, even if they opposed Tito and revered the memory of the executed wartime Chetnik leader Draža Mihailović, never dreamed of reshaping the Balkans with help from the U.S. superpower. In contrast, right-wing Croatian exile groups nursed dreams of restoring the short-lived "Independent Croatian State". In 1993, it was reported that "Croatia has built up the most effective lobbying and public relations network on Capitol Hill since the days when the Israel and Greek lobbies were at their peak." Croatian lobbying efforts, congressional investigators were quoted as saying, "could well exceed $50 million".[62]

In their effort to win separate states of their own, Croats, Albanians, and Bosnian Muslims shared a common enemy. That common enemy was multinational Yugoslavia. Politically, the formula for winning support from American politicians was to identify Yugoslavia with the Serbs and the Serbs with "communism".

The success of the three anti-Serb lobbies owed much to a young aide of Senator Robert Dole, Mira Radievolic Baratta, who went to work for Dole in June 1989. The daughter of Croatian nationalists who emigrated to California, Baratta was publicly credited with getting the Senate to adopt a resolution calling for lifting the arms embargo against the Bosnian Muslims.[63] In a bastion of ignorance about faraway places, Baratta easily became *the* Congressional expert on the Balkans. Baratta has "as good an understanding of the Balkans as anyone on Capitol Hill", *The Weekly Standard* reported admiringly, adding that "she is probably the only congressional staffer monitoring ex-Yugoslavia who speaks and reads both Croatian and Serbian" – a statement which itself indicates the prevailing ignorance, since Croatian and Serbian are the same language. In May 1995, Baratta received the "Award for Excellence in Politics" from the National Federation of Croatian Americans. Dole advisors Richard Perle, Paul Wolfowitz, and Jeane Kirkpatrick were described as "among Baratta's biggest boosters".[64] Perle, who advised the Bosnian Muslims at the Dayton Peace talks, called her "the most influential individual in shaping U.S. policy" in the Balkans next to Richard Holbrooke.[65]

One factor to explain such influence was the appeal of right-wing anti-communism, which portrayed Milošević's Serbia as the last bastion of unrepentant socialism. Another was the opportunity of using the Albanian wild card to create a Balkan satellite hospitable to NATO bases. An independent Albanian Kosovo would strengthen Turkey's renewed presence in the Balkans. This would bolster the key strategic partnership between the United States and Turkey, linked to Israel in the eastern Mediterranean and expanding northward into the oil-rich ex-Soviet republics. The region's geostrategic value was enhanced by little-known plans for oil pipelines. The mainstream media failed to inform the public of the fact that the U.S. government was funding feasibility studies for a billion dollar pipeline to be built by the Albanian, Macedonian and Bulgarian Oil Corporation (AMBO) of Pound Ridge, New York. This pipeline from the Black Sea port city of Burgas, in Bulgaria, to the Albanian Adriatic port of Vlora is designed to be the cheapest way to siphon Caspian oil off the European route on the way to the United States and its vast market.[66] The AMBO route also coincides approximately with "Corridor 8", part of the projected EU network known as the Pan-European Transport Corridors. In the next decade or so, the EU plans to invest over ten billion Euros in this major transport and communication project. Local governments politically indebted to the United States are likely to award construction contracts to major U.S. companies. Washington's support for the "Kosovar" cause has helped make Albania the most enthusiastically pro-American country in the world, whose leaders constantly plead for establishment of permanent U.S. bases. Albania is one of the rare former communist countries in Europe "where all the political forces, left and right, parliamentary and non-parliamentary, desire such an American military presence".[67]

Kosovo has been described as a "turntable" where east–west and north–south Balkan trade routes cross.[68] Immediately upon sending its troops into Kosovo, the Pentagon set about constructing a large permanent military base called Camp Bondsteel at a strategic crossroads. Without consulting NATO allies or bothering to compensate farmers deprived of their land, much less asking permission of the occupied country's authorities, the U.S. expropriated some 775 acres of rolling countryside, flattened it out and covered it with facilities for thousands of troops, including two chapels and a Burger King. Described as the biggest U.S. overseas military base since the Vietnam war, Camp Bondsteel is a solidly-built enclave which may be able to survive political upheavals in Kosovo just as the U.S. Guantanamo base has endured revolution in Cuba. It also happens to be located near two of the future European transport routes, "Corridor 8" and "Corridor 10". This military base commands the most strategically interesting corner of Kosovo, in close proximity to the two main north–south mountain passes allowing traffic to pass from northern Central Europe to the important Greek port of Thessalonika on the Aegean. If acquiring this new base was not one of Washington's motives for going to war, it looked that way to some of the United States' NATO allies.[69]

Camp Bondsteel is a self-sufficient high tech enclave. Everything it needs – water, electricity, laundry, meals, transport, fire department – is provided by the private contractor, Brown & Root Services, a subsidiary of Halliburton Corporation. Halliburton is the number one supplier of products and services to the oil industry and a major business partner of the Pentagon since being awarded its first big contracts by Dick Cheney when he was defense secretary under President Bush Sr. Halliburton gratefully took on Cheney as its CEO between 1995 and 2000, until Cheney left to become vice president under President Bush Jr. Brown & Root is not only the major employer in NATO-occupied Kosovo, it also carried out feasibility studies for the AMBO pipeline. And AMBO's president since 1997, Ted Ferguson, used to be director of oil and gas development in Europe and Africa for Brown & Root Energy services.

In July 2001, President George W. Bush chose to sign a Congressional bill increasing military spending by $1.9 billion in front of cheering troops in Camp Bondsteel. There is little doubt that Brown & Root had reason to cheer as well.[70]

Preparing for war

The UÇK, or KLA (Kosovo Liberation Army) in English, was founded by students influenced by Albanian dictator Enver Hoxha's dogmatic variety of Marxism-Leninism. The appeal of "Enverism" evidently had more to do with underground organization and illegal action than with bettering the lot of the working class. The first armed attack on Serb policemen and Albanian "collaborators" attributed to the group dates back to October 1992.[71] The UÇK dramatically escalated tension in Kosovo on 11 February 1996 with a series of night-time bomb and Kalashnikov attacks on half a dozen Serbian refugee camps in northern Kosovo. The makeshift camps sheltered a few hundred Serbs who had been driven out of the Croatian and Bosnian Krajina regions by the Croatian offensives of 1995. These wretched civilians, a small fraction of the over half million refugees parked throughout Serbia, were denounced as the vanguard of a diabolical plan to drive out the Albanians and repopulate Kosovo with Serbs. The UÇK demanded a stop to what it called the "colonization" of Kosovo and called on the United States to recognize the independence of Kosovo. It warned that any fellow Albanians who chose "Kosovo's autonomy within Serbia" would be assassinated.[72]

Violent intimidation followed. Kosovo Albanians killed or wounded by UÇK automatic weapons in 1998 ranged from postmen and foresters to prominent local members of Milošević's Serbian Socialist Party.[73] The UCK sought to destroy contacts between Serbs and Albanians by killing individuals who served as bridges between the two communities. Much later, the OSCE recalled reports that "UÇK forces killed not only moderate Kosovo Albanians but also Serbs who were well liked by both communities", giving the example of the 17 December 1998 abduction and murder of Polje, the Serb deputy mayor of Kosovo, "a moderate Kosovo Serb politician who had done much to improve social conditions in his area".[74]

These crimes were an embarrassment to those who were presenting the Kosovar struggle to the world as a model of non-violence. For a long time, Rugova and his colleagues denied the very existence of the UÇK, claiming that it was nothing but an invention of Serbian propaganda designed to discredit the Kosovar cause. However, since Western commentators readily justified UÇK violence by the failure of peaceful means to change Kosovo's status, it was Rugova's non-violence that was discredited. On 22 July 1998, eight years after it was established, the parliament of the shadow "Republic of Kosova" met for the first time and issued a statement officially recognizing the UÇK as a "legitimate Kosovar organization". Rugova himself added, "we should have done this long ago". So much for non-violence. Rugova's party went on to stigmatize Serbian police retaliation against the UÇK as "genocide".

In the months leading up to the NATO bombing, the rebels stepped up their armed attacks. The UÇK systematically exposed ethnic

Albanian villagers to reprisals by conspicuously turning villages into bases for attack on Serbian police. Inasmuch as the UÇK could not expect to defeat the Serbian police and army militarily, its murders of policemen can be understood only in the framework of a strategy of provocation. Civilian victims would help to bring in NATO. This strategy was obvious to Western observers:[75]

> The KLA had a simple but effective plan. It would kill Serbian policemen. The Serbs would retaliate, Balkan style, with widespread reprisals and the occasional massacre. The West would get more and more appalled, until finally it would, as it did in Bosnia, take action. In effect, the United States and much of Europe would go to war on the side of the KLA.
> It worked.

It worked because there were Great Powers that wanted it to work. Western intelligence services had forged links with the Kosovo Albanian rebels, whose success could be expected to increase Western influence in the region.[76] Behind the scenes, the CIA had been working closely with Albanian President Sali Berisha since 1992.[77] Berisha in turn was both supporting Rugova and turning northern Albania into a safe hinterland for armed Kosovo rebels. At least from 1996, the German BND provided training and equipment.[78] In the summer of 1998, as the Serbian government was trying to regain control of villages occupied by the UÇK, the main concern of the U.S. diplomatic observer mission in Kosovo was to unite the various factions of the UÇK into a single force. The U.S. Drug Enforcement Administration and other Western agencies were well aware of the close links between the UÇK/KLA and the Kosovo Albanian drug traffickers controlling the main flow of heroin into Western Europe from Afghanistan via Turkey.[79] The CIA has a long record of considering such groups as assets against governments targeted by the United States, whether in Southeast Asia, Africa or Central America.

"Bombing for peace"

In the winter of 1997–98, the UÇK announced the start of the battle for Kosovo's unification with Albania and stepped up its attacks on both police and civilians. At press briefings in both Priština and Belgrade on 23 February 1998, the special U.S. representative for former Yugoslavia, Robert Gelbard, declared that the "Kosovo Liberation Army" was "a terrorist group beyond any doubt" and "condemned very strongly" terrorist activities in Kosovo.[80] Four days later, the UÇK ambushed and killed four Serbian policemen. The Belgrade government thereupon undertook to do what the U.S. government itself would have done faced with such a group operating on its territory: eliminate them.

Led by the United States and Germany, the Contact Group issued strong condemnations and renewed sanctions against Yugoslavia. This Great Power intervention was constantly unclear in its aims and contradictory in its actions. While condemning the UÇK as terrorist, NATO condemned the Serbian offensive ... but tacitly allowed it to achieve its aim of recapturing territory from the "terrorists". The NATO powers insisted that Kosovo should remain part of Yugoslavia ... but also blamed Belgrade when negotiation were blocked by Kosovo Albanians' refusal to discuss anything but independence from Yugoslavia. Thus on the main political issue – the status of Kosovo – the NATO powers formally agreed with Belgrade, but condemned Yugoslavia for its use of excessive force ... which became the pretext for NATO to use even more excessive force to achieve the opposite political aim: de facto independence of Kosovo. No wonder if neither the Serbs nor the Albanians believed that the NATO powers meant what they said in public. But in the jargon of NATO power, "credibility" has nothing to do with truthfulness and everything to do with readiness to use force.

The West's treatment of the Kosovo situation was heavily influenced by the myth of a "pattern" in Bosnia that might be repeated in Kosovo. In 1995, Clinton administration officials had been eager to bomb the Bosnian Serbs, in part to gain U.S. control of the peace negotiations. At that time, as Richard Holbrooke recounts, Serbian president Slobodan Milošević was eager to work out a peace settlement in Bosnia-Herzegovina in order to have international sanctions against his country lifted.[81] Izetbegović wanted to continue the war, and it was only if the United States bombed the Bosnian Serbs that he would even consent to discuss negotiations.[82] In reality, the United States bombed the Bosnian Serbs to get Izetbegović to the negotiating table. But the version for the public was that bombing was necessary to get *Milošević* to the negotiating table.

This was repeated so often that even the U.S. officials who knew better seemed to believe it. It was on the basis of this myth that

"Milošević has to be bombed to the negotiating table" that the United States persuaded its NATO allies to issue its first activation order on 13 October 1998, thus formally starting to prepare for bombing Yugoslavia. On the eve of this order, Milošević accepted a peculiar unilateral cease-fire forced on him by U.S. envoy Holbrooke. The fact that Milošević had given in to bombing threats encouraged those like Madeleine Albright who saw Yugoslavia above all as an occasion to demonstrate the effectiveness of military force. What was overlooked was that Milošević had reason to expect something in return: that NATO would restrain the UÇK.[83] Indeed, with the UÇK threat removed, Rugova's party could be less intransigent and the opportunity existed for a negotiated settlement along the lines ostensibly sought by the United States. And yet it was then that the United States opened the way for a comeback by the UÇK which made compromise impossible.

In the October agreement with Holbrooke Milošević agreed to withdraw armed forces from Kosovo and allow 2,000 OSCE "verifiers" full access to Kosovo in order to monitor its application. Before the OSCE could formally establish this Kosovo Verification Mission (KVM), the United States persuaded Polish foreign minister Bronislaw Geremek, OSCE chairman at the time, to appoint an American official to head the KVM. Washington's choice was a veteran of Central American "banana republic" management, William Walker. Europeans were irritated, but acquiesced.[84]

The announced "humanitarian catastrophe" evaporated as civilians who had left their villages to escape the fighting returned to shelter. Serb forces were rapidly withdrawn as Milošević had promised.[85] But as Serb forces complied, the UÇK moved forward, taking up its offensive positions and provoking the Serbs to retaliate and thus break the cease-fire. UÇK commander Agim Çeku, who as an officer in the Croatian army had previously won notoriety by massacring Serb civilians, later explained: "The cease-fire was very useful to us. It enabled us to get organized, to consolidate, to grow."[86]

The "verifiers" dribbled into Kosovo in late autumn, mostly recruited from the ranks of the military or other intelligence services. By early November only 200 of the 2,000 KVM verifiers were in place, and 150 of them were modern mercenaries from the Virginia-based DynCorp, under contract from the U.S. government.[87] Walker and his British deputy, General John Drewienkiewicz, in charge of the security section, "cultivated privileged relations with UÇK factions".[88] The Anglo-Americans blocked cooperation with local Serbian police, while relying on information from local Albanian personnel friendly to the UÇK. European and Canadian verifiers complained that anyone who dared report UÇK human rights violations risked receiving death threats from the UÇK.[89] To get their bearings in this small province, the "verifiers" were invited to use the U.S. satellite geographic positioning system (GPS) which could fix the geographic coordinates of their position in relation to barracks, munitions depots, police stations, and other potential targets for subsequent NATO bombing.[90] According to one Swiss verifier, "We understood from the start that the information gathered by OSCE patrols during our mission was destined to complete the information that NATO had gathered by satellite. We had the very sharp impression of doing espionage work for the Atlantic Alliance."[91]

By the end of the year, complaints were mounting over the way Walker and Drewienkiewicz were directing the mission, with scant regard for the five other nations represented.[92] The fact that only the Serbian side had been obliged to accept the cease-fire, and therefore technically only the Serbian side could violate it, amounted to an open invitation to the UÇK to escalate hostilities and provoke Serbian retaliation. France's KVM deputy chief, Ambassador Gabriel Keller, complained that "every pullback by the Yugoslav army or the Serbian police was followed by a movement forward by UÇK forces". The UÇK took advantage of Serbian restraint "to consolidate its positions everywhere, continuing to smuggle arms from Albania, abducting and killing both civilians and military personnel, Albanians and Serbs alike". Privately, Keller said he believed that Walker deliberately sabotaged the mission, and that his only obsession was to "keep the UÇK for the Americans".[93] Later, the mission was bluntly described as a "CIA front" which exploited and destroyed a potential peace-making mission to help train the UÇK on how to fight the Serbs.[94]

Račak: *casus belli* for NATO

In January 1999, the UÇK stepped up its armed attacks. On the morning of 15 January, Serbian police encircled the village of Račak in pursuit of UÇK fighters who had recently ambushed and killed five policemen and two Albanian civilians. The KVM was informed in advance of the operation, which was filmed by a local Associated Press television team. That evening a Serbian Interior Ministry communiqué announced that the operation was a success as "several dozen terrorists were killed".

However, the UÇK rapidly reoccupied the village.

The next day, accompanied by selected Western and ethnic Albanian media, Walker was led by local UÇK to a gully on the edge of the village. It contained a score of dead bodies. Walker immediately described the scene as a "massacre, a crime against humanity" committed by Serbian government security forces.

"I see bodies like this with their faces blown away at close range in execution fashion and it's obvious people with no value for human life have done this", Walker told journalists. (Forensic studies later established that the victims' faces had *not* been "blown away at close range in execution fashion".) "I do not have the words to describe my personal revulsion at the sight of what can only be described as an unspeakable atrocity", Walker said, adding: "I have been in other war zones, and I have seen pretty horrendous acts, but this is beyond anything I have seen before."

Walker had no doubt seen a lot. His experience "in other war zones" had taken place in Central America, where the "pretty horrendous acts" were committed for the most part by forces he was supporting on behalf of his government. His postings in El Salvador and Honduras in the 1970s and 1980s involved setting up a fake "humanitarian" operation in El Salvador as a cover for running guns, ammunition, and supplies to Contra mercenaries attacking Nicaragua.[95] He worked with the Honduran army which formed death squads that "disappeared" some 200 politically suspect students and labor leaders.[96] As ambassador to El Salvador, Walker found excuses for that country's US-trained Atlacatl battalion, mostly graduates of the notorious "School of the Americas", who in the early hours of 16 November 1989 entered a dormitory at the University of Central America, dragged six Jesuit priests from their beds and blew their brains out with high-powered rifles at short range, before murdering the priests' cook and her 15-year-old daughter in the same way. Ambassador Walker demonstrated instant compassion ... for the killers' commander, Salvadoran army chief of staff Colonel Rene Emilio Ponce. "Management control problems exist in a situation like this", he observed. He was "not condoning it, but in times like these of great emotion and great anger, things like this happen".

After his long stint in Central America, Walker spent three years at the National Defense University before receiving his first European assignment, in 1996, as transitional administrator for the UN peacekeeping mission in eastern Slavonia, which transferred

Serb-occupied territory to Croatia. The least one can say is that this *curriculum vitae* scarcely seems ideal for the leader of a peace mission in a sensitive civil war area.

Walker's description of the Račak incident was indignantly denied by Serbian authorities. Serbian president Milan Milutinović angrily accused Walker of "a series of lies and fabrications" aimed at "diverting attention from terrorists, murderers and kidnappers and once again protecting them as he has been protecting them all along". Milutinović complained that Walker failed to recognize the illegality of the UÇK's terrorist attacks which had provoked the police and compelled them to defend themselves. Ignoring Serb protests, Walker's accusations were quickly echoed by NATO politicians and editorialists. The complex conflict in Kosovo was portrayed as a genocidal Serbian rampage against innocent Albanian civilian victims. "Račak" became the immediate justification for NATO war against Yugoslavia. The UÇK strategy of provocation had succeeded – with help from its American friends.

Why, instead of going to nearby Serbian police headquarters to demand an explanation, did Walker spend half an hour with UÇK commanders in Račak? Later, Walker denied having consulted U.S. officials on his cell phone, despite statements from both NATO commander Wesley Clark and Richard Holbrooke that Walker had called them from Račak.

The very next day, the NATO Council held an urgent session again threatening air strikes and declaring that events in Račak "represent a flagrant violation of international humanitarian law". In Washington, Clinton described the killings in Račak as "a deliberate and indiscriminate act of murder". Later, on the eve of the NATO bombing, Clinton declared: "We should remember what happened in the village of Račak back in January, innocent men, women and children taken from their homes to a gully, forced to kneel in the dirt, sprayed with gunfire – not because of anything they had done, but because of who they were." Germany's Green foreign minister Joschka Fischer declared that "Račak was the turning point for me", justifying German military intervention outside the NATO defense area.

"The killings at Račak", the *Washington Post* recalled two months later, "outraged the international community and became a turning point in the year-long conflict between security forces and the Kosovo Liberation Army ... Days later, both sides in the conflict agreed to take part in peace talks in France sponsored by the United States, Russia and four West European nations."[97]

Račak thus led directly to Rambouillet, the ultimatum to Serbia and NATO bombing.

Predictably, Walker's accusations were accepted uncritically throughout NATO countries, despite the fact that many members of his own Kosovo Verification Mission were privately critical of the biased and spectacular way he had handled the matter. The KVM had been well aware that Račak was a UÇK base. Strategically located only 500 yards south of the crossroads town of Stimlje, not far from the future "Camp Bondsteel", Račak was surrounded by trenches, a common practice of the UÇK which turned the villages it occupied into fortresses. UÇK units that had been mounting ambushes, abductions and murders in the vicinity were believed to have been operating out of Račak. A number of Kosovo Serbs had been abducted in the region, mostly during the summer of 1998, and not seen again.[98]

Serbs were not the only victims. In December 1998 and January 1999, the UÇK "arrested" 17 Albanians for various offenses including "friendly relations with Serbs" and "spying". (This behavior never ceased. The KVM reported that the UÇK even took advantage of the funeral for Racak victims, held on 11 February and attended by Walker, the world media, and thousands of Albanians, to kidnap nine more Kosovo Albanians accused of such crimes as "having a brother working with the police; being suspected of having weapons; drinking with Serbs; having Serb friends; or having a Serb police officer as a friend".)

On 8 January, a UÇK armed ambush on police vehicles left three policemen dead and one wounded. Three Kosovo Albanians in a passing taxi were wounded in the same ambush. "The ambush was well prepared: there was a camouflaged firing position for up to 15 men, which had been occupied for several days, and small arms, heavy machine-guns and rocket-propelled grenades were fired at the police convoy", the KVM reported. On 10 January, yet another policeman was fatally wounded in an ambush south of Stimlje. It was at this point that the Serbian police prepared their operation against the UÇK base in Račak.

Police the world over tend to be particularly angry when their colleagues are murdered. One may reasonably assume that Serbian police, cornering a group of men they assumed had done the killing, did not go out of their way to give them a chance to surrender but gunned them down mercilessly. If so, it might be called a "massacre". But the pertinent question is: was it or was it not a cold-blooded "massacre of civilians", killed only because of their ethnic identity, as part of a campaign of "ethnic cleansing"? That, after all, was the interpretation used to justify NATO bombing.

Doubts about Walker's version surfaced almost immediately. On 20 January, two leading French daily newspapers, *Le Figaro* and *Le Monde* published reports from their correspondents in Kosovo raising a number of disturbing questions, which have never been answered.[99] In particular, *Le Figaro*'s veteran Yugoslav correspondent Renaud Girard wondered: "What really happened? During the night, couldn't the UÇK have gathered up the bodies, in fact killed by Serb bullets, to create a scene of cold-blooded execution? ... Intelligently, did the UÇK seek to transform a military defeat into a political victory?"

The only scientific clues to what happened at Račak were to be found in the forensic tests carried out on the 40 bodies retrieved by Serbian authorities three days after the presumed time of death. (Five of the 45 reported bodies were retained by the Albanians and could not be examined.) The Serbian experts examining the Račak bodies were joined by a forensic team from Belarus as well as by a Finnish forensic team already under contract to the European Union to investigate alleged massacres in Kosovo. The initial forensic results were completed and available by the end of January.[100] But the Finnish forensic team, the only one the West would take seriously, kept postponing signing the report, despite the urgency of the matter.

Only on 17 March, as the second "Rambouillet negotiation" was ending in the inevitable impasse and the NATO bombing was about to begin, some 21 kg of undigested expert text accompanied by 3,000 photographs were turned over to the German government (as current occupant of the rotating European Union presidency), which kept the material under wraps. The only document made public was a rather vague "personal impression" written by Dr. Helena Ranta, the head of the Finnish team but by no means its most qualified forensic expert.[101]

On the very morning when Ranta was scheduled to present her conclusions in Priština, the *Washington Post*, in an article datelined Rome, jumped the gun and reported that the Finnish experts called the Račak deaths a "massacre" by Serbs.[102] Copiously citing "Western sources familiar with the report", "Western officials",

"Western sources", all unidentified, the *Washington Post* said the Finnish team had "concluded that the victims were unarmed civilians executed in an organized massacre, some of them forced to kneel before being sprayed with bullets". The *Washington Post* article was widely reprinted in American newspapers, and certainly had a greater impact than the timid reports from Priština the next day. It bore all the hallmarks of CIA disinformation.

In fact, the term "massacre" was carefully avoided by Ranta. At the Priština press conference, flanked by Walker and under persistent questioning by journalists, she nervously acknowledged that a "crime against humanity" had been committed, but quickly added that in her view, the death of any person was a crime against humanity. Many media reports snapped up only the first part of the statement, which in its entirety was virtually meaningless.

The very next day, the Albanian delegation in Paris, led by UÇK commander Hashim Thaqi, signed the "Rambouillet peace accord", thus providing the pretext for the NATO bombing that began six days later on 24 March. Hastily, Walker led the 1,381 members of the ill-starred "Kosovo Verification Mission" out of Kosovo into Macedonia on 20 March. Many were sorry to go. "The situation on the ground, on the eve of the bombing, did not justify a military intervention", said Swiss verifier Pascal Neuffer. "We could certainly have continued our work. And the explanations given in the press, saying the mission was compromised by Serb threats, did not correspond to what I saw. Let's say rather that we were evacuated because NATO had decided to bomb."

It was nearly two years before the Finnish report made it back into a few European newspapers – too late to matter. Certain key details of the Račak autopsies had been published in a specialist journal.[103] The forensic doctors stressed that political and moral questions were matters beyond their scope. Nevertheless, their very technical findings confirmed the following conclusions:

- There was no "execution at close range" in Račak. Almost all the victims were killed by multiple shots, fired from different directions and at a distance. Only one victim showed signs of possibly having been shot at close range.
- The inhuman mutilations of the corpses described by Walker were indeed inhuman. Tooth marks showed they were caused by animals that had had access to the bodies overnight, probably some of the many stray dogs roaming Kosovo.

- To speak of "innocent men, women and children", as President
  Clinton had done, was misleading. There was just one woman
  and one adolescent boy; all the others were men. The woman
  victim was killed from a distance by a single bullet through the
  thorax from the back, most plausibly while running away from
  the shooting.[104]

The Finnish conclusions were the same as those already published
by the Yugoslavs and the Belarussians at the end of January 1999,
but totally ignored by Western media.

The material evidence may be compatible with a pitiless assault
by angry Serbian police on men they considered to be – rightly
or wrongly – "terrorists" who had murdered their colleagues. Cases
of such police "overkill" occur in many countries, including,
notably, the United States. Rarely do such incidents result even
in reprimands, much less 78 days of bombing raids from outraged
foreign powers. In any case, the scientific evidence contradicts Walker's
emotionally charged description used to prepare Western opinion
for war.

The Rambouillet farce

The rise of the UÇK, hostile to any compromise and ready to
assassinate "traitors" who dealt with the Serbs, had made peaceful
negotiations over Kosovo more difficult than ever before. The U.S.-
directed "Rambouillet negotiations", which opened in France on
2 February 1999, under the looming threat of NATO bombing,
made them impossible. Rambouillet was an exercise in fake
diplomacy designed to "prove" that diplomacy had failed and that
war was unavoidable.

At Rambouillet, the official Serbian delegation, which pointedly
included representatives of Kosovo's diverse ethnic communities,
was prepared to make concessions to the more respectable nationalist
leaders such as Rugova, Fehmi Agani, or Veton Surroi. This was
never possible. The familiar Kosovo Albanian leaders were pushed
into the background. UÇK leader Hashim Thaqi, until then an
obscure outlaw, was now presented to the world as head of the
"Kosovar" delegation. Confronting the Serbian delegation with a
"terrorist" was a studied affront, contrary to all diplomatic practice.
Thaqi was treated as a special pet by Madeleine Albright's press
officer Jamie Rubin. The Kosovo Albanian delegation at Rambouillet
was counseled by top U.S. foreign policy guru Morton Abramowitz,

the former head of the Carnegie Endowment and who had acted as "founding father" of the International Crisis Group, leading Balkan policy designer for the "International Community", funded by governments and George Soros.[105] The main task of U.S. diplomats was to get the reluctant Kosovo Albanians to sign an American text on the future of Kosovo, which stopped short of meeting their demand for full independence. Albright enticed the reluctant rebels with the promise that if they signed, Yugoslavia could be bombed, but not otherwise.

In any normal negotiation, the long proposal presented by the Serbian government calling for extensive local self-government and guaranteed rights for all ethnic groups would at least have been acknowledged as a basis for discussion. The mere fact that the Serbian side was making such proposals was ignored. As for the Albanian side, it had only one proposal: secession from Serbia and total independence, if not today, then certainly in three years' time.

The "Rambouillet peace agreement", drafted mainly by State Department official Christopher Hill, was a U.S. ultimatum designed to bring NATO into Kosovo, get the Serbs out, and convince the Albanians to sign. It came in two parts, civilian and military.

According to the civilian part, Kosovo would in effect be independent of Serbia, but Serbia would not be independent of Kosovo. Kosovo would be able to influence Yugoslavia as a whole by sending its representatives to both Yugoslav and Serbian parliaments, governments and courts, whereas Yugoslavia would be barred from influencing Kosovo's internal affairs. Kosovo would have its own constitution, overruling the Yugoslav and Serbian constitutions, making it a "free market economy". Substantial economic aid was promised to Kosovo, while Serbia was to get nothing; the agreement did not even mention suspending economic sanctions against Serbia, much less any help to the 650,000 refugees in Serbia. In contrast to the parliamentary government proposed by the Serbs, "self-governing" Kosovo was to be a Western protectorate whose chief of mission would have the authority to issue binding directives on all important matters, hire and fire officials and security personnel, and overrule election results.

Aware of the forces aligned against it, the Serbian negotiating team at Rambouillet expressed readiness to accept this highly unfavorable arrangement. The real sticking point was the military side of the ultimatum. The Serbs had already agreed to accept international observers, and were ready to accept international peacekeepers. But late in the negotiations, the United States introduced new requirements spelled out in a section entitled "Annex B", giving NATO control not only of occupation forces in Kosovo but also complete freedom of operation throughout all of Yugoslavia. NATO was to be given "free and unrestricted access" to all Yugoslav territory, at Yugoslav expense, as well as immunity from all local jurisdiction or legal process. In short, NATO and its personnel could commit crimes or destroy property with impunity. This meant virtual unconditional surrender of sovereignty over the entire country.

Later, apologists for NATO claimed that the Serbs were responsible for war because they had not publicly challenged this military proposal, which was only a "bargaining position". However, since at a Rambouillet press conference on 20 February Albright herself blamed failure to reach an agreement on Serbian refusal to consider the presence of a NATO-led implementation force, it was clear that NATO was the sticking point and, if peace was the goal, it was on NATO presence that the "bargaining position" needed to be softened. Instead, it was deliberately hardened.

"The military provisions", observed Jan Oberg on 18 March, the day the Albanians signed, "have nothing to do with peacekeeping". The more appropriate term, he suggested, would be "peace prevention".[106] Oberg pointed out that none of the media, commentators, scholars, and diplomats who condemned the Serbs for refusing to sign had stopped to examine what was actually in the accords. Having followed the drafting process closely, Oberg concluded that "this document has been adapted to be acceptable to the Albanian delegates to such an extent that the Yugoslav side – ready to accept the political parts at an earlier stage – now find the changed document unacceptable". Why this change? "Because the worst case for the international community would be Yugoslavia saying yes and the Albanians saying no", Oberg concluded.

Rubin wrote later that the Serbs had been told the military annexe was negotiable. But he also recalled that when Italian foreign minister Lamberto Dini suggested dropping the demand that NATO rather than UN forces implement the agreement, Albright put him in his place by telling him: "The whole point is for the Serbs to accept a NATO force." The scenario, said Rubin, was this: "if the Serbs and the Albanians agreed to a settlement, NATO would implement it and U.S. troops would participate. If the Serbs balked, NATO would initiate air strikes. If the Kosovars balked, we would try to cut off international support for their rebellion." But, he added later, "I just didn't have the nerve to tell even a few sophisticated journalists that the only failure at Rambouillet would be a rejection by the Albanians."[107] In short, even if for some European governments the aim at Rambouillet was to make peace, the primary aim of the United States was to get NATO into Kosovo.

International law explicitly prohibits the use of military threats in international negotiations. In fact, a treaty obtained under threat is invalid. It could be said that the United States was deliberately invalidating any agreement made at Rambouillet, because Washington's intention was to impose its will by military force in any case.

Under heavy U.S. pressure, the UÇK finally agreed to sign once it was clear that Belgrade could not possibly do so, and that only in this way would the UÇK get the war it wanted, complete with NATO bombing of Yugoslavia.

The result was predictable and certain: streams of refugees, material devastation, innocent people killed, wounded and bereaved, homes and livelihoods lost. A less visible but equally disastrous consequence of this US–NATO decision to "solve" the Kosovo problem by war was an unprecedented wave of bitter hatred. In the name of "human rights" and "humanitarianism", hatred triumphed in Kosovo.

3. THE TRIUMPH OF HATRED

The fact that Albanians had invited foreigners to bomb their country was certain to stir violent resentment among Serbs. Some of this resentment found expression in acts of violence against Albanians. Walker's contested decision to pull outside observers out of Kosovo left the protagonists face to face under the bombs, alone to take vengeance or to tell lies. The fact that the "International Community" endorsed the belief that Serbs were intent on committing "genocide" confirmed Albanians in their most paranoid hatred of Serbs. Relations between Serbs and Albanians in Kosovo were already bad. NATO's war made them hopeless. The main psychological effect of the war was to endorse Albanian hatred of Serbs, recognize it as justified, and give free rein to subsequent persecution of Serbs as "revenge".

As the bombing began, the world's attention was focused on the stream of Albanian refugees fleeing into neighboring Albania and Macedonia. The refugees were retroactively turned into the justification of the bombing that set off their flight. In the absence of neutral observers, it is impossible for outsiders to know the precise reasons for that mass exodus – whether, as NATO and its Albanian allies claimed, it was the result of forced Serbian "ethnic cleansing" or whether, as the Serbian government claimed, the UÇK ordered people to leave in order to gain world sympathy for their cause. Or whether, as is equally plausible, various factors contributed to the refugee flow. In war after war, millions of civilians have abandoned everything in a desperate effort to escape the battleground. During NATO's bombing campaign, reliable estimates put the number of people who left the main cities in central Serbia itself (Belgrade, Niš, Novi Sad, and so on) to escape the bombing at about 900,000. Most were women and children, as with the Kosovo Albanians. The NATO assault had transformed the small province of Kosovo into a proving ground for advanced U.S. weaponry, cruise missiles, laser-guided bombs, cluster bombs, depleted uranium explosives. Terrifying Apache helicopters were massing across the border in Albania, threatening to rain down still more fire. The assault set off violent clashes between UÇK and Serb forces, determined to root out the traitors who were helping guide the NATO air strikes. The exodus was greatest in the western part of the province, on the border with Albania, where the fighting was fiercest. Serb forces had strategic reasons to clear the area of Albanians who could assist infiltration of arms and fighters from Albania.[108] Elsewhere in Kosovo, the exodus was far less than portrayed in the world media at the time. Kosovo is a small province; one can drive across it in about two hours. Kosovo Albanians could expect to find shelter with sympathetic fellow Albanians, in many cases family members, across the borders in Albania or Macedonia. After the fighting was over, they could hope to go home, which indeed they did, with a speed that astonished international observers who had been portraying this temporary departure as a tragic expulsion of people driven from their homes forever. In June 1999, when NATO troops marched into "emptied" Kosovo, they were hailed by huge crowds of Albanians in all the main towns.

What were the true objectives of the NATO war against Yugoslavia? And how did the means employed correspond to those objectives? The motives seem to have been mixed and shifting. The original stated objective was simply to force Milošević to sign the text presented at Rambouillet. For U.S. strategists, a less presentable but perhaps more decisive motive was to preserve "NATO's credibility". That was the "real issue", according to Albright mentor Zbigniew Brzezinski.[109] In the early days of the air strikes, the spectacle of masses of Albanian refugees leaving Kosovo provided a more emotionally appealing objective – to avert the humanitarian catastrophe that was underway. As the bombing continued, and the Yugoslav government failed to capitulate, the purpose increasingly shifted toward getting rid of Milošević. The method was to cause hardship to the Serbian people. This purpose continued after the bombing ended, using other means.

After one month of bombing, Senator Joe Lieberman (D-Conn), a favorite of the Albanian-American lobby, declared: "I hope the air campaign, even if it does not convince Milošević to order his troops out of Kosovo, will so devastate his economy, which it's doing now, so ruin the lives of his people, that they will rise up and throw him out."[110] After two months of bombing, asked whether NATO was "trying to make life miserable for regular, everyday Serbs", Lieberman answered: "Oh, we are, I mean that's what we've been doing for the last couple of months. We're not only hitting military targets, otherwise why would we be cutting off the water supply and knocking out the power stations – turning the lights out. We're trying through the air campaign to break the will of the Serbian people so they will force their leader to break his will and to then order his troops out of Kosovo."[111] Lieberman claimed that "the United States of America and the Kosovo Liberation Army stand for the same human values and principles ... Fighting for the KLA is fighting for human rights and American values."[112]

In his first wartime interview, NATO's air commander Lieutenant General Michael Short acknowledged that bombing was intended to cause distress among civilians as a way to strike at "the leadership and the people around Milošević to compel them to change their behavior":[113]

> I think no power to your refrigerator, no gas to your stove, you can't get to work because the bridge is down – the bridge on which you held your rock concerts and you all stood with targets on your heads. That needs to disappear at three o'clock in the morning.

In addition to "inflicting hardships in the daily lives of more Serbs", bombing the country's infrastructure also was seen as having a long-term political impact by destroying Serbia's economic self-sufficiency. An anonymous German official explained that the "kind of money that will be needed to rebuild bridges or even dredge the wrecks out of the Danube" was expected to provide "major leverage for Western countries".[114] The destroyed country would have to follow the dictates of the destroyers in the hope of ever obtaining desperately needed reconstruction aid. This cynical ploy eventually worked.

Meanwhile, the targeting of the civilian population – in flagrant violation of international law – was justified by commentators who found various ways of showing that the Serbian people fully deserved whatever punishment came their way. Most sophisticated was the columnist William Pfaff. "Much has been made, unwisely in my view," he wrote, "of NATO's being in conflict only with Serbia's leaders. Serbia's leaders have been elected by the Serbian people ... Serbian voters have kept Slobodan Milošević in power during the past decade. It is not clear why they should be spared a taste of the suffering he has inflicted on their neighbors."[115]

Newsweek reached a pitch of anti-Serb racism not easily surpassed with an article entitled "Vengeance of a Victim Race" describing Serbs as "expert haters", citing as evidence a "torrent of gutter invective about Bill Clinton's sex life" on commercial television in Serbia. "The Serbs are Europe's outsiders, seasoned haters raised on self-pity", this article proclaimed.[116] Indeed, if a group is earmarked for victimization, what better way to head off foreseeable sympathy than by proclaiming loud and long that those are people who always complain of being "victimized"?

NATO propaganda increasingly sought to justify destroying Yugoslavia by likening it to Nazi Germany and Milošević to Hitler. In a Memorial Day address, Clinton claimed that Milošević's government "like that of Nazi Germany rose to power in part by getting people to look down on people of a given race and ethnicity, and to believe they had ... no right to live". As the bombing intensified, Harvard professor Daniel Jonah Goldhagen came along with the ultimate justification not only for a "taste of suffering", but also for conquest and occupation of Serbia, by likening the temporary flight of Kosovo's civilians to the Holocaust, Milošević to Hitler and the Serbian people to "Hitler's willing executioners", to use the title of the book that gained him Harvard's chair of Holocaust studies. Goldhagen's false premise was that, like Germany and Japan in the early 1940s, Serbia in the 1990s "has been waging brutal imperial war, seeking to conquer area after area, expelling unwanted populations, and perpetrating mass murder".[117] Milošević was a "genocidal killer". He and the Serbian people were "beholden to an ideology which called for the conquest of Lebensraum". The majority of Serbs "believed fanatically" in the rightness of criminal actions and set out to eliminate the Albanian population of Kosovo, in an action reminiscent of the Holocaust. Therefore, the only remedy was the same remedy as that applied to Nazi Germany: Serbia must be conquered, de-Nazified and re-educated by the West.

Goldhagen claimed that, like the Germans and Japanese in the early 1940s, the Serbian nation "consists of individuals with damaged faculties of moral judgment and has sunk into a moral abyss from which it is unlikely, anytime soon, to emerge unaided". By "supporting or condoning Milošević's eliminationist policies", the Serbian people "have rendered themselves both legally and morally incompetent to conduct their own affairs". Therefore, "their country must be placed in receivership". NATO must take over and the Serbian people "need to be made to comprehend their errors and rehabilitated".

This was a call for an ideological crusade on the assumption that violence must be employed to correct the wrong thinking of an entire nation. This reference to Hitler and the Holocaust is symptomatic of an ideological transformation of the unique events of World War II into role-playing patterns that repeat themselves again and again, allowing the "good" power, the United States, to resort repeatedly to military conquest of Evil. The myth of the recurrent Holocaust can serve to justify countless wars of conquest needed to "re-educate" all the morally deficient populations in the world.

In the absence of international observers, the only information about wartime Kosovo was provided by Albanian sources close to the UÇK. The role of the Kosovo Albanian "Council for the Defence of Human Rights and Freedoms" as main source of reports on "human rights abuses" continued during the bombing, as before. The Council's "activists were often the first to interview refugees arriving in Macedonia", and contributed to helping the UÇK "form the West's wartime image of Kosovo".[118]

German defense minister Rudolf Scharping was in the forefront of the propaganda war. On 8 April, as the bombing campaign was going badly, he announced the discovery of a Serbian plan called "Operation Horseshoe" designed to empty Kosovo of its Albanian population. This was supposed to prove that Milošević had been planning to expel the Albanians from Kosovo before the NATO bombing. "Operation Horseshoe" was subsequently exposed as a hoax manufactured by military intelligence.[119]

Scharping eagerly passed along to the public any wild tale portraying the Serbs as monsters. On 26 March, he claimed that in Kosovo, "an ethnically based genocide is taking place". Two days later, he claimed that a concentration camp was being set up in the north of Priština where "teachers are being rounded up and shot before the eyes of their pupils". On 16 April, he outdid himself, choosing the most gruesome details from unsubstantiated horror stories told to eager interrogators by Kosovar refugees: "it is recounted that the foetus was cut out of the body of a dead pregnant woman in order to roast it and then put it back in the cut-open belly... that limbs and heads are systematically cut off, that sometimes they play football with heads..." These stories were "hard to bear for any normal human being", but Scharping bore them well. There was no material evidence, then or now, for these stories, which can take their place in the anthology of apocryphal wartime horror stories.

For the NATO powers, all this incitement to hatred was ephemeral war propaganda and could soon be forgotten. The effect on the peoples involved was much more damaging. Portraying the Serbs as inhuman could only further enflame a much more passionate and dangerous hatred: the hatred of the Albanians toward the Serbs. Albanian Kosovars could no longer resist the most extreme Albanian racist incitement against Serb neighbors when the greatest world powers, the United States and Germany, endorsed the view that Serbs were wicked people, plotting genocide.

The double standards of the NATO powers enforced the tendency of the Albanians themselves to say and believe the worst of the Serbs. The KVM, after leaving Kosovo, took charge of gathering reports on human rights in the refugee camps set up for Albanian refugees, relying on Albanians to collect testimony to help the ICTY prosecute Milošević. The standardized interview forms provided by the State Department amounted to a subtle form of "leading the witness" to confirm some 30 categories of possible human rights violations. In return for making accusations to be used by the ICTY, the refugees were given a promise of strict confidentiality, "to ensure the safety of the victims or witnesses". This method, already used in Bosnia, amounted to a call for anonymous denunciations. The temptation to invent or exaggerate was certain to be great. Telling Serb atrocity stories was the greatest service Kosovo Albanian refugees could render NATO and the UÇK, and there was no risk of being charged with perjury or slander. In reality, the number of Albanian victims in all categories turned out to be significantly lower than estimated during the bombing. Even though it emerged later that certain spectacular atrocity stories circulated during the war were totally invented, no serious doubt was ever cast on the credibility of Albanian refugee reports. Roma also suffered from the pro-Albanian bias of the Western investigators, who indulgently interpreted the traditional anti-Roma racism of the Albanians as a just resentment of Roma cooperation with the Serbs.[120]

When NATO entered Kosovo on 9 June 1999 and Serb forces withdrew, UÇK fighters – including Albanians from Albania – moved in and took over. They grabbed local economic assets and proclaimed themselves the new authorities. Albanian hatred of Serbs exploded into a campaign of violence. An estimated half of the Serbian population of Kosovo fled in terror to makeshift refugee camps in central Serbia. Roma, who had lived better in Serbian Kosovo than elsewhere in the region, were also terrorized and driven out. Elderly Serbs remaining in Priština were murdered and their apartments seized, sometimes by Albanians from Albania who then rented them to foreign aid workers. Serbian Orthodox churches and monasteries, many part of an artistic heritage dating from the Middle Ages, were systematically blown up.

The occupying powers paid little attention to these crimes being committed in their presence, absorbed as they were in the search for "mass graves" in an all-out effort to bolster the Tribunal indictment of Yugoslav president Slobodan Milošević. Well over a year after NATO occupied Kosovo, examination of the 345 most promising sites had yielded a total of 2,788 bodies of people of diverse origin who had died of various causes. The number of bodies plus the number of Albanians reported missing could total around 5,000 at the most, in any case far short of the alarmist declarations of NATO spokespeople during the bombing, suggesting that all Albanian men had been murdered in a campaign of "genocide". Asked when the Tribunal would exhume mass graves of Serb victims, ICTY prosecutor Louise Arbour replied that "the Tribunal has no money to undertake those exhumations". The significant fact is that the privately financed search for bodies was not part of an unbiased quest for the truth, but rather fit into a relentless campaign to make Milošević, and with him the Serbian people, the scapegoat for all the wrongs and suffering of ten years of Yugoslav disintegration.

Meanwhile, murders of Serbs in Kosovo continued apace. Kosovo was put under an occupation government, the United Nations Mission in Kosovo (UNMIK), whose first chief was Bernard Kouchner, founder of the French overseas medical aid organization "Doctors without Borders", and an early champion of the "right to humanitarian intervention". Kouchner did more to justify Albanian violence against the remaining Serb civilians than to stem it. "Human nature dictates this response among some Albanians, revenge being a direct antidote to the poison that has infected this war-ravaged region", prescribed the borderless doctor. Kouchner told Albanians that he felt very close to them, adding: "I love all peoples but some more than others and that is the case with you."[121] But "love" was not the prevailing mood. "You've got to be a little crazy to go to Kosovo!" Kouchner confessed, noting that "what is missing in Kosovo is love" – even between Albanians. "People don't like each other. They have clan and family ties, a tradition I respect ..." But what frightened him the most was "the spirit of vengeance". Kosovo, he concluded, "is not an affectionate place".[122]

Kouchner acknowledged "serious indications" of UÇK involvement in ongoing human rights abuses, noting that "these armed groups seem to operate in an organized fashion and have some form of hierarchy, command and control". But other manifestations of violence seemed to reflect the culture of hatred, liberated and even exalted by NATO's war against the Serbs. According to Kouchner, "One of the most alarming trends" documented by OSCE observers since NATO occupied Kosovo was "the increasing participation of juveniles in human rights violations". OSCE observers reported "case after case of young people, some only 10 or 12 years old, harassing, beating and threatening people, especially defenseless elderly victims, solely because of their ethnicity".[123]

This was the generation educated in Albanian chauvinism. The alleged Serbian oppression of Albanians had been a matter of police abuse of suspected terrorists, but never a matter of ordinary Serbs attacking their Albanian neighbors. This was not, as presented, a case of "getting even"; it was something new.

The upsurge of violence observed by the OSCE was not simply "revenge" or "ethnic cleansing in reverse", with Albanians murdering and persecuting Serbs. Albanians were also attacking other Albanians. This was in fact a *continuation* of the UÇK effort to seize control of the Albanian community in Kosovo. In response, the "International Community" appointed the chief fox to guard the chicken coop. After a phoney "disarmament" of the UÇK, its members were recruited into an ambiguous "Kosovo Protection Corps" – ambiguous because while its international sponsors pretend that "protection" refers to protection from natural disasters, the official word in Albanian, *"Mbrojtes"*, means not protection but "defense". The KPC considered itself the new army of Kosovo. Its commander was former UÇK commander Agim Çeku, notorious for massacring Serbs as an officer in the Croatian army. The salaries of these "protectors", widely accused of running Kosovo's flourishing crime operations, were paid by a special UN fund, fed by voluntary contributions – from the United States and Germany.

A favorite of the Americans and British, Ramush Haradinaj, was made second in command of the KPC. In 1998, while he was commanding the UÇK in his clan's stronghold in the western Decani region near the Albanian border, 40 civilians were murdered there. "Many of the bodies – of Serbs, Albanians and gypsies – bore marks of torture. Moderate Albanians in the Democratic League of Kosovo have implicated Haradinaj in the murders of civilians suspected of collaborating with Serbian forces."[124] Haradinaj was one of the senior UÇK commanders equipped with a satellite phone in 1999 to help guide NATO air strikes. Close to the Albanian lobby in the United States, Haradinaj was whisked off to a U.S. military hospital in July 2000 after he was wounded while leading an armed assault against the compound of the rival Musaj clan.

In March 2000, former Czech foreign minister Jiri Dienstbier reported to the UN Commission on Human Rights: "The bombing hasn't solved any problems. It only multiplied the existing problems and created new ones."[125] Most of Kosovo had been "ethnically cleansed of non-Albanians, divided, without any legal system, ruled by illegal structures of the Kosovo Liberation Army and very often by competing mafias". Dienstbier added that extremist KLA forces were supported in their desire to create Greater Albania by former President Sali Berisha and other leaders in Albania itself.

The 1999 war left a gaping wound in the Balkans. Triumphant Albanian nationalism, strongly encouraged by U.S. patronage, continues to threaten southern Serbia, Macedonia, and even Montenegro. War and resulting economic disaster have delivered the region to criminal enterprises, notably smuggling of drugs, arms, and women. These activities threaten to raise the level of criminal violence in the Western European NATO countries themselves.

4. DEMOCRACY IN THE NEW WORLD ORDER

Just as the medieval Crusades were proclaimed from churches, the 1999 crusade against the Serbs was proclaimed from the holiest of contemporary sites, the Holocaust Museum in Washington, by James Hooper, executive director of the Balkan Action Council.[126] In a 23 February 1999 speech at the invitation of the museum's "Committee of Conscience", Hooper stressed the need to accept the fact that "the Balkans are a region of strategic interest for the United States, the new Berlin if you will, the testing ground for NATO's resolve and U.S. leadership". Hooper accused Milošević of "successfully dividing" the United States from its allies, and for this he would have to be removed. "The administration should level with the American people and tell them that we are likely to be in the Balkans militarily indefinitely, at least until there is a democratic government in Belgrade."

Thus among the various stated and unstated aims of the U.S. war against Yugoslavia was the desire to determine the government in Belgrade. The adjective "democratic", in this context, certainly does not mean a government that wins a multiparty election, something Milošević himself had done on several occasions. And even simply letting him lose an election was not good enough. He had to be "overthrown", as befits a supposed "dictator", and then treated like a criminal in order to justify the war waged against his country and complete the demonstration of what can happen to foreign leaders who incur the wrath of the superpower. The lesson is not a lesson in favor of democracy. On the contrary. Had Milošević been a genuine dictator, he would simply have arrested dissidents and stayed in office.

As it was, the Yugoslav president called for early elections in 2000 that put his own office on the line. This was a risk a genuine dictator would have avoided. It was no secret that many Yugoslavs blamed Milošević for the country's misfortunes, including the *de facto* loss of Kosovo. Moreover, the constant message from the "International Community" that Serbia would continue to be an international pariah so long as Milošević was in office was a powerful form of blackmail. And for the first time, the voters were offered an acceptable alternative with the candidacy of Vojislav Koštunica, a conservative jurist with a rare reputation as an honest patriot. Behind the scenes, the United States persuaded the quarrelsome coalition calling itself the "democratic opposition of Serbia", or DOS, to back Koštunica. The United States was openly pouring money into the bombed country not to repair the damage (on the contrary, repair materials remained under embargo), but to support opponents of Milošević, such as the notoriously opportunistic and unpopular Democratic Party leader Zoran Djindjić. The U.S. National Endowment for Democracy provided millions of dollars and training in "methods of nonviolent action" to a network of young activists calling itself "Otpor" (resistance), with no political program other than the desire to "be normal" on Western terms.[127] The Otpor youth plastered walls with posters of clenched fists and tried to get arrested in order to denounce the "regime" as repressive. Their slogan was "He's through", meaning Milošević.

In the first round held on 24 September 2000, Milošević failed to gain re-election. Official results gave Kostunica over 48 per cent of the vote in a five-man race. This fell slightly short of the 50 per cent required to win, but indicated an almost certain landslide in the runoff against Milošević, who trailed by some ten percentage points. (Yugoslav electoral law calls for a second round if no candidate wins an absolute majority in the first round.) Not satisfied with this prospect of a certain victory at the ballot box, DOS claimed a first round victory and announced it would boycott the second round. This heightened tension and provided an opportunity for the Otpor agitators to take matters into their own hands. The DOS thereby moved the contest from the ballot box onto the streets. The result was the spectacle of the 5 October "democratic revolution", when a large crowd stormed the Skupština, the parliament building in the center of Belgrade. Presented to the world public as a spontaneous act of self-liberation, the event was staged for television cameras, which filmed and relayed the same scenes over and over again: youths breaking through windows, flags waving, flames rising, smoke enveloping the parliament building, described as "the symbol of the Milošević regime".

To storm and vandalize the scarcely guarded parliament, a gang of toughs was bussed in from the town of Čačak, whose fiercely anti-communist mayor, Velimir Ilić, boasted to the French news agency AFP that his armed "commando" of 2,000 men had set out on 5 October to "take control of the key institutions", including the parliament and the television. "Our action had been prepared in advance. Among my men were ex-parachute troops, former army and police officers as well as men who had fought in special forces." He added that "a number of us wore bullet-proof vests and carried weapons". Some of these former "special forces" commandos included veterans of the civil wars in Croatia and Bosnia. The peak of irony lies in the fact that such paramilitaries, primarily responsible for giving the Serbian people the reputation of "ethnic cleansers" and war criminals, were instantly promoted by Western media into heroes of a "democratic revolution".

The bogus "popular uprising" shoved the electoral process to the sidelines. The model was the 1989 overthrow and murder of the Romanian leader Ceaucescu and his wife, a piece of political theater contrived and staged by the Romanian secret service. Had Milošević and his wife met the same bloody fate as the Romanian ruling couple, that would be "proof" enough for the media that they too were dictators. Things did not go that far, but the street action opened a campaign of violence and intimidation aimed at changing the whole power structure in Serbia, outside of any democratic or legal process. Socialist Party headquarters were assaulted and demolished, officials were beaten and expelled from their functions by gangs of "democrats". The most lucrative enterprises were taken over. Strange parallel governments called "crisis headquarters" were set up without any democratic mandate to redistribute property and offices. The clear lesson: "democracy" is not defined by elections, but by "International Community" approval.

And IC approval required more. To gain admittance to the world, Serbia's new leaders would have to help NATO justify its bombing of their country by shipping their wartime president to The Hague for a show trial staged by NATO's partner, the International Criminal Tribunal. It was not enough to bomb Serbia and detach part of its territory. The Serbian people must be made to believe – or to pretend to believe – that they deserved it. The crime must be made to fit the punishment in the New World Order.

Postscript: Perpetual War

1. THE IDEALIZATION OF WAR

The Imperial Condominium

One of the great ironies of the Yugoslav intervention is that this operation, hailed by its ideological champions as uniting Europe around a noble cause, was an episode in the ongoing drive by the United States for supremacy over Europe as well as over the United Nations. The United States has continuously wielded its uncontested power and multifaceted influence to reduce the United Nations to a rubber stamp to be used or neglected as Washington sees fit. An agency such as UNESCO or a secretary general such as Boutros Boutros-Ghali who dares differ with Washington is soon brought into line or dismissed. Richard Holbrooke has emphasized that Kofi Annan "won the job" of UN secretary general the day he enabled the United States to bomb the Bosnian Serbs.[1] This bombing, as Holbrooke also made clear, demonstrated that the United States was "again Europe's leader".[2]

The Yugoslav conflicts of the 1990s were used to assert both U.S. dominance over the European Union through NATO, and NATO's dominance over the United Nations. The Kosovo war demonstrated NATO's willingness to act without UN permission. The political authority of the United Nations was replaced by the moral authority of a vague entity called the "International Community". The United Nations follows rules and procedures; it potentially offers all populations and states a voice in world affairs. In contrast, the "International Community" is vague in its composition and manner of operation. It does not automatically include the whole world. Determined by intangible "values", the IC is more like an English gentlemen's club, whose members are coopted according to unspoken criteria they alone need understand. Rich and powerful, the members are assumed to possess an innate moral sense of what is right and what is wrong, and need no outside authorization to exclude and chastise those who fail to meet their standards.

From its foundation in 1949, one of the major, unstated purposes of NATO was to bind together in a single alliance the European powers that had fought each other twice in the twentieth century. Instead of each defending its own national economic interests, together they can promote the extension of a political and economic order favorable to the trade arrangements, transnational corporations and financial institutions in which all, presumably, share a common interest. Bound together in a single military organization, under U.S. leadership, the leading industrial powers may have to fish together in troubled waters, rather than against each other as they did in the first half of the twentieth century, with such disastrous results. What is called the "International Community" is often a cover for this new Imperial Condominium.

The Kosovo war, officially dubbed by NATO "Operation Allied Force", gave the United States the advantage of asserting leadership over Europe, and European allies the momentary advantage of seeming to share in an equal partnership. However, the mere fact of "solving" the Yugoslav problem by resorting to military force rather than by diplomacy amounted to a victory of the United States over Europe, inasmuch as military force is the near-monopoly of the United States. The bombing of Yugoslavia confirmed the overwhelming military superiority of the United States, encouraging its next administration to go further in the aggressive use of military might without bothering to flatter the European allies.

Members of the Club

For European leaders, participation in US-led military expeditions offers at least the illusion of a share in world hegemony. British leaders strive to maintain their "special relationship" with Washington. Belonging to the *club des Grands* was French president François Mitterrand's avowed motive for taking part in the 1991 Gulf War against Iraq. This motive was confessed with disarming candor by the Italian prime minister Massimo D'Alema, who explained that taking part in the Kosovo war was a strategic imperative for Italy in order to "count as a major country". "If we hadn't done so, we would have ended up weakening the international prestige we had only just acquired", D'Alema explained to his fellow Italians, many of whom were deeply opposed to their country's involvement in bombing Yugoslavia. "The crisis of Kosovo created new networks of relations", D'Alema confided. "For example, the daily teleconferences between the Foreign Ministers of five countries: the United States, Germany, Great Britain, France and Italy. With Kosovo, we entered such a group. It isn't written in any official

document, but in fact, around Kosovo was born a sort of Club",
he proudly recalled.[3] "It's difficult to define the rules of membership
in the noble circle of the great, there exists no statute."

To be admitted to this exclusive club, with no known rules, the
Italian government violated the rules of the Italian Republic it
was sworn to defend. Article 11 of the Italian Constitution declares
that Italy "repudiates war as an instrument to resolve international
conflicts". The only exceptions are to defend the country if
attacked, or to defend an allied country under attack. Moreover,
Articles 78 and 87 specify that a declaration of war must be
submitted to parliament for deliberation. None of this was respected.
Italy's Constitution was a minor scrap of paper, readily sacrificed
to gain entrance to the "noble circle of the Great Powers". For
D'Alema, being admitted to the "Club" must have seemed the
crowning success of the transformation of what used to be the
Italian Communist Party – object of unrelenting U.S. hostility and
CIA plots – into an ordinary center-left party fit to take part in a
NATO government. The triumph was fleeting, as he and the center
left were voted out of office soon afterwards. The delight of this
former communist at being admitted into the "Club" is an eloquent
testimony to the moral collapse of the Western left on the occasion
of the war against Yugoslavia.

Partners in crime

The NATO war against Yugoslavia might be studied by ethnologists
as a contemporary example of the familiar role of blood rituals in
sealing the unity of groups. Joining in the ritual killing of a
scapegoat acts as a bond. Once the NATO governments had taken
part in devastating a country that had done them no harm, they
had to stick together, at least in maintaining the basic pretense
that this was a morally justified and even necessary war waged
for humanitarian values. The NATO governments found themselves
obliged to defend the concept of "humanitarian war", even if they
secretly knew better.

Only the French foreign minister, Hubert Védrine, dared
subsequently to warn publicly that NATO, or a future European
defense force, might be tempted to make dubious use of the "right
of humanitarian intervention". Védrine pointed out that the
concept was disturbingly similar to the "civilizing mission" of
nineteenth-century French imperialists and to the "white man's
burden" celebrated by Rudyard Kipling.[4]

The war against Yugoslavia set an extremely dangerous precedent. It showed how a "humanitarian calamity" could be used to conquer or destroy a targeted country. The procedure for leading NATO into war against Yugoslavia followed a series of steps that amounted to a formula for transforming contemporary internal conflicts into pretexts for military intervention.

1. Economic "reforms" weaken the state. Having fallen into the "debt trap", Yugoslavia had to follow the dictates of the IMF, which drastically weakened the financial and political power of the central government. In different ways, this is a standard feature of the cuts in public services imposed by IMF "structural reforms".

2. The weakening of the central state aggravates ethnic or regional particularities and conflicts. This process was particularly devastating in Yugoslavia because of its multinational composition and the very severe conflicts during World War II, which left their traces in the present generation. However, most existing countries are composed of different national, religious, or ethnic groups. When the security provided by the modern state is unattainable, people may readily turn to closed identity groups, Mafia-style "godfathers", religious sects, or regressive patriarchal protection rackets. This sort of regression is a likely reaction to "globalization".

3. The ethnic troubles are interpreted as a "human rights crisis". Especially if promoted by émigré lobbies in the United States, this interpretation can create an emotional bias that blocks realistic political analysis of the conflict and constructive diplomatic mediation.

4. The United States and/or NATO go to war to resolve the alleged "human rights crisis". The local clients rejoice, but the resulting death and destruction deepen poverty, antagonisms, and bitterness.

5. The resulting chaos is turned over to an "International Community" administration, which manipulates the local factions to create a semblance of "democracy". Any potentially independent government is decisively excluded, proving again that "there is no alternative".

The unilateral procedures adopted by NATO for Yugoslavia amounted to asserting a Western monopoly on determining what is a "humanitarian catastrophe" and what should be done about it. A genuine, unquestioned humanitarian emergency could be dealt with legally through the United Nations. In contrast, when real or potential rebel groups are made to understand that Great Powers can arbitrarily decide to intervene on the basis of a "humanitarian catastrophe", the incentive becomes enormous to manufacture just such a catastrophe, or the appearance of such a catastrophe, in order to get decisive military support from outside. How is the distinction to be made between a real "humanitarian calamity" and a staged imitation? What is to stop a ruthless group, ready to sacrifice some of its own people to reach its goals of taking power over a territory, from staging fake massacres in order to gain the prize of being able to "use NATO as its air force"? A declared policy of "humanitarian intervention" risks provoking far more unrest, violent repression, and humanitarian catastrophe than it can possibly deter or stop. But this leaves aside the possibility that the CIA, or its equivalent, will deliberately stir up the appropriate "humanitarian calamity" in a targeted area, then alert the media, allowing the Great Powers to be "forced to intervene" by "public opinion".

2. THE REAL EXISTING NEW WORLD ORDER

Another irony is that the crusade against "nationalism" in Yugoslavia was led by the United States, which has no qualms about pursuing its own national interest with the clamorous support of a population whose flag-waving nationalism has no rival in contemporary Europe, or perhaps even in the world. Even for the liberal elite, the eventual elimination of nations is envisaged essentially as a global expansion of the United States to encompass the whole world. This was expressed by President Clinton's deputy secretary of state, Nelson Strobridge Talbott III, in an essay significantly entitled "America Abroad; The Birth of the Global Nation".[5] Talbott "bet that within the next hundred years ... nationhood as we know it will be obsolete; all states will recognize a single, global authority". Such institutions as the International Monetary Fund and the General Agreement on Tariffs and Trade "can be seen as the protoministries of trade, finance and development for a united world". This attitude was echoed by British foreign secretary Robin Cook, who concluded that "the old independent nation-state is a thing of the past".[6] Once the concept itself is considered obsolete, smaller nations can no longer hope to evade the dictates of the "International Community" by invoking national sovereignty.

Whether in the soft idealistic version or the tough assertive version, U.S. leaders envision a future world necessarily shaped by U.S. will and U.S. power. In his State of the Union message on 29 January 1991, President Bush Sr. spoke of a "New World Order" under U.S. leadership for "the next American century". "Hegemony" is the term used unabashedly by the influential geostrategist Zbigniew Brzezinski – a hegemony based on military supremacy, ideological ascendancy, technological innovation, and domination of the world's financial system. This is achieved through a "new web of global linkages that is growing exponentially outside the more traditional nation-state system".[7] Brzezinski's forthright objective is "to perpetuate America's own dominant position for at least a generation and preferably longer still".[8] Building a "geopolitical framework" around NATO including Ukraine but excluding Russia will establish the geostrategic basis for controlling conflict in what Brzezinski calls "the Eurasian Balkans", the vast area between the eastern shore of the Black Sea to China, which includes the Caspian Sea and its petroleum resources, a top priority for U.S. foreign policy.

European liberals, in their alarm at the direction taken by the Bush administration's declaration of unilateral war against "the evil axis" and other assorted terrorist dens, risk looking back nostalgically to the happy days of "humanitarian warfare" when they were included in the action. It should be kept in mind that the essential aim of U.S. military policy remains the same, even if circumstances dictate changes in enemies and ideological explanations.

Globalization's fist

"For globalism to work, America can't be afraid to act like the almighty superpower that it is", announced the *New York Times* as the bombs began to fall on Belgrade. In the authoritative opinion of the *Times'* leading liberal commentator on foreign affairs, Thomas Friedman: "The hidden hand of the market will never work without a hidden fist – McDonald's cannot flourish without McDonnell Douglas, the designer of the F-15. And the hidden fist that keeps the world safe for Silicon Valley's technologies is called the United States Army, Air Force, Navy and Marine Corps."[9] In reality, the U.S. "fist" has never been hidden. It is merely cloaked in moral purpose, while being brandished conspicuously for the world at large. The "fist" was boastfully displayed throughout the bombing of Yugoslavia. The fist is meant to be seen and feared. The night fireworks over Baghdad in 1991 and over Belgrade in 1999 were displayed on television screens all around the world was a reminder of what happens to designated "rogues".

The obvious risks of being "outlawed" by the United States constitute a powerful incentive to all governments to stay within the good graces of Washington. As a German foreign policy specialist has observed, for the United States as a great power claiming unhindered access to markets the world over, "identifying and denouncing 'rogue states' in regions of economic interest offers the opportunity to ensure control over the markets of the rest of the region concerned, with help from security guarantees".[10] One "rogue" per region is ideal for bringing the rest into line. The war against the Serbs brought rapid subservience to NATO requirements on the part of governments of neighboring countries such as Bulgaria and Romania, who were not yet NATO members and whose populations disapproved of the NATO action. NATO membership is a coveted guarantee to avoid being the victim of aggression – especially from NATO itself. As a prized NATO member, Turkey can pursue massive internal repression with arms provided by NATO allies, burn villages, violate human rights, and invade neighboring Iraq in pursuit of Kurdish rebels without the slightest worry that Washington will deliver an ultimatum demanding Turkey withdraw its troops immediately from Kurdish-inhabited parts of Turkey, or else bombs will fall on Ankara. It is the United States alone that decides who enjoys protection of the law and who does not. Punishment may be visited on any state accused of violating human rights, supporting terrorism, or building weapons of mass destruction over which the United States intends to preserve its virtual monopoly.

NATO's birthday present

NATO's 50th birthday celebration was held in Washington between 23 and 25 April 1999. The bombing of Yugoslavia had been going on for a month. Thanks to Kosovo, NATO was already asserting its new role as a "humanitarian" strike force unlimited by geographical boundaries or international law.[11] The anniversary was the occasion for official adoption of NATO's new Strategic Concept, prepared by the Clinton administration and accepted by Allied leaders obliged to make a strong show of unity in the midst of a war. The

Strategic Concept includes three important elements which clinch the dominance of the United States over its European allies.

1. *Nuclear weapons.* The Strategic Concept emphatically laid to rest any remaining hope of nuclear disarmament since "the Alliance's conventional forces alone cannot ensure credible deterrence. Nuclear weapons make a unique contribution in rendering the risks of aggression against the Alliance incalculable and unacceptable. Thus, they remain essential to preserve peace." Moreover, nuclear weapons must remain *in Europe* "for the foreseeable future". The demand of the peace movement of the 1980s for a denuclearized Europe was thereby definitively rejected. "The presence of United States conventional and nuclear forces in Europe remains vital to the security of Europe, which is inseparably linked to that of North America." Thus, "the Alliance will maintain for the foreseeable future an appropriate mix of nuclear and conventional forces based in Europe and kept up to date where necessary ..."

2. *Interdependence.* The "inseparable link" between North America (that is, the United States) and Europe is central to the Strategic Concept. There will be no wriggling out of the grip of U.S.-dominated NATO on the part of the European Union or of individual member states. Thus, "The principle of collective effort in Alliance defence is embodied in practical arrangements that enable the Allies to enjoy the crucial political, military and resource advantages of collective defence, and prevent the renationalisation of defence policies, without depriving the Allies of their sovereignty."

3. *The prospect of more "out-of-area" war.* This is couched in the usual terms of reluctant acceptance of duty: "Regional and, in particular, geostrategic considerations within the Alliance will have to be taken into account, as instabilities on NATO's periphery could lead to crisis or conflicts requiring an Alliance military response, potentially with short warning times." The Concept points to the "special logistical challenges" involved in mounting and sustaining "operations outside the Allies' territory, where there may be little or no host-nation support". This can only mean invading countries where NATO is not wanted.

The vaguely defined "security interests" of NATO member states were seen to be threatened, no longer by Soviet communism, but by "risks of a wider nature, including acts of terrorism, sabotage and organized crime, and by the disruption of the flow of vital resources" as well as "uncontrolled movements of large numbers of people, particularly as a consequence of armed conflicts".[12]

Threats all around

After the suicide airliner bombings of the World Trade Center and the Pentagon, it was commonly said that "the world changed on September 11". One thing that had not changed, however, was the Pentagon's aggressive strategy. The attacks merely provided the most persuasive excuse for inflating the military budget since the Soviet threat. In the foreword to the Pentagon's Quadrennial Defense Review Report issued on 30 September 2001, defense secretary Donald Rumsfeld pointed out that the review and report were "largely completed before the September 11, 2001 attacks on the United States. In important ways, these attacks confirm the strategic direction and planning principles that resulted from this review." September 11 will "require the U.S. to move forward more rapidly in these directions".

The Pentagon's stated objective is to protect and advance U.S. national interests that "span the world". This involves precluding hostile domination of "critical areas, particularly Europe, Northeast Asia, the East Asian littoral, and the Middle East and Southwest Asia".

The essential innovation concerns the definition of "threats". From its pinnacle of power, the United States can scarcely perceive any tangible threats. Instead of feeling safer, the "defense" planners imagine potential threats everywhere. These go beyond invisible "terrorists" or recalcitrant "rogues". From now on, the United States fears the very potential of anybody, anywhere, to have the capability to pose any sort of threat. The Pentagon has undertaken to "shift the basis of defense planning from a 'threat-based' model that has dominated thinking in the past to a 'capabilities-based' model for the future". The question is not who might be an adversary, but what anybody might be able to do. In short, any country with the capability to be an adversary could be one, and so the strategy requires preventing any country from having the capability. Meanwhile, the United States will spend upwards of $500 billion a year to develop every possible "capability" of its own. A few direct quotes from this remarkable document give the tone:

- Although the United States will not face a peer competitor in the near future, the potential exists for regional powers to develop sufficient capabilities to threaten stability in regions critical to U.S. interests.
- US forces must maintain the capability at the direction of the President to impose the will of the United States and its coalition partners on any adversaries, including states or non-state entities. Such a decisive defeat could include changing the regime of an adversary state or occupation of foreign territory until U.S. strategic objectives are met.
- For the United States, the revolution in military affairs holds the potential to confer enormous advantages and to extend the current period of U.S. military superiority.
- A reorientation of the posture must take account of new challenges, particularly anti-access and area-denial threats. New combinations of immediately employable forward stationed and deployed forces; globally available reconnaissance, strike, and command and control assets; information operations capabilities; and rapidly deployable, highly lethal and sustainable forces that may come from outside a theater of operations have the potential to be a significant force multiplier for forward stationed forces, including forcible entry forces.

It is hard to see what "forcible entry forces" would be doing against "anti-access and area denial threats" other than invading foreign countries. Here is the bottom line to "globalization", and it signifies world economic domination enforced by military means.

Power has its own momentum. Whatever the declared motives, the war against Yugoslavia served as an exercise in the destruction of a country. The pretext is flexible: harboring terrorists, building weapons of mass destruction, or "humanitarian catastrophe" – all can be used to justify bombing as part of an unfolding strategy of global control.

With its military supremacy demonstrated, the United States shows signs of leaving its NATO allies on the sidelines as it pursues unilateral action in the rest of the world. The proclaimed intention to destroy an expandable list of designated enemies is causing growing alarm in the world at large, and even among European leaders. Should the tough unilateralist approach of the second Bush presidency cause serious disaffection among allies, U.S. leaders have the option of returning to the soft approach of "humanitarian war" that proved so successful in silencing critics and rallying support. To keep that option open, the partners in crime must continue to impose their own mythical version of the 1999 NATO crusade. The fiction must be told and retold of rescuing innocent victims from wicked villains. But the story is not over, and there is more truth to tell.

Notes

INTRODUCTION

1. The military action against Iraq aroused widespread opposition, even if the protests were muted by mainstream media. There was the beginning of a strong anti-war movement in the United States itself, nipped in the bud only by the extremely rapid announcement that the war was over. Thereafter, however, the United States and its British ally managed to go on bombing Iraq for years without arousing serious domestic opposition.
2. David Fromkin, *Kosovo Crossing: American Ideals Meet Reality on the Balkan Battlefields*, The Free Press, New York, 1999, pp.164–5.
3. Fred Hiatt, "A Standing War Crimes Tribunal Could Do Harm", *Washington Post/International Herald Tribune*, 20 June 2000.
4. On 7 March 1998, Madeleine Albright told Italian prime minister Lamberto Dini: "We are not going to stand by and watch the Serbian authorities do in Kosovo what they can no longer get away with doing in Bosnia" (Barton Gellman, "The Path to Crisis: How the Untied States and Its Allies Went to War", *Washington Post*, 18 April 1999; p. A1).
5. In 1993, when General Colin Powell questioned the usefulness of air strikes against Bosnian Serbs, Albright, then U.S. ambassador to the United Nations, retorted angrily: "What's the point of having this superb military that you're always talking about if we can't use it?" Colin Powell, *My American Journey*, Random House, New York, 1995, p. 576.
6. A report presented to President Vladimir Putin in October 2000 by Russian health minister Yury Shevchenko showed that Russia's population shrank by more than half a million people in the first eight months of the year, the steepest drop ever during peacetime. According to the study, Russians were dying younger and having fewer children due to rising rates of poverty, illness, stress, alcoholism, civil conflict, and industrial accidents. Drug abuse and sexually-transmitted diseases also contributed to the drastic decline of male life expectancy from 64 years in the 1980s to less than 59 years. The birth rate of 1.17 children per Russian woman was far below the 2.5 rate required to maintain the population. Shevchenko told a press conference: "The Russian nation is literally dying out." Fred Weir, "Russia May Soon be Empty of People", *Hindustan Times*, 26 October 2000.
7. A study entitled "Top 200: The Rise of Corporate Global Power", released in January 2001 by the Washington-based Institute for Policy Studies, confirmed that the balance of global economic power has shifted from governments to corporate boardrooms. The study, based on a comparison of corporate sales and gross domestic product, showed that 51 of the largest 100 economies in the world are corporations,

not countries. As an example, General Motors Corporation has more economic power than Denmark, IBM is bigger than Singapore, and Sony is bigger than Pakistan.

8. Interviewed by the French weekly *Le Nouvel Observateur*, 12 January 1998, Zbigniew Brzezinski revealed that the "official version" of history, according to which the CIA began to aid the mujahidin in 1980 after the Soviet Army invaded Afghanistan, was false. In reality, months earlier, on 3 July 1979, President Carter signed the first directive on clandestine aid to the Islamic rebels opposed to the pro-Soviet government in Kabul. At the time, Brzezinski said he had explained to Carter that this would trigger Soviet military intervention. That secret operation was "an excellent idea" because it sucked the Russians into the "Afghan trap", Brzezinski concluded. The former presidential National Security advisor made these revelations in Paris apparently as part of the promotion of the French edition of his book, *The Great Chessboard: American Primacy and its Geostrategic Imperatives*, Basic Books, New York, 1997.

9. John B. Roberts II, "Roots of Allied Farce", *The America Spectator*, June 1999. Roberts, a writer and television producer, was asked in February 1992 to design a publicity campaign to gain public support for the Carnegie Endowment's commission. In this connection he was invited to attend closed-door meetings of the commission, which organized its work to influence the next Democratic president, whoever he might be.

10. Morton H. Halperin and David J. Scheffer, with Patricia L. Small, *Self-Determination in the New World Order*, Carnegie Endowment for International Peace, 1992, Washington, D.C., p. 3.

11. Ibid., p. 108.

12. See the retrospective critique of the inward-looking campus left of the early 1990s by Naomi Klein: "In this new globalized context, the victories of identity politics have amounted to a rearranging of the furniture while the house burned down." *No Logo*, Flamingo, London, 2000, pp. 121–4.

13. It is fair to note that in the last half of the twentieth century, a number of Catholic missionaries risked their lives to take the side of the poor victims of U.S. imperialism in Latin America. There is a permanent tension between humanitarian organizations and the powers that use them as a pretext for intervention.

CHAPTER 1

1. The excerpts cited are faithful to the spirit of Milošević's speech, the full text of which was translated by the U.S. Commerce Department, published in an anthology in French, and has been available to officials and researchers for years. Yet the text has been constantly misrepresented, by selection of a single phrase out of context, "Six centuries later, now, we are being again engaged in battles and are facing battles. They are not armed battles, although such things cannot be excluded yet." To

interpret this patriotic rhetoric, typical of any head of state celebrating a historic battle, as a threat or declaration of genocidal war is either maliciously dishonest or paranoid. The passage concluded: "However, regardless of what kind of battles they are, they cannot be won without resolve, bravery, and sacrifice, without the noble qualities that were present here in the field of Kosovo in the days past. Our chief battle now concerns implementing the economic, political, cultural, and general social prosperity, finding a quicker and more successful approach to a civilization in which people will live in the 21st century. For this battle, we certainly need heroism, of course of a somewhat different kind, but that courage without which nothing serious and great can be achieved remains unchanged and remains urgently necessary."

2. William Pfaff, *International Herald Tribune*, 29 March 1996.

3. Quoted by Fred Hiatt, *Washington Post-International Herald Tribune*, 15 May 1999.

4. "Reporting 'Humanitarian' Warfare: Propaganda, Moralism and Nato's Kosovo War", by Philip Hammond, Senior Lecturer in Media at South Bank University, London.

5. For a handy anthology of wartime propaganda rhetoric (in French), see: David Mathieu, *Bombes et bobards: Propagande, bourrage de crâne, mensonges et manipulations de la guerre du Kosovo*, L'Age d'Homme, Lausanne, 2000.

6. *Le Journal du Dimanche*, Paris, 28 March 1999, in ibid., p. 19.

7. Lenard J. Cohen, *Serpent in the Bosom: The Rise and Fall of Slobodan Milošević*, Westview Press, Boulder, 2001. Milošević told the Eighth Session of the Central Committee of the Serbian League of Communists, held 22–24 September 1987: "Serbian nationalism today is not only intolerance and hatred of another nation or nations but is itself a serpent deep in the bosom of the Serbian people ... Serbian nationalists would do the greatest harm to the Serbian people today by what they offer as being allegedly the best thing, namely isolating the Serbian people ... No one can label us Serbian nationalists because we want to, and really will, resolve the problem of Kosovo in the interests of all the people who live there."

8. An important example is Branka Magaš, in *The New Left Review* and her book, *The Destruction of Yugoslavia*, Verso, London, 1993.

9. In 1981, the gross domestic product per inhabitant was $2,591 for Yugoslavia compared to $2,330 for Portugal. Yugoslav GDP exceeded Hungary, but not Czechoslovakia or Poland. Yugoslavia's overall development was greater under communism, as it had been far less developed than those countries before World War II.

10. Susan Woodward, *Balkan Tragedy*, Brookings Institution, Washington, DC, 1995, see pp. 47–57, etc.

11. Ibid., p. 56.

12. "Milošević's victory over the Serbian League of Communists is often cited, because of the war and Western policy in 1991–94, as the beginning of the end of Yugoslavia. But this view was not shared by Western banks and governments, or by other departments of the U.S. government. They supported him because he appeared to be an

economic liberal (with excellent English), who might have greater authority to implement the reform. Although Western governments were later accused of complicity, or foolishness in the extreme, Milošević was an economic liberal (and political conservative). He was director of a major Belgrade bank in 1978–82 and an economic reformer even as Belgrade party boss in 1984–86. The policy proposals commissioned by the 'Milošević Commission' in May 1988 were written by liberal economists and could have been a leaf straight out of the IMF book." Woodward, *Balkan Tragedy*, pp. 106–7.

13. Laura Silber and Allan Little, *Yugoslavia: Death of a Nation*, Penguin Books, London, 1996, p. 112.

14. Tito's most ruthless repression was of Yugoslav communists deemed to be "Stalinist" after the 1948 break with Moscow. This of course never aroused attention or concern in the West.

15. Warren Zimmermann, "The Last Ambassador: A Memoir of the Collapse of Yugoslavia", *Foreign Affairs*, March/April 1995, p. 2.

16. See Susan Woodward, *Balkan Tragedy*, p. 104.

17. Silber and Little, p. 119.

18. The first leader of the Krajina Serbs, Dr. Jovan Rašković, a psychiatrist, tried to work out a compromise in private talks with Tudjman. Tudjman's office leaked a transcript of the talks to the press, quoting Raskovic as calling the Serbs a "crazy people" and Milošević a "communist". Other writings of Rašković's suggest that he also considered the Croats crazy, but in a different way (he described the Serbs as "oedipal" and the Croats as "anal compulsive"). Thus disgraced, Rašković was rapidly replaced as leader of Krajina Serbs by a dentist, Milan Babić, who took a more intransigent position. See Silber and Little, *Yugoslavia*, p. 97.

19. Ibid., p. 86.

20. This notorious speech is quoted by, among many others, Dorothea Razumovsky, "Gott will es!", *Serbien muß sterbien*, Tiamat, Berlin, 1994, pp. 86–7.

21. Chris Hedges, "Kosovo's Rebels Accused of Executions in the Ranks", *New York Times*, 25 June 1999.

22. The Croats were trained for "Operation Storm" by the Virginia-based Military Professional Resources Incorporated (MPRI), described as an "outfit of former U.S. marines, helicopter pilots and special forces teams", which went on to train first the Kosovo Albanian rebels and then their adversaries in the Macedonian army. Christian Jennings, "Private U.S. Firm Training Both Sides in Balkans", *The Scotsman*, 3 March 2001.

23. Silber and Little, p. 174.

24. Interviewed by the author in Croatia in September 1996.

25. Mr. Bajramović told his story to the fearless Croatian satirical weekly, *The Feral Tribune*, from which it was picked up by leading Western newspapers. See Chris Hedges, "A Croatian Militiaman Recounts His Role as a Killer and Torturer", *New York Times*, 5 September 1997, pp. 1 and 3.

26. Ivica Djikić, "Investigation of the Pakrac Valley Crimes Reopened", AIM, Zagreb, 14 October 2000. AIM is a news service covering all of

former Yugoslavia and Albania, with financial support from the European Union.

27. Chris Hedges, "Croatian Whistle-Blowers Claim Persecution", *New York Times*, 15 February 1998.

28. See Robert Thomas, *Serbia under Milošević: Politics in the 1990s*, Hurst & Company, London, 1999, for a remarkably fair and detailed account of the conflicting currents in Serbian politics.

29. The peace plan devised for the International Conference on Former Yugoslavia by David Owen and Cyrus Vance would have established a decentralized Bosnia-Herzegovina no less favorable to the Muslims than the Dayton agreement nearly three years later. It was rejected by the Bosnian Serbs because it would have obliged them to give up considerable territory. However, Owen attributes its final failure to the United States, which accepted the Bosnian Serb veto to avoid committing U.S. ground troops and to prevent any solution not controlled by Washington. See David Owen, *Balkan Odyssey*, Victor Gollancz, London, 1995. The Clinton administration, in a confused way, was trying to pose as champion of the Muslims without having to commit itself in any concrete way.

30. These terms were applied to Serbia by Daniel Jonah Goldhagen in *The New Republic*, 17 May 1999.

31. Woodward, *Balkan Tragedy*, pp. 126–7.

32. For a thorough analysis, see: Barbara Delcourt and Olivier Corten, *Ex-Yougoslavie: Droit International, Politique et Idéologies*, Editions Bruylant, Editions de l'Université de Bruxelles, 1998.

33. The composition of this unusual body was prestigious. The presidents of three Constitutional Courts: Robert Badinter of France, Francisco Paolo Casavola of Italy, and Roman Herzog of Germany, as well as Elizabeth Palm (Judge at the European Court of Human Rights), and Jose Maria Ruda (former president of the International Court of Justice). However, this body was far from being a conventional court of arbitration, which is formed to settle disputes between states by judges of their own choice and with their full prior consent. Here, the countries of the European Union were issuing opinions to their own satisfaction over the heads of the parties concerned. Moreover, the jurists were experts in constitutional law, not international law, which was what they undertook to judge.

34. Delcourt and Corten, *Ex-Yougoslavie*, p. 161.

35. Ignoring the specific Yugoslav constitutional context, the Commission reached out and referred to a quite irrelevant principle, known in international law as *uti possidetis*, borrowed from Roman law, which had been applied solely to decolonization in Africa and South America. In those continents, where the colonies of European Great Powers covered territories with no previously defined national boundaries, *uti possidetis* meant that states emerging from decolonization would inherit the colonial administrative borders they held at the moment of independence. It had been a way of holding territories together, not breaking them up. But, as pointed out by a number of legal scholars, *uti possidetis* was totally inappropriate to the situation of an established European

country. See Matthew C.R. Craven, "The European Community Arbitration Commission on Yugoslavia", *British Yearbook of International Law*, 1995, p. 386. Also, Steven R. Ratner, "Drawing a Better Line: *uti possidetis* and the Borders of New States", *The American Journal of International Law*, vol. 90: 590, October 1996.

36. Craven, *British Yearbook of International Law*, p. 335.
37. Misha Glenny, *The Fall of Yugoslavia*, Penguin Books, Harmondsworth, 1992, p. 143.
38. In 1931, the Orthodox Christians (that is, Serbs) were counted as 1,028,723 or 44.3 per cent of the population of Bosnia-Herzegovina, the Muslims were 717,562 or 30.9 per cent, and the Catholics (Croats) were 557,836 or 24 per cent. There was no census in 1941 due to the war. Over twenty years after the 1931 census, the postwar baby boom had not yet wiped out the population losses of the war. In 1953, there were 1,261,405 Serbs (44.3 per cent), 891,798 Muslims (31.3 per cent) and 654,227 Croats (23 per cent). Serbs retained their traditional relative majority until around 1970. In the 1971 census, for the first time the Muslims registered a relative majority, with 1,482,430 (39.6 per cent), compared to 1,393,148 Serbs (37.2 per cent). The percentage of Croats had declined to 20.6 per cent. (*Hérodote*, No. 67, 4e trimestre 1992, p. 89.)
39. Interview with Zimmerman by David Binder, "U.S. policymakers on Bosnia admit errors in opposing partition in 1992", *New York Times*, 29 August 1993.
40. Glenny, *The Fall of Yugoslavia*, 1992, p. 183.
41. Jacob Heilbrunn and Michael Lind, "Third American Empire, With a Balkan Frontier", *International Herald Tribune*, 4 January 1996.
42. See in particular Owen, *Balkan Odyssey*, Chapter 4, on the disruptive effects of U.S. policy vacillation.
43. David Rieff, *Slaughterhouse: Bosnia and the Failure of the West*, Vintage, New York, 1995.
44. Ibid., p. 35.
45. Ibid., p. 10.
46. Ibid., p. 11.
47. Željko Vuković, "Das Potemkinsche Sarajevo", *Serbien muß sterbien*, 1994, p. 164.
48. Ibid., p. 166.
49. Malte Olschewski, *Von den Karawanken bis zum Kosovo: Die geheime Geschichte der Kriege in Jugoslawien*, Ethnos, Wilhelm Braumüller, Vienna, 2000, p. 245.
50. Ibid., p. 40.
51. Ibid., p. 223.
52. Ibid., p. 27.
53. Ibid., pp. 217–18: "if the Bosnian Serbs had any justice on their side, it came in about the same proportion as the Nazis' had, or the Khmer Rouge's. Again, what the Serbs were doing was *genocide*" (Rieff's emphasis).
54. Ibid., p. 23.
55. Jim Muir, "We Will Never Give Up", *The Christian Science Monitor*, 28 June 1993.

56. George Kenney, "The Bosnian Calculation", *New York Times*, Sunday, 23 April 1995, Section 6, Magazine, p. 42. Kenney resigned from the State Department in 1992 to protest U.S. policy in Yugoslavia. In this article, he noted that Bosnian prime minister Haris Silajdžić "routinely talks about genocide and the 'Bosnian holocaust' with nary an eyebrow raised in his audience. But there was no holocaust." After the Serbs secured the areas they wanted to control in 1992, "fighting declined steadily, reaching a virtual stalemate by autumn 1993". Combat casualties remained low, and there was no evidence of the systematic extermination that could take deaths into the hundreds of thousands. "Neither the International Committee of the Red Cross nor Western governments have found evidence of systematic killing. Nobody, moreover, has found former detainees of concentration camps who witnessed systematic killing. Random killing took place in the camps, but not enough to account for tens of thousands of dead. And, apart from the few well-known massacres, nobody sees signs of missing villages, either."

57. *1996 SIPRI Yearbook*, Oxford Press, London, 1997. *Los Angeles Times*, 2 June 1997.

58. Kenney, "The Bosnian Calculation".

59. These estimates were made a few months before the fall of Srebrenica. The "biggest massacre since World War II" alleged to have taken place on that occasion revived the flagging accusation of genocide. Once again, large figures went into circulation, never to be confirmed or retracted. Even if the top figure of 8,000 killed should turn out to be accurate (which is virtually impossible), that would not change Kenney's conclusion that the total number of persons killed falls far short of 200,000.

60. It is indicative of his reputation that in March 1997, Izetbegović received an award for "democracy development" from the U.S. Center for Democracy in Washington, DC.

61. An explanation offered by Silber and Little, *Yugoslavia*, is that in exchange for stepping aside, Abdić was able to choose his own man, Alija Delimustafić, as interior minister. Chris Hedges, *New York Times-International Herald Tribune*, 26 April 1996, called the deal "bewildering".

62. Alija Izetbegović, *Islam Between East and West*, American Trust Publications, Plainfield, Indiana, 1984. The book was published first in English in the United States by the author's friends at a time when Izetbegović was in jail in Yugoslavia for allegedly trying to transform Bosnia-Herzegovina into an Islamic state. The book could not be published in Bosnia-Herzegovina until after he was released in a general amnesty in 1988.

63. Alexandre Popovic, "Islamic Movements in Yugoslavia", in Andreas Kappeler, Gerhard Simon, Georg Brunner and Edward Allworth, *Muslim Communities Reemerge: Historical Perspectives on Nationality, Politics and Opposition in the Former Soviet Union and Yugoslavia*, Duke University Press, Durham, NC and London, 1994, p. 335.

64. Silber and Little, *Yugoslavia*, p. 211. "To the Serbs, this was a war cry", the authors add.

65. This opening shot in the civil war was generally attributed to Ramiz Delalic, called "Celo", a Bosnian Muslim gangster who became a paramilitary leader. He and his fellow criminal "Caco" murdered large numbers of Sarajevo Serbs in the early phase of the civil war, completely ignored by Western media which never missed a chance to publicize their Serbian counterpart, "Arkan".

66. Čengić recounted this in a November 1996 interview in the Bosnian Muslim publication *Liljan*.

67. Richard Holbrooke, *To End a War*, Random House, New York, p. 195.

68. Ousted in 1993 in favor of General Delić, Halilović made his accusations in his memoirs published in 1997 as *Lukava Strategija* (Cunning Strategy).

69. A Western diplomat calls Elfatih Hassanein "Izetbegović's bagman"; John Pomfret, *Washington Post*, 22 September 1996.

70. Craig Pyes, Josh Meyer and William C. Rempel, "Bosnia Seen as Hospitable Base and Sanctuary for Terrorists", *Los Angeles Times*, 7 October 2001; Željko Rogosić, "Vast Investigation in Bosnia-Herzegovina", *Nacional*, Zagreb, 27 September 2001. The GIA commander lent to the Bosnians was Abdelkader Mokhari, *nom de guerre* Abu el Maali.

71. Senad Advić, editor in chief of *Slobodna Bosna* (Free Bosnia), quoted in "Vast Investigation in Bosnia-Herzegovian", *Nacional*.

72. R. Jeffrey Smith, "A Bosnian Village's Terrorist Ties. Links to U.S. Bomb Plot Arouse Concern About Enclave of Islamic Guerrillas", *Washington Post*, 11 March 2000, p. A1. Alix Kroeger, "Bosnia's Holy Warriors Ready to Fight Evictions", *Observer*, London, 23 July 2000.

73. Chris Hedges, "Leaders in Bosnia Are Said to Steal up to $1 Billion", *New York Times*, 17 August 1999.

74. Ibid.

75. Agence France Press dispatch in the *International Herald Tribune*, 8 January 2002.

76. R. Jeffrey Smith, "High-Profile Bosnian Accused of Fraud", *Washington Post/International Herald Tribune*, 7 September 2001.

CHAPTER 2

1. "The 'Šibenik Ballad' of Lies and Death", AIM, Zagreb, 7 March 1999. The former Chief of Šibenik Military Police, Mario Barišić, said that on the eve of the Croatian parliamentary elections, he and another military policeman and two explosives experts staged the fake attack as directed for Croatian state television (HTV).

2. Mira Beham, *Kriegstrommeln: Medien, Krieg und Politik*, Deutscher Taschenbuch Verlag (dtv), Munich, 1996, pp.162, 169–70.

3. Ibid., p. 164.

4. Ibid., pp. 170–2.

5. Bernard-Henri Lévy, *Le Lys et la cendre*, Grasset, Paris, 1996, pp. 425–6.

6. Document reproduced in Jacques Merlino, *Les Vérités yougoslaves ne sont pas toutes bonnes á dire*, Albin Michel, Paris, 1993, pp. 265–6.

7. Ibid., p. 165.

8. Ruder Finn went from success to success. On the international stage, "Ruder Finn scored a public relations home run in helping its Bosnian Muslim clients dominate the June 1993 conference on human rights in Vienna, virtually hijacking the two-week agenda that climaxed with an 88-to-1 vote deploring the failure of the U.N. to stop the war and demanding that the arms embargo on Bosnia be lifted"; Peter Brock, "Dateline Yugoslavia: The Partisan Press", *Foreign Policy*, No. 93, Winter 1993–94, p. 160.

9. "News reports themselves showed that Bosnian Serbs were unusually cooperative in allowing international inspection of their camps, while Bosnian Muslims and Croats either refused or obstructed inspection of their camps – but that fact also received little public attention." Brock, 'Dateline Yugoslavia', p. 162.

10. "The Proof" was the headline which British tabloid the *Daily Mail* put on its front page above the ITN photo on 7 August 1992.

11. Thomas Deichmann, "Misinformation: TV Coverage of a Bosnian Camp", *Covert Action Quarterly*, No. 65, Fall 1998, pp. 52–5.

12. The two poster questions were, "Un camp où l'on purifie les ethnies, ça ne vous rappelle rien?" and "Les discours sur la purification ethnique, ça ne vous rappelle rien?" Under the photo of Fikret Alić and his companions, the text read: "Purification ethnique cela veut dire: camps, viols, assassinats, exécutions et déportations en masse des populations non serbes de Bosnie-Herzégovine et de Sarajevo. Les Nationalistes serbes iront jusqu'au bout de leur idéologie meurtrière. Médecins du Monde a choisi de continuer ses missions médicales et son aide d'urgence, mais n'a pas choisi de se taire. Se taire, c'est accepter ..." And finally: "Halte aux crimes contre l'humanité des nationalistes serbes." The poster is reproduced in Michel Collon, *Poker Menteur: Les grandes puissances, la Yougoslavie et les prochaines guerres*, EPO, Brussels, 1998, p. 34.

13. From Trnopolje, Fikret Alić emigrated to Scandinavia. He attended a press conference in Bonn on 10 March 1997.

14. This and other attempts by the Serbian diaspora in France to bring suits against various organizations and authors for defamation of the Serbian people are recounted by a lawyer involved in these cases, Vladimir Vukadinovic, in *Le Mur de Sarajevo*, L'Age d'Homme, Lausanne, 1995. For the case described here, see pp. 51–66.

15. Roy Gutman, "Death Camps: Survivors Tell of Captivity, Mass Slaughters in Bosnia" and "Witness's Tale of Death and Torture: In Sex-week Spree, at Least 3,000 Killed", *Newsday*, Long Island (New York), 3 August, 1992, dateline Zagreb. A film on Herak was screened at Bosnian film festivals to illustrate the bestial nature of the Serbs. Herak confessed to virtually any crime suggested to him, and even accused UNPROFOR General Lewis MacKenzie of raping Muslim women. Such details, which undermined Herak's credibility, were left out of Burns' report, distributed over the *New York Times* wire service on 26 November 1992, and featured in Sunday newspapers. Awarding a Pulitzer prize for recording the confession of a prisoner "under the approving eyes of

his Bosnian Muslim captors" raised disturbing questions about professional ethics. See Brock, "Dateline Yugoslavia", p. 163.

16. David Rohde, *Endgame: The Betrayal and Fall of Srebrenica, Europe's Worst Massacre Since World War II*, Farrar, Straus and Giroux, New York, 1997. A careful reading of this book shows that neither Rohde nor anyone else had any clear idea how many Muslim men were killed in and after the Serb conquest of Srebrenica.

17. A 2001 U.S. Justice Department survey found that 52 per cent of all women had been assaulted either in childhood or as adults, and that a woman is raped in the United States every 90 seconds. Bob Herbert, "A Rape in America Every 90 Seconds", *New York Times/International Herald Tribune*, 28 August 2001, p. 8.

18. Roy Gutman, *A Witness to Genocide*, Macmillan, London, 1993, p. 64.

19. Ibid., pp. 144–9.

20. In a statement transmitted to *Newsday* by the Bosnian Serb army, Željko Mejahić (accurate spelling) rudely denied the accusation: "In all responsibility I can state that there was no attempt at rape, and even less that I raped Jadranka Cigelj. I don't know why I would do that, because she is 45 years old, while I am 26, and I don't need a woman as old as that, particularly as she is a bad and unattractive woman. The way she was, I wouldn't lean a bicycle on her, let alone rape her." Any advisor in public relations could have warned that such crude machismo would make almost as bad an impression as confessing.

21. Aart Brouwer, "The Serb Femicide", *Groene Amsterdammer*, 3 September 1997.

22. Ibid.

23. Thomas Deichmann, "Roy Gutman, the Pulitzer Prize and Croatian Propaganda", an updated version of "Augenzeugen oder Propagandisten? Zur Rolle der Medien im Krieg auf dem Balkan" [Eye Witnesses or Propagandists? On the Role of the Media in the War in the Balkans], *Novo*, No. 12, September/October 1994, Frankfurt am Main. Main parts were also published in the German weekly *Die Woche*, 4 November 1994 as "Zeugin der Anklage" [Witness for the Prosecution] as well as in the Belgian Flemish daily *De Morgen* of 8 November 1994 and the Swedish daily *Helsingborgs Dagblad* on 26 November 1994.

24. Brouwer, "Serb Femicide".

25. Martin Lettmayer, "Da Wurde einfach Geglaubt, ohne Nachzufragen" [It was Simply Believed without Further Question], *Serbien muss sterbien: Wahrheit und Lüge im jugoslawischen Bürgerkrieg*, Tiamat, Berlin, 1994, pp. 37–49.

26. Alexandra Stiglmayer, "Die Demütigung als Waffe: In Bosnien-Herzegowina wird systematisch vergewaltigt, um die Moral des Gegners zu untergraben; Die totale Degradierung der Frau zur Ware", *Weltwoche*, 5 November 1992.

27. *Tageszeitung*, Berlin, 2 December 1992. The story was told to Erich Rathfelder, a ready conduit for unverified accusations against Serbs. In August 1998, his report of a "mass grave" of 567 Albanian civilians at Orahovac, based on hearsay, made international headlines before investigators were able to examine the site. There was no mass grave.

28. In its 21 January 1993 report on "Rape and Sexual Violence by Armed Forces in Bosnia-Herzegovina", Amnesty International called for caution, stressing that it was particularly difficult to obtain reliable information, and that the subject of rape of women was largely used as a propaganda weapon, all sides minimizing or denying exactions committed by their forces and exaggerating those of their adversaries.

29. Since the proceedings of the European Commission/Union Councils of ministers are not published, it is not possible to confirm reports that it was the German government which insisted on omitting rape of Serbian women from the delegation's investigation. See Merlino, *Les vérités yougoslaves*, pp. 65–71.

30. Mrs Josipa Milas-Matutinović from the Zagreb "Bedem Lubavi" movement.

31. Barbara Boxer, Susan M. Collins, Dianne Feinstein, Kay Bailey Hutchison, Mary L. Landrieu, Barbara A. Mikulski, Carol Moseley Braun, Patty Murray, Olympia J. Snowe.

32. Joseph Fitchett and John Vinocur, "At Summit, Allies Face Ground Forces Question", *International Herald Tribune*, 24 April 1999, pp. 1 and 4.

33. See Phillip Knightley, "Propaganda Wars", *Independent on Sunday*, London, 27 June 1999.

34. Rebecca Chamberlain and David E. Powell, "Serbs' System of Rape: The Crime is a Key Part of their Military Policy. Slobodan Milošević Must be Held Responsible", *Philadelphia Inquirer*, 24 May 1999.

35. Audrey Gillan, "The Propaganda War: Audrey Gillan tries to find the evidence for mass atrocities in Kosovo", *Guardian*, 21 August 2000. Audrey Gillan recounts that "Ron Redmond, the baseball-capped spokesman for the United Nations High Commissioner for Refugees, stood at the Blace border crossing from Kosovo into Macedonia and said there were new reports of mass rapes and killings from three villages in the Lipljan area ... He spoke to the press of bodies being desecrated, eyes being shot out. The way he talked it sounded as if there had been at least a hundred murders and dozens of rapes. When I pressed him on the rapes, asking him to be more precise, he reduced it a bit and said he had heard that five or six teenage girls had been raped and murdered. He had not spoken to any witnesses. 'We have no way of verifying these reports of rape', he conceded. 'These are among the first that we have heard of at this border.'" Ms Gillan observed that during a war like this, "you are not allowed to doubt atrocity".

36. Gillan concluded: "But among the rape victims arriving in Macedonia nobody spoke of anything like the camps the British Foreign Secretary referred to. Benedicte Giaever told me there had been rape, but not systematic and not on a grand scale. The same was true of the killing. 'We don't have big numbers,' she said ... Another senior OSCE source ... told me he suspected that the Kosovo Liberation Army had been persuading people to talk in bigger numbers, to crank up the horror so that Nato might be persuaded to send ground troops in faster. Robin Cook's rape camp was the same thing, he said: an attempt to get the British public behind the bombing. And wasn't all this a lesson in

how propaganda works in modern war? When I came back to London, I went to see the KLA's spokesman and recruiting officer in Golders Green. Dr. Pleurat Sejdiu, sitting beside the KLA flag and busts of the Albanian national hero Skenderbeg, said there were indeed rape camps ..."

37. Quoted by Thomas Roser, *Frankfurter Rundschau*, 1 November 1996.

38. Report of the Secretary General S/25704 of 3 May 1993.

39. "Punishing Serbs who committed war crimes, Western officials say, could relieve innocent Serbs of the burden of collective guilt." Richard Mertens, "Justice a Foreign Term in Kosovo", *Christian Science Monitor*, 1 August 2000. The fact that collective guilt is suggested *only* for Serbs indicates the underlying assumption.

40. This political use of the Tribunal was confirmed years later by French magistrate Claude Jorda, who observed, on a program broadcast by the Franco-German television channel "Arte" on 22 March 2000, that although Karadžić and Mladić could not be convicted because they hadn't been arrested, their mere indictment "played an important role in Dayton. The indictment prohibited Karadžić and Mladić from coming to Dayton, Paris, or London. And finally they were even definitively forced out of political life in their own countries. This is also a contribution of international justice."

41. For example, testifying before U.S. Senate hearings in August 1995, Professor Cherif Bassiouni insisted that there could be "no peace without justice".

42. Interview in *Wochenpost*, 6 June 1996. "White South Africans don't know how lucky they are in a country that doesn't cry for vengeance", he said.

43. Interview in the *Frankfurter Rundschau*, 22 August 1996.

44. "The ICTY has little support within Bosnian society," concludes David Chandler. "Poll findings that for Bosnian people of all three groups the question of war crimes is of little importance, with 6 per cent of people at the most giving it a high priority, would seem to indicate that the tribunal is acting more under international pressure than to meet Bosnian needs ... Accusations of war crimes, so far, seem to have done little to develop community reconciliation and much to promote tensions between the communities and international administrators." David Chandler, *Bosnia: Faking Democracy after Dayton*, Pluto Press, London, 1999; second edition 2000, p. 104.

45. This family name is pronounced, using English spelling, Dr-lya-cha. In Serbo-Croatian, "r" can stand alone as a vowel. Thus "brd" is pronounced the same as "bird" in English, and the "dr" in Drljača is like the English word "dirt" without the "t".

46. Rüdiger Göbel, "Tot oder lebend" [Dead or alive], *Junge Welt*, 30 June 1998.

47. Marlise Simons, "Controversy over the Death of a Serb War Crime Suspect", *New York Times*, 18 August 1998.

48. Charles Trueheart, "A Bosnian Serb Leader Is Arrested for Genocide", *Washington Post/International Herald Tribune*, 4 April 2000.

49. The September 1998 arrest of Stevan Todorovic and the April 2000

arrest of Dragan Nikolic, two Bosnian Serbs turned over to the Tribunal, were both secretly carried out by commandos who infiltrated Serbia and seized Todorovic in Zlatibor and Nikolic in Smederevo. In March 2000, NATO Secretary General Lord Robertson promised "rough justice" for men who defied the court, and vowed that they would have "no permanent hiding place" (6 May 2000 Associated Press report by Misha Savic from Smederevo).

50. Richard J. Newman, "Hunting War Criminals: The First Account of Secret U.S. Missions in Bosnia", U.S. *News & World Report*, 6 July 1998.

51. Christine Stone, British lawyer and co-founder of the British Helsinki Human Rights Group: "An Insider's View of the International War Crimes Tribunal at The Hague", Antiwar.com, 7 July 2000.

52. At times, however, it has been hard to distinguish the Prosecutor from the Presiding Judge. The first chief judge, Antonio Cassese, often seemed more zealous in his eagerness to prosecute Serb leaders than the first Prosecutor, Richard Goldstone. Cassese's successor, Gabrielle Kirk McDonald, was indistinguishable from Chief Prosecutor Louise Arbour in her hostility toward the Serbs.

53. Peter Brock, "The Hague: Experiment in Orwellian Justice", *Mediterranean Quarterly*, Volume 7, No. 4, Fall 1996.

54. At a joint press conference with Chief Prosecutor Arbour in The Hague on 5 November 1998, Kirk McDonald called Yugoslavia a "rogue state, one that holds the international rule of law in contempt", because it refused to allow Arbour into the country to investigate the Racak incident. Belgrade considered its refusal lawful since at Dayton it had accepted under duress the jurisdiction of the ICTY in Bosnia-Herzegovina only, not in Serbia.

55. The broadness of this definition was cited as a reason for the U.S. Senate to postpone ratification for 37 years.

56. The citation was read into the record not in the original Serbo-Croatian but as rendered in English, from Laura Silber and Allan Little, *Yugoslavia: Death of a Nation*, Penguin Books, Harmondsworth, p. 215.

57. Documents reproduced in: Prof. Kosta Čavoški *The Hague against Justice Revisited: The Case of Dr. Radovan Karadžić*, Serbian Sarajevo, 1997.

58. Silber and Little, *Yugoslavia*, p. 355.

59. David Owen, *Balkan Odyssey*, Victor Gollancz, London, p. 355.

60. This possibility was usually rejected indignantly by Western spokesmen as Serb cynicism, but in the spring of 1994, the German foreign ministry was obliged to admit that arms and munitions had been smuggled to Bihać in shipments of powdered milk for the hospital there.

61. Srebrenica Report: Report of the Secretary-General Pursuant to General Assembly Resolution 53/35 (1998), III. D.

62. Willem Honig and Norbert Both, *Srebrenica: Record of A War Crime*, Penguin Books, London, 1996, p. 133.

63. The Kravica massacre of 7 January 1993 was reported the next day only in the *Daily Telegraph*, and referred to in a CNN report on 23 March and in the *New York Times* of 22 April 1993 ("We Suffer Too, Serbs in Bosnia Cry", by John Darnton). This scant coverage

contrasts with widespread and repeated references to Serb attacks on Muslims.

64. Documentation of the death and destruction caused by Orić's raids has been turned over to the ICTY, which has failed to act on it. As of this writing, no indictment has ever been issued against Orić.

65. On 16 February 1994, the *Washington Post* reported that Orić, "the toughest guy" in Srebrenica, displayed his "war trophies" on videocassette tape: "burned Serb houses and headless Serb men, bodies crumbled in a pathetic heap". In the *Toronto Star* of 16 July 1995, Bill Schiller reported watching "a shocking video version of what might have been called Naser Orić's Greatest Hits. There were burning houses, dead bodies, severed heads, and people fleeing. Orić grinned throughout admiring his handiwork. 'We ambushed them,' he said when a number of dead Serbs appeared on the screen. The next sequence of dead bodies had been done in by explosives: 'We launched those guys to the moon', he boasted. When footage of a bullet-marked ghost town appeared without any visible bodies, Orić hastened to announce: 'We killed 114 Serbs there'...."

66. While other atrocities were committed during the Bosnian war, "the Muslims seem to have been the only ones to have practiced the method of beheading taken over from the Turks". Rewards were offered to Muslims for Serb heads. Malte Olschewski, *Von den Karawanken bis zum Kosovo: Die geheime der Kriege in Jugoslawien*, Braumüller, Vienna, p. 207.

67. One of Serbia's most famous monuments is the "skull tower", Ćele Kula, built with 952 skulls of beheaded Serbs in the outskirts of the city of Niš, by the Turkish governor in 1809.

68. These facts were established in the course of the 2001 trial of Bosnain Serb General Radislav Krstić, at the Hague Tribunal.

69. According to the five-year study of the Netherlands Institute for War Documentation (NIOR) comissioned by the Dutch government and released on 10 April 2002, the decision by Mladić to occupy the whole of Srebrenica "was primarily motivated by the lack of any significant resistance by both Muslim forces and the UN". This was also the consensus reched during the Kristić trial.

70. Interview with Mihailo Marković in *Newsweek*, 5 February 1996.

71. Malte Olschewski, op. cit., p. 157.

72. "The Presidency and the Chief of Staff Sacrificed Srebrenica", *Slobodna Bosna*, Sarajevo, 14 July 1996; translated into German for *Junge Welt*, Berlin, 26 July 1996.

73. Independent researcher George Pumphrey has taken the trouble to document the origin of this figure and subsequent estimates. See "Srebrenica", *Konkret*, 8 August 1999, pp. 18–22.

74. Chris Hedges, "Conflict in the Balkans: In Bosnia, Muslim Refugees Slip Across Serb Lines", *New York Times*, 18 July 1997, p. 7.

75. Michael Evans and Michael Kallenbach, "Missing Enclave Troops Found", *The Times*, 2 August 1995, p. 9.

76. Professor Milivoje Ivanisević of Belgrade University scrutinized the Red

Cross list and found the names of 500 people who had died before Srebrenica fell to the Serbs, as well as a total of 3,016 people listed as "missing" by the Red Cross on the lists of voters in the 1996 Bosnian elections. Either the persons were not missing or the elections were fraudulent.

77. In a particularly strange episode, the *Guardian* reported close to 1,000 Muslim POWs from Srebrenica and Žepa who were being transferred from camps in Serbia to Ireland, the United States, Australia, Belgium, Sweden, and France. Ed Vulliamy, "Bosnia: The Secret War: Serbs 'run secret camps'", *Guardian*, 17 January 2996.

78. Eric Schmitt, "Spy Photos Indicate Mass Grave at Serb-Held Town, U.S. Says", *New York Times*, 10 August 1995. Cited by Pumphrey, "Sebrenica".

79. Tim Weiner, "U.S. Says Serbs may Have Tried To Destroy Massacre Evidence", *New York Times*, 30 October 1995.

80. At the trial of General Krstic in the Hague, the defense acknowledged that Muslims were killed out of vengeance or "because they refused to surrender" or because they were potential killers who presented a "military risk". The defense readily admitted that such killings "were terrible war crimes", but argued that they did not constitute genocide, since women and children were spared and wounded men were given medical treatment and evacuated. The defense insisted that the Bosnian Serb army in general, and Krstic in particular, played no role in any executions, which it attributed to the 10th Sabotage Detachment under the command of Colonel Ljubo Beara, chief of military, operating outside the regular army hierarchy. Although not present during the alleged killings, Krstic was nevertheless found guilty of "genocide", inasmuch as the Tribunal judges evidently broadened the definition of "genocide" to include the motives mentioned above.

81. General Philippe Morillon, testifying on 25 January 2001 to the French National Assembly committee of investigation. The same opinion was voiced by UN military observer Carlos Martins Branco of the European University Institute on 4 March 1998 <http://www.balkanpeace.org/wcs/wctu/wctu08.html>.

82. Owen, *Balkan Odyssey*, p. 143.

83. In January 2000, the *International Herald Tribune* published two columns belittling and dismissing the formal complaints lodged by a group of international jurists with the International Criminal Tribunal in The Hague charging NATO leaders with war crimes for bombing civilians and employing such weapons as anti-personnel cluster bombs and depleted uranium. ("Professors Pursue War Crimes Case Against NATO" by Charles Trueheart, 21 January 2000, and "NATO Committed No War Crimes in Bombing Yugoslavia" by William Pfaff on 24 January 2000.) Although mentioned by name as the leader of the group, Professor Michael Mandel of York University in Toronto was unable to obtain publication in the same newspaper of his letter explaining the reasoning behind the initiative. Thus the IHT's important international readership was given access to only one side – the NATO side – of an important debate on international law and war crimes.

84. William Branigin, "The Shadow of Intelligence ... U.S. Gave Tribunal Classified Data", *Washington Post/International Herald Tribune*, 29 May 1999, p. 1.
85. Noam Chomsky, *The New Military Humanism: Lessons from Kosovo*, Common Courage Press, Monroe, Maine, 1999, pp. 152–3.
86. Thanks to Danilo Zolo, professor of international law at Florence University, for signaling the implications of these provisions.
87. A single U.S. officer, Lieutenant Calley, was convicted for the unprovoked massacre of Vietnamese civilians in the village of My Lai; there was no suggestion of seeking responsibility up the chain of command all the way to the Commander in Chief of the U.S. Armed Forces, that is, the President of the United States. In contrast, the proclaimed purpose of the ICTY has been to use individual crimes in the field to establish command responsibility of the top Serb leadership. Journalist Seymour Hersh has provided a careful, detailed account ("Annals of War; Overwhelming Force: What Happened in the Final Days of the Gulf War?", *The New Yorker*, 22 May 2000, pp. 49–82) of the unprovoked massacre of thousands of helpless Iraqi soldiers and civilians massacred in cold blood as they tried to surrender to U.S. soldiers after the 28 February 1991 cease-fire had technically ended the Gulf War. The motive described was sheer desire to kill more Iraqis, on the part of frustrated U.S. soldiers of the 24th Infantry division under the encouraging command of Major General Barry McCaffrey. Despite considerable evidence of a massive war crime, no charges were brought, least of all against McCaffrey, who was promoted to four star general and in 1996 put in charge of Clinton's war against drugs in Colombia as director of the Office of National Drug Control Policy. The 1991 massacre of Iraqis was more gratuitous and on a larger scale and better documented than the alleged "Srebrenica massacre" of 1995. The latter has become a household word while the former remains virtually unknown ... and unpunished.

CHAPTER 3

1. This ban was lifted only in 1830. It was reimposed by NATO on the largest urban Serbian community remaining in Kosovo in May 2001 "in order not to annoy the Albanians". *Glas Javnosti*, Belgrade, Yugoslavia, 27 May 2001, "KFOR doesn't want to irritate the Albanians: Church bells banned."
2. Leopold Ranke, *Die serbische Revolution* (second edition), Dunker und Humblot, Berlin, 1844. Translated into English by Mrs Alexander Kerr as *The History of Servia and the Servian Revolution*, George Bell & Sons, London, 1853, p. 33.
3. Ibid., p. 76. Georges Castellan, *Histoire des Balkans*, Fayard, Paris, 1991, p. 246.
4. For recent treatment of Garašanin's "Greater Serbia" project, see Tim Judah, *The Serbs*, Yale University Press, New Haven, 1997, pp. 56–9; Georges Castellan, *Histoire des Balkans*, Fayard, Paris, 1991, p. 305; and

Dušan Bataković, *The Serbs of Bosnia & Herzegovina*, Dialogue, Paris, 1996, pp. 48–51.

5. Leader of Polish exiles in Paris, Prince Adam Czartoryski, in 1843 wrote a memorandum of "Advice on Conduct to be Followed by Serbia". Poland was then fighting to free itself from repeated partition between Germany, Austria, and Russia. Czartoryski's Czech agent, Frantisek Zah, saw Serbia as the potential core of a future Slav state including the Czechs to be carved out of Habsburg lands.

6. Benjamin von Kallay, *Geschichte der Serben von der ältesten Zeiten bis 1815*, W. Lemffer, Vienna and Leipzig, 1878.

7. Misha Glenny notes that in the last 14 years of the nineteenth century, assassins claimed the lives of major public figures at an average rate of one a year (victims included Empress Elizabeth, the wife of Emperor Franz Josef of Austria). At the turn of the century, successful political murders suddenly increased, and from 1900 to 1913, 40 heads of state, politicians, and diplomats fell victim to the terrorist's bullet or bomb, including U.S. President William McKinley, four kings and six prime ministers. Glenny, *The Balkans, 1904–1999*, Granta, London, 1999, p. 303.

8. E.J. Hobsbawm, *Nations and Nationalism since 1780: Programme, Myth, Reality*, Cambridge University Press, Cambridge, 1990; second edition (Canto) 1992, p. 139.

9. Madeleine K. Albright, "The Balkans Stride Toward Europe's Mainstream", *Washington Post*, 8 April 2001.

10. Vera Vratusa-Zunjic, "The Intrinsic Connection Between Endogenous and Exogenous Factors of Social (dis)Integration: A Sketch of the Yugoslav Case", *Dialogue*, Paris, June 1997, p. 23.

11. On bureaucratic nationalism in both Yugoslavia and the Soviet Union, see Kosta Christitch, *Les Faux Frères: Mirages et réalités yougoslaves*, Flammarion, Paris, 1996, p. 28.

12. The complex political conflict between the Serbian and Slovenian Republics is recounted in detail by Susan Woodward in *Balkan Tragedy*, Brookings Institution, Washington, DC, 1995, especially in Chapter 4, "Escalation".

13. In conversation recorded by Dobrica Ćosić in his autobiographical *Un homme et son époque*, L'Age d'Homme, Paris, p. 78, cited by Christitch, *Les Faux Frères*, p. 39.

14. The *Arbeitsgemeinschaft Alpen-Adria* was founded in Venice on 20 November 1978. The working group brought together 19 regions including 43 million inhabitants: the German *Land* of Bavaria; the Italian Swiss region of Ticino; the Italian regions of Lombardy, Alto Adige (Sud Tirol), Emilia-Romagna, Friuli-Venezia-Giulia; Slovenia and Croatia in Yugoslavia; the five Hungarian states of Baranya, Kaposvar, Zala, Gyor-Moson-Sopron and Szombathely; and most of Austria.

15. The military court was accused of violating the defendants' human rights by conducting the trial in Serbo-Croatian, the majority national Yugoslav language (which the defendants spoke and understood perfectly well), rather than in Slovenian, a closely related Slavic language.

16. On 24 September 1988, I was visited at my home in Paris by three young Slovenian intellectuals from Ljubljana: Marko Hren (mathematician), Tomaž Mastnak and Braco Rolar (both sociologists). They presented in detail the facts and opinions recounted in these paragraphs.

17. Woodward, *Balkan Tragedy*, p. 440 (footnote to p. 98).

18. This astonishing message was cited by Professor Robert M. Hayden of the University of Pittsburgh, in "The Triumph of Chauvinistic Nationalisms in Yugoslavia: Bleak Implications for Anthropology", *Anthropology of East Europe Review*, Vol. 11, 1–2, Autumn 1993 (Special Issue on War among the Yugoslavs).

19. Walter Zimmermann, "The Last Ambassador", *Foreign Affairs*, March/April 1995, p. 7.

20. In his 1991 book, *Memories of the Beginning of the 1991 Armed Conflict in Yugoslavia*, as reported by Igor Mekina of AIM, "Ten Years Later", 7 July 2001.

21. These benefits to the elite are by no means shared by most of the population, who find themselves hemmed into a smaller territory with narrower prospects. Thus the need for an imaginary compensation in the form of "feel good" nationalist self-celebration.

22. The role of the Argentine diaspora in reviving the Slovenian far right is worthy of study.

23. AIM, 29 April 1998, "War Diplomacy – Controversial Armament Trade", by Igor Mekina reporting from Ljubljana.

24. AIM, 21 April 1998, "The Mystery of a Secret Agreement", by Igor Mekina in Ljubljana.

25. "Notre patrie commune, la Yougoslavie", entretien avec Marija Vogrič, écrivain slovène, par Alain Jejcic, *Dialogue*, n.19, Paris, Septembre 1996, pp. 49–60.

26. This is the semi-official message delivered by James Gow and Cathie Carmichael in their book, *Slovenia and the Slovenes: A Small State and the New Europe*, Hurst, London, 2000. The authors blame Slovenia's leaders for dragging their feet in abandoning the territorial nature of the Slovene army in order to meet NATO requirements. While recounting with sympathy Slovenian national feeling when it was turning against Yugoslavia, notably in the 1988 Mladina–Janša affair, they grow impatient with such attachment to *slovenstvo* ("Slovenianness") once it gets in the way of NATO demands. They also criticize Slovenia for failing to produce plans to work with Hungary to end Austria's neutral status and bring it into NATO.

27. Peter Kovačic Peršin in *Delo*, 15 December 2001, reported by Igor Mekina, "Slovenia & NATO: NATO Go Home!", AIM, 22 December, 2001.

28. Igor Mekina, "Slovenia & NATO: An Improperly Selected Lobbyist", AIM, 7 January 2002.

29. Christitch, *Les Faux Frères*, p. 194.

30. Radical party leader and longtime prime minister Nikola Pašić, Serbia's most influential politician, feared that Yugoslavia would not work. Joseph Rothschild, *East Central Europe between the Two World Wars*, University of Washington Press, 1974, p. 205.

31. See ibid., pp. 201–80.
32. At the time, Italian sources put the Croatian share of the total population of the NDH *including the Muslims* (the HDH included Bosnia-Herzegovina) at 4.8 million or 68.7 per cent, while the Serbs were put at 1.85 million or 26.5 per cent. As for Bosnia-Herzegovina, the proportions of the approximately two million inhabitants were estimated at 44 per cent Serbs, 32 per cent Muslims and 23 per cent Croats. German sources set the Serb share of the population much higher, at 33.9 per cent. However, according to the Third Reich's military envoy to Zagreb, Austrian General Edmund Glaises von Horstenau, the Serbs made up 30.6 per cent, the Muslims 11.9 per cent and the Croats 50.8 per cent of the population of the Independent State of Croatia in April 1941. Smilja Avramov, *Genocide in Yugoslavia*, BIGZ, Belgrade, 1995, p. 235.
33. "All undesirable elements will be exterminated without a trace", were the infamous words of Viktor Gutić in Banja Luka, 26 May 1941, who followed words with action. In Korica, 176 Serbs massacred; in Ljubuško district, some 4,500 people murdered. Even more in Čapljina. In Mostar, 135 Serbs and many Jews were killed by Stipe Varvarić. At an airfield between Svijče and Livno, 280 Serbs were thrown down wells and their bodies covered with lime. All the Serb families of Falinjevo were thrown off the Pristoj bridge, tied to each other by wire. On 28 June, the Orthodox basilica at Bihać was blown up while Ustashe pogroms murdered some 2,000 Serbs and Jews. Thousands of bodies were dumped in the Drina. In Herzegovina, 559 Serbs, all women, children, and elderly people, were thrown into a chasm named Golubinka by 14 Ustashe and two Catholic priests. In four years, thousands more victims would be dumped in the same place; Marco Aurelio Rivelli, *Le Génocide occulté*, L'Age d'Homme, Lausannem 1998, p. 54. Thousands more were killed in the districts of Srebrenica, Ozren, Vlasenica, Kladanj, Sanski Most, Ključ, etc.
34. A British surgeon with the partisans claimed in his memoirs (L. Rogers, *Guerrilla surgeon*, London, 1957, cited by Rivelli, *Le Génocide occulté*, p. 55) to have seen a sack full of human eyes. There are many other such reports. The most famous reference to this particular atrocity is found in *Kaputt* (New York, 1946, p. 266), Curzio Malaparte's account of the Nazi debacle. A diplomat and soldier in the Italian fascist regime, Malaparte called on Pavelić in Zagreb in late 1941. Noticing a basket full of slimy objects on Pavelić's desk, Malaparte asked whether they were Dalmatian oysters and was informed by the smiling *poglavnik* that this was "a present from my loyal Ustashe, forty pounds of human eyes". One may doubt the veracity of this grisly anecdote from the pen of a cynical writer who may have wished to shock his readers. The Italian press may have exaggerated, to bolster Fascist claims that Italy was more civilized than the Croats.
35. Avramov, *Genocide in Yugoslavia*, p. 298. It may be observed that a number of Croats and Slovenians were Germans remaining from the long period of Austro-Hungarian rule. The name "Zajc", for example, is Serbo-Croatian phonetic spelling for the German name "Seitz". This

German component facilitated the racist claim that Croats were really German "Aryans" who had simply adopted a Slavic language.

36. Notably the memoirs of the Third Reich's military envoy to Zagreb, the Austrian scholar General Edmund Glaises von Horstenau.

37. Reported in the 29 June 1941 issue of *Hrvatski Narod*, as cited by Rivelli, *Le Génocide occulté*, p. 64. The "Udbina operation" was so famous in Croatia that it was used in the title of the *Globus* articles by Darko Hudelist, cited below, on Tudjman's Canadian contacts plotting the next "Greater Croatia" incorporating Western Herzegovina.

38. Rivelli, *Le Génocide occulté*, p. 87.

39. Avramov, *Genocide in Yugoslavia*, p. 270.

40. The contrasting pretensions of the two principal Yugoslav peoples was brought out in the oft-quoted lament of the Croatian novelist Miroslav Krleža: "May God preserve me from Croat culture and Serb heroism!"

41. Avramov, *Genocide in Yugoslavia*, p. 248, from *Der Spiegel*, 5 June 1978.

42. Ibid. The coalition was made up of the Croatian Revolutionary Brotherhood (HRB), Croatian Illegal Organization (HIRO), Croatian National Resistance (HNO), United Croats of Germany (UNH), Croatian Youth (HM), World League of Croatian Youth (SHUMS), the Argentine-based Croatian Republican Party (HRP), the Croatian Socialist Party (HSP), and Croatian Freedom Fighters. Although some of these groups had actively fostered ties with Moscow, it was decided at this 1974 Toronto meeting that due to the weakening of the Eastern Bloc, the main ally to "liberate Croatia" should be the anti-communist forces of the West.

43. The remarkable ideological ambiguity, or indifference, of Croatian nationalists is illustrated by the figure of Ante Ciliga, alternately Cominform communist, critical dissident, internationalist communist and ardent nationalist. Philippe Bourrinet, *Ante Ciliga (1898–1992): Nazionalismo e comunismo in Jugoslavia*, Graphos, Geneva, 1996.

44. Literally "routeless territory of historic reality", Tudjman's book was published in English as "The Horrors of War", McEvans & Co., New York, 1996.

45. These conclusions were drawn primarily, but not exclusively, from a report by an ex-prisoner from Sarajevo, Vojislav Prnjatović, written in March 1942 for the refugee agency set up in Belgrade by the Nazi-controlled puppet government. Tudjman cited the communist Ante Ciliga who spent 1942 as a prisoner in Jasenovac and who also described the camp as being run by Jewish inmates. Ciliga sharply criticized the Jews for their alleged selfish behavior, which he attributed to their religion as "chosen people". Rather surprisingly, none of these texts seems to have been attacked for "revisionism".

46. A sign that this succeeded was the ardent defense of Tudjman's Croatia mounted in France by the prominent essayist Alain Finkielkraut, also an ardent defender of Israel.

47. The Norval meetings were recounted in detail, with photographs of the principal participants, in the 26 November and 3 December 1999 issues of the Croatian weekly *Globus*, numbers 468 and 469, by the prominent Croatian journalist Darko Hudelist.

48. Bataković, *Yougoslavie*, p. 196.

49. Ibid., p. 198.

50. Ibid., p. 197.

51. Emir Habul, "A Man Who Divided the People of Krajina: The Beginning of Fikret Abdić's Trial in Karlovac", AIM, 31 July 2001. This essentially unfriendly article by a Sarajevo-based journalist nevertheless describes Abdić's achievements as manager of Agrocommerce in glowing terms.

52. Woodward, *Balkan Tragedy*, p. 87. See footnotes p. 438.

53. Owen, *Balkan Odyssey*, p. 87.

54. For example, Noel Malcolm's *Bosnia: A Short History*, Macmillan, London, 1994, was hailed by Christopher Hitchens in a glowing review in the *Guardian* (1 May 1994) as "the finest anthem to the secular multicultural precept ever penned by a Church and King reactionary". Applauding Malcolm's thesis that "ancient hatreds" have been imported from outside, Hitchens then endorsed Malcolm's erroneous twist on that plausible thesis, by identifying as "outside" the Bosnian Serbs who in fact could not be more "inside". Hitchens claimed that: "Bosnia has been and is the victim of an invasion which had as its impossibly evil objective the fomenting of a civil war." This melodramatic thesis attributes everything to gratuitous "evil". It explains nothing. But its Manichean appeal to the real "outsiders" was enormous, as Leonard Cohen observed: "The view that Balkan ethnic conflicts are fundamentally driven by evil elites who have sought to disrupt 'healed' societies ... and that intervention by the International Community can relatively quickly reverse the damage done by local nationalist leaders in the region, naturally has strong appeal to foreign actors endeavoring to comprehensively transform Southeastern Europe" (Leonard Cohen, *Serpent in the Bosom*, Westview Press, Boulder, 2001, pp. 385–6).

55. Richard J. Aldrich, "America used Islamists to arm the Bosnian Muslims: The Srebrenica report reveals the Pentagon's role in a dirty war", *Guardian*, 22 April 2002. The source is the section on "Intelligence and the war in Bosnia, 1992–1995" by Professor Cees Wiebes in the 10 April 2002 report on Srebrenica by the Netherlands Institute for War Documentation.

56. 9 March 1994, Reuters dispatch from Dubai.

CHAPTER 4

1. Wolfgang Pohrt, "Entscheidung in Jugoslawien", *Bei Andruck Mord: Die deutsche Propaganda und der Balkankrieg*, Konkret, Berlin, 1997, p. 36.

2. This point is developed ibid.

3. The expression was immortalized in "Die letzten Tage der Menschheit" (Humanity's Last Days), 1915, a militant anti-war play by Austrian writer Karl Kraus caricaturing the slander, demonization, and war hysteria practiced by his country's press.

4. In Belgrade, a puppet government was set up under General Milan Nedić who, like Maréchal Pétain of France, was a military hero of World

War I persuaded that collaboration with a triumphant Germany was the only way to save his people. Also like Pétain, Nedić had long advocated a purely defensive military strategy, totally inappropriate for countering German *Blitzkrieg* tactics. The parallel with France goes further. Just as Charles de Gaulle had criticized the defensive Maginot Line strategy before the defeat of France, and afterwards proclaimed himself chief of the Resistance, so Colonel Draža Mihailović, who had urged a defensive guerrilla strategy more suited to Yugoslavia's rough terrain and poor infrastructure, refused to accept defeat and formed the first armed guerrilla resistance to Nazi occupation in all of Europe.

5. These facts, thoroughly documented, are recalled by Ralph Hartmann in *Die ehrlichen Makler*, Dietz, Berlin, 1998, p. 52.

6. At the 6th Fürstenfeldbrucker Symposium "for leaders of the Bundeswehr and business", on 23 and 24 September 1991, organized by the Bavarian educational association, a branch of the Federal association of German employers (*Bildungswerk der Bayerischen Wirtschaft e.V*, Munich, *Bundesvereinigung der Deutschen Arbeitgeberverbände*) Scholz argued that as a part of the "Western value community" – the German moralizing version of the IC – Germany could no longer claim that its Constitution prevented it from taking part in foreign military operations. For one thing, Germany was unquestionably "the biggest motor" for Europe's political integration, and political union required "security union". Second, NATO will be engaged in more and more "out of area" engagements, as shown by the Gulf War, so Germany cannot stay on the sidelines. Scholz told his business leaders several years in advance that the NATO Treaty would be changed to deal with "greater global risk control" and changed weapons systems.

7. Rupert Scholz, "Das Festhalten an ungewollten Staaten schafft keine Stabilität", *Die Welt*, 12 December 1991, cited in Matthias Küntzel, *Der Weg in den Krieg*, Elefanten Press, Berlin, 2000, p. 93.

8. "Der Staat ist en Mittel zum Zweck. Sein Zweck liegt in der Erhaltung und Förderung einer Gemeinschaft physisch und seelisch gleichartiger Lebewesen". "Staaten, die nicht diesem Zecke dienen, sind Fehlerscheinungen, ja Missgeburten" (Hitler, *Mein Kampf*, cited in Werner Maser, *Adolf Hitler Mein Kampf; Geschichte, Auszüge, Kommentare*, Moewig, Munich 1981, pp. 272–3).

9. This play on words was made by Matthias Küntzel. See the section, "Eth(n)ischer Imperialismus", in his *Der Weg in den Krieg*, Elefanten Press, Berlin, 2000, p. 95.

10. *Denkschrift über den ethischen Imperialismus*, quoted by Walter von Goldendach and Hans-Rüdiger Minow, *Von Krieg zu Krieg: Die deutsche Aussenpolitik und die ethnische Parzellierung Europas*, Berlin, Verlag, 8 May 1996.

11. Pierre Hillard, *Minorités et Régionalismes dans l'Europe Fédérale des Régions: Enquête sur le plan Allemand qui va bouleverserl'Europe*, François-Xavier de Guibert, Paris, 2001, p. 88.

12. Von Goldendach and Minow, *Von Krieg zu Krieg*, p. 18.

13. Ibid., p. 17.
14. Ibid. This procedure was also followed by ethnic Albanian clans in Kosovo in the period leading up to the 1989 crisis.
15. Cited in Küntzel, *Der Weg in den Krieg*, p. 97.
16. Franz Neumann, *Behemoth: The Structure and Practice of National Socialism 1933–1944*, Oxford University Press, 1944, Oxford, p. 145.
17. Küntzel, *Der Weg in den Krieg*, p. 96.
18. Heinrich Himmler, "Einige Gedanken über die Behandlung der Fremdvölkischen im Osten", Geheime Reichssache, 15 May 1940, cited in *Bei Andruck Mord*, p. 10.
19. Neudeck's testimony to the Bundestag committee was reproduced in French in *Le Livre Noir de l'ex-Yougoslavie*, Arléa, Paris, March 1993, pp. 445–9.
20. Neudeck claimed that "ethnic cleansing" and "an incredible terror" reigned throughout Yugoslavia, including Voivodina – a region where in reality the civil wars raging elsewhere failed to disturb the harmony between Yugoslavia's greatest mix of populations. Equally absurd, he claimed that Bosnian Serbs and Bosnian Muslims were separated by "race". Presented as an "eye witness", Neudeck recycled all the most extreme anti-Serb press reports of events outside his experience. However, Neudeck made an impression as an authentic emotional witness to his own childhood memories.
21. Zayas's article was published in the 1995 *Criminal Law Forum*; Hillard, *Minorités et Régionalismes*, p. 207.
22. Hillard, *Minorités et Régionalismes*, p. 202. Born in Chicago in 1947 of Franco-Spanish parentage, Zayas obtained doctorates from both the Harvard Law School and Göttingen University. He worked for Cyrus Vance from 1970 to 1973. Ibid., p. 201.
23. Hillard, *Minorités et Régionalismes*, pp. 222–3.
24. These include Rudolf Stehr, an active promoter of Nazi racist policy in Denmark, whose German minority made it a major focus of German *Volkspolitik*; Hans Schmidt-Oxbüll, who also concentrated on Denmark; and Count Hans-Christoph Matuschka, first as Nazi consul in occupied Hungary concerned with *Volksgruppen*, and after the war as a president of FUEV and its main contact with the Bonn Foreign Ministry. Count Matuschka stressed the need to "overcome" the concept of the modern State. Von Goldendach and Minow, *Von Krieg zu Krieg*, pp. 30–5.
25. Hillard, *Minorités et Régionalismes*; "Le cheval de Troie de l'Alpen-Adria", *Balkan infos*, Paris, No. 55, May 2001.
26. Need it be noted that the "intervention by the international community" in Kosovo, which took place a little over two years after this speech, exacerbated inter-ethnic tension to such a point that the presence of the "international community" is thereafter considered necessary for an indefinite period as the only way to prevent wholesale massacre of the non-Albanian minorities. *Divide ut regnes*.
27. Hillard, *Minorités et Régionalismes*, pp, 160–1.
28. Expressed by Silvo Devetak, director of ISCOMET, speaking at the 1998 FUEV congress in Prague; Hillard, p. 154.
29. "Von deutschen Boden wird in Zukunft nur Frieden ausgehen. Wir

sind uns bewußt, daß die Unverletzlichkeit der Grenzen und die Achtung der territorialen Integrität und der Souveränität aller Staaten in Europa eine grundlegende Bedingung für den Frieden ist."

30. Rupert Scholz, "Deklamationen reichen nicht. Das Selbstbestimmungsrecht und die deutsche Politik", *Internationale Politik* 4, 1995, p. 51. Cited by Küntzel, *Der Weg in den Krieg*, pp. 97–8.

31. It is notorious that Germany used the Maastricht negotiations for the treaty transforming the EC into the European Union to get its way. The French government was totally obsessed with persuading Bonn to go ahead with monetary union, despite German reluctance to give up the Deutschmark. In addition to monetary union, the Maastricht Treaty promised to create a common foreign policy. Scarcely a week after the treaty was signed on 10 December 1991, the German government announced that it was going ahead with the controversial recognition. Bonn's European partners had the choice between doing the same or killing the "common foreign policy" before it was born and holding the newly conceived European Union up to ridicule. This was recounted by Horst Grabert, who had served as West Germany's ambassador to Yugoslavia in the 1980s, in his article: "Jugoslawien: Der Grosse Umweg", *Blätter für deutsche und internationale Politik*, 2, 1993, p. 156.

32. The 6 December 1995 motion to send 4,000 *Bundeswehr* soldiers into Bosnia was adopted by a vote of 543 to 107, with six abstentions. Those voting against included all 30 members of the Party of Democratic Socialism (the successor to the East German Communist Party) and 55 SPD members (out of 243). The Greens split evenly, 22 for and 22 against, with five abstentions. One SPD member also abstained.

33. Through Hans-Jürgen Wischnewski, a close advisor to Willy Brandt, German Social Democrats provided clandestine assistance to the Algerian national liberation movement during its war against France. Top secret at the time, this has subsequently been acknowledged with pride by Wischnewski himself. But it can be assumed that other operations contrary to the interests of "friendly allies" may also have been pursued.

34. In his memoirs published a year after his death as *Verschlußsache*, Mainz, 1980, p. 144, published a year after his death in 1979, Gehlen warned that "Tito's heirs ... will not be in a position to ensure the country's non-alignment in the long run. The Soviet Union for its part has long since made all necessary preparations to exploit a situation favorable to its ends." This reflected the habitual over-estimation of Soviet expansionism characteristic of professional Cold Warriors. In reality, the main threat to Yugoslavia's non-alignment turned out to be the implosion of the Soviet Bloc, which robbed non-alignment of its geopolitical significance.

35. Erich Schmidt-Eenboom, *Der Schattenkrieger: Klaus Kinkel und der BND*, Econ, Düsseldorf, 1995, p. 217.

36. Ibid., p. 212. In return, Yugoslav agents passed to the BND a copy of Nikita Khrushchev's famous secret February 1956 speech to the 20th Soviet Party Congress.

37. Schmidt-Eenboom, *Der Schattenkrieger*, p. 216.
38. Ibid., p. 223.
39. Quoted by Ralph Hartmann, *Die ehrlichen Makler*, Dietz Verlag, Berlin, 1998, p. 139.
40. Andreas Zumach, "Die internationale Politik in Südosteuropa hat versafgt", *Bosnien-Herzegowina: Die Chancen einer gerechten Lösung*, Frieden und Abrüstung, January 1995; p. 53. Cited by Mira Beham, *Kriegstrommeln: Medien, Krieg und Politik*, Deutscher Taschenbuch Verlag, Munich, 1996, p. 214.
41. During the NATO bombing of Yugoslavia, UÇK chief and NATO ally Hashim Thaqi held consultations in Tirana with *Balli Kombetar* leader Shpetim Rroqi Matthias Küntzel, *Der Weg in den Krieg*, pp. 55, 80–9.
42. KPD (Kommunistische Partei Deutschlands), KPD/ML (Kommunistische Partei Deutschlands/Marxist-Leninist), KBW (Kommunistische Bund Westdeutschland), KABD (Kommunistische Arbeiterbund Deutschlands). Founded in a few years around 1970 by radical students, these "K-groups" were all characterized by a pro-China orientation and hostility toward the "revisionism" of the Soviet Union and the old Communist Party of Germany, the KPD. The KPD had been banned in West Germany in 1956. It was revived in 1968 as the Deutsche Kommunistische Partei (DKP), more present in the labor movement than the K-groups, less radical and closer to the left wing of the Social Democratic Party.
43. Christian Schmidt, *Wir sind die Wahnsinnigen: Joschka Fischer und seine Frankfurter Gang*, Econ Verlag, Munich, 1999.
44. See, *inter alia*, David Owen, *Balkan Odyssey*, Indigo edition, 1996, pp. 261–2 and 278–9.
45. Interview with Dany Cohn-Bendit, "Schluss mit den Halbherzigkeiten", *Die Tageszeitung*, 2 August 1995.
46. "Grosser Bruder", *Der Spiegel*, 42/96, 14 October 1996.
47. Speech by Gerhard Schröder on "Germany's foreign policy responsibility in the world" before the Deutsche Gesellschaft für Auswärtige Politik in Berlin, published in *Internationale Politik* 10,1999, p. 69. Cited and commented by Küntzel, *Der Weg in den Krieg*, p. 87.
48. The Archduke, who speaks perfect Hungarian in addition to flawless German, French, Spanish, and English, has described how his family cooperated with the reformist Hungarian communist leadership in shaping events leading directly to the fall of the Berlin Wall. "The decisive turning point for the U.S. was 19 August 1989, when we succeeded in opening the border separating Hungary from Austria, near the town of Sopron", according to Habsburg. This allowed over 600 East Germans to cross the border on their way to West Germany. Habsburg recalled that the idea "had germinated at one of our meetings in Debrecen, at a time when the communists, at least on paper, governed the country ... We had decided to organize an international picnic not far from the iron curtain on Hungarian territory under a double presidency: on the Hungarian side, the State minister Pozsgai; on the Pan-European side, myself. Not wanting our presence to draw the fire of the communists from the start, we delegated ... State Secretary Vass, and my daughter Walburga. They are the ones who opened the border and

had the joy of living that hour of freedom which caused the infamous Honecker to say that it was the mortal blow struck against his regime." *Otto de Habsbourg: Mémoires d'Europe*, entretiens avec Jean-Paul Picaper, Criterion, Paris, 1994, pp. 135–6.

49. By French minister delegate to European Affairs Alain Lamassoure, in his preface to *Mémoires d'Europe*, p. xii.

50. Jean-Paul Picaper, *Otto de Habsbourg: Mémoires d'Europe*, Criterion, Paris, 1994, pp. 209–10.

51. Author's personal experience during sessions of the European Parliament in Strasbourg in 1991.

52. Otto von Habsburg, "¿Dónde están los Balcanes?" *ABC*, Madrid, 27 September 1995. Praising the military capacity of the Croats, as displayed in western Slavonia and the Krajina, Habsburg spoke rather scornfully of those who "attribute this to some retired U.S. generals and to Israeli technology. The latter was important; as for the former, a great doubt exists."

53. Claudia Lagler, "VP-Positionen unklar, Spektrum zu breit", interview with Karl Habsburg, *Die Presse*, Vienna, 12 June 1996.

54. The year before, in January 1996, von Habsburg himself sponsored an exhibition of photographs in the hall of the European Parliament in Strasbourg designed to show that Croatia is "in the very heart of Europe". A feature of the exhibit was a pair of photos, one of an Austrian-style public building in Vukovar entitled "Croatian culture" and the other, of the same building in ruins, entitled, "Serbian culture". Nobody would know that Vukovar had been a multinational town in the Austro-Hungarian Empire when that building was constructed and that it was no more "Croatian" than "Serb", just as the civil war that devastated it was no more Serb than Croat.

55. See Annie Lacroix-Riz, *Le Vatican, l'Europe et le Reich de la Première Guerre mondiale à la guerre froide*, Armand Colin, Paris, 1996, pp. 99–112.

56. Ibid., p. 101.

57. Ibid., p. 102.

58. Dušan T. Bataković, *Yougoslavie: Nations, Religions, Idéologies*, L'Age d'Homme, Lausanne, 1994, pp. 169–72.

59. The Trepča mining complex in Kosovo, for example, was British-owned and operated.

CHAPTER 5

1. Gardan Gashi and Ingrid Steiner, *Albanien: Archaisch, orientalisch, europäisch*, Promedia, Vienna, 1997, p. 68.

2. Ibid., p. 56.

3. Ibid., p. 72. Miranda Vickers, *Between Serb and Albanian: A History of Kosovo*, Columbia University Press, New York, 1998 p. 57. Here as elsewhere, the attributions differ slightly.

4. Ibid., p. 47.

5. Ibid., p. 49.

6. Dušan T. Bataković, *The Kosovo Chronicles*, Plato, Belgrade, 1992.

7. In December 1920, Albania's first independent government took

office under President Solejman Delvina. Italy's economic influence was predominant. The interior minister, Ahmet Zogu, went on to declare himself King of the Albanians in September 1928, before being deposed in April 1939 by the Italians, who took full control. After Germany invaded Yugoslavia, Vittorio Emmanuele III of Italy, declared on 12 August 1941 Kosovo, West Macedonia, and parts of northern Greece to be attached to "Greater Albania". After Italy accepted defeat on 8 September 1943, the German *Wehrmacht* occupied Albania. Civil war broke out between the fascists and the Yugoslav-backed communist partisans led by Enver Hoxha, who took power in Tirana on 28 November 1944.

8. The cruel repression of the Albanians was denounced by Dimitrije Tucović, founder of the Serbian Social Democratic Party, among others.

9. Vickers, *Between Serb and Albanian*, pp. 116–17; Noel Malcolm, *A Short History of Kosovo*, Macmillan, London, 1998, p. 284; Mirko Grmek, Marc Gjidara and Neven Simac, *Le Nettoyage ethnique*, Fayard, Paris, 1993, pp. 150–85, reproduces the full French translation published by the information center of the "Republic of Kosova" in 1992.

10. The first decree revoking rights of settlers in Kosovo-Metohija and Macedonia was issued by the presidency of the Antifascist Committee of National Liberation of Yugoslavia on 6 March 1945. It was confirmed by a decree of 5 November 1946. Specifically deprived of their rights were settlers installed on land abandoned by Albanian emigrants after 1918 (Article 4b). The context is peculiar, since under the Ottoman regime Muslim landlords *de facto* disposed of the land, without "owning" it.

11. Bataković, *The Kosovo Chronicles*, p. 17.

12. As of 1979, the natural population growth of Kosovo Albanians was 26.1 per 1,000 compared with 8.6 for Yugoslavia as a whole. Vickers attributes this partly to the need for an Albanian woman to produce a son as quickly as possible after marriage to ensure her status, avoid being divorced, and hasten the day when she can hand over a large part of her domestic work to a daughter-in-law. "Having a large number of children, apart from other perceived advantages, was also seen as ensuring for Kosovo an Albanian as opposed to a Serbian future." Vickers, *Between Serb and Albanian*, p. 172.

13. The 1961 census registered 646,605 Albanians, making up 67.2 per cent of the total population of Kosovo (of the seven listed minorities, Serbs numbered 227,061, accounting for 23.6 per cent). The 1971 census registered 916,167 Albanians, making up 73.7 per cent (with Serbs at 228,261 or 18.4 per cent). The 1981 census counted 1,227,000 Albanians – roughly double the number of 20 years earlier – with the Serb population declining to 210,000 or 13.2 per cent. From then on, Kosovo Albanians boycotted the census, but claimed vastly greater numbers and "90 per cent of the population". This percentage, impossible to verify, was accepted and constantly repeated by international news media throughout the Kosovo crisis of 1998–99.

14. A high birthrate is normally associated with economic under-

development and an unfavorable social position of women, two obvious characteristics of Kosovo Albanian society. However, the Kosovo birthrate was high even in comparison with Albania. "Thus, during the 1980s the women in Kosovo, on the average, had one child more than the women in Albania, despite the fact that the economic and cultural development was at a higher level and more accelerated in Kosovo than in Albania"; Dušan Janjić, "National Movements and Conflicts of Serbs and Albanians", *Conflict or Dialogue: Serbian–Albanian Relations and Integration of the Balkans*, Open University, European Civic Centre for Conflict Resolution, Subotica, Serbia, 1994, p. 120.

15. Vickers, *Between Serb and Albanian*, p. 74.
16. Gashi and Steiner, *Albanien*, pp. 140–1.
17. Quoted in Vickers, *Between Serb and Albanian* p. 58. Trotsky reported on the 1912–13 Balkan wars as a correspondent for *Pravda*.
18. Vickers, *Between Serb and Albanian* p. 153.
19. Ibid., 176–7, citing R. Gremaux, "Politics of Ethnic Domination in the Land of the Living Past", in G. Duijzings, D. Janjic and S. Maliqi, *Kosovo:Kosova : Confrontation or Coexistence*, University of Nijmegen, p. 19.
20. Arshi Pipa, *Albanian Stalinism*, East European Monographs, Boulder (Colorado), 1990, p. 50.
21. Arshi Pipa, "The Other Albania: a Balkan Perspective", in *Studies in Kosova*, edited by Arshi Pipa and Sami Repishti, East European Monographs, No. CLV, Boulder, distributed by Columbia University Press, 1984, p. 245. The authors use the Albanian spelling of Kosovo.
22. "The pressure of unemployment was channeled into an explosive growth in the number of educational establishments and education itself. Young people graduated from secondary school or university with little chance of finding work, which was made more difficult by their ignorance of other languages besides Albanian." Vickers, *Between Serb and Albanian*, p. 191.
23. Interview with Professor Hajredin Hoxha in *Vjesnik*, Zagreb, 9 May 1981; cited by Vickers, *Between Serb and Albanian*, p. 193.
24. Vickers, *Between Serb and Albanian*, p. 200.
25. Illiteracy remained at 31.5 per cent, compared to 15.2 per cent for Yugoslavia as a whole. Of a population of over 1.5 million, only 178,000 people had jobs, while most of the population lived off unproductive family agriculture, especially herding goats and sheep. Pipa, *Albanian Stalinism*, pp. 100–1.
26. Vickers, *Between Serb and Albanian*, p. 191.
27. An example is Catherine Samary, a leading member of the French Trotskyist *Ligue Communiste Révolutionnaire* who has published numerous books and articles on Yugoslavia.
28. Pipa, *Albanian Stalinism*, p. 202.
29. Matthias Küntzel, *Der Weg in den Krieg*, Elefanten Press, Berlin, 2000, p. 21.
30. "Il n'existait pas de tissue social réel en Albanie mais des cellules juxaposées entre lesquelles régnaient la méfiance ou l'indifférence.

La force de la médisance, la volonté d'abaisser le mérite, la jalousie de la réussite d'autrui étaient considérables. Parler d'une 'culture de la haine' comme cela a été fait parfois est trop fort, mais à tout le moins peut-on évoquer une 'culture de la hargne'. Abaisser le clan voisin était un moyen de rehausser le sien, aussi la délation a-t-elle énormément sévi." Jean-Paul Champseix, "Communisme et tradition: un syncrétisme dévastateur", *Albanie Utopie: Huis clos dans les Balkans,* Editions Autrement, Paris, 1996, p. 58.

31. Pierre Milza and Serge Berstein, *Histoire terminale,* Hatier, Paris, 1993, p. 330.

32. Defending themselves against a lawsuit for slander brought by the Serbian Academy, the textbook authors and publishers presented in their defense 91 newspaper articles to substantiate their accusations, but not the memorandum itself! (In November 1993 the suit was thrown out of a Paris court on a technicality.) French opinion was heavily influenced by Florence Hartmann, the press spokesperson at the French embassy in Belgrade who was hired as correspondent for *Le Monde* to cover Yugoslavia's disintegration. Aside from her own consistently anti-Serb articles, she provided her own orientation to visiting correspondents unfamiliar with Yugoslavia. Ms Hartmann was married to a Croat, Emil Domankušić, an engineer employed at Belgrade airport, whose father , General Stjepan D. Domankušić, was a top counter-intelligence officer under Tito. In January 2001, Ms Hartmann appeared in The Hague as the new spokeswoman for the Office of the Prosecutor at the International Criminal Tribunal.

33. According to Mihailo Marković, one of the 16 members of the Academy's committee on the memorandum, the first section on the economy had been written by Kosta Mihailović, among others, and had been discussed and approved. The second part had been written by Professor Vasilije Krestić alone and was yet to be discussed when the draft text was published. Interview with Mihailo Marković, "Titos Kapitulation", *Konkret,* Berlin, May 2000, p. 25. See especially Kosta Mihailović and Vasilije Krestić, *Memorandum of the Serbian Academy of Sciences and Arts: Answers to Criticisms,* Belgrade, 1995.

34. Susan Woodward points out (*Balkan Tragedy,* Brookings Institution, Washington, DC, 1995, p. 78) that the same Serbian leaders who attempted to denounce the intellectuals' nationalism by leaking the incomplete "memorandum" wanted to reduce Kosovo's autonomy for purely economic reasons but saw no way to do it. The former banker Slobodan Milošević found the political excuse to do so by defending the Kosovo Serbs: the political combination that built his power base.

35. Conversation with the author in Paris, 16 April 1998. Professor Krestić said it would have been more appropriate to speak only of "cultural genocide" (also a questionable term).

36. The interview appeared in the 6 April 2001 issue of *Le Vif/Express,* which never published the letter to the editor from Belgian journalist Georges Berghezan setting the facts straight.

37. For example, in the *New York Times* of 12 July 1982, Marvine Howe,

in a report from Priština entitled "Exodus of Serbians Stirs Province in Yugoslavia", quoted Becir Hoti, an executive secretary of the Communist Party of Kosovo and an ethnic Albanian, as saying: "The [Albanian] nationalists have a two-point program, first to establish what they call an ethnically clear Albanian republic and then the merger with Albania to form a greater Albania." And in the 1 November 1987 *New York Times*, David Binder reported from Belgrade ("In Yugoslavia, Rising Ethnic Strife Brings Fears of Worse Civil Conflict") that: "As Slavs flee the protracted violence, Kosovo is becoming what ethnic Albanian nationalists have been demanding for years ... an 'ethnically pure' Albanian region, a 'Republic of Kosovo' in all but name."

38. Vllasi's show trial for "counter-revolutionary activity" opened in October 1989 and ended in his acquittal in April 1990.

39. *The Kosovo Report*, by The Independent International Commission on Kosovo, Oxford University Press, London, 2000, p. 43.

40. At the time, some 400 radio and television stations had been operating in Yugoslavia with temporary licenses, or none at all. The vast majority were in Serbia, a country of less than ten million inhabitants on a small territory of only 88,361 km^2.

41. As of June 1998, there were 2,319 print publications and 101 radio and television stations in Yugoslavia, over twice the number that existed in 1992. Belgrade alone had 14 daily newspapers. Six state-supported national dailies had a joint circulation of 180,000, compared to around 350,000 for seven leading opposition dailies. Figures come from "State Media Circulation Slips", on p. 3 of the 8 June 1998 issue of *The Belgrade Times*, an English-language weekly. Press diversity in Serbia no doubt profited from the extremely acrimonious contest between government-backed media (by no means as bad or as uniform as alleged) and opposition media seeking foreign backing. Without this ongoing battle, the government might well have established a media monopoly. But it is also fair to point out that the champions of independent media needed to keep exaggerating the perils of their situation in order to attract ongoing financial backing from the West, notably from the European Union and the Soros Foundation. After Milošević was defeated and sent to The Hague, Serbia's press was more uniform than before, but in the opposite, pro-Western, direction.

42. *International Herald Tribune*, 18 March 1998.

43. Shkelzen Maliqi, "Characteristics and Perspectives of the Albanian Movement", *Conflict or Dialogue: Serbian–Albanian Relations and Integration of the Balkans*, Open University, European Civic Centre for Conflict Resolution, Subotica, Serbia, 1994, pp. 237–47.

44. On 14 October 1992 in Priština, Rugova's mentor Fehmi Agani confirmed this widely held impression in conversation with journalist Tim Judah: "Frankly, it is better [for us] to continue with Milošević. He is not prepared for such a long war. Milošević was very successful in destroying Yugoslavia and, in the same way, if he continues, he will destroy Serbia." Tim Judah, *Kosovo: War and Revenge*, Yale University Press, New Haven and London, 2000, p. 79.

45. Interview at Serbian Ministry of Education on 22 March 2000, with Milivoj Simonović, in charge of education in Kosovo before the NATO bombing.

46. Judah, *War and Revenge*, p. 71.

47. *The Kosovo Report* of the "Independent International Commission on Kosovo" concludes that "most experts seem to accept the theory of mass hysteria; there have been similar occurrences in situations of heightened tension". Footnote 18, p. 343.

48. A late example of this hyperbole: in an interview in *Politique Internationale* in 2000, Bernard Kouchner, at the time UN administrator for Kosovo, sought to excuse the Albanians for their failure to cooperate by claiming that "after ten years of apartheid, during which they lived as sub-humans, the Albanians no longer have confidence in anybody".

49. Judah has observed that "many Kosovars successfully convinced many Westerners that the question of Kosovo was really one of human rights. In fact it was not. At the heart of the matter was a fundamental struggle between two peoples for the same piece of land" (*War and Revenge*, p. 84). The question Judah neglects to raise is to what extent certain Western officials deliberately let themselves be convinced of something that all informed observers of the area knew was untrue.

50. Sandro Provvisionato, *Uck: l'armata dell'ombra*, Gamberetti, Rome, 2000, p. 67.

51. Such as Predrag Simić, for several years director of the Institute of International Politics and Economics in Belgrade, and subsequently foreign policy advisor to Yugoslav president Vojislav Koštunica; and historian Dušan Bataković, Koštunica's ambassador to Greece.

52. "While he was president of Yugoslavia in 1992 and 1993, Dobrica Ćosić made discreet contact with Kosovo Albanian leaders. He wanted to discuss the territorial division of the province, with the Albanian part, except for a number of Serbian enclaves, leaving Serbia. This was rejected by Albanian leaders." Tim Judah, *The Serbs*, Yale University Press, New Haven, 1997, p. 307.

53. Ćosić's analysis of the Kosovo situation, as expressed before and during his term as president (cut short in mid-1993 by Milošević, who may have concluded that his domestic prestige was not exportable and thus of no use), is to be found in a 1994 collection of his writings published by L'Age d'Homme under the title *L'Effondrement de la Yougoslavie*.

54. In an interview given to Julia Ferguson of Reuters on 27 May 1998, Albanian prime minister Fatos Nano suggested that "a compromise could be reached by giving Kosovo the status of the third republic without the right of succession from the Federal Republic of Yugoslavia, under international guarantees".

55. One NGO, Jan Oberg's Transnational Foundation for Future and Peace Studies, based in Lund, Sweden, distinguished itself by attempting to work toward peaceful reconciliation. But its efforts were undermined by the conflictual approach of the "international community".

56. The summer 1998 issue of the NED's magazine *Democracy* ran the slogan on its cover: "Kosovo – World's Largest NGO?" adding that Veton Surroi "likes to tell people" this, and that "he is only partly joking". The *bon mot* was published earlier in the March 1998 report of the International Crisis Group, a particularly influential international governmental-non-governmental organization, entitled "Kosovo Spring".

57. *Democracy*, NED, summer 1998.

58. These documents, dated from October 1998 until 15 March, less than ten days before the NATO bombing began, were obtained by the International Association of Lawyers Against Nuclear Arms (IALANA) which sent them to various media. Several texts were published in the daily *Junge Welt* on 24 April 1999. Either the authorities were downplaying the plight of the Kosovo Albanians in order to reject asylum-seekers, or they were exaggerating the plight to justify war. Either way, the hypocrisy is manifest.

59. For example, the mountain people of Indochina were used by the United States against the Vietnamese; the United States attempted to use the Misquito Indians against Sandinista Nicaragua; Savimbi's CIA-backed *Unita* stressed Ovimbundu claims to weaken Angola; apartheid South Africa allied with separatist Zulu tribal leaders against the racial unity of the anti-apartheid African National Congress.

60. From a 1 January 1988 interview, cited by SIRIUS, Benjamin C. Works, 28 February 1999 archive.

61. Ian Mather, "Ethnic Europeans Lend Clinton a Hand", *The European*, 7 November 1996.

62. *Defense & Foreign Affairs Strategic Policy*, London, 31 March 1993.

63. Mira Baratta's grandfather fought with the pro-Nazi Ustashe army, while her father Petar Radievolic carried on the Croatian nationalist cause in the United States, publicly defending Pavelić's interior minister Andrija Artuković in Los Angeles when his extradition was belatedly demanded in 1985. Brian Mitchell, "The GOP's Tangled Foreign Policy", *Investor's Business Daily*, 4 March 1999.

64. Brian Mitchell, "The GOP's Tangled Foreign Policy", *Investor's Business Daily*, 4 March 1999.

65. Matthew Rees, "Bosnia's Mira Image", *The Weekly Standard*, 25 December 1995.

66. "The underground pipeline, 913 kilometres long, is designed to carry 750,000 barrels a day, or 35m metric tons per year, which will represent 40 per cent of the crude oil from newly-developed oil-fields that will enter the Black Sea in the next five years, or 30 percent of the new oil over the next 10 years. It would ship Russian, Azerbaijani, Kazakh and Turkmenian oil from around the Black Sea to the markets of Western Europe and North America. It will also bypass Turkey's heavily traveled Bosphorus Straits ... Big tankers carrying 300,000 tonnes of crude can anchor at the port of Vlora, which makes the transit journey to the United States economic, while the biggest tankers passing the Bosphorus can only carry 150,000 tonnes, AMBO officials said. A holding structure with three separate companies in

Bulgaria, Macedonia and Albania will build the pipeline." "Albania Gives AMBO Corporation Exclusivity", *Albanian Daily News*, 20 September 2000.

67. Shaban Murati, "Albanie: Le retour des Etats-Unis", AIM (Alternativna informativna mreza/Association of Independent Media), Tirana, 7 March 2000.

68. Pipa, *Albanian Stalinism*, p. 97.

69. An illustrated report on Camp Bondsteel in a French weekly magazine announced: "Not secret, but very discreet: the immense solidly-built base that the Americans have constructed in Kosovo is there to last. And the allies of the United States are starting to wonder whether its implantation wasn't the real objective of the war ..." Victor Loupan, "La base américaine inconnue du Kosovo", *Le Figaro Magazine*, 9 June 2000, pp. 30–4.

70. Paul Stuart, "Camp Bondsteel and America's Plans to Control Caspian Oil", 29 April 2002, World Socialist web-site http://www.wsws.org/articles/2002/oil-a29.shtml.

71. Provvisionato, *Uck*, p. 74.

72. Ibid., p. 83.

73. Targets included Chamijl Gasi, a member of the Yugoslav Assembly from Glagovac; Gugna Adem, president of the Suva Reka Municipal Board; and Ibro Vait, member of the Serbian National Assembly from Prizren.

74. This was acknowledged by the OSCE in its report *Kosovo/Kosova: As Seen, as Told*, an analysis of the human rights findings of the Kosovo Verification Mission October 1998 to June 1999, OSCE, Vienna, 1999, p. 137. By then NATO had won the UÇK's war for it. Such facts were never publicized when they might have influenced public opinion to oppose war against Yugoslavia.

75. Richard Cohen, "The Winner in the Balkans is the KLA", *International Herald Tribune/Washington Post*, 18 June 1999.

76. In 2000, UÇK commander Shaban Shala, by this time involved in seizing villages in southern Serbia, just across the border from Camp Bondsteel, boasted of having been in contact with the CIA as well as with British and Swiss agents in northern Albania since 1996. Tom Walker and Aidan Laverty, "CIA Aided Kosovo Guerrilla Army", *Sunday Times*, 12 March 2000.

77. According to a 20 November 2001 front page feature in the *Wall Street Journal* by Andrew Higgins and Christopher Cooper ("CIA-Backed Team Used Brutal Means to Break up Terrorist Cell in Albania"), CIA agents began arriving in Albania "when the country's doctrinaire communist regime collapsed in 1992". The CIA "found an eager partner in Sali Berisha, a cardiologist elected Albania's president in 1992. 'Total cooperation', is how Mr. Berisha described his relationship with the American intelligence agency. 'They worked in Albania as if they were in New York or Washington', he added."

78. Provvisionato, *Uck*, p. 85.

79. Jerry Septer, "KLA Finances War with Heroin Sales", *Washington Times*, 3 May 1999.

80. During the summer of 1998 Serbian security forces pursued classic anti-insurgency operations aimed at recapturing territory under UÇK control. Washington backed away from Gelbard's earlier description of the UÇK as a "terrorist group". At a Pentagon press conference on 29 June 1998, a spokesman explained that the "Secretary of State determines through a special procedure when an organisation is a 'terrorist organisation'. Such a determination was not done in the case of the KLA, that is all." Thus Madeleine Albright alone had the power to define the nature of the UÇK.

81. Richard Holbrooke, *To End a War*, Random House, New York, 1998. Holbrooke repeatedly credits Milošević with saving the Dayton peace negotiations by making concessions to a stubborn Izetbegović, who wanted to keep the war going.

82. Holbrooke, *To End a War*, pp. 91–2, 96. On 28 August, Holbrooke arrived in Paris to work out a negotiating position with Izetbegović and his foreign minister Muhamed Sacirbey. That day, CNN reported a particularly gruesome bomb massacre in downtown Sarajevo, with scores of civilian victims. The timing was perfect. Izetbegović, wearing "a sort of paramilitary outfit, complete with loose khakis, a scarf, and a beret bearing a Bosnian insignia", demanded that NATO launch strikes against the Bosnian Serbs immediately. Izetbegovic was exclusively "focused on the necessity for immediate NATO bombing, and wary of negotiations ... From Pale the Bosnian Serbs accused the Bosnian Muslims of staging the incident to draw NATO into the war", Holbrooke recalls. Within NATO, experts disagreed, and UN Secretary General Boutros Boutros-Ghali called for an investigation. "None of this mattered much", according to Holbrooke. "What counted was whether the United States would act decisively and persuade its NATO allies to join in the sort of massive air campaign that we had so often talked about but never even come close to undertaking." American experts instantly attributed the massacre to the Serbs. Holbrooke failed to mention that British ammunition experts serving with the UN in Sarajevo said they found no evidence that Bosnian Serbs had fired the lethal mortar round and suspected the Bosnian government army might have been responsible (Hugh McManners, "Serbs 'Not Guilty' of Massacre: Experts Warned U.S. that Mortar was Bosnian", *Sunday Times*, 1 October 1995, p. 15).

83. The October 1998 Holbrooke–Milošević agreement allowed 20,000 Serb police officers and soldiers to remain in Kosovo. "This point is crucial: NATO did not expect or intend for its agreement with Belgrade to stop all Serb security operations in Kosovo. When KLA activities and Serb retaliations spiraled up in the following months, what failed most of all were NATO's promises and threats to restrain the KLA. Belgrade could not be expected to give up recourse to self-defense if NATO could not deter and control the KLA." Timothy W. Crawford, "Pivotal Deterrence and the Kosovo War: Why the Holbrooke Agreement Failed", *Political Science Quarterly*, No. 4, Vol. 116, 22 December 2001, p. 499.

84. Brigadier General (Ret.) Heinz Loquai, military advisor to the German

delegation to the OSCE in Vienna, in "Die OSZE-Mission im Kosovo – eine ungenutzte Friedenschance?", *Blätter für deutsche und internazionale Politik*, September 1999, recounts the following: "On 25 October 1998, the OSCE standing council decided to set up the Kosovo Mission, a day after the UN Security Council cleared the way with resolution 1203. Already on October 17, that is, even before the Mission was officially established, the OSCE president, Polish foreign minister Bronislaw Geremek, named the American diplomat William Walker to head the KVM." And Roger Cohen reported to the *New York Times* from Berlin on 9 July that "Europeans were also angry at how the appointment of an American, William Walker, to head the mission to Kosovo of the Organization for Security and Cooperation in Europe had been decided. 'We provide two-thirds of the expense and the personnel, and then the appointment is made with almost no consultation', said an official."

85. German NATO General Klaus Naumann, who had helped design the ultimatum, told the BBC, "He really did what we had asked him to do. He withdrew within 48 hours some 6,000 police officers and the military back into the barracks. This was also confirmed by the OSCE verification mission." On 12 March 2000, the BBC broadcast "Moral Combat: NATO at War", hosted by Allan Little (*Daily Telegraph* correspondent and co-author with Laura Silber of *The Death of Yugoslavia*), first broadcast on BBC2, 12 March 2000).

86. Ibid.

87. "The U.S. contracted a private firm from Virginia, DynCorp, to send 150 experts. The enterprise, which had already gathered experience in Bosnia, employed primarily veterans of American armed forces – modern mercenaries, whose loyalty is to their employer, not necessarily to the OSCE or NATO." *Der Spiegel* 46/1998, 9 November 1998, "Wehrlose Aufpasser", p. 210.

88. Ulisse (pseudonym), "Come gli Americani hanno sabotato la missione dell'Osce", *Limes*, supplemento al n.1/99, p. 113, L'Espresso, Rome, 1999.

89. Incident reported by both *Limes* and *La Liberté*, articles cited.

90. *Limes*, ibid.

91. Pascal Neuffer, a 32-year-old geologist, quoted in *La Liberté*, Genève, 22 April 1999.

92. Walker's other deputies represented the rest of the Contact Group plus Norway as current OSCE president.

93. According to *Figaro* correspondent Renaud Girard, interviewed 25 January 2000.

94. Walker and Laverty, "CIA Aided Kosovo Guerrilla Army".

95. By an odd coincidence, the Agence France Presse reported on 18 January 1999 that one of Walker's sons was currently working for a non-governmental organization in Kosovo.

96. Don North, "Irony at Račak: Tainted Diplomat", *The Consortium*, Arlington, Virginia, 8 February 1999, p. 2.

97. R. Jeffrey Smith, "Kosovo Attack Called a Massacre", *Washington Post*, 17 March 1999, p. 1.

98. All this was acknowledged when it was too late to matter, in the November 1999 OSCE report on human rights, *Kosovo/Kosova: As Seen, As Told*, p. 353.

99. Renaud Girard, "Kosovo: zones d'ombre sur un massacre", *Le Figaro*, 20 janvier 1999, p. 3; and Christophe Châtelet, "Les morts de Račak ont-ils vraiment été massacrés froidement?", *Le Monde*, 21 janvier 1999, p. 2.

100. The Finns subsequently stressed the professional accord between themselves and their colleagues from Yugoslavia and Belorussia. Indeed they reached the same conclusions, but Western media never showed any interest in the findings of Yugoslav or Belorussian experts.

101. A dentist, Dr. Ranta's expertise is limited to dental identification, which had no bearing on the critical issue of the circumstances in which the persons were killed. Her team included Antti Penttilä, considered one of the world's top forensic experts, who remained discreet.

102. R. Jeffrey Smith, "Kosovo Attack Called a Massacre", *Washington Post*, 17 March 1999, p. 1.

103. J. Rainio, K. Lalu and A. Penttilä, "Independent forensic autopsies in an armed conflict: investigation of the victims from Račak, Kosovo", *Forensic Science International*, 116 (2001), pp. 171–85.

104. The fact that the men were not wearing military uniforms cannot be conclusive evidence that they were not UÇK fighters forced into battle at a time and place not of their choosing by the Serb police assault.

105. In a 1 August 2001 column in the *International Herald Tribunal*, senior ICG political analyst Anna Husarska recounted meeting Albanian activists "in 1997 when traveling with Mort Abramowitz, the International Crisis Group's founding father". At Rambouillet, Abramowitz was accompanied by Washington-based international lawyer Paul Williams, Assistant Secretary of State for Southeastern Europe in the Bush administration before serving on the State Department's Serbian Sanctions Task Force under Clinton, and by Marc Weller, a German scholar at Cambridge University specializing in the Kosovo Albanian cause.

106. Jan Oberg of the Swedish-based Transnational Foundation for Future and Peace Studies had made dozens of visits to Kosovo as advisor to Ibrahim Rugova.

107. James Rubin, "Countdown to a Very Personal War", *Financial Times*, 30 September 2000, and "The Promise of Freedom", *Financial Times*, 7 October 2000.

108. This was a considerably more realistic fear than the fear of the U.S. government in World War II that its citizens of Japanese origin would assist a Japanese invasion, the pretext for "ethnically cleansing" the region by putting Japanese-Americans in concentration camps.

109. Tyler Marshall, "U.S. in Kosovo for the Long Haul", *Los Angeles Times*, 10 June 2000.

110. "Meet the Press", 25 April 1999.

111. Fox News, 23 May 1999.

112. *Washington Post*, 28 April 1999.

113. Michael R. Gordon, "NATO General Urges Hits on Serbian Leaders;

Belgrade People Must Suffer, Too, He Says", *New York Times/ International Herald Tribune*, 14 May 1999.

114. Joseph Fitchett, "Is Serb Economy the True Target? Raids Seem Aimed at Bolstering Resistance to Milošević", *International Herald Tribune*, 26 May 1999, p. 1.

115. *International Herald Tribune*, 31 May 1999.

116. Rod Nordland, "Vengeance of a Victim Race", *Newsweek*, 12 April 1999.

117. Daniel Jonah Goldhagen, "If You Rebuild It ... A New Serbia", *The New Republic*, 17 May 1999.

118. Daniel Pearl and Robert Block, "Despite Tales, the War in Kosovo Was Savage, but Wasn't Genocide", *Wall Street Journal*, 31 December 1999.

119. The fraud of "Operation Horseshoe" was authoritatively exposed by Brigadier General Heinz Loquai, former German military advisor to the OSCE in Vienna, in his careful study entitled *Der Kosovo-Konflikt: Wege in einen vermeidbaren Krieg* [The Kosovo Conflict: Ways into an Avoidable War], edited by the Institute for Peace Research and Security Policy of the University of Hamburg, Nomos, Baden-Baden, 2000, pp. 138–44.

120. In the KVM report's chapter on the Roma people in Kosovo, the Roma were referred to as "Gypsies (Maxhupet)", because that is what Kosovo Albanians call them – despite recognition that "Maxhupet" is "derogatory" and that "there was clearly prejudice against and negative perceptions of Gypsies (Maxhupet) among Kosovo Albanians". But since "virtually all of the information in this chapter of the report derives from information provided by Kosovo Albanian refugees", the derogatory Albanian term was retained. Why, if the KVM was interested in Roma, did it not interview some of them? Why did it relay Albanian accusations against Roma for aligning themselves with Serbs, without drawing the obvious conclusion that the widely mistreated Roma were better off in Serbia than in most of southeastern Europe and had no desire to exchange Serbs for Albanians? Why should it be acceptable to call Roma "Maxhupet" and wrong to call Albanians "Shqiptar", the term used by the Albanian people themselves?

121. Bernard Kouchner, "The Long Path Toward Reconciliation in Kosovo", *Los Angeles Times/International Herald Tribune*, 27 October 1999.

122. Interview with Bernard Kouchner by Catherine Perron, "Kosovo: Le courage de Sisyphe", *Politique Internationale*, Paris, winter 1999–2000, pp. 69–90.

123. From Kouchner's preface to an OSCE report on human rights abuses, published as the second volume of the November 1999 OSCE Report, *Kosovo/Kosova: As Seen, As Told*. It was compiled by a new OSCE Mission in Kosovo called OMIK, headed by Dutch diplomat Daan Everts, which in July 1999 began on the spot investigation intended to help "positively influence the development of civil society" and "establish the rule of law".

124. Tom Walker, "Cook Held Talks with War Crime Suspect", *Sunday Times*, London, 29 April 2001.

125. Dienstbier's findings were reported by all major news agencies and

in newspapers such as the *Detroit Free Press*, March 30, 2000, without making any noticeable dent in public opinion.

126. The Balkan Action Council is a gathering of established warhawks including Zbigniew Brzezinski, Frank Carlucci, Jeane Kirkpatrick, and Paul Wolfowitz. The group's web-site is <www.balkanaction.org>. It is logical that the executive director of such a group saw Kosovo primarily as a "test of will" for NATO rather than as a humanitarian problem, even when speaking at the Holocaust Museum. Hooper's view that "the Balkans are the new Berlin; the test of Western will" was echoed in a column by Anthony Lewis, *New York Times/International Herald Tribune*, 12 April 1999.

127. Roger Cohen, "Who Really Brought Down Milošević?", *New York Times Sunday Magazine*, 26 November 2000.

POSTSCRIPT: PERPETUAL WAR

1. Richard Holbrooke's, *To End a War*, Random House, New York, 1998. On p. 202, he recounts that it was "Kofi Annan's strength on the bombing in August" that had "made him the private favorite" of American officials to replace Boutros Boutros-Ghali. "Although the American campaign against Boutros-Ghali, in which all our key allies opposed us, was long and difficult ... the decision was correct, and may well have saved America's role in the United Nations." The key event was the 30 August 1995 bombing. On p. 99, Holbrooke recounts the eve of that bombing. "In New York, Ambassador Albright continued her vigorous campaign with those United Nations officials she could round up; fortunately, Secretary-General Boutros-Ghali was unreachable on a commercial aircraft, so she dealt instead with his best deputy, Kofi Annan, who was in charge of peacekeeping operations. At 11:45 a.m., New York time, came a big break: Annan informed Talbott and Albright that he had instructed the U.N.'s civilian officials and military commanders to relinquish for a limited period of time their authority to veto air strikes in Bosnia. For the first time in the war, the decision on the air strikes was solely in the hands of NATO – primarily two American officers ... " To sum it up, p. 103: "Annan's gutsy performance in those twenty-four hours was to play a central role in Washington's strong support for him a year later as the successor to Boutros Boutros-Ghali as Secretary General of the United Nations. Indeed, in a sense Annan won the job on that day."

2. Ibid., p. 103.

3. Massimo D'Alema, *Kosovo. Gli italiani e la guerra*, Mondadori, Milan, 1999, pp. 52–3.

4. Hubert Védrine, "Droit d'ingérence, démocratie, sanctions: Refonder la politique étrangère française", *Le Monde diplomatique*, December 2000. While apologizing for the Kosovo intervention as an exceptional case, Védrine argued that it should not serve as a precedent – not the view of Ms Albright nor of a strong "humanitarian intervention" lobby in France itself.

5. Published in the 20 July 1992 edition of *Time* magazine.
6. *Die Welt* interview with Robin Cook, 8 August 1998.
7. Zbigniew Brzezinski, *The Grand Chessboard: American Primacy and its Geostrategic Imperatives*, New York: Basic Books, 1997, p. 215.
8. Ibid.
9. Thomas Friedman, "A Manifesto For a Fast World", *New York Times Magazine*, 28 March 1999. This surprising candor did not mean that the *Times* editors got the facts straight. Friedman declared complacently: "It's true that no two countries that both have a McDonald's have ever fought a war since they each got their McDonald's. (I call this the Golden Arches Theory of Conflict Prevention.)" In reality, there were several McDonald's restaurants in Belgrade, enjoying advantageous sites and considerable publicity. This did not deter the United States from bombing Belgrade.
10. CDU parliamentarian Willy Wimmer, vice president of the OSCE parliamentary assembly and former foreign ministry official, in an interview with the *Berliner Zeitung*, 6 September 1999.
11. *New York Times*, 11 April 1999: "War Teaches NATO What its Role is", Craig Whitney from Brussels, referring to the new "strategic concept" defining NATO's role in the twenty-first century, wrote that "that role is being defined in practice in Kosovo, not on paper in Washington".
12. NATO's Strategic Concept, 24 April 1999; Part II.

Index

CPSIA information can be obtained
at www.ICGtesting.com
Printed in the USA
FSOW02n0944051116
27024FS